Bioarchaeology of Frontiers and Borderlands

Bioarchaeological Interpretations of the Human Past: Local, Regional, and Global Perspectives

BIOARCHAEOLOGY OF
Frontiers and Borderlands

Edited by Cristina I. Tica and Debra L. Martin

Foreword by Clark Spencer Larsen

UNIVERSITY OF FLORIDA PRESS
Gainesville

Copyright 2019 by Cristina I. Tica and Debra L. Martin
All rights reserved
Published in the United States of America

This book may be available in an electronic edition.

24 23 22 21 20 19   6 5 4 3 2 1

Library of Congress Cataloging-in-Publication Data
Names: Tica, Cristina I., editor. | Martin, Debra L. (Professor of Biological
   Anthropology), editor. | Larsen, Clark Spencer, author of foreword.
Title: Bioarchaeology of frontiers and borderlands / edited by Cristina I.
   Tica and Debra L. Martin ; foreword by Clark Spencer Larsen.
Other titles: Bioarchaeological interpretations of the human past.
Description: Gainesville : University of Florida Press, 2019. | Series:
   Bioarchaeological Interpretations of the Human Past: Local, Regional, and
   Global Perspectives | Includes bibliographical references and index.
Identifiers: LCCN 2018055525 | ISBN 9781683400844 (cloth : alk. paper)
Subjects: LCSH: Human remains (Archaeology) | Excavations (Archaeology) |
   Borderlands—History.
Classification: LCC CC79.5.H85 B544 2019 | DDC 930.1—dc23
LC record available at https://lccn.loc.gov/2018055525

University of Florida Press
2046 NE Waldo Road
Suite 2100
Gainesville, FL 32609
http://upress.ufl.edu

Contents

List of Figures   vii
List of Tables   xi
Foreword   xiii

Introduction: Bioarchaeology and the Study of Frontiers   1
Cristina I. Tica and Debra L. Martin

PART I. THE COMPLEXITY AND LIMINALITY OF THE FRONTIER

1. Across the River: Romanized "Barbarians" and Barbarized "Romans" on the Edge of the Empire (Third–Sixth Centuries CE)   13
Cristina I. Tica

2. Funerary Practice and Local Interaction on the Imperial Frontier, First Century CE: A Case Study in the Şərur Valley, Azerbaijan   41
Selin E. Nugent

3. Queering Prehistory on the Frontier: A Bioarchaeological Investigation of Gender in Mierzanowice Culture Communities of the Early Bronze Age   55
Mark P. Toussaint

PART II. MOVEMENT ACROSS BORDERS

4. Isotopes, Migration, and Sex: Investigating the Mobility of the Frontier Inhabitants of Roman Egypt   83
Amanda T. Groff and Tosha L. Dupras

5. Temporal and Spatial Biological Kinship Variation at Campovalano and Alfedena in Iron Age Central Italy   107
Evan Muzzall and Alfredo Coppa

PART III. ADAPTABILITY AND RESILIENCE ON THE FRONTIER

6. Living on the Border: Health and Identity during Egypt's Colonization of Nubia in the New Kingdom Period 135
Katie Marie Whitmore, Michele R. Buzon, and Stuart Tyson Smith

7. Life on the Northern Frontier: Bioarchaeological Reconstructions of Eleventh-Century Households in North Iceland 160
Guðný Zoëga and Kimmarie Murphy

PART IV. VIOLENCE ON THE FRONTIER

8. A Mass Grave outside the Walls: The Commingled Assemblage from Ibida 187
Andrei Soficaru, Claudia Radu, and Cristina I. Tica

9. A Line in the Sand: Bioarchaeological Interpretations of Life along the Borders of the Great Basin and the American Southwest 212
Aaron R. Woods and Ryan P. Harrod

PART V. CHALLENGES AND LIMITATIONS OF BIOARCHAEOLOGICAL METHODS AND THEORY

10. Mortuary Practices in the First Iron Age Romanian Frontier: The Commingled Assemblages of the Măgura Uroiului 233
Anna J. Osterholtz, Virginia Lucas, Claira Ralston, Andre Gonciar, and Angelica Bălos

11. Marginalized Motherhood: Infant Burial in Seventeenth-Century Transylvania 252
Jonathan D. Bethard, Anna J. Osterholtz, Zsolt Nyárádi, and Andre Gonciar

Conclusion: The Future of Bioarchaeology and Studies at the Edges 273
Cristina I. Tica

List of Contributors 279

Index 285

Figures

1.1. Map of Romania showing Târgşor and Ibida (Slava Rusă) 14

1.2. Demographics of the Ibida sample 23

1.3. Demographics of the Târgşor sample 23

1.4. Periosteal reaction on the right tibia in a mature adult female from Ibida 27

1.5. Right parietal cranial depression fracture in an old adult male from Ibida 31

1.6. Right femur fracture in a young female from Târgşor 32

2.1. Map of the South Caucasus and Oğlanqala 42

2.2. Burial WWE.B1 43

2.3. Silver denarii accompanying WWE.B1 44

2.4. Bronze and glass-paste Isis and Serapis signet ring 47

2.5. Strontium and oxygen isotope values for WWE.B1 in relation to Şərur Valley bioavailability 50

3.1. Burial orientations by estimated sex 66

3.2. Hierarchical clustering based on entheseal scores 69

3.3. Burial 6 from Żerniki Górne showing a probable female with a variation of a Le Fort type I fracture 71

3.4. Burial 6 from Żerniki Górne showing a probable female with symphyseal fracture of the mandible 72

3.5. Burial 6 from Żerniki Górne showing a probable female with possible decapitation or artificial widening of the foramen magnum 72

4.1. Map showing the location of the Dakhleh Oasis and Kellis in Egypt 86

4.2. Comparison of oxygen isotope ranges from Nile Valley sites and the Kellis 2 cemetery, Dakhleh Oasis 96

4.3. Bone apatite $\delta^{18}O$ values from eight females identified as possible foreigners plotted against the remaining Dakhleh Oasis adult females and Tombos (Sudan) $\delta^{18}O$ values 99

4.4. Bone apatite $\delta^{18}O$ values from eighteen males identified as possible foreigners plotted against the remaining Dakhleh Oasis adult males and Tombos (Sudan) $\delta^{18}O$ values   101

5.1. Locations of Campovalano and Alfedena in Central Italy   111

5.2. Multidimensional scaling scatterplot of geometric mean–scaled dental data showing the six metric samples from Campovalano and Alfedena   118

5.3. Neighbor-joining clustering of the five ASUDAS samples from Campovalano and Alfedena   120

5.4. ANCOVA scatterplot of distal premolar and second molar data for females and males   121

6.1. Map illustrating the changes in the border between Egypt and Nubia during the Middle and New Kingdom periods   136

6.2. Map of location and excavations at Tombos cemetery   140

6.3. Scatter chart of $^{87}Sr/^{86}Sr$ values in the Nile Valley   141

6.4. Examples of Egyptian-style burials and grave goods   142

6.5. Examples of Kerma-style burials   143

7.1. A map showing cemeteries excavated in the Skagafjörður area with Keldudalur and Seyla underlined   161

7.2. Distribution of age in the Keldudalur and Seyla cemeteries   170

7.3. Overviews of Keldudalur and Seyla cemeteries showing sex distribution   170

7.4. Defects of dental enamel at Keldudalur and Seyla   173

7.5. Location of coffin graves in the Keldudalur and Seyla cemeteries   175

8.1. Map of the Roman province of Scythia Minor showing the site of Ibida   189

8.2. Map of funeral discoveries from Ibida   193

8.3. Diagram of multistage process that led to formation of M141 deposit   199

8.4. Cranial fragment with perimortem bone modification from the M141 deposit   200

8.5. Femur fragment with postmortem bone modification from the M141 deposit   201

8.6. Femur fragment with postmortem bone modification from the M141 deposit   201

8.7. Newborn frontal fragment with left orbit from the M141 deposit   202

9.1. Map showing the location of the Fremont and Ancestral Puebloan border areas in southern Utah and southern Nevada 213

9.2. Histogram showing sex ratios of Fremont, Kayenta Branch, and Virgin Branch samples 220

9.3. Histogram showing distribution of Fremont, Kayenta Branch, and Virgin Branch samples by age groups 220

10.1. Map of Romania showing location of the Măgura Uroiului monument 235

10.2. Distribution of cranial trauma and an example of a large healed cranial depression fracture on an adult female at the Măgura Uroiului 238

10.3. Porotic hyperostosis and cribra orbitalia from a juvenile and an adult female at the Măgura Uroiului 241

10.4. Gray wolf skull in situ at the Măgura Uroiului 245

10.5. Gray wolf metacarpal close to human remains at the Măgura Uroiului 245

10.6. Carving of a Dacian dragon at the base of the Măgura Uroiului site 246

11.1. Google Earth map of Eastern Europe depicting how the Carpathian Arch formed the eastern borderland of the Principality of Transylvania 257

11.2. Photograph of Burial 54 at the Telekfalva Reformed Church excavation 258

11.3. Original plan view of the Telekfalva Reformed Church excavation 259

11.4. Age distribution of all individuals recovered from the Telekfalva Reformed Church 260

Tables

1.1. Frequency and percent of physiological stress conditions mentioned in text in the Ibida sample by sex and age at death   25

1.2. Frequency and percent of physiological stress conditions mentioned in text in the Târgşor sample by sex and age at death   26

1.3. Frequency and percent of antemortem trauma in the two samples by sex   29

2.1. Strontium and oxygen values for the WWE.B1 young adult male   50

3.1. Frequency of osteoarthritis of the major joint systems by sex and burial orientation   67

3.2. Frequency of dental pathologies by sex and burial orientation   68

3.3. Frequency of antemortem and perimortem trauma by sex and burial orientation   68

4.1. Oxygen isotope data for adult females   92

4.2. Oxygen isotope data for adult males   94

4.3. Comparison of $\delta^{18}O$ values for Nile Valley sites and Kellis 2 cemetery, Dakhleh Oasis   97

5.1. Samples used in this study   114

5.2. Cranial landmarks used in this study   115

5.3. ANOVAs and Tukey HSDs for Iron Age Campovalano, Medieval Campovalano, and Alfedena   119

6.1. Chronologies of Ancient Egypt and Nubia   137

6.2. Number of individuals exhibiting linear enamel hypoplasia, cribra orbitalia, and osteoperiostitis by sex and age category   146

6.3. Number of individuals exhibiting abscesses, antemortem tooth loss, and carious lesion by tooth (total number of individual teeth observed) and by individual (with at least one tooth observable)   148

7.1. Comparison of the stature of human remains in medieval cemeteries in the North Atlantic   172

7.2. Summary of pathologies at Keldudalur and Seyla by frequency and percent 173

8.1. Distribution of identified cranial fragments from feature M141 by age category and sex 195

8.2. Sagittal and transverse diameter (in millimeters) of femoral shaft and head for the five groups included in this study 196

8.3. Distribution of modifications to bone surface 197

9.1. Indications of nutritional stress among the Fremont, Kayenta Branch, and Virgin Branch groups 221

9.2. Nonlethal trauma among the Fremont, Kayenta Branch, and Virgin Branch groups 222

10.1. Demography of the human Măgura Uroiului assemblages 237

10.2. Cranial depression fractures by demography, size, location, and depth 239

10.3. Nonhuman species represented at the Măgura Uroiului 243

Foreword

Beginning with founding of the discipline of anthropology in the late nineteenth century, the topic of frontiers and borderlands has been a lead topic of study and discussion, in large part because anthropology encompasses all peoples in all places at all times. The history of our science reveals that humans are extraordinarily adaptable, are fluid in their living circumstances, and continuously adjust to challenges. Indeed, the adaptive success of modern humans and their ancestors is reflected in their remarkable ability to adjust and to respond to challenges via the biocultural processes that are uniquely human.

My own experience with the bioarchaeology of frontiers focuses on the Spanish borderlands of eastern North America. The Spanish borderlands, called La Florida as they pertain to the American Southeast, have an extraordinary record of native adaptation and native responses to new and novel challenges arising from the arrival of new cultures, new economic systems, and new people. The arrival of explorers and the establishment of the mission system in the sixteenth century set into motion a series of changes to the landscape and for the people that had far-reaching consequences.

Given my interests in borderlands biocultural adaptation, I was excited to read Tica and Martin's book and to see the expansion of interest in and scholarship on frontiers and borderlands. The foregoing chapters underscore the vital importance of interpreting a large, complex record via the integration of data sets and methods that historians, archaeologists, and bioarchaeologists have developed. This robust and integrative approach provides a unique perspective that is not possible from discipline-specific investigation. Today, few of us could image developing a research program without integrating knowledge that was once discipline-specific. The findings presented in this volume document and interpret the record of dominance and outcomes for exploited peoples. More important, these findings underscore the remarkably dynamic nature of human interactions in frontiers and borderlands.

The developing record clearly shows that there are negative outcomes for frontier groups living in the shadow of a dominant society (e.g., the *limes* of the Roman empire Cristina Tica discusses), including conflict and violence, exposure to new pathogens, social inequality, and the associated processes of emerging living conditions. In bioarchaeological research on the Spanish borderlands, various authorities have documented similar outcomes with regard to oral health, iron deficiency anemia, trauma, and alterations in well-being in general (e.g., see Larsen 2001; Murphy and Klaus 2017).

The various settings discussed in this book present a record of economic, social, and cultural change that ranges from changes in diet to remarkably rapid alterations in mortuary programs. The chapters reveal the fundamental importance of integrating historical, archaeological, and bioarchaeological data sets in order to characterize and interpret life and living circumstances. The contributors to the book provide case and regional studies that underscore the central role of human remains for addressing these issues.

I am especially excited to see that the bioarchaeological research presented in this volume challenges long-held notions of what it means to be a dominant power. Although a long historical record contains innumerable accounts of violence and outcomes of warfare for their victims, that record is only a part of the larger picture of expansionism and exploitation. There is no question about it: our science is showing the vital importance of combining methods and data in interdisciplinary research agendas. It is clear that integrating method and theory and developing new tools, new approaches to the study of behavioral dynamics, and new ways of thinking about the past are changing how we study earlier humans. The integrative approaches many of the chapters in this book present provide a more informed understanding of societies that were expanding from core to peripheral landscapes (e.g., Roman colonization) or those being encountered by newly arriving dominant societies (e.g., Nubia). Violence and exploitation were and continue to be a part of the record of domination of one society or state over another. Equally important, however, are records of adjustment and adaptation. It is that record that makes the focus on frontiers and borderlands such an interesting and compelling discussion about human adaptation and behavior.

Clark Spencer Larsen
Series Editor

References Cited

Larsen, C. S., ed. 2001. *Bioarchaeology of Spanish Florida: The Impact of Colonialism.* Gainesville: University Press of Florida.

Murphy, M. S., and H. D. Klaus, eds. 2017. *Colonized Bodies, Worlds Transformed: Toward a Global Bioarchaeology of Contact and Colonialism.* Gainesville: University Press of Florida.

Stojanowski, C. M. 2013. *Mission Cemeteries, Mission Peoples: Historical and Evolutionary Dimensions of Intracemetery Bioarchaeology in Spanish Florida.* Gainesville: University Press of Florida.

Introduction

Bioarchaeology and the Study of Frontiers

CRISTINA I. TICA AND DEBRA L. MARTIN

Frontiers, territorial borders, and the process of boundary making are important aspects of the natural history of the human species, since human consciousness and social organization are deeply influenced by territoriality (Anderson 1996, 189). Borders and frontiers are means through which humans assign meaning to their existence, as these delimitations connect and relate people to one another as being part of something special because it is separate (Williams 2006, 119). Territorial borders are an integral part of the way human societies work. They are fundamental contributors to our sense of belonging and our sense of place in the world; they allow us to relate to one another based on trust, commonality, and security (Williams 2006, 119). Thus, frontiers are intrinsically linked to the entities they encompass (Anderson 1996, 10).

Why We Should Care

Every culture defines and is affected by territorial borders. Defining, defending, and protecting the borders of a homeland are a fundamentally important social practice, since they divide political communities, political authority, and political rights and obligations. Accordingly, borders and frontiers lay the basis for collective identity formation. They require complex social processes that serve to protect people—or to put them at risk (Williams 2006, 124,133). The frontier includes and excludes while encompassing both the inside and the outside, the identity and the difference (Vaughan-Williams 2009, 1). Borders and frontiers are protecting and imprisoning, at once gateways and barriers, zones of contact and conflict, cooperation and competition, opportunity and insecurity, ambivalent identities and aggressive assertion of difference, and dichotomies that can coexist simultaneously in the same people (Anderson and O'Dowd 1999, 595).

The daily news is a constant reminder of why a scholarship of borders and frontiers is not only still relevant but crucially needed. The portrayal of frontiers and borderlands as either a menacing threat or an optimistic prospect for sociocultural interactions is based on a weak (and frequently wrong) grasp of the past and therefore of the complexity of these phenomena. Their contradictory, problematic, and multifaceted nature makes borders and frontiers hard to conceptualize and define. Frontier is more of a set of processes rather than a "thing"; it is "a busy field of intersecting forces," and defining it narrowly "will not tame these forces or unite them in a single pattern" (Rodseth and Parker 2005, 16). And as Rodseth and Parker (2005, 16) argue, all aspects of the frontier should be investigated, from all different points of view, in all its specific times and places; thus, the frontier should be investigated "in the wild," so to speak.

As Thomas Nail (2016, 7) asserts, borders are dynamic and fluid. They never finish "including" people or things because they are never stable or immutable; they are easily changed in response to shifting politics or cultural changes. Borders and frontiers are also never successful in keeping everyone in or out (8), and as Nail emphasizes, they all "leak precisely because all borders are constituted by and through a process of leakage, which is only temporarily stabilized into border regimes" (13).

One of the definitions of frontier is a zone that separates civilization from the wilderness (Donnan and Haller 2000, 11), a territorial expansion into formerly "empty" areas (Baud and Van Schendel 1997, 213). However, during colonization, one group's homeland becomes another's frontier (Lightfoot and Martinez 1995, 473). The frontier is a place in and of itself but it is also a link in a larger network (Wendl and Rösler 1999, 10). Therefore, a change in one group's frontier requires the other group to also make accommodations and changes. And exchanges between two groups often underscore their interdependence (Green and Perlman 1985, 4). An example is the agricultural/hunter-gatherer frontier in temperate prehistoric Europe: as Dennell (1985) posits, the spread of agriculture was probably generated by the actual interaction between foragers and farmers, by a close dialogue between those on either side of the Mesolithic-Neolithic frontier.

To a certain extent, the notion of "frontier" is used interchangeably with "border" (Wendl and Rösler 1999, 3). Borders are spaces of "meaning-making" and "meaning-breaking." They are liminal zones that put in sharp relief the full range of "multivocal and multilocal" identities. Donnan and Wilson (1999, 64) maintain that this can be especially seen in the case of ethnic and national identities expressed at peripheries and borders in ways that often differ from how the same identities are configured in core areas of the state.

For the people who live on the frontier or in frontier regions, the meaning of what a frontier is is deeply influenced by the rules and regulations that frontier imposes on their lives (Anderson 1996, 2–3), rules and regulations created and enforced by those with more power who often live at the center. Borders and frontiers are rarely natural; they are almost always socially and politically constructed. They are subjective, negotiated, and contested; they derive meaning and function from the people they divide (Diener and Hagen 2010a, 3–4). Furthermore, borders and frontiers are lived; they are "historically contingent, politically charged, dynamic phenomena that first and foremost involve people and their everyday lives" (Vaughan-Williams 2009, 1).

A Bioarchaeology of Frontiers and Borderlands

This volume of case studies illustrates the ways that borders and frontiers have both material and symbolic uses (Anderson and O'Dowd 1999, 595). Each chapter demonstrates in different ways the complexity and the versatility of the border. What makes border theory so difficult to grasp is that there are many types of borders and frontiers: regional and geographical, political, religious, cultural, generational, ethnic, racial, based on class and socioeconomic stratification, and so forth (Vaughan-Williams 2009, 1). At the same time, borders are "equally aterritorial, apolitical, nonlegal, and noneconomic [phenomena]" (Nail 2016, 2–3) (for example, see chapter 3, this volume).

The study of borders and frontiers should not be exclusively undertaken based on any single type of division or social force because what is common to all these types of borders is the status of the "between" (Nail 2016, 2). Borders and frontiers can exist at different levels and scales: between individual and society, among individuals, among communities or groups, and among societies. Borders are places of (ethnic) conflict and accommodation because of their geographical location and their role as areas of immigration (Donnan and Wilson, 1999, 5). People at the borders adapt to the social, economic, cultural, and political necessities of living with, or in spite of, their cross-border neighbors, whom they might consider as friends, enemies, or neutral parties (Donnan and Wilson, 1994, 3).

Frontiers, borders, and borderlands are complex composites. Each border is actually made up of multiple borders that are never given or static but are mobile and reproduced (Nail 2016, 1–2, 7). Borders and frontiers are "the mobile cutting blades of society" (Nail 2016, 7). As Nail (2016) notes, and as the chapters in this volume suggest, frontiers and borders have always been complex, multiple, mobile, and embodied, emerging in the landscape from the identities individuals and groups carry in themselves (Diener and Hagen 2010b, 193). The case studies in this volume, which are largely based on analysis of human skeletal remains, can add to this dimensionality of borders and frontiers by providing a look at what the lived experience was for people in a variety of border contexts.

The aim of this edited volume is to present a series of cases that address how living on or interacting with the frontier can affect health and socioeconomic status. The goal is to explore how people in the past might have maintained, created, or manipulated their identity while living in a place of liminality. The zone of "in-betweenness," of demarcation between two or more spheres of influence, is a very dynamic and potentially violent place. Because borders and frontiers are often places where those with more power can exert more influence and coercion, violence is often at the core of border and frontier studies. This book aims to explore how different groups living in these zones were affected and how they lived their lives "on the edge."

Bioarchaeology is a powerful tool that brings invaluable empirical data on health and trauma. Since the topics of frontiers, borders, emigration, immigration, refugees and the building of walls occupy a central place in today's global political milieu, the aim of this book is to draw attention to the relevance of these kinds of studies and what can be learned from the past. A bioarchaeological approach to frontiers and borderlands can offer a new outlook, and, sadly, today more than ever, we need new perspectives on this topic. The more understanding we have on how frontier zones and migration processes affected health and social (in)stability in the past, the better chances we have to make sense of it all in the present.

The case studies presented address questions of how living on the frontier or near borders might have affected the health and disease of these groups, how conflict and violence might have been expressed, and how social inequalities might have been manifested. How did these groups maintain their identity? What overall effect did the "frontier" have on the existence of those who called it home? Some chapters address situations where the people involved might not have lived permanently in the borderland zone but had extensively interacted with it or were deeply marked by it. A frontier delineates, at least mentally, an end for one group, for one zone and the beginning for another.

The Structure of the Book

The chapters in this volume discuss one or more aspects of frontiers and borders, each presenting archaeological case studies that integrate the evidence from human remains with the historical and cultural context. The chapters are divided into five thematic sections: The Complexity and Liminality of the Frontier, Movement across Borders, Adaptability and Resilience on the Frontier, Violence on the Frontier, and Challenges and Limitations of Bioarchaeological Methods and Theory. The theme of complexity, in one form or another, permeates all the chapters in this volume.

In chapter 1, Cristina I. Tica integrates insights gleaned from bioarchaeology with what we know from archaeology and the historical sources in the case of the lower Danube frontier in the Late Roman Empire. She looks at how the daily life of people under Roman control compared to that of their neighbors to the north, the "barbarians," and she shows that there are health, demographic and mortality differences.

In chapter 2, Selin E. Nugent takes a different approach to the notion that powerful empires (here, Rome and Parthia) seek the expansive use of violence and militarism to define all relationships with frontier populations. As it turns out, this may not be the case. Nugent's nuanced look demonstrates that the relationships between Rome and Parthia blurred the boundaries between empire and frontier and were mutual and beneficial.

This volume also aims to emphasize the ways that frontiers and borderlands are liminal zones that demand a reconceptualization of many of our most deeply held assumptions about the relationships between people-place-identity and culture. The most personal of spaces to inscribe borders on is the body. Today, in an age of international travel, through risk-based border securitization and biometric bordering practices, the individual has become a walking, talking border (Popescu 2015, 103–104). The body is thus an ideal border to interrogate. As Popescu (2015, 103) notes, the body has long been a canvas for bordering practices, and Mark P. Toussaint shows us that in chapter 3. His chapter explores the geographically and culturally liminal spaces in Central Europe. He sees the whole of the Bronze Age as a sociocultural frontier for which gendered roles and identities were contested and formulated, resulting in surprising configurations.

Part 2, which includes two studies, deals with movements across borders. In chapter 4, Amanda T. Groff and Tosha L. Dupras use stable oxygen isotope analysis in conjunction with textual evidence to discuss the mobility of individuals buried in the Kellis 2 cemetery in the Dakhleh Oasis, Egypt. Their data complement the limited textual evidence, allowing for a more detailed reconstruction of economics, kinship, and residence patterns during the Romano-Christian era and lead to a definition of Egyptian frontier identity. They considered archaeological, historical, and ethnographic records to help provide a more detailed view of the socioeconomic context, labor, kinship patterns, and mobility of individuals in this remote location.

In chapter 5, Evan Muzzall and Alfredo Coppa examine temporal and spatial boundaries with a series of burials from Campovalano and Alfedena in Central Italy to see if marriage and residence rules were negotiated within the cultural and ideological borders that separated wealthy coastal groups from the less economically important interior groups. They use a biodistance approach to investigate social borders of the past in time and space.

Part 3 examines the human costs and benefits of adaptability and resilience on the frontier. Scholars have recognized that borders and borderlands are areas of transition and sites of cultural interaction, exchange, and hybridity. While all too often border regions are zones of military conflict and cultural animosity, they can also constitute sites of opportunities and cultural exchange (Diener and Hagen 2010a, 10). The two chapters in this part show how people negotiate and adapt to the frontier situations.

In chapter 6, Katie Marie Whitmore, Michele R. Buzon, and Stuart Tyson Smith discuss the boundary between Egypt and Nubia and the site of Tombos during the New Kingdom. Traditionally, it was thought that during the Egyptian Colonial New Kingdom period, Egyptians subjected native Nubians to harsh labor and impoverishment. However, Whitmore and colleagues show that at the frontier community of Tombos, biological and/or ethnic identity was more integrated and fluid. By using archaeological and bioarchaeological evidence, the authors suggest that the individuals living at Tombos incorporated both Egyptian and Nubian practices in their social spheres, resulting in a biologically and culturally entangled community.

An integral aspect of frontiers and borders relates to the fact that they are often both gateways to and (natural or artificial) exclusions from resources, water, food, hunting grounds, and so forth. Chapter 7 addresses frontiers as natural limits to the habitable environment. Guðný Zoëga and Kimmarie Murphy explore how the advent of a new religious reality appears in the archaeological record in the Skagafjörður region of North Iceland and discuss the impacts of frontiers and borderland spaces on the settlers' biology and culture during the eleventh century. Icelandic settlers operated in numerous frontiers and borderlands. Zoëga and Murphy note that unlike many frontier lands that are eventually transformed into stable, permanent settlements, northern Icelanders occupied a liminal space on the landscape, continually forced to adjust and adapt to environmental instability.

Part 4 addresses violence on the frontier. There is a deep connection between violence and borders that is historical, structural and colonial (Vaughan-Williams 2009, 67). Frontiers are often used as instruments of oppression and restrict the movements of people. Frontiers and borders are the primary mechanisms through which "outsiders" are denied asylum, travel, settlement, work, or citizenship (Anderson 1996, 150). Anderson and O'Dowd (1999, 597) note that territorial borders and frontiers "are generally imposed through force and intimidation in the course of wars, conquests and state formation" and their political economy reveals unequal and asymmetrical relationships. The process of bordering is often inherently violent.

Returning to the lower Danube frontier during the Late Roman Empire, Andrei Soficaru, Claudia Radu and Cristina I. Tica (chapter 8) present the case of feature M141, a mass grave discovered outside the walls of the Roman city of Ibida in the province of Scythia Minor. Based on their findings, the authors conclude that this is a case of political violence against a particular group of people that sought to completely eradicate their presence from collective memory.

In chapter 9, Aaron R. Woods and Ryan P. Harrod explore the boundaries archaeologists have drawn between the Fremont and Ancestral Pueblo groups in the ancient Southwest. They show the challenges of defining the frontier as people living in and near it would have done, and they question the practice of defining borders using only pottery and architecture to delineate presumed "lines in the sand" where one ethnic/political group ends and another may begin. The authors aim to contribute to a more nuanced understanding of borders that are often defined solely by the material culture.

Finally, part 5 addresses the challenges and limitations of bioarchaeological methods and bioarchaeological theory. Two chapters examine cultural representations of borders and the role these play in the construction and contestation of identities and their social formations and the potential challenges researchers face when making forays into new areas of scholarship.

In chapter 10, Anna J. Osterholtz and colleagues present a complex mortuary program on an Iron Age Romanian frontier in the form of unusual feasting and sacrifice associated with the primary burials of women and children. Even though the assemblage they examine is small, it gives a glimpse into one of the processes operating at the Romanian frontier.

Jonathan D. Bethard and his team argue for a consideration of boundaries that goes beyond geography; in chapter 11, they aim to engage in "boundary-bending bioarchaeological scholarship." They apply this concept to an examination of infant burials in Székely communities on the frontier of Transylvania by exploring a range of borders (church/state, mothers/infants, Roman Catholic/Hungarian Reformed Church, locals/nonlocals). Their goal is to illuminate a complex and nuanced set of accommodations that occurred around infant burials during the seventeenth century CE. The authors argue that their approach to the understanding of frontier has enriched their interpretations of the bioarchaeology of Transylvanian Székely communities.

Conclusions

Each of these studies offers a view of border and frontier existence from the ground up—how ordinary people ascribe, deny, or assume cultural differences and how they actively enact and modify their notions of belonging and identity in specific temporal-spatial contexts. The type of frontier varies based on what each author is exploring and on the specific aspect the researchers chose to investigate in each chapter. Thus, the aim of this volume is to examine the multitude of meanings and definitions borders and frontiers can have. No exhaustive, all-encompassing, and overarching definition is provided at the beginning of the volume. We believe that such an attempt would be reductionist and would detract from our intended objective. Instead, we ask the reader to go with what each author defines and be open to exploring the individual aspects of frontiers and boundaries each chapter examines. The chapters are intended to start the conversation about a crucial contemporary issue. We hope that these case studies will nudge the reader to delve deeper into frontiers and borderlands scholarship.

Many of these chapters get at the biocultural dimensions of borders and frontiers. This is the unique perspective that bioarcheology can offer. In some way, each chapter gets at the cultural dimensions of borders and the physical and metaphorical borderlands that radiate outward from the centers of these less stable and more contested spaces. Finally, these chapters argue for the re-conceptualization of borders and frontiers as socially charged places where innovative cultural constructs are created and transformed. They all advocate for a broadening of the conceptual framework of borders so that they are considered as zones of cultural interfaces in which cross-cutting and overlapping social units can be defined and recombined at different spatial and temporal scales.

References

Anderson, M. 1996. *Frontiers: Territory and State Formation in the Modern World.* Cambridge, UK: Polity Press.

Anderson, J. and L. O'Dowd. 1999. "Borders, Border Regions and Territoriality: Contradictory Meanings, Changing Significance." *Regional Studies* 33(7): 593–604.

Baud, M., and W. Van Schendel. 1997. "Toward a Comparative History of Borderlands." *Journal of World History* 8(2): 211–242.

Dennell, R. W. 1985. "The Hunter-Gatherer/Agricultural Frontier in Prehistoric Temperate Europe." In *The Archaeology of Frontiers and Boundaries*, edited by S. W. Green and S. M. Perlman, 113–139. Orlando: Academic Press, Inc.

Diener, A. C. and J. Hagen. 2010a. "Introduction: Borders, Identity, and Geopolitics." In *Borderlines and Borderlands: Political Oddities at the Edge of the Nation-State*, edited by A. C. Diener and J. Hagen, 1–14. Plymouth, UK: Rowman & Littlefield Publishers

———. 2010b. "Conclusion: Borders in a Changing Global Context." In *Borderlines and Borderlands: Political Oddities at the Edge of the Nation-State*, edited by A. C. Diener and J. Hagen, 189–194. Plymouth, UK: Rowman & Littlefield Publishers.

Donnan, H., and D. Haller. 2000. "Liminal No More. The Relevance of Borderland Studies." *Ethnologia Europaea* 30(2): 7–22.

Donnan, H., and T. M. Wilson. 1994. "An Anthropology of Frontiers." In *Border Approaches: Anthropological Perspectives on Frontiers*, edited by H. Donnan, T. M. Wilson, and Anthropological Association of Ireland, 1–14. Lanham, MD: University Press of America.

Donnan, H. and T. Wilson. 1999. *Borders: Frontiers of Identity, Nation and State.* Oxford: Berg.

Green, S. W., and S. M. Perlman. 1985. "Frontiers, Boundaries, and Open Social Systems." In *The Archaeology of Frontiers and Boundaries*, edited by S. W. Green and S. M. Perlman, 3–13. Orlando, FL: Academic Press, Inc.

Lightfoot, K. G., and A. Martinez. 1995. "Frontiers and Boundaries in Archaeological Perspective." *Annual Review of Anthropology* 24: 471–492.

Nail, T. 2016. *Theory of the Border.* Oxford: Oxford University Press.

Popescu, G. 2015. "Controlling Mobility: Embodying Borders." In *Borderities and the Politics of Contemporary Mobile Borders*, edited by A.-L. Amilhat Szary and F. Giraut, 100–115. London: Palgrave Macmillan.

Rodseth, L., and B. J. Parker. 2005. "Introduction: Theoretical Considerations in the

Study of Frontiers." In *Untaming the Frontier in Anthropology, Archaeology, and History*, edited by B. J. Parker and L. Rodseth, 3–21. Tucson: University of Arizona Press.

Vaughan-Williams, N. 2009. *Border Politics. The Limits of Sovereign Power.* Edinburgh: Edinburgh University Press.

Wendl, T., and M. Rösler. 1999. "Introduction: Frontiers and Borderlands: The Rise and Relevance of an Anthropological Research Genre." In *Frontiers and Borderlands: Anthropological Perspectives*, edited by M. Rösler and T. Wendl, 1–27. Frankfurt am Main: Peter Lang.

Williams, J. 2006. *The Ethics of Territorial Borders: Drawing Lines in the Shifting Sand.* London: Palgrave Macmillan.

I

The Complexity and Liminality of the Frontier

1

Across the River

Romanized "Barbarians" and Barbarized "Romans"
on the Edge of the Empire (Third–Sixth Centuries CE)

CRISTINA I. TICA

The aim of this research is to assess differences in overall health between two groups that have been characterized in the literature as "Romans" and "barbarians." I have used skeletal remains to address how the daily life of people under Roman-Byzantine control compared to that of their neighbors, the "barbarians" to the north. By looking at two contemporaneous populations from the territory of modern Romania that date to the third–sixth centuries CE, I aim to examine pathological conditions and traumatic injuries in order to gain a better understanding of the general quality of life for these populations. One collection comes from the site of Ibida (Slava Rusă) from the Roman frontier province of Scythia Minor and the other originates from the Târgșor site, located to the north of the Lower Danube frontier, in what was considered the *barbaricum* (figure 1.1).

This chapter seeks to contribute to the field of frontier studies with bioarchaeological data that will add to our understanding of how living in relative proximity but under different sociopolitical organizations may affect health. Human remains have the potential to provide information about age, sex, health status, accrued trauma and injury, and other factors related to resilience and adaptability under different political regimes (Martin et al. 2013).

The Greeks and Romans coined the label "barbarian," a word that "has helped define Europe itself, and European civilization" (James 2009, 1). "Barbarian" primarily meant non-Roman, or coming from outside the empire; a second meaning was someone who was not civilized, a pejorative label Romans

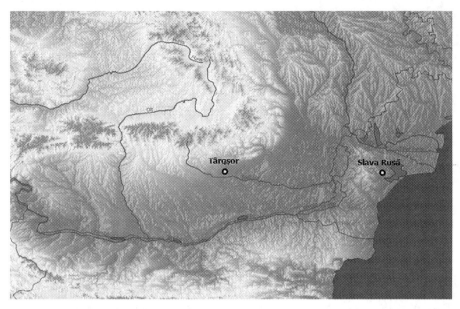

Figure 1.1. Map of Romania with the Danube River, showing the sites of Târgșor and Ibida (Slava Rusă). Map by Trent Skinner.

applied to others (James 2009, 5). Historians have continued this stereotyping to divide the world into "us" and "them" long after the end of the Roman world (Geary 2002, 52). Scholars continue to use the term "barbarian," stripped of its original value judgment and taken to encompass "all those elements of the landmass population who were not part of any great European empires of the era, whether Roman, Byzantine, or Frankish/Ottonian," justifying it as a "useful collective term" (Heather 2010, 605). It is all too convenient to have a catch-all term to characterize unknown or little-known groups from this time period. It seems almost ironic that the more information we gain through our innovative and insightful methodological and theoretical approaches in order to better understand the complexities, nuances, and sheer multitude of the group identities that were coalescing at this time, the easier and less problematic the current use of "barbarian" or "barbarian societies" appears to be. That might be so because there is still so much to learn about these groups.

Barbarians were interspersed at all social levels of the Roman Empire, including prisoners of war, slaves, merchants, ordinary soldiers in the Roman army, and commanders-in-chief and imperial advisors (James 2009, 157). The policy of settling defeated barbarians in the empire, a practice the Romans initiated in the 250s CE, could initially have made good economic and military sense. But as it accelerated in the fourth century CE, it brought the seeds of trouble for the empire (Zahariade 2006, 28). In Scythia, the massive Carps settlement dates from the third and early fourth centuries CE and is detectable well into the fourth century. The Goths were also settled in towns along the Danube frontier after Constantine's victory in 323. The new groups usually received land for agriculture on the border areas; thus, they performed both economic and military duties (Zahariade 2006, 129).

Theoretical Approaches: Frontier Studies

In the later empire, *limes* came to mean a fortified frontier region (Elton 1996, 70) that was usually, although not exclusively, associated with rivers (Graham 2006, 62–63). The Roman *limes* was not a frontier in a modern sense or a clear line on the map. Even in the case of a river, such as the Lower Danube, the frontier was a zone as much as a line. The defense of the empire consisted of troops and fortifications, but more important, Romans used constant diplomacy and negotiation, striving to encourage the barbarians through persuasion and economic trade to become willing partners of the Roman Empire (James 2009, 30).

After Constantinople became the eastern capital of the Roman Empire and the principal residence of the emperors, the Lower Danube and Scythia became a vital strategic axis for the focused attention of the imperial administration. From the fourth until the seventh century CE, the Roman policy was to maintain the Danube not only as a military and political frontier between the Romans and *barbaricum* but also as a mental barrier between the two worlds. Whether dealing with the Carpic, Sarmatian, or Gothic tribes, the older and more established groups north of the Danube, or with the Huns, Avars, and Slavs, the adversaries that emerged later in the region, the Roman administration had to continuously adjust its military and diplomatic strategies to an ever-changing challenge (Zahariade 2006, 21).

The Danube, however, was no barrier in the strictest sense of the term. Since the first half of the first century BCE, different powers sought to control both of its banks, because without control of the Danube, no power could control the Balkans (Burns 2003, 198). However, the Romans did not see the river as a "definite frontier." While it was a useful tactical impediment, it did not bar the flow of people and trade (Burns 2003, 198; Whittaker 2004, 8–9). In this regard, the Danube was just like any other Roman *limes*, a flexible, closed/open space where groups migrated, interacted, intermarried, and adapted (Whittaker 2004, 193). The Roman frontier was actually a frontier zone, a permeable, dynamic, and fluid gradual transition from Roman to non-Roman society (Drijvers 2011, 17).

The Roman frontier was a magnet zone that attracted people and products from all directions. Its expanding infrastructure began to influence the various groups in the hinterlands of Eastern Europe. On the one hand, trade and diplomatic contacts seem to have been the means through which a gradual increase of wealth and the use of items imported from Rome were concentrated in the hands of the military-political "barbarian" elites (Burns 2003, 185–187). On the other, violence in one society inevitably affected the other (Burns 2003, 18). The frontier played a central role in developing politically useful stereotypes, such as the Roman portrayal of the Germanic barbarians as slayers of empires. The stereotyping is necessary for an expansionist ideology that promotes the conquest and occupation of the frontier zone. The invasion and subsequent building of the frontier becomes justified by portraying the indigenous peoples living in the area as subhuman, while the frontier zone is depicted as uninhabited (Miller and Savage 1977, 109–131).

The Roman frontiers have been conceptualized as social and geographical spaces where ethnic identity was created. Many scholars see the period from the fourth to the eighth centuries CE as the time when the barbarian identities arose through interactions with the Roman Empire (Curta 2001, 2005; Hu 2013, 389–390). Thus, the lives of the "barbarians" were shaped on the Roman frontier (Weik 2014, 298).

While Roman legal and literary sources promoted a policy of exclusion at the imperial frontiers, in reality, total exclusion was never the objective. Rome's goal was to control the process of inclusion, first among occupied provincials and then among the groups living beyond the frontier (Burns 2003, 18). There was never a situation where the Romans were neatly separated on one side and the "barbarians" on the other (Cooter 1977, 84).

Romanization has been defined in the literature as the "cultural processes which result from the interaction between two supposedly distinct cultures. The nature of this change has been assumed by most to involve the progressive adoption of Roman culture by indigenous populations, including Roman speech and manners, political franchise, town life, market economy, material culture, architecture, and so on" (Jones 1997, 33). This concept has been rejected as a uniform process (Jones 1997, 129–135) or as a passive and blanket phenomenon that promoted a very restricted perception of "Roman versus native" (Pitts

2007, 693–695). The Roman Empire was a heterogeneous society; individuals and groups adopted different means of "becoming Roman" while maintaining their core, inherited identities in a global empire that recreated itself through local engagement. Heterogeneity was the binding force of imperial stability in a network of local groups that was "roughly held together by directional forces of integration that formed an organized whole and lasted for several centuries" (Hingley 2009, 60–61). While the imperial administration created, articulated, and manipulated local contexts for locals to integrate themselves into the imperial society, locals adopted a range of responses to these situations, from resistance to exploitation, for their own benefit. In these local societies, marginalized and assimilated were not discrete categories; in most cases, these categories overlapped (Hingley 2009, 70). Being or becoming Roman was not a standardized process. Different groups constructed different versions of what Roman and non-Roman identity meant, either by resisting or embracing the empire (Mattingly 2004, 22). On the *limes*, the reality of these groups (the "civilized" Romans and the "uncivilized" intruders) coalescing, assimilating, and adapting to the pressures of living on the frontier was a lot more complicated and more interesting than we understand it to be. At times, it was uncertain who the Romans were and who the barbarians were (Whittaker 1994, 132–133).

Archaeological investigations of frontiers have primarily taken place at broad regional or pan-regional scales, which is not to say that macroscale approaches have not resulted in many contributions to the field. However, multiscalar temporal and regional approaches are needed in order to give a more balanced perspective that can address issues on the order of individuals and sectional groups in specific frontier contexts (Lightfoot and Martinez 1995, 477,487). It is necessary to reconstruct microcosms in order to build a more inclusive picture. Scholars should start with the premise that this was a world of individuals who were making conscious and unconscious decisions in order to survive and prosper (Wood 1998, 301). This study looks at the community level in order to tease out how living in close proximity to the frontier affected the health and identity of people.

Both sides of a border need to be taken into account in order to better understand the cultural, social, and economic dynamics of frontiers and borderlands and their historical transformations (Baud and Van Schendel 1997, 229, 241). The current study satisfies this point as well: it includes the analysis of two communities living across the frontier on both sides of the border. This is especially relevant, since the border divides people who may have had a long history of contact. The border also unites them in their dependence on it (Baud and Van Schendel 1997, 242). Before the Romans under Emperor Trajan defeated the independent Dacian state under King Decebal in two wars in the period 101–106 CE (Ellis 1996, 105; Ellis 1998, 221), the "barbarian" Dacians showed a strong level of cohesion, beginning in the first century BCE, when Burebista unified the different Dacian groups for the first time (Burns 2003, 185; Ellis 1996, 105).

The Archaeological Site of Ibida (Slava Rusă)

Slava Rusă is located in Tulcea County, 40 kilometers southwest of Tulcea, a port on the Danube River. The climate is continental and arid, dry in the summer and cold in the winter. Based on historical sources, the site has been identified with the Roman town of Ibida (Soficaru 2014, 308). The Romans built a military camp at the end of the first century CE. In the fourth century and again in the middle of the sixth century, they built a 2,000-meter-long stone wall with 24 towers that were 10 meters tall and 3 meters wide. The wall enclosed the urban habitation area. Outside it were many farms and a military fortification. The town was abandoned at the beginning of the seventh century, presumably when nomadic peoples invaded the Roman Empire. The town flourished during the Late Roman and Early Byzantine periods (Soficaru 2014, 308). Agriculture was the main occupation of the inhabitants; archaeological investigations have revealed fragments of shovels, scoops, hoes, and mills. A granary-like structure was identified near the northwest part of the city. Fishing, hunting, and animal husbandry were also practiced (Soficaru 2014, 308–309). The walled town benefited from a very favorable position on the commercial road that traversed the center of the province and terminated at Constantinople. Goods from all provinces were transported to Ibida by this road. Workshops for producing glass, ceramics, tiles, bronze and lead also sustained the economy of Ibida (Soficaru 2014, 309).

The site has been systematically investigated by archaeologists and bioarchaeologists since 2001. A total of 174 graves have been excavated, mostly single inhumations (10 percent were double burials). A family vault with thirty-nine skeletons was also discovered. The human bones and graves have been discovered in an area of about 20 hectares around the town. The graves, which were of a variety of types, contained coffins, tiles, and stones. The human remains were found in the extended position; half were oriented along the west-east axis. Where grave goods were found, they were minimal. They included coins, rings, brooches, beads, and glass items. Several graves have been disturbed by agricultural practices (Soficaru 2014, 309).

The Archaeological Site of Târgşor

Located in Prahova County, Târgşor is a multi-period site. Its occupation began in the second century BCE and extends all the way to present. The Romans briefly occupied the site, from the time of Trajan's conquest (101–106 CE) until sometime in the middle of the second century CE (Diaconu 1965). It has been postulated that during the third and fourth centuries CE, after Aurelian withdrew from the region, this area might have been part of a buffer zone the Romans developed and maintained between the Danubian *limes* to the south and local and migratory groups to the north. The groups that lived in this buffer zone presumably were friendly toward the empire (Mitrea and Preda 1966, 158–159). This would support the view of some scholars that the Roman frontier was not meant as a border defense but as a deep zone that included the *limes* itself, the frontier provinces, and sometimes even territories on the other side in the *barbaricum* (Curta 2005, 173–174).

Only the necropolis from Târgşor had been excavated. In the 1960s, the first archaeologists to work at the site proposed, based on their analysis of the stratigraphy and of the mortuary remains, that a Sarmatian population used the necropolis during the third century and that groups belonging to the Sântana de Mureş/Černjakhov Culture used it during the fourth century. No traces of domestic structures for the third and fourth centuries CE have been found. The settlement and burials dating to the fifth and sixth centuries CE were destroyed during the eighteenth century when a local princely court was rebuilt (Diaconu 1965).

Sântana de Mureş Culture

Dating to the later third and fourth centuries CE, the Sântana de Mureş Culture in Romania and the Černjakhov Culture in the Ukraine and the Republic of Moldova constituted a rich and relatively homogeneous cultural complex that spread across large areas in southeastern Europe between the Danube and the Don Rivers (Ellis 1996, 106; Heather and Matthews 1991, 47). Although there still are some divergent and contradictory opinions about who this fourth-century culture should be attributed to and about whether or not there was a temporal discontinuity (Ellis 1996, 107; Heather and Matthews 1991, 47–50), most European historians and archaeologists associate its material remains with the spread of Goth power north of the Black Sea (Heather 2010, 117; Heather and Matthews 1991, 50; Lee 1993, 26, 158). While the material remains of this system are relatively similar during the fourth century from the Carpathians in the west to the Dnieper River in the east, it does not follow that there were not distinct cultural or ethnic identities in it (Heather 2010, 165). The finds from settlements and burials have been attributed to four different groups: Dacians, Romans, Sarmatians, and Goths (Ellis 1996, 107). The well-established agrarian Dacian population did not disappear after the Romans withdrew to the south of the Danube in the early 270s. The withdrawal of Aurelian opened up ties of communication and cultural interchange throughout the region: Dacian, Sarmatian, Goth, and Roman frontier populations interacted on a regular basis (Ellis 1996, 107). Ellis (1996) calls these processes of acculturation a "stabilized pluralism," where the cultures in contact did not lose their character during the fourth century but became multicultural societies. The Sarmatians, who were present in the Black Sea region for hundreds of years, had fought alongside Dacians in the wars against Trajan. The Dacians, the Bastarnae, the Sarmatians, and the Goths collaborated against the Romans during the third century. Roman veterans married local women and settled in Dacia. It is no wonder then that the single most striking feature of the whole Sântana de Mureş/Černjakhov phenomenon is its uniformity, although its constituent elements have different origins (Ellis 1996, 106–119; Heather and Matthews 1991, 47–88).

Since prehistoric times, the region had been characterized by the coexistence of settled agricultural populations and semi-nomadic pastoralists. Despite this coexistence, the Sântana de Mureş/Černjakhov Culture was primarily agricultural. Settlements were concentrated along river valleys (Kulikowski 2007, 89), and, as was the case with all northern barbarian societies, this culture was decidedly rural (Burns 2003, 190, 345). Wheat, barley, and millet were the staple grains; the grinding seemed to have been done at home by hand. Handmade and wheel-turned pottery were used for cooking. There is evidence for commercial workshops and for trade in fine wares with Scythia Minor (Kulikowski 2007, 90). Trade with distant regions of the barbaricum and with the Roman Empire is well attested. Roman glass, fine ceramics, and wine were presumably high-value items that were not available locally and that served the needs of the culture's elites. The presence of Roman coins close to the frontier illustrates the monetization of the local economy. Gift exchange distributed some of these luxury goods from the immediate vicinity of the frontier into more remote parts of the barbaricum. As the many grave goods from the region attest, the ability to dispose of and display valuable items was an important sign of social distinction among the Sântana de Mureş/Černjakhov elites (Kulikowski 2007, 91–94).

Burial practices in the Sântana de Mureş/Černjakhov Culture generally progressed chronologically from cremation toward inhumation. While the material culture of the living was relatively uniform, the burial goods were highly differentiated both between and within cemetery sites. These artifacts show a mixture of local, Roman, nomadic, and northern European traditions (Kulikowski 2007, 94–95). While most Sântana de Mureş/Černjakhov burials were unfurnished, some had only pottery and some had brooches. Many graves contained belt buckles. Burials containing weapons are very rare (Kulikowski 2007, 95). Bone combs, spindle whorls, and iron implements (other than weapons) have also been found with the dead (Heather and Matthews 1991, 55).

Materials

Both the Ibida and Târgşor collections have been stored at the "Francisc I. Rainer" Institute of Anthropology in Bucharest, Romania. Romanian bioarchaeologists have extensively studied the assemblage from Ibida (Aparaschivei et al. 2012; Miriţoiu and Soficaru 2003; Rubel and Soficaru 2012; Soficaru et al. 2004; Soficaru 2011; Soficaru 2014). Archaeologists have dated this collection based on stratigraphy, analysis of material culture, burial typology, body positioning in the grave, and radiocarbon dating for some individuals (Soficaru 2011; Soficaru 2014). The sample size was thirty-two adults (fourth–sixth centuries CE).

The skeletal collection from Târgşor had not been analyzed before this research. The sample size is thirty-two adults. The original archaeologists dated the burials based on stratigraphy and the analysis of the funerary contents (Diaconu 1965). No radiocarbon dating has been carried out on this collection. The entire Târgşor collection is in a poor state of preservation. It includes both cremations and inhumations, but meaningful data could be collected only from adult inhumations that also broadly overlapped the time frame under consideration in the present study (the third–fourth centuries CE). As mentioned earlier, the burials dating to fifth and sixth centuries CE were destroyed during the eighteenth century.

Methods

A biological profile was developed for each individual using standardized data collection. This included using standard osteological methods to estimate age at death and sex (Bass 1995; Buikstra and Ubelaker 1994; Işcan 1989; White et al. 2012). Only individuals with an age at death of 20 years and older were selected. This was determined based on eruption of the third molar and fusion of the epiphyses. Adult individuals were assigned to three age categories corresponding to young adult (20–34), mature adult (35–50), and old adult (over 50).

Pathology and trauma were also analyzed following well-established protocols (Aufderheide and Rodríguez-Martín 1998; Buikstra and Ubelaker 1994; Ortner 2003). The criteria Aufderheide and Rodríguez-Martín (1998) and Ortner (2003) have outlined were used in order to make decisions about possible differential diagnoses. All pathological changes were recorded as present or absent. Special attention was paid to recording health-related stress markers. Cribra orbitalia was assessed for every individual with at least one observable orbital roof. Where sufficiently well-preserved crania or cranial fragments were available for analysis, porotic hyperostosis was recorded. The long bones were analyzed for periosteal reaction. At least 50 percent of a bone had to be present to be included in the analysis.

The skeletons were examined for signs of antemortem and perimortem trauma and for fractures on the skull and the postcranial elements. Aufderheide and Rodríguez-Martín (1998) and Ortner (2003) were used to identify different potential signs of traumatic injuries.

Results

Demographic Profile

The analysis of biological descriptors such as sex and age of each individual provides the baseline data for creating the demographic profile for a community. A comparison of multiple sites starts with this basic biological community profile; without it, the comparison becomes meaningless.

The sample for the individuals from Ibida included eighteen males and fourteen females. The demographic profile for this sample is presented in figure 1.2. A Fisher's exact test was conducted to test whether there was any bias by sex and age at death. The results showed that there was no significant difference ($p = 0.519 > 0.05$).

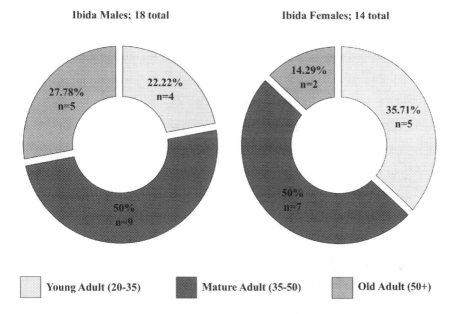

Figure 1.2. Demographics of the Ibida sample. Pie graph by Trent Skinner.

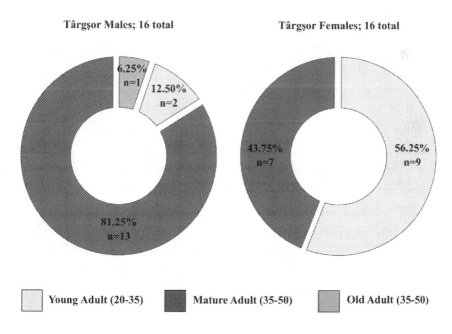

Figure 1.3. Demographics of the Târgșor sample. Pie graph by Trent Skinner.

A total of thirty-two individuals from Târgşor were selected for analysis, sixteen males and sixteen females. Figure 1.3 shows the demographic profile for this sample. It appears that the sex of the individual had an effect on the age at death in the "barbarian" population. The results of Fisher's exact test show that there was a significant difference; more women than men died at a younger age ($p = 0.023 < 0.05$).

Cribra Orbitalia and Porotic Hyperostosis

Cribra orbitalia (localized porotic lesions on the orbital roof) and porotic hyperostosis (abnormal porosity on the cranial vault), two of the most frequent pathological conditions seen in ancient human skeletal collections, have been shown to relate to anemia (Meyer 2016; Pētersone-Gordina et al. 2013; Walker et al. 2009). Anemia is a pathological symptom, not a specific disease (Walker et al. 2009, 110). It can be caused by multiple factors, such as poor nutrition; blood loss; vitamin A, B_6, B_{12}, and C deficiencies; and folic acid deficiencies (Meyer 2016; Pētersone-Gordina et al. 2013; Walker et al. 2009), or inadequate levels of iron (Oxenham and Cavill 2010). Chronic dietary deficiencies and malabsorption of folic acid and vitamin B_{12}, in particular, have been suggested as the most likely causes for cribra orbitalia in archaeological populations (Pētersone-Gordina et al. 2013; Walker et al. 2009).

In the Ibida sample, cribra orbitalia was observed on only three individuals out of twenty-six (11.54 percent) observable adults. The frequencies for cribra, broken down by sex and age categories, are listed in table 1.1. Porotic hyperostosis affected fourteen of twenty-eight (50 percent) observable individuals from the Ibida sample. These are presented by age and sex category in table 1.1. It is of interest that there are more males than females in all age categories. While this pattern is not statistically significant (Fisher's exact test, $p = 0.252 > 0.05$), it does suggest that adult males and females were both nutritionally stressed at times.

In the Târgşor sample, five of twenty (25 percent) observable individuals showed signs of cribra orbitalia, as shown in table 1.2, with no statistical difference by sex (Fisher's exact test, $p = 1 > 0.05$). Porotic hyperostosis was observed in five of twenty-five (20 percent) assessable Târgşor individuals. Table 1.2 also illustrates the frequency of porotic hyperostosis by sex and age categories in the Târgşor sample, showing that there is no statistical difference by sex (Fisher's exact test, $p = 1 > 0.05$).

Table 1.1. Frequency and percent of physiological stress conditions mentioned in text in the Ibida sample by sex and age at death

	Cribra Orbitalia (CO)		Porotic Hyperostosis (PH)		Periosteal Reaction (PR)		Comorbidity (PH and PR)	
	N	%	N	%	N	%	N	%
FEMALES								
Young adult (20–34)	0/4	0.00	2/4	50.00	4/5	80.00	2/3	66.67
Mature adult (35–50)	1/6	16.67	2/6	33.33	4/7	57.14	2/4	50.00
Old adult (50+)	0/2	0.00	0/2	0.00	1/1	100.00	0/0	0.00
Total	1/12	8.33	4/12	33.33	9/13	69.23	4/7	57.14
MALES								
Young adult (20–34)	0/4	0.00	3/4	75.00	3/4	75.00	2/2	100.00
Mature adult (35–50)	1/6	16.67	5/7	71.43	6/7	85.71	4/4	100.00
Old adult (50+)	1/4	25.00	2/5	40.00	5/5	100.00	2/2	100.00
Total	2/14	14.29	10/16	62.50	14/16	87.50	8/8	100.00
Total both sexes	3/26	11.54	14/28	50.00	23/29	79.31	12/15	80.00

Periosteal Reaction

Another pathological condition that is commonly encountered in archaeological human skeletal remains is periosteal reaction (abnormal periosteal new bone formation), also known as periostitis (figure 1.4). While it can affect any bone, it is often observed on the long bones, especially the tibiae (Klaus 2014, 295; Weston 2012, 492). Infection, metabolic diseases, nutritional deficiencies, comorbidity with other diseases, trauma, neoplasms, and circulatory disorders can all trigger periosteal new bone formation (Klaus 2014, 296; Weston 2009, 186). Historically, bioarchaeologists have looked at periosteal reaction as an indicator of stress, especially of nonspecific infectious disease (Weston 2008, 48). This assertion has been contested through macroscopic, radiographic, and mi-

Table 1.2. Frequency and percent of physiological stress conditions mentioned in text in the Târgşor sample by sex and age at death

	Cribra Orbitalia (CO)		Porotic Hyperostosis (PH)		Periosteal Reaction (PR)		Comorbidity (PH and PR)	
	N	%	N	%	N	%	N	%
FEMALES								
Young adult (20–34)	3/6	50.00	3/8	37.50	6/8	75.00	2/3	66.67
Mature adult (35–50)	0/4	0.00	0/5	0.00	2/7	28.57	0/3	0.00
Old adult (50+)	0/0	0.00	0/0	0.00	0/0	0.00	0/0	0.00
Total	3/10	30.00	3/13	23.08	8/15	53.33	2/6	33.33
MALES								
Young adult (20–34)	0/1	0.00	0/1	0.00	1/1	100.00	0/0	0.00
Mature adult (35–50)	2/8	25.00	2/10	20.00	6/10	60.00	1/3	33.33
Old adult (50+)	0/1	0.00	0/1	0.00	0/1	0.00	0/1	0.00
Total	2/10	20.00	2/12	16.67	7/12	58.33	1/4	25.00
Total both sexes	5/20	25.00	5/25	20.00	15/27	55.56	3/10	30.00

croscopic studies of museum specimens (Weston 2008, 2009, 2012). However, a complete rejection of periosteal reaction as a skeletal stress marker does not fit within the current molecular and pathophysiological fields of study. Also, after all other potential differential diagnoses have been ruled out, systemic nonspecific infection should still remain a contextually or biologically plausible diagnosis for periosteal reaction (Klaus 2014). Having said that, it is imperative to acknowledge that periosteal reaction is a complex phenomenon and that its biocultural significance is highly context-specific and challenging to interpret. In addition, while breakthrough studies on molecular signaling factors in bone have significantly advanced our current knowledge in this area, there is still a lot we do not fully understand (Klaus 2014, 299).

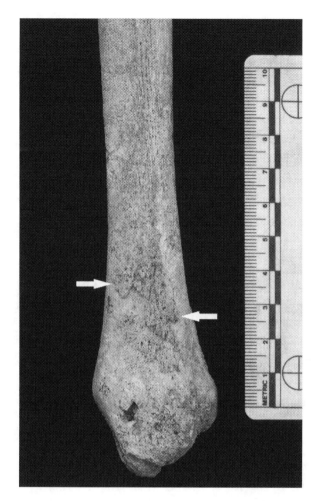

Figure 1.4. Severe, active periosteal reaction on the distal end and medial malleolus of the right tibia in a mature adult female from Ibida. Photo courtesy of Andrei Soficaru.

Periosteal reactions could be assessed for twenty-nine of the individuals from the Ibida sample. A large portion (n = 23, 79.31 percent) showed signs of this pathology (table 1.1). There is no statistically significant difference by sex (Fisher's exact test, $p = 0.364 > 0.05$) or by age (Fisher's exact test, $p = 0.417 > 0.05$). Males and females in all age categories carried a morbidity burden that included nonspecific infections. Possible reasons for this are addressed in the discussion section below.

In total, fifteen of twenty-seven (55.56 percent) observable individuals from Târgșor had periosteal reaction; table 1.2 presents frequencies by age and sex categories. There is no statistically significant difference by sex (Fisher's exact test, $p = 1 > 0.05$) or by age (Fisher's exact test, $p = 0.157 > 0.05$).

Comorbidity

The cause of death, overall health status, and medical history for an individual are not always written in his/her bones. Acute diseases, for example, were probably more common causes of death before antibiotics than the conditions that have left an osteological evidence (van Schaik et al. 2014). Most diseases, especially the fatal ones, often leave no marks or indicators on the skeletal remains (Meyer 2016).

Individuals accumulate pathology as they age, and the severity and number of these conditions depend on a multitude of factors, among which sex, age, hormones, comorbidities, genetics, socioeconomic status, and nutritional and metabolic stress play an important role. Thus, it is difficult to infer the disease burden an individual experienced during life based only on pathological analysis of skeletal remains (van Schaik et al. 2014). Nevertheless, bioarchaeological studies continually strive to get a better and more contextualized understanding of the general quality of life for past people. The tendency in bioarchaeological population studies is to focus on the general indicators of stress presented above because these types of pathological conditions refer to the body's nonspecific adaptive response to stressors such as malnutrition and metabolic stress (Meyer 2016, 1–2). Taken together, these stress indicators can provide a more nuanced picture of health for the populations and individuals under study. My research looks at porotic hyperostosis in conjunction with periosteal reaction as two indicators of comorbidity.

In the Ibida sample, fifteen individuals could be assessed for both pathologies. Twelve (80 percent) of these had signs of both porotic hyperostosis and periosteal reaction. A frequency of comorbidity for males and females by age categories is presented in table 1.1. Males in all age categories carried a comorbidity burden and more males than females showed signs of both conditions. It appears that the sex of the individual (Fisher's exact test, $p = 0.077 > 0.05$, close to significant) but not age (Fisher's exact test, $p = 1 > 0.05$), could have been a factor in developing both nutritional anemia and nonspecific systemic infection.

In the Târgșor sample, three of ten (30 percent) observable individuals showed signs of comorbidity. The only affected male was a mature adult and the two affected females were young adults, as shown in table 1.2. No statistically significant difference by sex (Fisher's exact test, $p = 1 > 0.05$) or by age (Fisher's exact test, $p = 0.458 > 0.05$) is observed in this sample.

Trauma

Skeletal remains have the potential to provide a powerful empirical record of pathology and trauma. No pathological analysis of human remains can ever reveal a complete picture of an individual's health status without a study of injuries and trauma. The trauma, pathological conditions, and irregular and abnormal changes in the skeleton can be collectively used to assess what health effects living in the proximity of the frontier had on communities and individuals. In this study, the primary focus is on injuries and fractures that happened during a person's lifetime and had time to heal. Table 1.3 reports the findings for antemortem trauma for both cranial and postcranial elements.

There is evidence of some form of antemortem trauma for thirteen of thirty-one (41.94 percent) observable individuals in the Ibida sample: ten males and three females suffered traumatic injuries during their lifetime (table 1.3). These injuries range in severity from shallow, small cranial depression fractures and small-rib bony spurs to fractures of the radius, ulna, or ribs. The most common cranial injuries are cranial depression fractures and the most common

Table 1.3. Frequency and percent of antemortem trauma in the two samples by sex

	Antemortem Cranial Trauma		Antemortem Postcranial Trauma		Individuals with Some Form of Antemortem Trauma (Cranial or Postcranial)		Individuals with Some Form of Trauma and Comorbidity	
	N	%	N	%	N	%	N	%
IBIDA								
Females	2/11	18.18	2/11	18.18	3/13	23.08	2/3	66.67
Males	4/15	26.67	9/17	52.94	10/18	55.56	7/10	70.00
Total	6/26	23.08	11/28	39.29	13/31	41.94	9/13	69.23
TÂRGȘOR								
Females	2/9	22.22	3/11	27.27	4/14	28.57	2/4	50.00
Males	3/11	27.27	5/8	62.50	8/13	61.54	1/8	12.50
Total	5/20	25.00	8/19	42.11	12/27	44.44	3/12	25.00

postcranial injuries are rib fractures. Males and individuals from older age categories were the most affected by rib fractures. The frequency of males who suffered some type of trauma is more than double the frequency of females, although there is no statistically significant difference by sex (Fisher's exact test, p = 0.139 > 0.05). Of the thirteen individuals with healed injuries, eight carried a comorbidity burden for porotic hyperostosis and periosteal reaction and one carried a comorbidity factor for cribra orbitalia and periosteal reaction (table 1.3). It is of interest that all but one of the individuals with cranial or postcranial trauma also showed signs of at least one general stress indicator (one could not be assessed).

Five (38.46 percent) individuals from the Ibida sample had healed cranial depression fractures (an example is presented in figure 1.5): three males (two in the young adult and one in the old adult age categories) and two females (both in the mature adult age category). All of these five individuals showed signs of periosteal reaction and three of them also showed porotic hyperostosis. All of the cranial depression fractures (CDFs) were located above the hat brim line (HBL). In forensic literature, the HBL is defined as the area located between two lines parallel to a line inspired by the Frankfort horizontal plane (a horizontal plane that passes through the right and left porion points and the left orbitale, the superior margin passing through the glabella and the inferior margin passing through the center of the external auditory meatus) (Guyomarc'h et al. 2010, 423–424; Kremer et al. 2008, 716; Kremer and Sauvageau 2009, 923). Being able to discriminate between falls and blows is a major issue in forensic practice. Historically, the HBL rule has been used as the most useful single criterion. According to this rule, an injury inside the HBL is more likely due to a fall, while a wound located above this line is likely the result of a blow (Guyomarc'h et al. 2010; Kremer et al. 2008; Kremer and Sauvageau 2009). Recent studies, however, have shown the HBL rule to be far from a perfect criterion; using it on its own is not recommended (Guyomarc'h et al. 2010; Kremer et al. 2008; Kremer and Sauvageau 2009; Lefèvre et al. 2015). In conjunction with other tested criteria, such as the side lateralization and number and length of lacerations, the HBL rule might sometimes be partially useful in discriminating falls from blows (Guyomarc'h et al. 2010; Kremer et al. 2008; Kremer and Sauvageau 2009). In terms of side lateralization, it has been suggested left for blows and right for falls due to the fact that most people are right-handed: most perpetrators would hit the left side of their victims' head but in a fall, most people would interpose their right hand and the right side of the head would be more

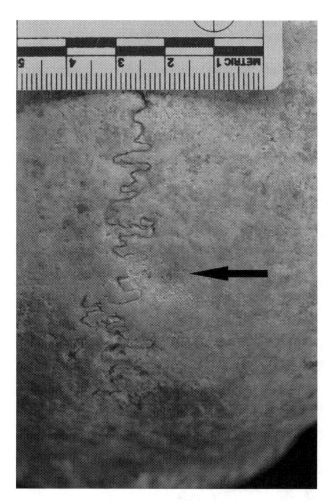

Figure 1.5. Right parietal cranial depression fracture in an old adult male from Ibida. Photo courtesy of Andrei Soficaru.

prone to hit the ground (Guyomarc'h et al. 2010; Kremer et al. 2008; Kremer and Sauvageau 2009). Three of the five Ibida individuals with CDFs had cranial injuries on the left side.

In the Târgşor sample, twelve (44.44 percent) of twenty-seven observable individuals had signs of healed fractures and injuries. Similar to the Ibida sample, twice as many males as females suffered from trauma: eight males and four females (table 1.3). However, sex differences in the prevalence of trauma were not statistically significant (Fisher's exact test, $p = 0.128 > 0.05$). In this sample, the bones of the lower limbs (see figure 1.6), especially the tibiae, seem to have been most affected by trauma. Just as in the Ibida sample, most individuals suffering from some form of trauma also had osteological evidence of at least one general

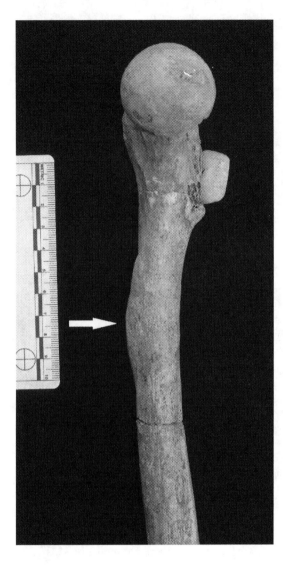

Figure 1.6. Right proximal femur fracture in a young adult female from Târgșor. Photo courtesy of Andrei Soficaru.

stress indicator discussed above. Three of these individuals suffered from all three pathologies: cribra orbitalia, porotic hyperostosis, and nonspecific periosteal lesions (table 1.3).

CDFs were also found in the Târgșor sample. Three mature adult males and one young adult female had healed cranial depression fractures; for three of them the CDFs were located above the HBL and for one male the CDF was in the HBL zone. Most CDFs were on the left parietal, although one mature adult male displayed a right parietal fracture.

Population-level analyses give critical information. They give perspective on what the general quality of life was like for these communities. The summary statistics and population tendencies help place the individuals who suffered stress indicators and trauma in the context of their respective groups or communities. In the Ibida sample, both males and females carried a comorbidity burden and more males than females suffered from both porotic hyperostosis and periosteal reaction. Males also suffered more from trauma. In the Târgşor sample, women had a higher mortality risk and lower survivorship rate than men. And although the finding was not statistically significant, more women than men suffered from cribra orbitalia, porotic hyperostosis, and periosteal reaction. Similar to the finding for the Ibida sample, however, more males than females showed signs of trauma in the Târgşor sample.

Discussion

In this study, I looked at the differences in health and trauma between two groups living on the Lower Danube frontier. The results, which were close to statistical significance, show that the "barbarians" from Târgşor had a higher mortality risk and a lower survivorship rate. By comparison, the "Romans" from Ibida lived longer (Fisher's exact test, $p = 0.087 > 0.05$, nearly significant). When broken down by sex, there was no statistical difference in mortality rates between "Roman" and "barbarian" males, or between "Roman" and "barbarian" females. However, the "Romans" had a higher morbidity burden and showed a higher frequency of stress indicators. The prevalence of porotic hyperostosis was statistically higher in the "Roman" sample (Fischer's exact test, $p = 0.043 < 0.05$, significant). The prevalence of nonspecific periosteal lesions was also higher in the "Roman" sample than for the "barbarians" (Fisher's exact test, $p = 0.086 > 0.05$, nearly significant). When I looked at these two stress markers in combination, the results show that the "Romans" had a higher comorbidity burden than their "barbarian" neighbors to the north (Fisher's exact test, $p = 0.034 < 0.05$, significant). The "Romans" were living longer but were sicker, while the "barbarians" were dying younger but were healthier. In order to see which sex was driving this difference, Fisher's exact tests were run on "Roman" versus "barbarian" males and on "Roman" versus "barbarian" females. While there is no statistical difference between "Roman" females and "barbarian" females in terms of comorbidity ($p = 0.592$), the "Roman" males were more likely to be affected by both porotic hyperostosis and periosteal reaction than their "barbarian" counterparts ($p = 0.018$). Thus, the "Roman" males had more allostatic loading. There was no statistical difference in the incidence of trauma in the two groups (Fisher's exact test, $p = 1$). Further breakdown by sex did not reveal a statistical difference between "Romans" and "barbarians" for trauma.

Alternatively, according to Wood et al.'s (1992, 356) osteological paradox, which states that "better health makes for worse skeletons," the individuals that exhibited more stress indicators could actually, under some circumstances, have been relatively healthier than at least some of the "barbarian" individuals who died before a bony response had time to develop. Researchers have used contextually informed osteological collections from both Rome and Britain to show that living inside the empire did not necessarily imply a healthier and more hygienic way of life: urbanization, malnutrition, hygiene, sanitation, and comorbidity of parasites and numerous infections may have increased people's general stress and frailty (Killgrove 2014, 880). Nevertheless, the fundamental paradox in bioarchaeology is that we are trying to recreate the lives and health patterns of past people by using intrinsically biased samples of dead individuals (DeWitte and Stojanowski 2015, 406). It is crucial to recognize the challenges we are facing. For this study in particular, we need to acknowledge the small sample size and the poor preservation of some of the skeletons, particularly from the Târgşor collection.

The overall results of this study agree with some of the previous investigations into the health, demographic, and mortality differences between rural and urban populations in Roman Britain (Redfern et al. 2015). Redfern and colleagues (2015) have been able to show that rural populations in Dorset experienced lower frequencies of indicators of stress and metabolic diseases than their urban neighbors did and that urban dwellers had higher survivorship than their rural counterparts. Their study, however, compared populations living under Roman rule inside a Roman province. For the present study, an additional level of complexity should be considered: the two populations represent not only rural and urban environments but also different sociopolitical and economic backgrounds in a frontier setting.

The differences in poor health indicators between the two samples can be explained by looking at the historical context of the Lower Danube frontier in late antiquity. Scythia Minor was one of the most exposed provinces of the empire. The written sources mention that in the first half of the sixth century, raids by groups the empire regarded as barbarians took place yearly (Curta 2006, 53). This prompted Emperor Justinian to begin his unprecedented fortification project on the Danube frontier. It is no surprise then that during the fourth–sixth centuries, there was a remarkable increase in the number of military settlements and increased construction of large military forts in Scythia Minor, transforming it into a highly militarized province (Curta 2001, 124, 182; Curta 2006, 53–54; Zahariade 2006, 16).

According to Ammianus Marcellinus, a Roman army officer turned historian, in 376 CE two groups of Goths driven from their homes by the Huns, newcomers to the region, were roaming the plains in the Lower Danube region, asking the Romans for permission to cross the river. The emperor allowed one group, but not the other, to cross into the empire. However, the officials responsible for the operation miscalculated the number of refugees who were given asylum (Ammianus Marcellinus 1986, 416–417). A mass migration of refugees into the empire was followed by a notorious example of abuse by corrupt Roman officers. The Roman officers robbed the refugees of their possessions and their women while they were negotiating the terms of the asylum (Whittaker 2004, 210). If Ammianus Marcellinus is to be believed, the same officers were selling dog meat in exchange for slaves, among whom were the sons of the Goths' chieftains, giving the Goths no choice but to fight back (which they had promised not to do) or starve (Ammianus Marcellinus 1986, 418–421). The migration of this large group into an area that could not possibly support it followed by the Goths' revolt and the ensuing Roman military action resulted in a human-induced famine (Stathakopoulos 2004, 204).

Continuous migrations, invasions, and raids in the province severely disrupted country life. Farms were devastated and farmers were no longer safe as they worked in their fields (Liebeschuetz 2015, 425–464). This led to a switch in crops from field-grown cereal to garden-cultivated millet and legumes, crops that could be grown close to the city or inside fortified settlements (Liebeschuetz 2015, 439). Because millet was considered a substandard grain in the Roman Empire and was associated with famine and the poor (Killgrove and Tykot 2013, 36), a difference in foodways between the "Roman" sample from Ibida and the "barbarian" sample from Târgşor could partially explain the higher rates of stress markers affecting the "Romans."

Demographic imbalances, epidemics, and failures of subsistence systems along the frontier coupled with external inputs (such as demographic surfeits beyond the frontier) or internal embarrassments (such as civil wars within the empire) (Cooter 1977, 99) might have all contributed to nutritional stress and metabolic diseases. No single and simple explanation can account for the complexity of these peoples' lives on the frontier and their health differences.

Conclusion

I have highlighted the health, demographic and mortality differences between frontier provincials and populations living outside the Roman Empire in Romania during the third–sixth centuries CE. Overall, I found that the "Romans" had lower mortality, higher rates of survivorship, and a higher comorbidity burden than their "barbarian" counterparts across the Lower Danube frontier. This pilot study opens new areas of research for the future. These differences should be further investigated through the use of biogeochemical and biomolecular techniques, while additional bioarchaeological health studies need to be conducted on larger skeletal samples.

The term "barbarian" is alive and well and still denotes any group that goes against western societal values. The current project aims to give a broader historical perspective to contemporary issues. In the past, ethnic and group identity was a function of power relations and a matter of daily social practice (Curta 2007, 184); the interplay between these practices and power relations left indelible marks on the bones.

Killgrove (2014) has observed that Imperial Roman bioarchaeology in the twenty-first century is still mostly focused on Italy, Greece, and Britain. That is not to say that bioarchaeological research is not being conducted at the periphery of the empire, on its frontiers and borderlands, such as Romania (this chapter; chapter 8), Azerbaijan (chapter 2), and Egypt (chapter 4). In line with Killgrove's (2014) call to action, this chapter expands bioarchaeological research from the center of the Roman world to the lesser-studied provinces of the empire.

Acknowledgments

I wish to thank the staff from the "Francisc I. Rainer" Institute of Anthropology in Bucharest for access to the collections, and for providing excellent facilities. Special thanks are due to Dr. Andrei Soficaru, without whom this research would not have been possible. I also thank Trent Skinner for his assistance with figures 1.1, 1.2, and 1.3. Versions of this paper were presented at the Society for American Archaeology 81st Meeting in Orlando, April 2016, and at the 21st European Meeting of the Paleopathology Association in Moscow, August 2016. I greatly benefited from questions and discussion points received from audience members.

References

Ammianus Marcellinus. 1986. *The Later Roman Empire (A.D. 354–378)*. Introduction by Andrew Wallace-Hadrill. Translated by Walter Hamilton. New York: Penguin Books.

Aparaschivei, D., M. Iacob, A. D. Soficaru, and D. Paraschiv. 2012. "Aspects of Everyday Life in Scythia Minor Reflected in Some Funerary Discoveries from Ibida (Slava Rusă, Tulcea County)." In *Homines, Funera, Astra. Proceedings of the International Symposium on Funerary Anthropology. 5–8 June 2011. '1 Decembrie 1918' University (Alba Iulia, Romania)*, edited by R. Kogălniceanu, R.-G. Curcă, M. Gligor, and S. Stratton, 169–182. Oxford: Archaeopress.

Aufderheide, A. C. and Rodríguez-Martín, C. 1998. *The Cambridge Encyclopedia of Human Paleopathology*. Cambridge: Cambridge University Press.

Bass, W. M. 1995. *Human Osteology: A Laboratory and Field Manual*. Columbia: Missouri Archaeological Society.

Baud, M., and W. Van Schendel. 1997. "Toward a Comparative History of Borderlands." *Journal of World History* 8(2): 211–242.

Buikstra, J. E., and D. H. Ubelaker. 1994. *Standards for Data Collection from Human Skeletal Remains*. Arkansas Archaeological Survey Research Series No. 44. Fayetteville: Arkansas Archaeological Survey.

Burns, T. S. 2003. *Rome and the Barbarians: 100 B.C.–A.D. 400*. Baltimore, MD: John Hopkins University Press.

Cooter, W. S. 1977. "Preindustrial Frontiers and Interaction Spheres: Prolegomenon to a Study of Roman Frontier Regions." In *The Frontier: Comparative Studies*, edited by D. H. Miller and J. O. Steffen, 81–107. Norman: University of Oklahoma Press.

Curta, F. 2001. *The Making of the Slavs: History and Archaeology of the Lower Danube Region, c. 500–700*. Cambridge: Cambridge University Press.

———. 2005. "Frontier Ethnogenesis in Late Antiquity: The Danube, the Tervingi, and the Slavs." In *Borders, Barriers, and Ethnogenesis: Frontiers in Late Antiquity and the Middle Ages*, edited by F. Curta, 173–204. Belgium: Brepols Publishers.

———. 2006. *Southeastern Europe in the Middle Ages, 500–1250*. Cambridge: Cambridge University Press.

———. 2007. "Some Remarks on Ethnicity in Medieval Archaeology." *Early Medieval Europe* 15(2): 159–185.

DeWitte, S. N., and C. M. Stojanowski. 2015. "The Osteological Paradox 20 Years Later: Past Perspectives, Future Directions." *Journal of Archaeological Research* 23: 397–450.

Diaconu, G. 1965. *Târgșor. Necropola din secolele III–IV e.n.* București: Editura Academiei Republicii Populare Române.

Drijvers, J. W. 2011. "The Limits of the Empire in the Res Gestae of Ammianus Marcellinus." In *Frontiers in the Roman World: Proceedings of the Ninth Workshop of the International Network Impact of Empire (Durham, 16–19 April 2009)*, edited by O. Hekster and T. Kaizer, 13–29. Leiden: Brill.

Ellis, L. 1996. "Dacians, Sarmatians, and Goths on the Roman-Carpathian Frontier: Second–Fourth Centuries." In *Shifting Frontiers in Late Antiquity*, edited by R. W. Mathisen and H. S. Sivan, 105–125. Aldershot, Hampshire and Brookfield, Vt.: Variorum.

Ellis, L. 1998. "'Terra deserta': Population, Politics, and the [De]Colonization of Dacia." *World Archaeology* 30(2): 220–237.

Elton, H. 1996. *Frontiers of the Roman Empire*. Bloomington: Indiana University Press.

Geary, P. J. 2002. *The Myth of Nations: The Medieval Origins of Europe*. Princeton, NJ: Princeton University Press.

Graham, M. W. 2006. *News and Frontier Consciousness in the Late Roman Empire*. Ann Arbor: University of Michigan Press.

Guyomarc'h, P., M. Campagna-Vaillancourt, C. Kremer, and A. Sauvageau. 2010. "Discrimination of Falls and Blows in Blunt Head Trauma: A Multi-Criteria Approach." *Journal of Forensic Science* 55(2): 423–427.

Heather, P. 2010. *Empires and Barbarians: The Fall of Rome and the Birth of Europe*. Oxford: Oxford University Press.

Heather, P., and J. Matthews. 1991. *The Goths in the Fourth Century*. Liverpool: Liverpool University Press.

Hingley, R. 2009. "Cultural Diversity and Unity: Empire and Rome." In *Material Culture and Social Identities in the Ancient World*, S. Hales and T. Hodos, 54–75. Cambridge: Cambridge University Press.

Hu, D. 2013. "Approaches to the Archaeology of Ethnogenesis: Past and Emergent Perspectives." *Journal of Archaeological Research* 21: 371–402.

Işcan, M. Y. 1989. *Age Markers in the Human Skeleton*. Springfield, IL: Charles C. Thomas Publisher.

James, E. 2009. *Europe's Barbarians, AD 200–600*. London: Pearson Education Limited.

Jones, S. 1997. *The Archaeology of Ethnicity: Constructing Identities in the Past and Present*. London: Routledge.

Killgrove, K. 2014. "Bioarchaeology in the Roman Empire." In *Encyclopedia of Global Archaeology*, edited by C. Smith, 876–882. New York: Springer.

Killgrove, K., and R. H. Tykot. 2013. "Food for Rome: A Stable Investigation of Diet in the Imperial Period (1st–3rd centuries AD)." *Journal of Anthropological Archaeology* 32: 28–38.

Klaus, H. D. 2014. "Frontiers in the Bioarchaeology of Stress and Disease: Cross-Disciplinary Perspectives from Pathophysiology, Human Biology, and Epidemiology." *American Journal of Physical Anthropology* 155: 294–308.

Kremer, C., S. Racette, C. A. Dionne, and A. Sauvageau. 2008. "Discrimination of Falls and Blows in Blunt Head Trauma: Systematic Study of the Hat Brim Line Rule in Relation to Skull Fractures." *Journal of Forensic Science* 53(3): 716–719.

Kremer, C., and A. Sauvageau. 2009. "Discrimination of Falls and Blows in Blunt Head Trauma: Assessment of Predictability through Combined Criteria." *Journal of Forensic Science* 54(4): 923–926.

Kulikowski, M. 2007. *Rome's Gothic Wars: From the Third Century to Alaric*. Cambridge: Cambridge University Press.

Lee, A. D. 1993. *Information and Frontiers: Roman Foreign Relations in Late Antiquity*. Cambridge: Cambridge University Press.

Lefèvre, T., J. C. Alvarez, and G. Lorin de la Grandmaison. 2015. "Discriminating Factors in Fatal Blunt Trauma from Low Level Falls and Homicide." *Forensic Science, Medicine, and Pathology* 11(2): 152–161.

Liebeschuetz, W. 2015. *East and West in Late Antiquity: Invasion, Settlement, Ethnogenesis and Conflicts of Religion.* Leiden: Brill.

Lightfoot, K. G., and A. Martinez. 1995. "Frontiers and Boundaries in Archaeological Perspective." *Annual Review of Anthropology* 24: 471–492.

Martin, D. L, R. P. Harrod, and V. R. Pérez. 2013. *Bioarchaeology. An Integrated Approach to Working with Human Remains.* New York: Springer.

Mattingly, D. 2004. "Being Roman: Expressing Identity in a Provincial Setting." *Journal of Roman Archaeology* 17: 5–25.

Meyer, A. 2016. "Assessment of Diet and Recognition of Nutritional Deficiencies in Paleopathological Studies: A Review." *Clinical Anatomy* 29(7): 1–8.

Miller, D. H., and W. W. Savage Jr. 1977. "Ethnic Stereotypes and the Frontier: A Comparative Study of Roman and American Experience." In *The Frontier: Comparative Studies,* edited by D. H. Miller and J. O. Steffen, 109–137. Norman: University of Oklahoma Press.

Mirițoiu, N., and A. D. Soficaru. 2003. "Studiul antropologic al osemintelor din cavoul Romano-Bizantin 'Tudorca' de la Slava Rusă (antica Ibida)." *PEUCE* 1: 511–530.

Mitrea, B., and C. Preda. 1966. *Necropole din secolul al IVlea E.N. in Muntenia.* Bucureşti: Editura Academiei Republicii Socialiste România.

Ortner, D. J. 2003. *Identification of Pathological Conditions in Human Skeletal Remains.* San Diego: Academic Press.

Oxenham, M. F., and I. Cavill. 2010. "Porotic Hyperostosis and Cribra Orbitalia: The Erythropoietic Response to Iron-Deficiency Anaemia." *Anthropological Science* 118(3): 199–200.

Pētersone-Gordina, E., G. Gerhards, and T. Jakob. 2013. "Nutrition-Related Health Problems in a Wealthy 17–18th Century German Community in Jelgava, Latvia." *International Journal of Paleopathology* 3: 30–38.

Pitts, M. 2007. "The Emperor's New Clothes? The Utility of Identity in Roman Archaeology." *American Journal of Archaeology* 111(4): 693–713.

Redfern, R. C., S. N. DeWitte, J. Pearce, C. Hamlin, and K. E. Dinwiddy. 2015. "Urban-Rural Differences in Roman Dorset, England: A Bioarchaeological Perspective on Roman Settlements." *American Journal of Physical Anthropology* 157: 107–120.

Rubel, A., and A. D. Soficaru. 2012. "Infant Burials in Roman Dobrudja. A Report of Work in Progress: The Case of Ibida (Slava Rusă)." In *Homines, Funera, Astra. Proceedings of the International Symposium on Funerary Anthropology. 5–8 June 2011. '1 Decembrie 1918' University (Alba Iulia, Romania),* edited by R. Kogălniceanu, R.-G. Curcă, M. Gligor, and S. Stratton, 163–168. Oxford: Archaeopress.

Soficaru, A. D. 2011. *Populația provinciei Scythia în perioada Romano-Bizantină (sf. Sec. III–înc. Sec. VII).* Iaşi, Romania: Editura Universităţii "Alexandru Ioan Cuza."

———. 2014. "Anthropological Data about the Funeral Discoveries from Slava Rusă, Tulcea County, Romania." *PEUCE* 12: 307–340.

Soficaru, A. D., N. Mirițoiu, N. M. Sultana, M. M. Gătej, and M. D. Constantinescu. 2004. "Analiza antropologică a osemintelor descoperite în campania din 2002, în necropola Romano-Bizantină de la Slava Rusă (Jud. Tulcea)." *PEUCE* 2: 329–386.

Stathakopoulos, D. C. 2004. *Famine and Pestilence in the Late Roman and Early Byz-*

antine Empire: A Systematic Survey of Subsistence Crises and Epidemics. Burlington, VT: Ashgate.

van Schaik, K., D. Vinichenko, and F. Rühli. 2014. "Health Is Not Always Written in Bone: Using a Modern Comorbidity Index to Assess Disease Load in Paleopathology." *American Journal of Physical Anthropology* 154: 215–221.

Walker, P. L., R. R. Bathurst, R. Richman, T. Gjerdrum, and V. A. Andrushko, 2009. "The Causes of Porotic Hyperostosis and Cribra Orbitalia: A Reappraisal of the Iron-Deficiency-Anemia Hypothesis." *American Journal of Physical Anthropology* 139: 109–125.

Weik, T. M. 2014. "The Archaeology of Ethnogenesis." *Annual Review of Anthropology* 43: 291–305.

Weston, D. A. 2008. "Investigating the Specificity of Periosteal Reactions in Pathology Museum Specimens." *American Journal of Physical Anthropology* 137: 48–59.

———. 2009. "Brief Communication: Paleohistopathological Analysis of Pathology Museum Specimens: Can Periosteal Reaction Microstructure Explain Lesion Etiology?" *American Journal of Physical Anthropology* 140: 186–193.

———. 2012. "Nonspecific Infection in Paleopathology: Interpreting Periosteal Reactions." In *A Companion to Paleopathology*, edited by A. L. Grauer, 492–512. Malden: John Wiley & Sons.

White, T. D., M. T. Black, and P. A. Folkens. 2012. *Human Osteology*. 3rd ed. Boston: Elsevier Academic Press.

Whittaker, C. R. 1994. *Frontiers of the Roman Empire: A Social and Economic Study*. Baltimore, MD: John Hopkins University Press.

———. 2004. *Rome and Its Frontiers: The Dynamics of Empire*. London: Routledge.

Wood, I. 1998. "Conclusions: Strategies of Distinction." In *Strategies of Distinction: The Construction of Ethnic Communities, 300–800*, edited by W. Pohl and H. Reimitz, 297–303. Leiden: Brill.

Wood, J. W., G. R. Milner, H. C. Harpending, K. M. Weiss, M. N. Cohen, L. E. Eisenberg, D. L. Hutchinson, R. Jankauskas, G. Česnys, M. A. Katzenberg, J. R. Lukacs, J. W. McGrath, E. A. Roth, D. H. Ubelaker, and R. G. Wilkinson. 1992. "The Osteological Paradox: Problems of Inferring Prehistoric Health from Skeletal Samples." *Current Anthropology* 33(4): 343–370.

Zahariade. M. 2006. *Scythia Minor: A History of a Later Roman Province (284–681)*. Amsterdam: Adolf M. Hakkert.

2

Funerary Practice and Local Interaction on the Imperial Frontier, First Century CE

A Case Study in the Şərur Valley, Azerbaijan

SELIN E. NUGENT

Despite their geographic distance from centers of power, imperial frontiers are spaces of intense interaction and identity formation that engage disparate social networks that create and re-create sociopolitical boundaries. The South Caucasus has exhibited the physical and social qualities that characterize a frontier or borderland region throughout much of its history. The South Caucasus refers to the region to the south of the Greater Caucasus Mountains that is between the Caspian and Black Seas and is intersected by the Kura and Aras Rivers. The geology and geography of the South Caucasus form a boundary between the Europe and Asia. The Lesser Caucasus range crosses the entirety of the region, forming a rugged, highland barrier at the intersection of Anatolia, the Northern Caucasus, and the Iranian Plateau. This physical boundary mirrors a cultural boundary that has existed between western and eastern societies over centuries. This geographical division was amplified in the Classical period, when this region served as a buffer zone between the Greco-Roman and Persian Empires as they competed for territorial expansion.

Seemingly isolated from centers of imperial power, the South Caucasus often attracted political tensions and hostilities related to border protections and territorial expansion. Instead of functioning as a segregated space of minimal or passive interaction, the South Caucasus was a dynamic space for negotiating identities and alliances among diverse individuals and groups from local and distant territories.

This chapter focuses on the South Caucasus as a Roman and Parthian frontier during the first century AD. Imperial neighbors wrote many historical accounts of interactions in this region through the perspective of institutional authority. Military campaigns and conflict between the Roman and Parthian Empires and frontier communities defined the years leading to the first century CE. During this time, local alliances were cyclically forged, broken, and mended in the quest for control of the territory (Campbell 1993; Swain and Davies 2010). The dynamic and fluid nature of imperial interaction and influence raises questions about actors involved and the material realities of social relations, intersections of identity, and individual and collective agency that forged lived experiences on the frontier.

This study explores a particular instance of the confluence of empire and frontier that is evident in an unusual burial and its associated human skeletal remains from the first century CE that was discovered at the Oğlanqala fortress in the Şərur Valley of Naxçıvan, Azerbaijan (figure 2.1). It integrates osteological and isotopic data from human skeletal remains and a regional approach to funerary practices in order to examine status, individual identity, and the various influences on funerary practices. By delving into the distinct

Figure 2.1. Map of the South Caucasus and Oğlanqala. Map by Selin Nugent.

42   Selin E. Nugent

biography of individual and the regional mortuary context, this chapter offers a bottom-up perspective on the relationship between local and foreign actors on a frontier in order to reconsider and expand on institutional narratives of domination and violence.

The Lone Westward-Facing Burial

During the 2011 research season of the Naxçıvan Archaeological Project, excavators discovered an isolated urn burial (WWE.B1) placed at the exterior of the west-facing stone fortification wall surrounding an Iron Age hilltop fortress at Oğlanqala. The urn was an approximately 1 meter tall pithos that was resting horizontally and was oriented south to north. It was capped by a large ceramic sherd (figure 2.2). The skeleton within rested on the left side in tightly flexed position, oriented south to north and facing west.

Four identical silver Roman *denarii* recovered at the bottom of the pithos date the burial to the first decade of the first century CE. The obverse of the coins depicts a laureate Caesar Augustus with the inscription "CAESAR AVGVSTVS

Figure 2.2. Burial WWE.B1. Photograph by Selin Nugent.

Figure 2.3. Obverse and reverse view of silver denarii accompanying WWE.B1. Photograph by Selin Nugent.

DIVI F PATER PATRIAE." The reverse depicts the standing, togated figures of Gaius Caesar and Lucius Caesar and is inscribed with "AVGVSTI F COS DESIG PRINC IVVENT, C L CAESARES" (figure 2.3). The inscription translates to "G[aius] and L[ucius] Caesars, sons of Augustus, consuls designate, leaders of youth." These coins were minted in 2 BCE (at the earliest) to celebrate the priesthood bestowed upon both Gaius and Lucius, heirs of Emperor Augustus. Minting ended in 14 CE (at the latest) after the death of Augustus (Mousheghian and Depeyrot 1999).

While the construction of the Oğlanqala citadel dates to the Iron Age, the burial corresponds to Period II, a later period of occupation that has been radiocarbon dated to the first century BCE through the first century CE. Evidence of Period II at Oğlanqala consists of several sparse domestic structures and large feasting pits. The feasting pits, which are located at the center of the citadel complex, contained abundant charred sheep and goat fragments and broken ceramic eating and drinking vessels (Ristvet et al. forthcoming).

In the South Caucasus, reuse of abandoned Iron Age fortresses in later periods for both settlement and funerary purposes was a common practice (Khatchadourian 2007). The substantial and sturdy stone walls, which survive to the present day, likely offered visibility of the valley and protection to inhabitants. However, the Period II assemblages at Oğlanqala do not appear to be associated with extensive permanent local residence or cemetery space. Rather, the combination of large-scale feasting refuse paired and minimal domestic architecture and mortuary features may suggest a brief period of use by a large group. The mortuary assemblage from Burial WWE.B1 in context with osteo-logical and isotopic data from the interred individual points to the possibility of an alternative use of the fortress that involved hosting foreign travelers. The presence of such travelers in the region is well documented.

The South Caucasus during the Roman Campaign in the Early First Century CE

During the first century BCE and the first century CE, the South Caucasus, and particularly the Aras River Basin, which intersects with the Şərur Valley, was at the center of mounting political and military tensions between Rome and Parthia. While the region was ultimately under the rule of the Artaxiad dynasty of the kingdom of Armenia, both Rome and Parthia continuously mounted campaigns in the region to preserve and expand their imperial borders and imperial representatives maintained their regional interests by negotiating the degree of Roman and Parthian political influence with local authorities and the Artaxiad court (Campbell 1993).

After Augustus became emperor in 14 BCE, the Romans began vigorous cam-paign against Parthia to end a century of fluctuating borders in the South Cau-casus region. Rome's reputation rested on its ability to reassert its power over its frontier regions (Benario 1999; Cooley 2009). Concurrent with the decade of the Oğlanqala burial, Augustus ordered by his heir, Gaius Caesar, to lead a cam-paign to expand the territory Rome controlled in the South Caucasus (Augustus 1924, 27.2). Although the *Res Gestae divi Augusti* described the campaign in vio-lent, militaristic terms, it included a brief reflection on a moment of diplomacy (Romer 1979). Velleius Paterculus wrote that Gaius met with King Phraataces of Parthia on the banks of the Euphrates River, where they established a treaty designed to ensure peace in the Caucasus (Velleius Paterculus 1924, 2. 101). How-ever, in 3 CE, the campaign descended into violence in the South Caucasus when Gaius's troops attacked and captured the hilltop fortress at Artageira. This was an effort to suppress a local revolt against the Roman presence. Gaius did not survive this campaign (Dio Cassius 1917, 55.10a; Strabo 1928, 11.14.6; Velleius Pa-terculus 1924, 2.102). The fact that the Roman chroniclers reported contradictory accounts of diplomacy and military operation may have been part of an attempt to come to terms with the complex reality of imperial efforts on the frontier.

Gaius's campaign provides significant context for Burial WWE.B1 because the interment took place in the same decade and because the four *denarii* placed in the burial depict Gaius. This mortuary assemblage of traditionally Roman artifacts plus biogeochemical data offer evidence that the individuals who used this site operated in proximity to the Roman military presence in the region. This offers a unique opportunity to investigate individual-level experiences on the frontier during a period of intense military presence and to study how these experiences relate to the identity formation that is evident in mortuary traditions.

Mortuary Assemblage

Burial WWE.B1 consists of a small assemblage of burial goods of a decidedly Roman character. Yet the pithos jar and a smaller ceramic vessel found directly adjacent to the southern side of the pithos were produced locally (Fishman 2016). Similar ceramic styles and urn burial forms are common locally and are widely attested in the South Caucasus as a classical feature of funerary practice in the kingdom of Armenia, in Media Atropatene, and in Parthia (Fard 1995; Zardarian and Akopian 1995). However, this mortuary tradition is more commonly found in shared cemetery spaces than it is in an isolated burial, as is the case with WWE.B1.

Three pomegranate-shaped, blown-glass *unguentaria* (small bottles), were discovered attached to the left lateral side of the pelvis at the bottom of the pithos. The location and clustering of the *unguentaria* suggest that they may have been tied to the waist. This was a common way of carrying the vessels. *Unguentaria* carried precious liquids such as perfume, oils, or powders. In the Roman mortuary tradition, these vessels were typical luxury items among grave goods. The quantity of the intricate vessels in the WWE.B1 interment suggests that the individual may have been wealthy enough to own such luxury items or may have had a high social status that mandated funerary offerings.

A single horned eye bead made of glass was recovered near the *unguentaria*. The style and form of the bead closely resembles horned beads produced in Phoenicia. The bead may have been produced in the Levant or it may have been made elsewhere in imitation of the Phoenician style. In the Mediterranean and Near East during the Roman period, the horned eye bead was a popular personal adornment. Similar examples have been documented in other jar burials in the South Caucasus (e.g. Fard 1995) and across the broader region.

The individual also wore seven signet rings. This is a large number of rings for a typical Roman burial, and is another likely indicator of high status. Two of the rings had visible engravings preserved.

The first ring is bronze band set with a circular intaglio made of glass paste

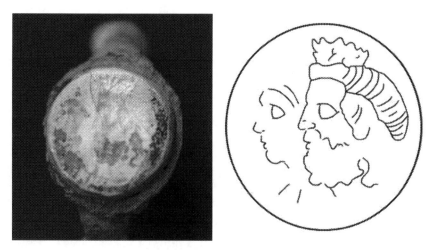

Figure 2.4. Bronze and glass-paste Isis and Serapis signet ring. Photograph by Selin Nugent.

(figure 2.4). The profiles of the deities Isis and Serapis are carved into the glass paste and are inlaid with gold. The mystery cult of Isis and Serapis, which originated in the third century BCE, had a wide following, particularly among soldiers and sailors in the Roman period (Alvar 2008).

The second identifiable signet ring is an iron band set with a scaraboid carnelian intaglio that depicts the profile of a bull inlaid with gold. The gem is Graeco-Persian from approximately the third–fourth century BCE. It is likely that it was removed from its original setting and reset in a Roman band. The remaining five rings are bronze bands set with intaglio carnelian and glass-paste stones, but they were not preserved well enough for identification.

Osteological and Biogeochemical Findings

Due to the alkaline soil of the site, the human skeletal remains were poorly preserved and it was not possible to develop a complete osteological profile of the individual. However, positioning and features related to dentition could be examined.

The narrow dimensions of the pithos restricted the position of the skeleton, which was tightly flexed in a seated position in the pithos. The head, which was oriented to the west, faced inferiorly and rested atop the lower limbs. The arms were wrapped tightly around the lower limbs and the hands rested on the forehead.

Poor preservation of the pelvic region and portions of the cranium limited the estimation of biological sex to the better-preserved portions of the mandible. A prominent gonial eversion and a roughly 90-degree gonial angle indicate that the individual was probably male. Biological age was estimated using the preserved dentition and bones of the hand. The partial eruption of the third molar and nearly complete epiphyseal fusion of the phalanges suggest that this individual was a young adult approximately 18 to 20 years old (Gilsanz and Ratib 2005).

The individual exhibited severe wear on the right dentition of the maxilla and mandible, particularly on the first and second molars. This degree of wear on a young adult may be attributable to a number of factors, including a hard diet, asymmetrical grinding, and bruxism, a disorder that involves excessive grinding or clenching of the teeth due to habit and to psychological stressors (Xhonga 1977). No other signs of trauma or pathology were evident in the preserved elements of the skeleton.

Residential mobility and geographic origin are key considerations when discussing interaction on the imperial frontier. Distinguishing between local and nonlocal individuals in the archaeological record help clarify the relationship between place of origin and mortuary treatment.

This study employed biogeochemical methods of investigating residential mobility using radiogenic strontium and stable oxygen isotope analysis of dental enamel. Strontium isotopes ($^{87}Sr/^{86}Sr$) reflect mobility using data about the composition of bedrock (Bentley 2006; Price et al. 2002). The strontium values of bedrock enter the food chain through weathering processes that incorporate these values in the water, plants, and fauna of a given ecosystem, which humans then ingest. Local versus nonlocal status may be determined by comparing $^{87}Sr/^{86}Sr$ values of the local environment to those of dental enamel, which provides data about the minerals an individual consumed during childhood. My analysis of modern plants collected in the Şərur Valley determined that local $^{87}Sr/^{86}Sr$ values ranged from 0.70760 to 0.70780 (Nugent 2017).

Oxygen isotopes ($\delta^{18}O$) reflect mobility in relation to data about the influence of climate on water sources (Knudson and Price 2007; Luz et al. 1984). The $\delta^{18}O$ values of a certain region are determined by the location's temperature, altitude, and distance from coastlines, which affect how $\delta^{18}O$ is represented in meteoric sources and in standing water (Dansgaard 1964; Longinelli 1984; Luz et al. 1984). These values are incorporated in the human skeleton through the ingestion of water. My analysis of modern water samples collected from springs, wells, rivers, and streams across Naxçıvan determined that the local $\delta^{18}O$ values of the Şərur Valley ranged from -10 to -8‰ (Nugent 2017).

Strontium and oxygen isotopes incorporate in the mineral component of the dental enamel, referred to as hydroxyapatite, during enamel mineralization in childhood. Each tooth mineralizes at a different age during dental development, and sampling of enamel from a certain tooth reflects the isotopic values of food and water consumed during the specific period of time when that tooth mineralized. Samples for this study were taken from the first, second, and third left mandibular molars (M1, M2, and M3). The first molar mineralizes between birth and three years of age. The second molar mineralizes between three and six years of age. The third molar mineralizes between eight and eleven years of age (Reid and Dean 2006). Intra-individual sampling makes it possible to determine an individual's residential mobility between birth and death and to determine whether the individual was mobile in childhood.

The dental enamel samples were prepared for radiogenic strontium analysis at the Archaeological Isotopes Laboratory at The Ohio State University following methods adapted from Knudson and Price (2007). The enamel was first mechanically abraded using a Dremel tool with a tungsten carbide burr attachment to remove a thin layer from the surface of the enamel, which is most prone to diagenesis. Then, 4–6 milligrams of enamel were removed for strontium analysis and 2 milligrams were removed for oxygen analysis using the Dremel tool across the growth axis of the tooth. For strontium analysis, powdered samples were dissolved in 5 M (mole) nitric acid (HNO_3). Then strontium was chemically isolated using column chemistry in the Class 100 Radiogenic Isotopes Clean Laboratory. $^{87}Sr/^{86}Sr_{bioapatite}$ was measured using a Finnigan MAT261A thermal ionization mass spectrometer at the Ohio State University Radiogenic Isotopes Laboratory.

For oxygen analysis, powdered samples were prepared following methods adapted from Koch et al. (1997). Samples were cleaned with 2 percent sodium hypochlorite (NaOCl) at room temperature for twenty-four hours followed by five rinses with 0.5 milliliters MilliQ H_2O. Samples were then treated with 0.1 M acetic acid (CH_3COOH) at room temperature for twelve hours followed by five rinses with MilliQ H_2O. After the final rinse, samples were placed in a drying oven at 40°C until dry. Dr. David Dettman measured samples on an automated carbonate preparation device (KIEL-III) coupled to a gas-ratio mass spectrometer (Finnigan MAT 252) at the Environmental Isotope Laboratory at the University of Arizona.

Table 2.1. Strontium and oxygen values for the WWE.B1 young adult male

Element	Mineralization Age	$^{87}Sr/^{86}Sr$	$\delta^{18}O$ (‰)
LLM1	Birth–3 years	0.70692	-9.1
LLM2	3–6 years	0.70699	-8.4
LLM3	8–11 years	0.70692	-11.5

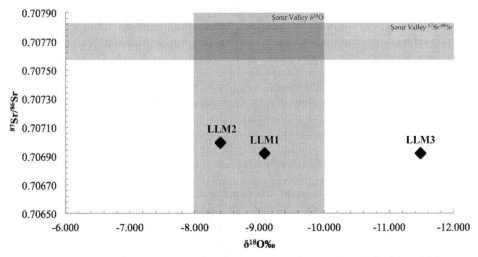

Figure 2.5. Strontium and oxygen isotope values for WWE.B1 in relation to Şərur Valley bioavailability.

Table 2.1 presents the strontium and oxygen isotopic measurements from WWE.B1. Figure 2.5 represents these values in relation to local bioavailability of both isotopes in the Şərur Valley.

All three teeth exhibited similar $^{87}Sr/^{86}Sr$ values, which suggests the individual was not mobile during childhood. However, the represented values are significantly lower than the local bioavailability of strontium. These values are also not consistent with neighboring geological zones represented in the Naxçıvan Autonomous Republic (Nugent 2017). This suggests the individual was not local to the Şərur Valley or the surrounding region.

In contrast, $\delta^{18}O$ values of these three teeth varied over the course of the childhood of this individual. The $\delta^{18}O$ values for M1 and M2 fall within the ranges of the local Şərur Valley (-10–-8‰), while the $\delta^{18}O$ value for M3 is more

Selin E. Nugent

depleted. The variation in oxygen values suggests that the individual consumed various sources of water during childhood. The consistency of strontium values suggests that these shifts may not have been related to mobility but rather that the individual may have been acquiring water from different types of sources in the same geological context. The nonlocal strontium values of the three teeth tell us that this individual spent his childhood in an area with a climate that was mostly similar to that of the Şərur Valley but with different bedrock geology.

Foreign Identity and Local Interactions at Oğlanqala

Historical, biological, and archaeological evidence converges to offer a glimpse into the identity of a foreign, young adult male of high standing buried in the ruins of an abandoned citadel during a period of Roman campaigning in the South Caucasus. Despite the Roman character of burial accompaniments, this individual received a burial treatment that was similar to a local funerary tradition using locally produced ceramic wares. These features may indicate that local people participated in the funerary events by supplying materials for burial of the deceased. Yet this burial's position outside the fortress and in isolation from other burials in a shared cemetery space suggests that this individual, perhaps because of his personal identity, did not have access to funerary spaces afforded to local inhabitants of the Şərur Valley. Instead, the isolation of this burial positions this individual as an outsider or as someone who was exceptional in other ways.

While it may not be possible to definitively link this individual to the campaign of Gaius Caesar in the South Caucasus, commemorative coins celebrating Gaius that were commissioned during the period of the campaign and a signet ring that is closely related to cultic worship in the Roman imperial military echo the concurrent events documented in the region's history. This may indicate that the individual came to the Şərur valley as part of a military campaign.

The evidence of short-term, large-scale feasting activities during Period II possibly point to an occupation that could be associated with a camp. Oğlanqala's location on a travel corridor along the Aras River, where historical accounts document the presence of Roman armies, raises this possibility. Furthermore, much like the settlements established in other Iron Age fortresses in the region, Oğlanqala's large defensive walls and commanding view of the valley would have offered the advantage of protection. However, it is difficult to conclusively identify a camp, since little is known about the logistics of campaigning in this region for either the Roman or the Parthian empire (Kennedy

1996). Nevertheless, as part of a historically attested influx of foreigners affiliated with Imperial Rome, this individual's treatment in death raises important insight into individual-level interaction with local inhabitants on the frontier. These small-scale interactions that seem insignificant on their own form a part of the broader tactics of imperial influence in this critical region.

The contexts of this foreign individual's treatment offer insight into archaeological representations of negotiation through the intersection of outsider status and identity with local traditions and material realities. The mortuary treatment of WWE.B1 reveals how foreign or outsider identity was preserved in the burial assemblage on the body itself and through the physical separation of the interment from spaces where local funerary customs were enacted. Yet a negotiation through either the influence of the deceased on the local community in life or through the relationship of mourners to the local community allowed access to the vessels used for burial and to the knowledge needed to reproduce and reenact aspects of local burial tradition. This evident acquisition of materials, ideas, and possible assistance from locals speaks to processes of quotidian negotiations outside the macro-scale narratives of travel and life in the borderlands.

The traditional understanding of the role of the South Caucasus at the frontier of the two powerful empires of Rome and Parthia is that it was a battleground for the competing interests of major historical figures and armies. Historical accounts rarely discuss the populations that inhabited this region or how the imperial representatives engaged and interacted with them beyond relationships of domination and violence. This perspective undermines the active role of frontier populations in shaping the empire, whether through defining its extent or through determining its influence in a dynamic intersection of social networks. During the period of Gaius Caesar's campaign in Armenia, the Romans who sought to impose their rule faced an open rebellion that ultimately led to Gaius's untimely death. Yet the WWE.B1 burial exhibits a complex negotiation of belonging and exclusion in a local mortuary tradition that may also have broader implications for how identities converged, how resources and ideas were exchanged, and how influence was formed on the frontier.

While this burial and this individual do not speak to the broader themes of Roman campaign strategies or to the interactions of the Roman military with local populations, the unique qualities of this burial and the study of it using multiple lines of evidence begin to provide information about the frontier that are not evident in the Roman accounts of Rome's presence. An approach that integrates osteological and archaeological data offers a critical view of textual histories and is significant for understanding Roman imperialism in a way that does not simply continue to underwrite the strict division between empire and frontier. This approach provides an opportunity to understand how various levels of Romans' interactions with locals blurred the boundaries between empire and frontier.

Acknowledgments

I thank Lauren Ristvet, Hilary Gopnik, Emily Hammer, and Veli Bakhshaliyev, the directors of the Naxçıvan Archaeological Project, for granting access to these materials and for their consistent support and guidance. George Armelagos, Clark Spencer Larsen, and Mark Hubbe also provided invaluable advice on this study, for which I am very grateful. This project was supported by the National Science Foundation (BCS 1430404).

References

Alvar, J. 2008. *Romanising Oriental Gods: Myth, Salvation and Ethics in the Cults of Cybele, Isis and Mithras.* Religions in the Graeco-Roman World vol. 165. Leiden: Brill.

Augustus. 1924. *Res Gestae Divi Augusti.* In *Compendium of Roman History.* Translated by Frederick W. Shipley. Loeb Classical Library no. 152. Cambridge, MA: Harvard University Press.

Benario, H. W. 1999. "Augustus, Rome, and the Romans." In *Veritatis Amicitiaeque Causa: Essays in Honor of Anna Lydia Motto and John R. Clark*, edited by Shannon N. Byrne, Anna Lydia Motto, and John R. Clark, 1–20. Wauconda, IL: Bolchazy-Carducci.

Bentley, R. A. 2006. "Strontium Isotopes from the Earth to the Archaeological Skeleton: A Review." *Journal of Archaeological Method and Theory* 13(3): 135–187.

Campbell, B. 1993. "War and Diplomacy: Rome and Parthia, 31 BC–AD 235." In *War and Society in the Roman World*, edited by John Rich and Graham Shipley, 213–240. London: Routledge.

Cooley, A. E. 2009. *Res gestae divi Augusti.* Cambridge: Cambridge University Press.

Dansgaard, W. 1964. "Stable Isotopes in Precipitation." *Tellus* 16(4): 436–468.

Dio Cassius. 1917. *Roman History.* Vol. 6, *Books 51–55.* Translated by Earnest Cary and Herbert B. Foster. Loeb Classical Library 83. Cambridge, MA: Harvard University Press.

Fard, K. 1995. *Parthian Pithos-Burials at Germi (Azerbaijan).* Tehran: Iran University Press.

Fishman, S. G. 2016. "The Space Between: Ceramic Production and Exchange in Roman-Parthian Period Oğlanqala, Azerbaijan." *Journal of Archaeological Science: Reports* 9: 12–24.

Gilsanz, V., and O. Ratib. 2005. *Hand Bone Age: A Digital Atlas of Skeletal Maturity.* Berlin: Springer.

Kennedy, D. L. 1996. "The Parthia and Rome: Eastern Perspectives." *Journal of Roman Archaeology* supplementary series 18: 67–90.

Khatchadourian, L. 2007. "Unforgettable Landscapes: Attachments to the Past in Hellenistic Armenia." *Negotiating the Past in the Past: Identity, Memory, and Landscape in Archaeological Research*, edited by Norman Yoffee, 43–75. Tucson: University of Arizona Press.

Knudson, K. J., and T. D. Price. 2007. "Utility of Multiple Chemical Techniques in Archaeological Residential Mobility Studies: Case Studies from Tiwanaku- and Chiribaya-Affiliated Sites in the Andes." *American Journal of Physical Anthropology* 132(1): 25–39.

Koch, P. L., N. Tuross, and M. L. Fogel. 1997. "The Effects of Sample Treatment and Diagenesis on the Isotopic Integrity of Carbonate in Biogenic Hydroxylapatite." *Journal of Archaeological Science* 24(5): 417–429.

Longinelli, A. 1984. "Oxygen Isotopes in Mammal Bone Phosphate: A New Tool for Paleohydrological and Paleoclimatological Research?" *Geochimica et Cosmochimica Acta* 48(2): 385–390.

Luz, B., Y. Kolodny, and M. Horowitz. 1984. "Fractionation of Oxygen Isotopes between Mammalian Bone-Phosphate and Environmental Drinking Water." *Geochimica et Cosmochimica Acta* 48(8): 1689–1693.

Mousheghian, A. and G. Depeyrot. 1999. *Hellenistic and Roman Armenian Coinage (1st. c. BC–1st c. AD)*. Wetteren: Moneta.

Nugent, S. E. 2017. "Pastoral Mobility and the Formation of Complex Settlement in the Middle Bronze Age Serur Valley, Azerbaijan." PhD diss, The Ohio State University.

Price, T. D., J. H. Burton, and R. A. Bentley. 2002. "The Characterization of Biologically Available Strontium Isotope Ratios for the Study of Prehistoric Migration." *Archaeometry* 44(1): 117–135.

Reid, D. J., and M. C. Dean. 2006. "Variation in Modern Human Enamel Formation Times." *Journal of Human Evolution* 50(3): 329–346.

Ristvet, L., H. Gopnik, and V. Bakhshaliyev. Forthcoming. *Local Identities and Imperial Resistance: The Naxçivan Archaeology Project, 2006–2011*. Philadelphia: University Museum Press, University of Pennsylvania.

Romer, F. E. 1979. "Gaius Caesar's Military Diplomacy in the East." *Transactions of the American Philological Association* 109: 199–214.

Strabo. 1928. *The Geography of Strabo*. Vol. 5, *Books 10–12*. Translated by Horace Leonard Jones. Loeb Classical Library 211. Cambridge, MA: Harvard University Press.

Swain, H., and M. E. Davies. 2010. *Aspects of Roman History 82BC–AD14: A Source-Based Approach*. New York: Routledge.

Velleius Paterculus. 1924. *Compendium of Roman History*. Translated by Frederick W. Shipley. Loeb Classical Library 152. Cambridge, MA: Harvard University Press.

Xhonga, F. A. 1977. "Bruxism and Its Effect on the Teeth." *Journal of Oral Rehabilitation* 4(1): 65–76.

Zardarian, M. H., and H. P. Akopian. 1995. "Archaeological Excavations of Ancient Monuments in Armenia, 1985–1990." *Ancient Civilizations from Scythia to Siberia* 1(2): 169–195.

3

Queering Prehistory on the Frontier

A Bioarchaeological Investigation of Gender in Mierzanowice
Culture Communities of the Early Bronze Age

MARK P. TOUSSAINT

> Throughout history . . . societies
> have been formed and transformed
> in relation to their frontiers.
>
> *(Rodseth and Parker 2005, 3)*

Definition and Characteristics of "Frontiers"

According to Rodseth and Parker (2005, 10), borders and frontiers are subtypes
of boundaries that serve to delimit and differentiate various entities. Whereas
borders are typically distinct and codified, frontiers are "zones of transition
between two core areas, each of which contains a population center and usually
a center of political power." It is this transitional and dynamic character that is
most applicable to this particular study.

Boundaries need not necessarily be physical; they can also be conceptual.
Conceptual boundaries can be based on perception, ideology, and world view
(Pellow 1996). Cultural boundaries, which correspond to "different worlds
of meaning" (Donnan and Wilson 1999, 19), are not mutually exclusive with
more concrete geopolitical boundaries. In fact, boundaries of meaning may be
defended as passionately as more material boundaries of territories (Casimir
1992). In some cases, conceptual and cultural boundaries arise first, creating de
facto territorial boundaries in their wake (Pellow 1996).

The construct of gender is subject to the forces and possibilities of the social landscape of the frontier. One crucial variable in frontier situations that influences the negotiation of gender is power. In highly stratified and centralized societies, for example, the integrity of the border and the allegiance and conformity of peoples on the frontier is often seen as necessary because borders are the "first lines of defence, institutions of social coercion, and symbols of a variety of state powers" (Wilson and Donnan 1998, 10). Thus, "it is often precisely at borders that state power is most keenly marked and felt" (17). Conversely, individuals can strategically use the nature of boundary regions and frontiers to exercise their *power to* (as defined in Pitkin 1972). As Barth ([1969] 1998) points out, social or ethnic boundaries do not necessarily circumscribe populations with static, unchanging membership but are maintained even in the face of changing personnel. As individuals move across boundaries, they can use the power that they possess "as an attribute of the person, emphasizing potency or capability" (Wolf 1990, 586) in order to manipulate and contest meaning. Because gender is culturally salient in many situations, it is an attribute that can be used in this way (Levy 1999).

The Mierzanowice Culture of the Central European Early Bronze Age

The Mierzanowice Culture is the name given to an archaeological complex that existed from about 2400/2300–1600 BCE in the Early Bronze Age of Central Europe (Górski et al. 2013; Kadrow and Machnik 1997). At its largest extent, the Mierzanowice Culture covered parts of Moravia (Czech Republic), eastern Slovakia, southern Poland, and western Ukraine to the north of the Carpathian Mountains (Kadrow and Machnik 1997). Mierzanowice Culture populations appear to have been settled, at least since their Early Phase, and their subsistence practices seem to have been a mixture of an agricultural component and a reliance on animal husbandry (Kadrow et al. 1995). Despite the existence of long-term settlements, few archaeological remains of structures have been found. Using data from settlement pits, researchers have inferred that each pit corresponded to a single house structure that was used by something like a nuclear family unit (i.e., they were not large enough for an extended family; I do not use the term "nuclear family" to imply any particular definition of family) (Kadrow 1991, 1994). The site of Babia Góra II in Iwanowice, Poland (about 20 kilometers north of Kraków), is perhaps the most well investigated Mierzanowice Culture settlement. At this site, the house structures originally appear to have been arranged in a lens- or eye-shaped manner with one structure in the middle. In later phases, the arrangement of house structures became more open. Their arrangement became more linear and there was increasing distance between settlement pits. In addition, in the later phase, there were fewer house structures (Kadrow 1991).

Mierzanowice Culture cemeteries were usually associated with main, long-term sites in settlement microregions and were located close to—but separate from—settlement areas. The cemetery at Babia Góra gives the impression that it was planned and that its boundaries were delimited at the beginning of its use, in part through the creation of a ditch between the cemetery and the settlement area (Kadrow et al. 1995). Graves were likely marked, since overlapping or intersecting graves are unknown at Babia Góra and at the cemetery of Szarbia Zwierzyniecka (approximately 50 kilometers northeast of Kraków), for example (Baczyńska 1994; Kadrow et al. 1992, 1995). The only obvious spatial pattern at these two cemeteries is a chronological one, in which the cemetery was filled in from one end to the other in a fairly sequential manner (Baczyńska 1994; Kadrow et al. 1992).

At Mierzanowice Culture cemeteries in general, the biological sex of individuals, as estimated by previous anthropologists (who presumably used the classical visual assessments of the greater sciatic notch and characteristics of the ischiopubic region, as per Phenice [1969]) seems to correspond strongly to several burial characteristics. Although there is some variation, both chronologically and site to site, the principal axis of the body in the grave is east-west (Kadrow and Machnik 1997; Kadrow et al. 1992). Males are typically arranged with their heads to the west and females with their heads to the east. Both sexes are usually in a crouched position and their faces are directed to the south. Males are most often lying on their right sides and females on their left. Deviations from the east-west axis have been variously explained as relating to the topography and orientation of the site, the chronological phase of the Mierzanowice Culture, and potentially to sunrises and sunsets at different times of year (Bąbel 2013; Kadrow et al. 1992).

Grave goods can be found in male, female, and children's graves (which appear to follow the same patterns), although for many types of goods, there is more fluidity than might be indicated by the burial orientations. Items that are primarily reserved for male graves include stone battle axes, arrowheads, stone wrist guards, boar-tusk pendants, disks or badges made of bone or copper, and pins and antler artifacts. Predominantly female items include necklaces made of animal teeth, copper spiral-shaped earrings, and needles (Baczyńska 1994;

Kadrow 1994; Kadrow and Machnik 1997). Although they are more prevalent in female graves, beads made of bone and mussel shell (used in necklaces and other types of jewelry) can be found in the graves of both males and females. Other more universal items (for adults) included faience beads, simple earrings of copper wire, and pottery. The presence and amount of each item depends on the chronological phase.

The Mierzanowice Culture and related groups of the so-called Circum-Carpathian Epi-Corded Culture Circle bordered populations of the Únětice Culture (in western Germany, northeastern Austria, the Czech Republic, and western Poland) and the Otomani-Füzesabony Culture (in adjacent parts of Slovakia, Hungary, Romania, and Ukraine), both of which seem to have been more centralized than the Mierzanowice Culture, judging by monumental architecture, prestige items, and other archaeological evidence (Harding 2000; Jiráň et al. 2013; Kadrow 1994; Marková and Ilon 2013; Vandkilde 2007). In the Únětice Culture, the most archaeologically visible and discussed signs of this stratification are the so-called princely burial mounds and hoards of bronze weapons and jewelry. Fourteen such mounds are known to have existed at Łęki Małe in Poland near the fortified site of Bruszczewo. Janusz Czebreszuk (2013, 782) states that the phenomenon at Bruszczewo and Łęki Małe "may be interpreted in terms of proto-state structures possessing a stable governing body, an extensive network of extra-regional contacts, varied artisanal production, and a well-organized food economy."

Gender differentiation in flat inhumations of the Únětice Culture is far less pronounced in both orientation and grave furnishings than in the Mierzanowice Culture region. Males, females, and subadults are usually all buried on their right sides in a crouched or fetal position on a north-south axis with their heads to the south and their faces to the east (Pokutta 2013; Vandkilde 2007). Although princely burials are most often associated with males throughout the Únětice region, some burial mounds in Poland also include females (Pokutta 2013; Vandkilde 2007).

The Otomani-Füzesabony Culture in the Carpathian Basin is found primarily in parts of Hungary, Slovakia, Romania, and Ukraine. There is ample evidence that it also permeated lower-lying mountains and hills of the Carpathian chain into southeastern Poland (Jaeger 2010; Marková and Ilon 2013; Przybyła and Skoneczna 2013). The Otomani-Füzesabony Culture is most well known for its prolific and advanced metallurgy; many of the dead were buried with copper, bronze, and gold (Jaeger and Olexa 2014; Jaeger 2014; Marková and Ilon 2013), including "85–90% of the 784 discovered burials" at the site of Nižná Myšľa in Slovakia (Jaeger and Olexa 2014, 172). At some of the fortified sites, deposits of metals have been found under dwellings, which Jaeger and Olexa (2014, 165) posit is a possible indication of private property and the ability to amass wealth. Like other cultural paradigms in the Carpathian region, Otomani-Füzesabony Culture groups maintained the tradition of sex-differentiated burials. Those in closer contact with the Epi-Corded groups used the east-west orientation and others adopted the north-south orientation (Marková and Ilon 2013).

Sex and Gender in Mierzanowice Culture Groups

Over the 700 or so years the Mierzanowice Culture endured, the one thing that remained the most constant throughout the region was the tradition of mirror-opposite, sex-differentiated burials, despite increasing regionalization and influences from surrounding cultural paradigms (Kadrow 1994). Although the precise orientations of the bodies varied over time and space, this dichotomous aspect persisted from the time of the Corded Ware and Bell Beaker cultures of the Final Neolithic until the end of the Early Bronze Age in the Mierzanowice Culture region (Kadrow 1994; Milisauskas and Kruk 2011; Włodarczak 2014). This represents a span of some 1,200 years. Although it is impossible to know the exact symbolic and ideological significance of these burial traditions—let alone the degree to which meaning and symbolism changed from region to region and throughout the generations—it is clear that some kinds of distinctions were made, whether they were based on socially salient categories of sex or on gender. Such distinctions must have been an important aspect of identity in Mierzanowice Culture communities.

However, perhaps the binary nature of the burial characteristics has been overstated. There is no shortage of exceptions that have been documented in the data. For example, at the site of Babia Góra, one woman appeared to have been on her right side (typically reserved for males) with her head to the east (typical for females) and her face directed to the north (atypical) (Kadrow et al. 1992). An individual estimated to be male was on a north-south axis with his head to the north and his face to the east, which is singular at this cemetery and rare in this region for Mierzanowice Culture graves but is not unheard of throughout the Circum-Carpathian region. Also, among nine graves with two or more individuals, one grave included two young males who were both on their backs on an east-west axis with their heads to the west, one completely supine and looking south, the other with legs and face turned to the north. Their bodies were touching, and they had the appearance of looking at one another. In addition, they are both recorded as having perimortem cranial injuries (Kadrow et al. 1992).

At the site of Szarbia Zwierzyniecka exceptions were even more common. Of the burials that were well preserved enough to estimate sex and/or burial orientations, twenty-one were in the orientation typical for males. Two of these individuals were estimated to be female (9.5 percent) and five were undetermined (23.8 percent) (Baczyńska 1994). Among thirty typically female burial orientations, five individuals were estimated to be males (16.7 percent) and nine were undetermined (30 percent). Of the fourteen multi-individual burials, one contained two males who were both in the usual male position. One individual was missing the cranium and only the lower limbs were in anatomical position; the rest of his bones were piled together where the cranium would be. Another double burial was of a male with a small child on his chest. He was on an east-west axis on his right side (typical for males), but his head was place to the east (which was typical for females) and face was directed to the north (atypical) (1994).

There are a variety of potential explanations for the many nontypical burial arrangements, including the possibility that those who were treated differently were not local. Given how strong the association is between the axis of the body, the side the body is laid on, and the estimated sex of the individual, however, I believe that most permutations of these characteristics are likely to have held meaning relating to social conceptions of gender. Thus, I will focus on the bioarchaeology of sex and gender.

Theorizing Sex and Gender

It is all too easy for the general public and for bioarchaeologists alike to interpret the past through our own contemporary cultural lenses. As a case in point, the London *Telegraph* described a burial of a male individual of the Corded Ware Culture that deviated from the typical male burial pattern and was found in the Czech Republic some years ago as the "first homosexual caveman."[1] How do we make sense of the cultural logic behind the apparent pattern of burying anthropologically sexed males and females in mirror-opposite positions without discounting burials that deviate from this pattern as mere exceptions or otherwise assigning our own cultural significance to such differences?

Pamela Geller (2008, 2017) urges bioarchaeologists to resist the "presentism" of framing studies of the past in terms of the modern heteronormative discourse of the binaries of male/female, man/woman, and productive/reproductive. Thus, a first step for bioarchaeologists—especially bioarchaeologists of prehistory—is to allow for the possibility that the people we study did not see only binaries but may have acknowledged more than two gender categories or even a fluidity between the categories. Furthermore, we must resist the urge to uncritically attach our own significance to potential social categories that we encounter. For example, the assumption that a biological male who was buried in a manner typically reserved for females was homosexual ignores the complexity of historical and ethnographic examples in which sexual behavior is not a primary characteristic of gender categories.

The concept of the sex/gender system is useful for understanding and discussing ethnohistoric examples of gender variants. Gayle Rubin defines the sex/gender system as "a set of arrangements by which the biological raw material of human sex and procreation is shaped by human, social intervention and satisfied in a conventional manner, no matter how bizarre some of the conventions may be" (Rubin 1975, 165). It has been convincingly argued elsewhere that—biological differences notwithstanding—salient categories of sex are socially constructed and are therefore culturally and historically contingent (Fausto-Sterling 2000; Laqueur 1990). In her characterization of the relationship between sex and gender, Judith Butler notes that "gender is not to culture as sex is to nature; gender is also the discursive/cultural means by which 'sexed nature' or 'a natural sex' is produced and established as 'prediscursive,' prior to culture, a politically neutral surface *on which* culture acts" ([1990] 2006, 10, Butler's italics). In other words, variations in both human biology and behavior are real, but how such variation is classified and the significance that is attached to these categories are products of each specific time and place. The particular forms that constructions of sex and gender take serve the purpose of making possible and reinforcing political, economic, and other arrangements and systems in a given society.

It is not surprising, therefore, that numerous different sex/gender systems have been documented historically and ethnographically. In the fifth century BCE, Herodotus (2014, 1:105, 4:67) wrote of a category of "effeminate" men among the Scythians called Enarees, who were "afflicted . . . with a feminizing disease," at least some of whom were soothsayers. Thomas Laqueur (1990) argues that a one-sex model existed among the ancient Greeks in which differences between males and females were of degree and not of kind. More recently, but still in the western cultural sphere, there is the example of the "sworn virgins," or *burneshas*, of Albania and the western Balkans, attested from at least the early nineteenth century (Grémaux 1996; Nanda 2014). These are biological females who transition socially to assume traditionally male roles and who enjoy male privileges in a patriarchal society. Often they assume male roles because of needs that arise in their family homes, such as a lack of male heirs. They wear masculine clothing and adopt masculine mannerisms and ways of talking. René Grémaux (1996) documents one example of a *burnesha* who was buried in traditional masculine ceremonial clothing but could not be given the customary male funerary lamentation due to the customs of the local tribe. In addition, Serena Nanda (2014) documents many nonwestern examples of gender variants, including Navajo *nádleeh*, Mohave *alyha* and *hwame*, and Indian *hijras* and *sādhins*. In many cases, the gender variance of such individuals is not recognized as a complete transition from man to woman or vice versa but rather as a different status altogether. Often this involved being seen as having qualities of both men and women or of being biologically one sex while embodying the gender typically associated with another sex. In nearly all of these examples, one of the defining characteristics of a gender variant is the type of labor the individual does.

Taking all of this into account, I propose that while it is still important for bioarchaeologists to continue to estimate and take into account "biological sex" in their research, as Pamela Geller urges (2017), they must bear in mind that the ways they assess and define sex are also a product of social and historical forces. Thus, we cannot assume that what we deem as "male," for example, was seen as such by past societies. However, by keeping our eyes and minds open to the nuances, to the blurry edges of our constructions, by letting go sometimes of the need to force ambiguous features into male or female categories and by comparing the differences we notice in biology to embodied differentials in labor, nutrition, resources, and interpersonal conflict, we may begin to tease apart aspects of the sex/gender system.

A Case Study

For this preliminary study, a total of twenty-six adult individuals from the Mierzanowice Culture cemeteries at Żerniki Górne (n = 19) and Szarbia (n = 7)—approximately 25 kilometers east-northeast of Kraków in the Koniusza commune (not to be confused with Szarbia Zwierzyniecka)—were assessed for sex and age estimation, health and diet indicators, trauma, and musculoskeletal stress. Due to taphonomic considerations, not all individuals were included in every analysis. Żerniki Górne represents graves from the Classic and Late Phases of the Mierzanowice Culture (Krenz-Niedbała 1999). Based on the extensive presence of faience beads and metal jewelry (Kadrow and Machnik 1997), many graves from Szarbia are also likely from the Late Phase. Both sites are located in the upland regions of southeastern Poland. Andrzej Kempisty excavated Żerniki Górne from 1965 to 1968 (Kempisty 1978), and Barbara Baczyńska excavated Szarbia in the summer of 2000 (Baczyńska 2000a).

Methods

Multiple methods were applied in the estimation of the sex and age of individuals and a composite result was used. For age estimation, the methods of Brooks and Suchey (1990), Todd (1920, 1921), Lovejoy and colleagues (1985), Ubelaker (1978), Buikstra and Ubelaker (1994), Scheuer and Black (2000), and Meindl and Lovejoy (1985) were used. Where such methods were of little use due to lack of diagnostic features or taphonomy, dental attrition (Lovejoy 1985) was used. Where possible, greater weight was given to indicators of the pelvic region for adults with fully fused epiphyses. Estimation of sex was carried out using the heuristics described in Buikstra and Ubelaker (1994), including the characteristics of the ischiopubic region as described by Phenice (1969). However, given the lack or taphonomic degradation of the ischiopubic region for many individuals and the subjective nature of categorical assessments of the greater sciatic notch (especially in cases of individuals who do not fall at the extremes), the multicomponent method of Jaroslav Bruzek (2002) was also used. Where there was a slight disagreement between methods (e.g., probable male vs. male or indeterminate vs. male), the more robust methods were given extra weight. However, in the case of extreme disparity in results or where a high degree of ambiguity existed, the sex was considered "indeterminate."

As Joanna Sofaer (2006) argues, the skeleton can be seen as a material record of embodied social arrangements and constructs that manifest as markers of health, disease, trauma, and musculoskeletal stress that are the result of constraints placed upon—or privileges conferred to—individuals. Here, musculoskeletal stress is used to signify any load or biomechanical demand placed upon the skeletal system. Markers of musculoskeletal stress that were investigated here include osteoarthritis (marginal osteophytes, eburnation, new bone formation, pitting), which is pathological and is related to multiple factors, including age and biomechanical stresses (Waldron 2009), and entheseal development, which in many cases is nonpathological. In this study, entheseal robusticity was recorded rather than pathological changes to entheses. There has been much debate about the degree to which entheses can be informative about past activity (e.g., Henderson et al. 2013; Villotte et al. 2010). Age has consistently been found to be closely related to entheseal changes (Havelková et al. 2013; Henderson et al. 2013; Mariotti, Facchini, and Belcastro 2007; Villotte et al. 2010), but there have been conflicting results regarding the relationship between activity and entheses; some studies have not found a link (e.g., Cardoso and Henderson 2010; Milella et al. 2012; Niinimäki and Baiges Sotos 2013), while others have (e.g., Mariotti, Facchini, and Belcastro 2007; Niinimäki 2011; Niinimäki et al. 2013; Villotte et al. 2010; Villotte and Knüsel 2013). Although the etiology of entheseal morphology and changes is clearly multifactorial and there is much research yet to be done before the relationship between entheses and activity can be clarified, I believe that researchers should proceed in collecting data on entheses in a standardized manner and interpret their results cautiously.

To that end, entheseal robusticity is scored in this study using the methods of Mariotti et al. (2007) and analyses are conducted not in order to link the development of specific entheses to specific activities but rather to investigate overall patterns in entheseal development across the sample. The idea behind such an approach is that no individual or group of individuals was doing only one activity or one type of movement over and over. Rather, one would expect that if entheseal development does reflect activity to some degree, then the skeleton is a palimpsest of all of the major types of activity that an individual did in his or her lifetime. Of course, the activities that produced the greatest loads or were carried out most repetitively would likely have had the greatest influence. And hypothetically, if activities were at least to some degree the purview of particular segments of society (i.e., a gendered division of labor or status differences in activity), we might reasonably expect to see overall patterns show up through the individual noise.

In an attempt to discern any such patterns, a clustering algorithm was used. Data were taken for a total of 28 entheses of the upper and lower body (14 left, 14 right; 20 upper body, 8 lower body). However, because of missing skeletal elements or taphonomy, many individuals were missing data for several entheses. Thus, a subset of entheses were chosen for this analysis in order to ensure as large a sample size as possible and to avoid having to impute missing values for this preliminary study. The scores from the left and right deltoids, pectoralis majors, and glutei maximi were used from a total of nineteen individuals. Manhattan distances between individuals were calculated and hierarchical clustering with complete linkage was performed using the R Statistical Computing Package.

A large literature exists in bioarchaeology regarding differential disease risk (e.g., Bird and Rieker 2008; Grauer and Stuart-Macadam 1998; Koziol 2012; Martin 1997) and exposure to violent trauma (e.g., Grauer and Stuart-Macadam 1998; Koziol 2012; Martin 1997; Robb 1997; Tung 2012; Walker 1997) that is based on salient social categories such as sex, gender, age, and occupation. The exact patterns and directionality of differential risk are culturally and historically contingent, but categories of social significance nearly always play a role. Accordingly, this study attempted to document skeletal indicators of nutritional insufficiency (e.g., porotic hyperostosis, cribra orbitalia, rickets, scurvy), dental disease (e.g., caries, antemortem tooth loss, abscesses), infection (e.g., osteomyelitis, periostitis), and general indicators of health, such as adult stature (Ortner 2003; Ruff et al. 2012; Waldron 2009). Blunt force and sharp force trauma were also recorded, including cranial depression fractures, radiating fractures, spiral fractures, parry fractures, cut marks, and percussion marks (Wedel and Galloway 2014). Due to taphonomic considerations, however, it was generally not possible to observe porotic hyperostosis and periosteal reaction. Furthermore, too few individuals had femora or tibiae complete enough to allow for a meaningful reconstruction and consideration of adult stature in this study.

Results

Unsurprisingly, the small sample size for this study likely hindered the ability to find statistically significant differences between sex or burial orientation and variables such as musculoskeletal stress markers, disease indicators, and trauma. Furthermore, the sex of several individuals could not be confidently estimated as male or female by the given criteria and were listed as indeterminate. Almost certainly some fraction of those individuals were indeed viewed in life as either male or female, but one goal of this study was to resist the urge to force individuals into one category or another for analysis. In addition, it is quite possible that some of these individuals may have been seen in life as something other than "male" or "female."

Each analysis with regard to the different variables was done with respect to both estimated sex and burial orientation. The hypothesis was that burial orientation might be more informative of how Mierzanowice Culture communities viewed individuals within their sex/gender system. Figure 3.1 shows the frequencies of burial orientation by estimated sex. The majority of "indeterminate" individuals was buried in the manner typical for males, but one of the individuals who was buried in an atypical orientation (facing north) was of indeterminate sex (Szarbia, grave 21) and was found without any grave equipment. The other atypical burial (Szarbia, grave 37) was of a probable female who was laid in a typically male orientation but on her left side, facing north. She was found with equipment that included some materials typically given to males and some typically given to females. In any case, her assemblage of grave goods was rather rich for this cemetery (Baczyńska 2000b).

Frequencies of osteoarthritis were calculated for major joint systems (spine, knee, shoulder, elbow, hip, and ankle) (Table 3.1). None of them reached significance ($p < 0.05$) for either sex or burial orientation. The closest any of the variables came to statistical significance was osteoarthritis of the shoulder and of the hip by sex ($p = 0.3566$ for both; Fisher's exact test; two-tailed). The small sample size does not allow for a high degree of confidence in any apparent patterns.

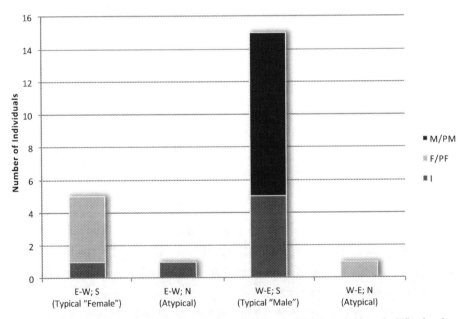

Figure 3.1. Burial orientations by estimated sex. "M" is male, "PM" is probable male, "F" is female, "PF" is probable female, and "I" is indeterminate or unable to estimate.

Table 3.1. Frequency of osteoarthritis of the major joint systems by sex and burial orientation

	Spine	Knee	Shoulder	Elbow	Hip	Ankle
SEX						
Male/Probable male	3/6	2/7	3/7	3/7	3/7	2/6
Female/Probable female	1/2	1/3	1/3	1/3	1/3	0/2
Indeterminate	3/4	0/4	0/4	1/4	0/4	0/3
ORIENTATION						
Body oriented west to east, face directed to the south	3/7	2/8	3/8	4/8	3/8	2/7
Body oriented west to east, face directed to the north	1/1	0/1	0/1	0/1	0/1	0/1
Body oriented east to west, face directed to the south	2/3	1/4	1/4	1/4	1/4	0/3
Body oriented east to west, face directed to the north	1/1	0/1	0/1	0/1	0/1	0/0

Note: Frequencies are given as the number of affected individuals among the total number for whom the condition could be assessed in each category.

In order to analyze the rates of linear enamel hypoplasia (LEH) and dental caries, frequencies were calculated per tooth. These were not calculated on an individual level because their observation depends on the number of teeth present. The rates of antemortem tooth loss (AMTL), however, were calculated per individual, since diagnostic criteria do not depend on the presence/absence of teeth but rather on signs of remodeling in the dental alveoli. Frequencies are given in table 3.2. The only test that reached significance was for LEH by sex (p = 0.02661; Fisher's exact test; two-tailed). Pairwise comparison showed a difference between the rates of LEH in male/probable male and indeterminate individuals, which was significant below the 0.05 confidence level. However, this result is not significant after applying the Bonferroni correction, which in this case requires a critical value of 0.017. It is interesting to note that the single "indeterminate" individual from which the three teeth with LEH came was buried in a typical "male" fashion.

Table 3.2. Frequency of dental pathologies by sex and burial orientation

	LEH (# teeth)	Caries (# teeth)	AMTL (# individuals)
SEX			
Male/Probable male	*1/107*	6/107	3/5
Female/Probable female	*2/50*	3/50	1/2
Indeterminate	*3/31*	0/31	1/1
ORIENTATION			
Body oriented west to east, face directed to the south	4/138	6/138	4/6
Body oriented west to east, face directed to the north	0/0	0/0	0/0
Body oriented east to west, face directed to the south	2/50	3/50	1/2
Body oriented east to west, face directed to the north	0/0	0/0	0/0

Note: Frequencies are given as the number of affected individuals among the total number for whom the condition could be assessed in each category. Italics indicate a statistically significant difference.

Table 3.3. Frequency of antemortem and perimortem trauma by sex and burial orientation

	Antemortem	Perimortem	Either
SEX			
Male/Probable male	2/7	2/7	4/7
Female/Probable female	3/3	1/3	3/3
Indeterminate	1/4	1/4	2/4
ORIENTATION			
Body oriented west to east, face directed to the south	*2/8*	3/8	5/8
Body oriented west to east, face directed to the north	*0/1*	0/1	0/1
Body oriented east to west, face directed to the south	*4/4*	1/4	4/4
Body oriented east to west, face directed to the north	*0/1*	0/1	0/1

Note: Frequencies are given as the number of affected individuals among the total number for whom the condition could be assessed in each category. Italics indicate a statistically significant difference.

Data on trauma was collected and frequencies of antemortem, perimortem, and either kind of trauma were calculated per individual (Table 3.3). The only relationship that reached significance was that between burial orientation and antemortem trauma ($p = 0.02431$; Fisher's exact test; two-tailed). Among pairwise comparisons, the difference between rates of antemortem trauma in the typical male (head to the west, lying on the right side, facing south) and typical female (head to the east, lying on the left side, facing south) burial orientations reached a significance of $p = 0.0606$ (two-tailed). Again, after controlling for the family-wise error rate, this did not reach significance.

Hierarchical clustering of individuals (based on Manhattan distances calculated from entheseal scoring) resulted in two main clusters. Figure 3.2 shows the resulting clusters, along with the estimated sex, the burial orientation, and the estimated age of the individuals (in broad age categories: Young Adult, Middle Adult, etc., per Buikstra and Ubelaker 1994). Multiple logistic regression was performed with the cluster as the response variable and sex, burial orientation, and age as the independent variables. There was no statistically significant relationship between any of the independent variables and the cluster. Age came the closest to significance ($p = 0.119$ when the model used only "age" as an in-

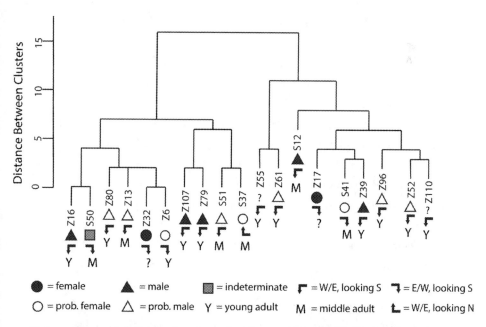

Figure 3.2. Hierarchical clustering based on entheseal scores. The symbols below the individuals represent the estimated sex, the burial orientations, and the age groups of the individuals.

dependent variable), with younger individuals being more strongly associated with the right-branch cluster.

Discussion

Mierzanowice Culture cemeteries provide a unique opportunity to investigate and theorize the relationship between sex and gender in prehistory, due to their "bipolar" burial orientations, which seem to give a window into social constructions of identity, including perhaps sex, gender, and status. Resisting the urge to foist modernist notions of sex onto past societies and leaving space for ambiguity in the estimation of biological sex of skeletal remains opens up the possibility of seeing intersections of identity that may otherwise be invisible. The flipside to this approach is that there is almost certainly not a one-to-one correspondence between remains that are difficult to sex anthropologically and individuals who may have been seen as other than simply male or female in life. Some of the individuals who are put into the "indeterminate" category were quite likely male or female—particularly in societies such as those of the Mierzanowice Culture, where there is evidence of a pseudo-binary categorization.

Aside from the ambiguities involved in estimating the sex of skeletal remains in general, missing skeletal elements and taphonomic considerations greatly increased the number of individuals of indeterminate sex in this sample, and the amount of missing data. This compromised the ability to find statistically significant relationships in an already small data set. Nonetheless, there are some patterns that were beginning to emerge in this study, and which may become clearer when more data are collected.

First of all, this study confirms the close relationship between burial orientations and sex. All of the male individuals in this study were buried on a west-east axis, with their heads to the west, and faces directed southward. All of the females except one were buried on an east-west axis, with their heads to the east, and faces also directed southward. It is interesting to note that, aside from this one female buried in an atypical fashion, there is also an individual of indeterminate sex (Szarbia, grave 50) who is buried in the typical "female" fashion, but whose grave goods included a flint arrowhead, which is typically reserved for males. Although the available data certainly do not prove the existence of nonbinary gender categories, they invite further study and hint at such possibilities, and the very real possibility that some manner of gender fluidity was allowed.

In terms of embodied social structures, this study also points to an increase in the risk of early childhood malnutrition or disease for "indeterminate" individuals versus males, and an increase in the incidence of antemortem trauma for females versus males. With regard to the indication that individuals of indeterminate sex showed higher rates of LEH than males, this should be taken as extremely provisional, since there were only three individuals, total, that showed signs of LEH. With regard to antemortem trauma, however, all three females for which data on trauma was available had suffered some form of antemortem injury. The difference between males and females here may point to an increased risk for females of non-lethal trauma during their lives. One female individual in the study (Żerniki Górne, grave 6) suffered both antemortem and perimortem trauma. She showed signs of a healed rib fracture, a variation on a Le Fort type I fracture of the right midface (Figure 3.3), a symphyseal fracture of the mandible (Figure 3.4), and one or two other possible perimortem blunt-force traumas to the cranial vault. She also showed signs of potential decapitation (Figure 3.5) or—as reported for two individuals at the cemetery at Szarbia (Skalbmierz commune; different from the Szarbia included in this

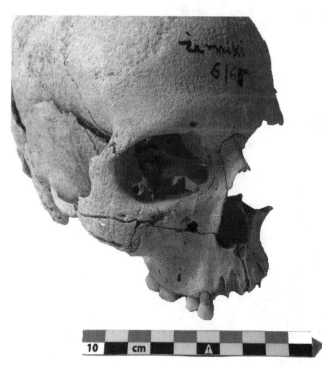

Figure 3.3. Image of burial 6 from Żerniki Górne showing a probable female 25–30 years of age with a variation of a Le Fort type I fracture of the right midface. Photo by Mark P. Toussaint.

Queering Prehistory on the Frontier: Early Bronze Age Mierzanowice Culture   71

study)—an "artificially widened spinal aperture... evidence of endocanibalism [*sic*]" (Baczyńska 1994, 58). It should be noted that another (male) individual from Żerniki Górne (grave 52) showed almost the same trauma to the area surrounding the foramen magnum.

The lack of statistically significant results in the cluster analysis is likely due to a combination of factors: the small sample size, the small number of entheses

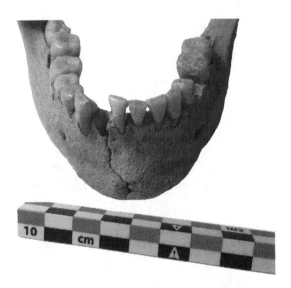

Figure 3.4. Burial 6 from Żerniki Górne showing a probable female 25–30 years of age with symphyseal fracture of the mandible. Photo by Mark P. Toussaint.

Figure 3.5. Image of burial 6 from Żerniki Górne showing a probable female 25–30 years of age with indications of possible decapitation or artificial widening of the foramen magnum. Photo by Mark P. Toussaint.

per individual, and the confounding factor of age. As described above, age is known to significantly correlate with entheseal development. Ideally, an analysis such as this would control for age. However, given the sample size for this case study, it would not have been feasible to do that. In future studies, after more data are gathered, cluster analyses will be conducted on individuals in the same age category or after statistically controlling the raw data for age. Another factor to consider is that sex or gender may not be the primary drivers of differences in labor patterns. It is likely that overlapping social identities and roles existed that affected the types of stress placed on the musculoskeletal system. Nonetheless, I believe that this is a fruitful approach to the investigation of entheseal development in populations. For example, Porčić and Stafanović's (2009) study of an Early Bronze Age cemetery in Serbia used a similar cluster analysis to show that "vertical status" (indexed by grave goods) interacted with sex and that different labor patterns were reflected in entheseal development depending on these categories. Such an approach has the potential to be particularly informative about individuals buried in unorthodox orientations and other "atypical" individuals.

Conclusion

Instead of presenting blank-slate landscapes waiting to be colonized, frontier zones are regions of interaction and exchange. They can be places where power is exercised in a stringent manner and where conformity is policed or they can be places where individual agency, creativity, and hybridity flourish. The structural, spatial, and ideological particularities of frontier societies all impact the specific character of the frontier zone. Gender provides a powerful lens through which to examine these phenomena because it is a nexus where power, agency, and identity meet.

The Mierzanowice Culture populations in the northern Carpathian region provide a unique opportunity to study the interactions between gender and the frontier. Their dead were buried in particular orientations depending on sex and/or gender, perhaps among other variables. Furthermore, Mierzanowice Culture populations showed signs of regionalization and differentiation in the Late Phase, quite likely due to the interactions between Mierzanowice communities and communities of the Únětice and Otomani-Füzesabony cultural paradigms.

Although the case study explored in this chapter was based on a small sample of individuals, a few patterns have begun to emerge. Certain aspects of burial orientations may correspond more to gender than to sex, as evidenced by one female who was buried along a typically male axis but was lying on her left side, which is typical for females. It is not out of the realm of possibility that such atypical burial orientations may correspond to a nonbinary gender category. This preliminary study also indicated that while all individuals were at fairly equal risk of perimortem trauma, females were more likely than males to incur antemortem trauma.

In future studies, more data will be gathered from these and other Mierzanowice Culture cemeteries to allow for the expansion of the sample size. Due to the limitations of the current sample size, changes in gender constructions over time in the "frontier zone" of the Mierzanowice Culture region could not be explored. The majority of individuals included in this study were from the Late Phase of the Mierzanowice Culture. However, in the future, I will endeavor to collect data from earlier cemeteries or cemeteries of longer duration in order to more fully investigate the influence of surrounding cultural paradigms on how gender was conceptualized, actualized, and embodied in Mierzanowice Culture communities.

Acknowledgments

Deep gratitude is owed to Dr. Piotr Włodarczak and to the Institute of Archaeology and Ethnology of the Polish Academy of Sciences, without whose assistance, hospitality, and permission to use collections this study would not have been possible. Sincere thanks are due also to Dr. Debra Martin, whose guidance and support have been crucial. Finally, I would like to thank the University of Nevada Las Vegas Graduate and Professional Student Association and the UNLV International Programs for financial support for this project. In particular, big thanks go to Lizbeth Arias for her help in facilitating this international work.

Note

1. "First Homosexual Caveman Found," *The Telegraph* (London), April 6, 2011, https://www.telegraph.co.uk/news/newstopics/howaboutthat/8433527/First-homosexual-caveman-found.html.

References

Bąbel, J. T. 2013. *Cmentarzyska Społeczności Kultury Mierzanowickiej Na Wyżynie Sandomierskiej*. Część 1, *Obrządek Pogrzebowy*. Rzeszów, Poland: Instytut Archeologii Uniwersytetu Rzeszowskiego.

Baczyńska, B. 1994. *Cmentarzysko Kultury Mierzanowickiej W Szarbi, Woj. Kieleckie: Studium Obrządku Pogrzebowego*. Kraków: Secesja.

———. 2000a. "Szarbia: Stanowisko 14, Gm. Koniusza, Woj. Małopolskie." Unpublished site report, Instytut Archeologii i Etnologii Polskiej Akademii Nauk.

———. 2000b. "Szarbia, Gmina Koniusza, Województwo Małopolskie, Stanowisko 14, Wykop I/2000: Opisy Obiektów 1–51." Unpublished site report, Instytut Archeologii i Etnologii Polskiej Akademii Nauk.

Barth, F. (1969) 1998. *Ethnic Groups and Boundaries: The Social Organization of Culture Difference*. Long Grove, IL: Waveland Press.

Bird, C. E., and P. P. Rieker 2008. "Gender Differences in Health: Are They Biological, Social, or Both?" In Bird and Rieker, *Gender and Health: The Effects of Constrained Choices and Social Policies*, 16–53. Cambridge: Cambridge University Press.

Brooks, S., and J. Suchey 1990. "Skeletal Age Determination Based on the Os Pubis: A Comparison of the Acsádi-Nemeskéri and Suchey-Brooks Methods." *Human Evolution* 5: 227–238.

Bruzek, J. 2002. "A Method for Visual Determination of Sex, Using the Human Hip Bone." *American Journal of Physical Anthropology* 117(2): 157–168.

Buikstra, J. E., and D. H. Ubelaker 1994. *Standards for Data Collection from Human Skeletal Remains*. Fayetteville, AR: Arkansas Archaeological Survey.

Butler, J. (1990) 2006. *Gender Trouble: Feminism and the Subversion of Identity*. New York: Routledge.

Cardoso, F. Alves, and C. Y. Henderson. 2010. "Enthesopathy Formation in the Humerus: Data from Known Age-at-Death and Known Occupation Skeletal Collections." *American Journal of Physical Anthropology* 141(4): 550–560.

Casimir, M. J. 1992. "The Dimensions of Territoriality: An Introduction." In *Mobility and Territoriality: Social and Spatial Boundaries among Foragers, Fishers, Pastoralists, and Peripatetics*, edited by Michael J. Casimir and Aparna Rao, 1–26. New York: Berg.

Czebreszuk, J. 2013. "The Bronze Age in the Polish Lands." In *The Oxford Handbook of the European Bronze Age*, edited by Harry Fokkens and Anthony Harding, 767–786. Oxford: Oxford University Press.

Donnan, H., and T. M. Wilson 1999. *Borders: Frontiers of Identity, Nation and State*. Oxford: Berg.

Fausto-Sterling, A. 2000. *Sexing the Body: Gender Politics and the Construction of Sexuality*. New York: Basic Books.

Geller, P. L. 2008. "Conceiving Sex: Fomenting a Feminist Bioarchaeology." *Journal of Social Archaeology* 8(1): 113–138.

———. 2017. *The Bioarchaeology of Socio-Sexual Lives: Queering Common Sense About Sex, Gender, and Sexuality*. Cham, Switzerland: Springer International.

Górski, J., P. Jarosz, K. Tunia, S. Wilk, and P. Włodarczak. 2013. "New Evidence on the Absolute Chronology of the Early Mierzanowice Culture in South-Eastern Poland." In *From Copper to Bronze: Cultural and Social Transformations at the Turn of the 3rd/2nd Millennia B.C. in Central Europe*, edited by Martin Bartelheim, Jaroslav Peška, and Jan Turek, 105–118. Gewidmet PhDr. Váslav Moucha, CSc. anlässlich seines 80. Langenweißbach: Beier & Beran.

Grauer, A. L., and P. Stuart-Macadam, eds. 1998. *Sex and Gender in Paleopathological Perspective*. Cambridge: Cambridge University Press.

Grémaux, R. 1996. "Woman Becomes Man in the Balkans." In *Third Sex, Third Gender: Beyond Sexual Dimorphism in Culture and History*, edited by Gilbert Herdt, 241–281. New York: Zone Books.

Harding, A. F. 2000. *European Societies in the Bronze Age. Cambridge World Archaeology*. Cambridge: Cambridge University Press.

Havelková, P., M. Hladík, and P. Velemínský. 2013. "Entheseal Changes: Do They Reflect Socioeconomic Status in the Early Medieval Central European Population? (Mikulčice–Klášteřisko, Great Moravian Empire, 9th–10th Century)." *International Journal of Osteoarchaeology* 23(2): 237–251.

Henderson, C. Y., V. Mariotti, D. Pany-Kucera, S. Villotte, and C. Wilczak. 2013. "Recording Specific Entheseal Changes of Fibrocartilaginous Entheses: Initial Tests Using the Coimbra Method." *International Journal of Osteoarchaeology* 23(2): 152–162.

Herodotus. 2014. *Histories*. Edited by James Romm. Translated by Pamela Mensch. Indianapolis, IN: Hackett Publishing.

Jaeger, M. 2010. "Transkarpackie Kontakty Kultury Otomani-Füzesabony." In *Transkarpackie Kontakty Kulturowe w Epoce Kamienia, Brązu i Wczesnej Epoce Żelaza*, edited by Jan Gancarski, 313–330. Krosno, Poland: Muzeum Podkarpackie w Krośnie.

———. 2014. "The Stone Fortifications of the Settlement at Spišský Štvrtok. A Contribution to the Discussion on the Long-Distance Contacts of the Otomani-Füzesabony Culture." *Praehistorische Zeitschrift* 89(2): 291–304.

Jaeger, M., and L. Olexa. 2014. "The Metallurgists from Nižná Myšľa (Okr. Košice-Okolie/SK): A Contribution to the Discussion on the Metallurgy in Defensive Settlements of the Otomani-Füzesabony Culture." *Archäologisches Korrespondenzblatt* 44(2): 163–176.

Jiráň, L., M. Salaš, and A. Krenn-Leeb. 2013. "The Czech Lands and Austria in the Bronze Age." In *The Oxford Handbook of the European Bronze Age*, edited by Harry Fokkens and Anthony Harding, 787–812. Oxford: Oxford University Press.

Kadrow, S. 1991. "Iwanowice, Babia Gora Site: Spatial Evolution of an Early Bronze Age Mierzanowice Culture Settlement (2300–1600 BC)." *Antiquity* 65(248): 640–650.

———. 1994. "Social Structures and Social Evolution among Early-Bronze-Age Communities in South-Eastern Poland." *Journal of European Archaeology* 2(2): 229–248.

Kadrow, S., and J. Machnik. 1997. *Kultura Mierzanowicka: Chronologia, Taksonomia I Rozwój Przestrzenny*. Kraków, Poland: Polska Akademia Nauk, Oddział w Krakowie.

Kadrow, S., A. Machnikowa, and J. Machnik. 1992. *Iwanowice Stanowisko Babia Góra. Część II, Cmentarzysko Z Wczesnego Okresu Epoki Brązu*. Kraków, Poland: Secesja.

———. 1995. "Early Bronze Age Settlement on 'Babia Góra' Site at Iwanowice Against the Background of the Contemporary Settlement Network in an Upper Vistula River Basin (SE Poland)." *Science Dell' Uomo* 4: 203–220.

Kempisty, A. 1978. *Schyłek Neolitu i Początek Epoki Brązu na Wyżynie Małopolskiej w Świetle Badań nad Kopcami*. Warsaw: Wydawnictwa Uniwersytetu Warszawskiego.

Koziol, K. M. 2012. "Performances of Imposed Status: Captivity at Cahokia." In *The Bioarchaeology of Violence*, edited by Debra L. Martin, Ryan P. Harrod, and Ventura R. Pérez, 226–250. Gainesville: University Press of Florida.

Krenz-Niedbała, M. 1999. "Harris Lines in a Skeletal Sample of the Neolithic and of the Early Bronze Age, Żerniki Górne (Poland)." In *Biological and Cultural Consequences of the Transition to Agriculture in Central Europe*, edited by Dobrochna Jankowska, Marta Krenz-Niedbała, Janusz Piontek, and Jacek Wierzbicki, 105–114. Poznań, Poland: Monografie Instytutu Antropologii UAM.

Laqueur, T. 1990. *Making Sex: Body and Gender from the Greeks to Freud*. Cambridge, MA: Harvard University Press.

Levy, J. E. 1999. "Gender, Power, and Heterarchy in Middle-Level Societies." In *Manifesting Power: Gender and the Interpretation of Power in Archaeology*, edited by Tracy L. Sweely, 62–78. London: Routledge.

Lovejoy, C. O. 1985. "Dental Wear in the Libben Population: Its Functional Pattern and Role in the Determination of Adult Skeletal Age at Death." *American Journal of Physical Anthropology* 68: 47–56.

Lovejoy, C. O., R. S. Meindl, T. R. Pryzbeck, and R. P. Mensforth. 1985. "Chronological Metamorphosis of the Auricular Surface of the Ilium: A New Method for the Determination of Adult Skeletal Age at Death." *American Journal of Physical Anthropology* 68(1): 15–28.

Mariotti, V., F. Facchini, and M. G. Belcastro. 2007. "The Study of Entheses: Proposal of a Standardised Scoring Method for Twenty-Three Entheses of the Postcranial Skeleton." *Collegium Antropologicum* 31(1): 291–313.

Marková, K., and G. Ilon. 2013. "Slovakia and Hungary." In *The Oxford Handbook of the European Bronze Age*, edited by Harry Fokkens and Anthony Harding, 813–836. Oxford: Oxford University Press.

Martin, D. L. 1997. "Violence Against Women in the La Plata River Valley (A.D. 1000–1300)." In *Troubled Times: Violence and Warfare in the Past*, edited by David W. Frayer and Debra L. Martin, 45–76. Boca Raton, FL: Taylor & Francis Group.

Meindl, R. S., and C. O. Lovejoy. 1985. "Ectocranial Suture Closure: A Revised Method for the Determination of Skeletal Age-At-Death Based on the Lateral-Anterior Sutures." *American Journal of Physical Anthropology* 68(1): 57–66.

Milella, M., M. G. Belcastro, C. P. E. Zollikofer, and V. Mariotti. 2012. "The Effect of Age, Sex, and Physical Activity on Entheseal Morphology in a Contemporary Italian Skeletal Collection." *American Journal of Physical Anthropology* 148(3): 379–388.

Milisauskas, S., and J. Kruk. 2011. "Late Neolithic/Late Copper Age 3500–2200 BC." In *European Prehistory*, edited by Sarunas Milisauskas, 293–325. New York: Springer.

Nanda, S. 2014. *Gender Diversity*. 2nd ed. Long Grove, IL: Waveland Press.

Niinimäki, S., and L. Baiges Sotos. 2013. "The Relationship Between Intensity of Physical Activity and Entheseal Changes on the Lower Limb." *International Journal of Osteoarchaeology* 23(2): 221–228.

Niinimäki, S. 2011. "What Do Muscle Marker Ruggedness Scores Actually Tell Us?" *International Journal of Osteoarchaeology* 21(3): 292–299.

Niinimäki, S., M. Niskanen, J. Niinimäki, M. Nieminen, J. Tuukkanen, and J. A. Junno. 2013. "Modeling Skeletal Traits and Functions of the Upper Body: Comparing Archaeological and Anthropological Material." *Journal of Anthropological Archaeology* 32(3): 347–351.

Ortner, D. J., ed. 2003. *Identification of Pathological Conditions in Human Skeletal Remains*. 2nd ed. San Diego: Academic Press.

Pellow, D. 1996. "Introduction." In *Setting Boundaries: The Anthropology of Spatial and Social Organization*, edited by Deborah Pellow, 1–8. Westport, CT: Bergin and Garvey.

Phenice, T. W. 1969. "A Newly Developed Visual Method of Sexing the Os Pubis." *American Journal of Physical Anthropology* 30(2): 297–301.

Pitkin, H. F. 1972. *Wittgenstein and Justice: On the Significance of Ludwig Wittgenstein for Social and Political Thought*. Berkeley, CA: University of California Press.

Pokutta, D. A. 2013. "Population Dynamics, Diet and Migrations of the Únětice Culture in Poland." PhD diss., University of Gothenburg.

Porčić, M., and S. Stefanović. 2009. "Physical Activity and Social Status in Early Bronze Age Society: The Mokrin Necropolis." *Journal of Anthropological Archaeology* 28(3): 259–273.

Przybyła, M. S., and M. Skoneczna. 2013. "The Fortified Settlement from the Early and Middle Bronze Age at Maszkowice, Nowy Sącz District (Western Carpathians). Preliminary Results of Studies Conducted in the Years 2009–2012." *Recherches Archéologiques* (3): 5–66.

Robb, J. 1997. "Violence and Gender in Italy." In *Troubled Times: Violence and Warfare in the Past*, edited by David W. Frayer and Debra L. Martin, 111–144. Boca Raton, FL: Taylor & Francis Group.

Rodseth, L., and B. J. Parker. 2005. "Introduction: Theoretical Considerations in the Study of Frontiers." In *Untaming the Frontier in Anthropology, Archaeology, and History*, edited by Bradley J. Parker and Lars Rodseth, 3–21. Tucson: University of Arizona Press.

Rubin, G. 1975. "The Traffic in Women: Notes on the 'Political Economy' of Sex." In *Toward an Anthropology of Women*, edited by Rayna R. Reiter, 157–210. New York: Monthly Review Press.

Ruff, C. B., B. M. Holt, M. Niskanen, V. Sladék, M. Berner, E. Garofalo, H. M. Garvin, M. Hora, H. Maijanen, S. Niinimäki, K. Salo, E. Schuplerová, and D. Tompkins. 2012. "Stature and Body Mass Estimation from Skeletal Remains in the European Holocene." *American Journal of Physical Anthropology* 148(4): 601–617.

Scheuer, L., and S. Black. 2000. *Developmental Juvenile Osteology*. San Diego, CA: Elsevier Academic Press.

Sofaer, J. R. 2006. *The Body as Material Culture: A Theoretical Osteoarchaeology*. Cambridge: Cambridge University Press.

Todd, T. W. 1920. "Age Changes in the Pubic Bone. I: The Male White Pubis." *American Journal of Physical Anthropology* 3(3): 285–334.

———. 1921. "Age Changes in the Pubic Bone. II: The Pubis of the Male Negro-White Hybrid, III: The Pubis of the White Female, IV: The Pubis of the Female Negro-White Hybrid." *American Journal of Physical Anthropology* 4(1): 1–70.

Tung, T. A. 2012. "Violence against Women: Differential Treatment of Local and Foreign Females in the Heartland of the Wari Empire, Peru." In *The Bioarchaeology of Violence*, edited by Debra L. Martin, Ryan P. Harrod, and Ventura Pérez, 180–198. Gainesville: University Press of Florida Gainesville.

Ubelaker, D. H. 1978. *Human Skeletal Remains: Excavation, Analysis, Interpretation.* Chicago: Aldine.

Vandkilde, H. 2007. *Culture and Change in Central European Prehistory: 6th to 1st Millennium BC.* Aarhus, Denmark: Aarhus University Press.

Villotte, S., and C. J. Knüsel. 2013. "Understanding Entheseal Changes: Definition and Life Course Changes." *International Journal of Osteoarchaeology* 23(2): 135–146.

Villotte, S., D. Castex, V. Couallier, O. Dutour, C. J. Knüsel, and D. Henry-Gambier. 2010. "Enthesopathies as Occupational Stress Markers: Evidence from the Upper Limb." *American Journal of Physical Anthropology* 142: 224–234.

Waldron, T. 2009. *Palaeopathology: Cambridge Manuals in Archaeology.* Cambridge: Cambridge University Press.

Walker, P. L. 1997. "Wife Beating, Boxing and Broken Noses: Skeletal Evidence for the Cultural Patterning of Violence." In *Troubled Times: Violence and Warfare in the Past*, edited by David W. Frayer and Debra L. Martin, 145–180. Boca Raton, FL: Taylor & Francis Group.

Wedel, V. L., and A. Galloway, eds. 2014. *Broken Bones: Anthropological Analysis of Blunt Force Trauma.* 2nd ed. Springfield, IL: Charles C. Thomas.

Wilson, T. M., and H. Donnan. 1998. "Nation, State and Identity at International Borders." In *Border Identities: Nation and State at International Frontiers*, edited by Thomas M. Wilson and Hastings Donnan, 1–30. Cambridge: Cambridge University Press.

Włodarczak, P. 2014. "The Traits of Early-Bronze Pontic Cultures in the Development of Old Upland Corded Ware (Małopolska Groups) and Złota Culture Communities." *Baltic-Pontic Studies* 19: 7–52.

Wolf, E. R. 1990. "Distinguished Lecture: Facing Power—Old Insights, New Questions." *American Anthropologist* 92(3): 586–596.

II

Movement across Borders

4

Isotopes, Migration, and Sex

Investigating the Mobility of the Frontier
Inhabitants of Roman Egypt

AMANDA T. GROFF AND TOSHA L. DUPRAS

By the Romano-Christian period in Egypt (50 to 450 CE), Rome had successfully expanded its empire, which included the incorporation of the remote Egyptian oases via caravan routes. The oases were dynamic borderlands where culture, economic practices, and politics diverged from those of the Nile Valley. While managing these routes fell to the empire, the people who moved along these routes were often local to the oases and used them for livelihood. The cultural identities of these individuals are mostly lost to history, save for scant textual sources that describe socioeconomic activities. In this chapter we explore these identities further by using stable oxygen isotope analysis in conjunction with textual sources to discuss the mobility of adults from the Kellis 2 Cemetery, Dakhleh Oasis, Egypt. These data complement the limited textual evidence, allowing for more detailed reconstruction of economics, kinship, and residence patterns during the Romano-Christian era and add to a definition of Egyptian frontier identity.

Isotope Analysis

Oxygen Isotopes

Oxygen is the most abundant light chemical element on the planet. It constitutes nearly 21 percent of the earth's atmosphere and 90 percent of our drinking water (Emsley 2001; Meier-Augenstein 2010). Oxygen exists in nature in three stable isotope forms, ^{16}O, ^{17}O, and ^{18}O. Due to its abundant nature, the

[18]O isotope is frequently used as a natural tracer for measuring groundwater mineral interactions and local rainfall and for tracking migration (e.g., Bowen and Wilkinson 2002; Meier-Augenstein 2010; White et al. 1998). In humans, drinking water is responsible for 60 percent to 70 percent of the oxygen incorporated into body tissues. Food consists of 30 to 40 percent oxygen (Bryant and Froelich 1995; Hedges et al. 2005). Incorporating oxygen isotopes into human tissue follows three primary principles. First, specific factors, including climate and geography, regulate the oxygen composition of rainfall. Second, the composition and amount of oxygen in drinking water reflects its original source. Finally, a strong linear relationship exists between the oxygen composition of drinking water and the oxygen composition of bone and tooth enamel (e.g., Dupras and Schwarcz 2001; Longinelli 1984; Luz and Kolodny 1989; White et al. 1998). The balance of this relationship is maintained through oxygen-containing compounds that are constantly entering and exiting the body. Sources for oxygen-containing compounds that enter the body include atmospheric oxygen, water consumed, and water contained in food (e.g., Dupras and Schwarcz 2001; Meier-Augenstein 2010; White et al. 1998).

Oxygen isotope values found in human tooth enamel and bone apatite are influenced primarily by consumed water produced from local rainfall. If an individual consumes foreign water, their oxygen isotope values may differ from the local population (White et al. 1998). Oxygen isotope analysis can be used to create life histories of migration or movement during an individual's lifetime. From birth to 12 years of age, oxygen isotope values are integrated into tooth enamel during mineralization. Because enamel does not remodel, it captures a permanent record of oxygen values at the time of formation (Wright and Schwarcz 1998) and provides a way to both track the timing of migration in childhood and reveal the geographic origin of that individual (e.g., White et al. 1998; White et al. 2000; White et al. 2004). Bone apatite functions in a similar fashion, but it does remodel. While it models at different rates depending on age and bone type, turnover of a load-bearing bone such as a femur takes ten to twenty years (Hedges et al. 2005). Thus, adult oxygen isotope values from bone apatite can be used to document the environment of the area where a person was just before they died. A life history pertaining to mobility and migration of an individual can be created by combining stable oxygen isotope data from tooth enamel and bone apatite (e.g., Buzon and Bowen 2010; White et al. 1998).

The Archaeological Context: The Movement of Goods and People in Roman Egypt

The trade and movement of goods from the Nile Valley and Nubia (present-day Sudan) was essential for the survival of oasis inhabitants (Bagnall 1985; Morkot 1996; Worp 1995). To the archaeologist, the movement of trade items is highly relevant for understanding intrapersonal relationships and population movement across Egypt. In ancient Egypt, a series of caravan routes ran through the Western Desert, connecting the north and south and moving from one oasis to the next (Adams 2007; Morkot 1996). Although the oases of the Western Desert were not the focus of luxury trade items, it is clear that they were linked to the Nile Valley and generated wealth through trade connections (Adams 2007). The distances traveled along these desert routes were great (thousands of kilometers) (figure 4.1) and it is certain that luxury and nonluxury items such as olive oil, pack animals, and wine were transported in these regions (Adams 2007; Bagnall 1985; Bagnall 1997). A natural effect of this trade was the movement of people around the landscape.

Socioeconomic Activities of Females in Roman Egypt

During the Roman period in Egypt, young girls acquired numerous skills that prepared them to become wives and mothers. Although most girls learned these skills from their mothers and older female family members, some girls were professionally trained to prepare for a life as a servant (Rowlandson 1998). Girls were free born (from elite or wealthy families), born of a lower status and trained to be domestic servants, or born into slavery (Lewis 1999). Spinning, weaving, making clothes, and preparing food were among the most common training activities for all young girls (Lewis 1999; Rowlandson 1998). Unfortunately, written documentation detailing these training activities is virtually nonexistent for free-born girls in Roman Egypt. Paradoxically, the training of slave girls in weaving and other activities is much better documented (Rowlandson 1998). Apprenticeships for both free-born and slave girls typically started around the age of 10 and would last one to three years but could run an additional one to two years longer (Lewis 1999; Westermann 1914). Contracts from the Oxyrhynchus papyri collection supports this age and duration (e.g., Westermann 1914, P.Oxy.II.275, P.Oxy.IV.724, P.Oxy.IV.725) and indicate that children would be relocated away from family to training facilities or under the supervision of a training official (Grenfell and Hunt 1899; Westermann 1914).

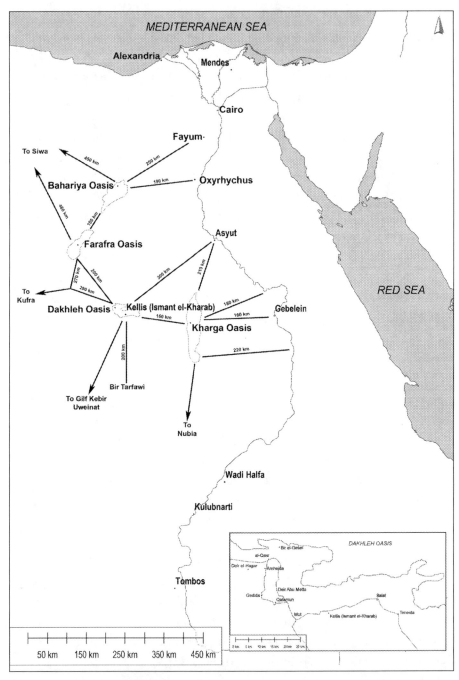

Figure 4.1. Map showing the location of the Dakhleh Oasis and Kellis (*inset*) in Egypt. Trade routes and estimated distances from the Dakhleh Oasis are also illustrated. Map by Amanda Groff.

Slavery in rural villages like Kellis was relatively rare; occurring in only about 11 percent of households (Bagnall and Frier 2006). An example of slavery at Kellis is documented in a letter from House 3: "I acknowledge that I have given to you . . . for the current year [the] daughter of my house-born slave for learning the weavers trade" (Worp 1995, P. Kell. I Gr. 19A). The context of this document indicates that the slave girl was local to the Dakhleh Oasis. While few females moved to Dakhleh Oasis to become slaves or to serve as apprentices, it can be assumed that young girls left the oasis to go to the Nile Valley to train or to fulfill slavery contracts. Wet nursing was a job typically performed by slave women who nursed free-born and slave children for a fee paid to their owner. Ancient contextual evidence for these types of arrangements include P.Oxy.I.91, in which a man acknowledges to a woman that he has received the wages she has paid to him for the wet-nursing service his female slave provided for her baby daughter (in Rowlandson 1998). Slave women may have also been engaged in prostitution; a letter about trade in prostitutes mentions the activities of two males who were trading in female slaves as prostitutes (Rowlandson 1998, PSI. IV.406).

Numerous documents written in both Greek and Coptic during the fourth century CE indicate the socioeconomic status of females. For example, documentation indicates that women owned land and agricultural tracts, managed the selling and purchasing of camels, sold beer or wine, entertained as flute players or dancers, and performed other waged jobs that were not formal enough to document (Rowlandson 1998). Ancient leasing contracts also indicate the socioeconomic independence of women. In Dakhleh, P. Kell. I Gr. 32 (in Worp 1995) is a contract for leasing a room between a woman named Aurelia Marsis from the village of Kellis who had moved to Aphrodite in the Antaiopolite nome and a man named Aurelius Psais. Documents also indicate that a woman named Tehat conducted a tailoring business in conjunction with her son or her husband in House 3 in the village of Kellis (Bowen 2001; Gardner et al. 1999; Worp 1995, P. Kell. V Copt. 18). While the status of women involved in Tehat's business is unknown, letters recovered from House 3 indicate that the women workers were free (Bowen 2001).

Marriage was likely the primary reason that females moved. According to census returns, marriage was largely monogamous and females typically married at 16 to 20 years old (Bagnall 1993). Patrilocality was a common practice in Roman Egypt (Bagnall and Frier 2006; Rowlandson 1998). Mitochondrial DNA (mtDNA) studies indicate evidence of thirteen genetic lineages in the

Kellis 2 cemetery and demonstrate a pattern of patrilocal residential organization (Parr 2002). However, in contrast, nonmetric skeletal traits (Molto 2001) and nonmetric dental traits (Haddow 2012) suggest that the population buried in Kellis 2 cemetery was homogenous and came from similar genetic lines, perhaps indicating inbreeding, intermarrying, or infrequent migration. While it is almost impossible to compare these two types of data, they provide interesting evidence that can be supported or refuted by isotopic analyses.

Socioeconomic Activities of Males in Roman Egypt

Both free and enslaved young boys of Roman Egypt were expected to participate in apprenticeships starting between the ages of 10 and 13, learning their trade in one to three years with the option for a two-year extension. Evidence from papyri suggests that boys apprenticed to be builders, coppersmiths, mat plaiters, nail makers, pipers, wood carvers, and wool shearers (Lewis 1999). Weaving was also a common apprenticeship for young males (Rowlandson 1998). As documented in P. Oxy. II 275 (in Rowlandson 1998), in 54 CE a man named Tryphon purchased a loom and taught his sons the weaving trade. Twelve years later, in 66 CE, his youngest son was recorded as learning the weaving craft from another weaver. Additionally, P. Kell. I Gr. 12 (in Worp 1995) records that a man from Kellis sent his son to a monastery to learn the linen-weaving trade. It would appear that leaving home for apprenticeships was a common practice and it is likely that young boys traveled both short and long distances to acquire desired skills.

Adult males fulfilled various positions in society, including farmer, slave, and statesman. However, three socioeconomic activities were directly linked to male mobility in Roman Egypt: professional transporter, compulsory worker, and military soldier. Trade in the Western Desert connecting remote oases to the Nile Valley and other locations throughout northern Africa. The oases of the Western Desert produced products such as wine, dates, and olive oil (Adams 2007; Bagnall 1985; Bagnall 1997), and traders transported coveted minerals such as alum to the Nile Valley for tanning hides or for pigments for dyeing (Hope et al. 2009). The majority of evidence for trade in the oases is preserved in customs and transport receipts (Adams 2007). For example, P. Kell. I Gr. 51–52 (in Worp 1995) consists of transport receipts from 320 CE that record that Aurelius Horos, son of Mersis, a camel-driver from the village of Kellis, transported olives, palm fibers, dried figs, dried grapes, and linen to and from the Nile Valley city of Hermopolis (approximately 300 kilometers from Mothite [Dakhleh]).

Most slaves in Roman Egypt performed domestic duties rather than agricultural tasks (Biezunska-Malowist 1977; Lewis 1999; Straus 1988). However, there is documentation that indicates that while some males were not considered slaves, they were assigned to compulsory work parties that would take them to other locations to work in mines or fields. In most instances, the distance between a male's village of residence and his assigned work site did not exceed more than 10–12 kilometers, although it could be much further (Lewis 1999). A document from 213 CE–214 CE indicates that sixty male workers were transferred more than 32 kilometers for work.

Evidence for the Roman military's presence in Egypt is well known. The Roman military built various forts and fortresses around the country, including at the oases of the Western Desert (Kucera 2010). Roman soldiers would collect supplies in considerable quantities from the Western Desert and the presence of soldiers in remote locations further encouraged trade (Adams 2007). The local recruitment system did not exist in Egypt until the end of the second century, when the Roman military sought to build up its forces. The standard age of recruitment for Roman soldiers and legions was 17 years old (Roth 1999). Upon retirement or discharge, military men would typically settle near their assigned camp, as they may have already founded a home and family nearby (Alston 1995). Based on available ancient source materials and archaeological evidence, it is evident that males were more likely to travel for economic purposes than females in Roman Egypt. The socioeconomic status of male and male-oriented work increased the opportunities for male family members to traverse the landscape.

Dakhleh Oasis

The Dakhleh Oasis is one of five major depressions located in the Western Desert of Egypt. It is located approximately 250 kilometers west of the Nile River (see figure 4.1). This oasis stretches approximately 80 kilometers (50 miles) east to west and 25 kilometers (16 miles) north to south. It has been continuously inhabited since the Old Stone Age and has been in contact with the Nile Valley since the Pharaonic era (Mills 1999). Dakhleh is bordered by a large escarpment to the north and is located roughly 100 meters below the surrounding desert (Kleindienst et al. 1999).

Kellis (Ismant el-Kharab)

The Roman period settlement of Kellis (Ismant el-Kharab), which was occupied from the mid-first to second centuries CE to the third and fourth centuries CE, was an important economic and political center for the Dakhleh Oasis (Hope 1988, 2001). At its peak, Kellis likely housed several thousand people and was supported by many surrounding agricultural fields. The abandonment of Kellis was likely caused by encroaching sand dunes, failing water supplies, salinization of agricultural fields, or a combination of these factors (Hope 2001). Two major cemeteries are associated with the village: Kellis 1 or West Cemetery (Late Ptolemaic–Early Roman period, ca. 60 BCE–100 CE) (Birrell 1999) and Kellis 2 or the East Cemetery (Roman period, ca. 50 CE–450 CE) (Birrell 1999; Stewart et al. 2003).

Kellis 2 is estimated to contain 3,000 to 4,000 burials (Molto 2002a). As of 2011, 761 graves had been excavated by the Dakhleh Oasis Project "bone team." Of these 761 graves, 724 individuals have been aged. The remains of juveniles under the age of 15 years represent 64 percent (n = 463) of the individuals who have been aged; the remaining 36 percent (n = 261) are adults. The mean ages range from 21 weeks gestation to 72 years (Wheeler 2009). The mean age at death for adults was 39.4 for females and 36.0 for males. Of the 261 adults, 153 (59 percent) are females, 105 are males (41 percent), and 3 adult individuals are of undetermined sex. The age range of 16 to 35 years represents the peak of mortality for adult females and males. The excellent preservation of human remains provides the opportunity for stable isotopes analysis to address questions of mobility and migration among the sexes.

Materials and Methods

Enamel and bone samples were collected from 81 individuals (36 females, 45 males) from the Kellis 2 cemetery at Dakhleh Oasis in Egypt. Sex and age estimation of all individuals was based on standard osteological methods (Buikstra and Ubelaker 1994). Where possible, multiple enamel and bone samples were collected from each individual; if either enamel or bone was missing, then only the available enamel and/or bone sample was tested.

In total, thirty-six adult female enamel (n = 6) and bone (n = 35) samples were analyzed for their stable oxygen isotopes. When possible, enamel samples were collected from multiple teeth from the adult females. In this study, both enamel samples (from the first, second, and third molars) and bone samples were collected from the femurs of two adult females. For these two females, B131 and B279, a complete migration life history can be created.

Samples of tooth enamel and bone were collected from forty-five adult males excavated from the Kellis 2 cemetery. Apatite samples were collected from either the humerus or the femur of 43 of the 45 adult males; enamel samples were collected from 12 of the 45 adult males. In some cases, enamel samples were collected from multiple teeth from the adult males. Both enamel samples (from the first, second, and third molars) and bone samples (from the femur) were collected from three adult males. For these three males, B111, B124, and B139, a complete migration life history can be created. A baseline for stable oxygen isotope (δ^{18}O) values in the Dakhleh Oasis was established from mice femurs and humeri excavated from a Ptolemaic site in the oasis. While mice are mobile creatures, their size and lifespan make them a reliable source because it is likely that they lived and died in the Dakhleh Oasis.

Because the turnover rates for tooth enamel and bone are different, the isotopic value from each sample represents a different age. The time period when different teeth are calcified serves as a marker for the stages in life when migration may have occurred. For this study, the oxygen isotope value from an adult first molar represents birth to 2.5 years of age, the second molar 3.8 to 6 years of age, and the third molar 9.5 to 12 years of age (Dupras and Tocheri 2007). If a value does not fall within the accepted δ^{18}O range for a specific location, then that individual might not be local. For apatite in adults, bone remodels about 1.5–5.1 percent per year (Hedges et al. 2007). Given these estimations, it would take around or over 10 years for an adult human skeleton to be replaced. Thus, bone isotope values are likely representative of an average of the final ten years of an individual's life.

All enamel and bone samples were processed at the University of Central Florida Laboratory for Bioarchaeological Sciences using protocols modeled after Wright and Schwarcz (1998) and Sullivan and Krueger (1983). All isotope results are reported in standard delta notation relative to VPDB and converted to VSMOW to facilitate comparison with previously published oxygen data from Egypt (e.g., Buzon and Bowen 2010; Dupras and Schwarcz 2001; Iacumin et al. 1996). The following equations are the generally accepted method for converting VPDB and VSMOW:

δ^{18}OVSMOW = (δ^{18}OVPDB) + 30.92 (original VSMOW, conversions before 2006)

δ^{18}OVSMOW = 1.03092 [x] (δ^{18}OVPDB) + 30.92 (VSMOW2, conversions after 2006)

δ^{18}OVPDB = 0.97002 [x] (δ^{18}OVSMOW)—29.98

Results

The analytical precision for isotope analyses was ± 0.048‰ for $\delta^{18}O$. The average $\delta^{18}O$ value for the mice is 27.9‰ ± 0.3‰. This baseline is further supported by the average $\delta^{18}O$ values of 27.5‰ ± 2.0‰ for human enamel and bone apatite samples; although the overall average $\delta^{18}O$ value for enamel of 26.9‰ ± 2.7‰ is slightly lower.

Female Tooth Enamel and Bone Apatite Results

Results from adult female enamel reveal that the $\delta^{18}OVSMOW$ values for five of the six females fall within or below the average range of 27.9‰ ± 0.3‰ established for the Dakhleh Oasis (table 4.1). For these five females, the average $\delta^{18}OVSMOW$ values were 26.3‰ for the first molar, 25.1‰ for the second molar, and 25.2‰ for the third molar. One female (B437) whose first and third molar were analyzed revealed $\delta^{18}OVSMOW$ values of 31.0‰ for the first molar and 31.59 percent for the third molar. These values fall outside the average range for the oxygen isotope in the Dakhleh Oasis.

Table 4.1. Oxygen isotope data for adult females

Burial number	Est. age at death	$\delta^{18}O$ (‰) Enamel M1	$\delta^{18}O$ (‰) Enamel M2	$\delta^{18}O$ (‰) Enamel M3	$\delta^{18}O$ (‰) Bone Apatite
2	25				27.0
19	45				27.6
21	45				26.6
25	19				28.7
26	19				26.7
27	30				27.3
44	63				24.3
52	30				25.8
53	38				24.8
58	48				26.8
105	58				28.4
131	23	26.79	25.52	25.45	27.61
141	42	25.9			25.9

Burial number	Est. age at death	$\delta^{18}O$ (‰) Enamel M1	$\delta^{18}O$ (‰) Enamel M2	$\delta^{18}O$ (‰) Enamel M3	$\delta^{18}O$ (‰) Bone Apatite
160	22				26.7
165	55				28.8
169	23				26.5
170	26				28.4
172	45				27.9
177	55				28.4
189	50				25.1
190	19				30.3
191	48				27.3
198	38				27.3
202	66				29.6
207	60				28.5
210	54				26.8
214	23				27.6
269	55				25.3
270	27				26.9
271	31				27.4
279	23	25.6	24.8	25.5	26.6
282	27	26.9	25.3		26.8
289	34			24.6	26.5
307	23				26.8
327	21				26.9
437	40	31.0		31.6	

Bone apatite data (Table 4.1) reveal an average δ^{18}OVSMOW value of 27.1‰ ± 1.3‰. B190 had a δ^{18}OVSMOW value of 30.3‰, indicating that she had been living away from the Dakhleh Oasis but had relocated to the oasis before she died. Seven other females (B25 [28.7‰], B105 [28.4‰], B165 [28.8‰], B170 [28.4‰], B177 [28.4‰], B202 [29.6‰], and B207 [28.5‰]) have bone apatite values that border on being "foreign" δ^{18}OVSMOW values. There are no enamel samples for these seven females to indicate if they were born outside the Dakhleh Oasis.

Male Tooth Enamel and Bone Apatite Results

Analysis of adult male enamel reveals that the δ^{18}OVSMOW values for eight of the twelve males fall within or below the average range of 27.9‰ ± 0.3‰ established for the Dakhleh Oasis (table 4.2). The average δ^{18}OVSMOW values were 25.5‰ for the first molar, 25.5‰ for the second molar, and 25.0‰ for the third molar. Analysis of enamel from three of the males revealed δ^{18}OVSMOW average values of 31.9‰ for the first molar (B6, B111, B116); 31.9‰ for the second molar (B111 only, as he was the only male in the population with second molar available); and 31.6‰ for the third molar (B6, B111, B116). These values fall outside the average range of δ^{18}OVSMOW values in the Dakhleh Oasis. Results from the enamel of burial B139 reveal a dramatic change in δ^{18}O values between the second molar (25.3‰) and third molar (31.8‰).

Table 4.2. Oxygen isotope data for adult males

Burial number	Est. age at death	δ^{18}O (‰) Enamel M1	δ^{18}O (‰) Enamel M2	δ^{18}O (‰) Enamel M3	δ^{18}O (‰) Bone Apatite
4	50				27.4
6	29			30.0	28.4
16	29				27.9
42	46				26.5
60	37				27.6
81	40				27.2
87	70				28.4
93	23				30.6
107	27	23.4	25.3		28.7
111	37	32.0	31.9	32.2	29.7
116	23	31.9		32.2	32.5
119	35				28.3
124	30	26.3	25.1	24.8	26.9
132	19	25.9	25.2		28.3
136	30				28.1
139	29	26.0	25.3	31.8	30.5
143	19				27.6
159	20				27.2
194	23				27.9
199	35				31.2

Burial number	Est. age at death	$\delta^{18}O$ (‰) Enamel M1	$\delta^{18}O$ (‰) Enamel M2	$\delta^{18}O$ (‰) Enamel M3	$\delta^{18}O$ (‰) Bone Apatite
211	55				29.1
213	55				26.9
218	29				28.8
220	35				26.8
222	29	26.0	25.5	25.2	
225	35				29.3
227	23				30.4
228	35				27.9
240	46				27.7
242	25				26.6
245	35				28.5
250	45				26.7
259	44				27.2
262	23				28.4
264	23				26.7
265	50				28.68
268	23				26.9
274	20				31.7
281	60	26.51			26.92
293	45		26.7		29.3
303	23				26.2
305	29				30.1
308	35				28.7
392	40	25.5		25.0	
543	25	25.1		24.9	28.0

Bone apatite oxygen isotope values revealed an average $\delta^{18}OVSMOW$ value of 28.3‰ ± 1.5‰. This average is high due to the inclusion of values from seven males whose bone apatite values fall outside the oxygen isotope range for Dakhleh Oasis. Burials B222 and B392 did not have any bone apatite available for testing. Burials B116, B199, and B274 had an average $\delta^{18}OVSMOW$ value of 31.8‰, indicating they had been living away from the Dakhleh Oasis but had relocated to the oasis before they died. Eighteen males had bone apatite values that bordered on "foreign" $\delta^{18}O$VSMOW values (average 28.7‰) outside the baseline range for oxygen values established for the Dakhleh Oasis.

Discussion

The results from adult oxygen isotope analysis from Kellis 2 were compared against published values from the sites of Asyut (Iacumin et al. 1996), Gebelein (Iacumin et al. 1996), Kulubnarti (Turner et al. 2007), Mendes (Prowse et al. 2007), Tombos (Buzon and Bowen 2010), and Wadi Halfa (White et al. 2004). Table 4.3 and figure 4.2 establish the mean and range for $\delta^{18}O$ values at these sites as compared to the Kellis 2 cemetery. Oxygen stable isotope values greater than 31.0‰ are considered representative of time spent in the Nile Valley. This is the value established for the Nile Valley based on the value common to all Nile Valley sites. Four sites that were used for comparison—Asyut, Gebelein, Mendes, and Tombos—have outlier values that indicate that these sites likely had travelers buried in their cemeteries. Those who had oxygen stable isotope

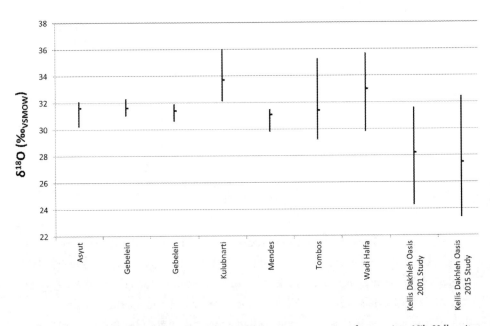

Figure 4.2. Gantt chart showing comparison of oxygen isotope ranges from various Nile Valley sites and the Kellis 2 cemetery, Dakhleh Oasis.

Amanda T. Groff and Tosha L. Dupras

Table 4.3. Comparison of $\delta^{18}O$ values for Nile Valley sites and Kellis 2 cemetery, Dakhleh Oasis

Site	Time period	Mean $\delta^{18}O$ ‰VSMOW	Range $\delta^{18}O$ ‰VSMOW	Sample	Reference
Asyut	1st Intermediate (2150–2050 BCE)	31.6	30.2–32.1	Enamel carbonate	Iacumin et al. 1996
Gebelein	Predynastic (3500–2600 BCE)	31.6	31.0–32.3	Bone carbonate	Iacumin et al. 1996
Gebelein	1st Intermediate (2150–2050 BCE)	31.4	30.6–31.9	Bone carbonate	Iacumin et al. 1996
Kulubnarti	Christian (500–800 CE)	33.7	32.1–36.0	Bone carbonate	Turner et al. 2007
Mendes	Greco-Roman (332 BCE–395 CE)	31.1	29.8–31.5	Enamel carbonate	Prowse et al. 2007
Tombos	New Kingdom and 3rd Intermediate Period (1400–1050 BCE)	31.4	29.2–35.3	Enamel carbonate	Buzon and Bowen 2010
Wadi Halfa	X-Group (350–550 CE) and Christian (500–1400 CE)	33	29.8–35.7	Bone and enamel carbonate	White et al. 2004
Kellis Dakhleh Oasis 2001 Study	Byzantine-Romano (50–450 CE)	28.2	24.3–31.6	Bone carbonate	Dupras and Schwarcz 2001
Kellis Dakhleh Oasis 2014 Study	Byzantine-Romano (50–450 CE)	27.5	23.35–32.45	Bone and enamel carbonate	

values ranging from 28.0‰ to 30.9‰ are considered possibly foreign to the Dakhleh Oasis and are referred to as "travelers." It is likely that individuals with these values were either traveling between Dakhleh Oasis and the Nile Valley and returned long enough for low oxygen values to begin cycling out of their bone or they had been living along the Nile and moved to the Dakhleh Oasis before they died. Individuals with values lower than 28.0‰ (that range was 23.4‰ to 27.9‰) are considered indigenous and continuous inhabitants of the Dakhleh Oasis.

Adult Female Mobility

For both free-born and slave girls, apprenticeships began around the age of 10 and would last one to three years but could run an additional one to two years longer (Lewis 1999; Westermann 1914). During the time a girl would be in training, the third molar, which calcifies from 9.5 to 12 years of age, would capture the oxygen isotope value of where she was apprenticing. Of the adult females from the Kellis 2 cemetery, four had the third molar available for testing. Three of these four females (B131, B279, B289) had third-molar oxygen values that were reflective of the Dakhleh Oasis. If these women were slaves or apprentices, their travel would have been local in the Dakhleh Oasis. Two additional adult females (B141 and B282) who were lacking a third molar but had values for the first and second molar also reflect values that are representative of the Dakhleh Oasis.

Burial 437, who was approximately 40 years old, was the outlier among enamel values. She had a distinctive first-molar $\delta^{18}O$ value (31.0‰) that indicated that she had been born along the Nile River. Her third-molar $\delta^{18}O$ value (31.6‰) shows that she also spent her childhood along the Nile River. Coincidentally, B437 is one of six diagnosed cases of leprosy found in the Kellis 2 cemetery (Molto 2002b). Her migration to the Dakhleh Oasis perhaps relates to regaining health or healing (Groff et al. 2017) or perhaps to relocation for marriage.

If patrilocal marriage was a motivating factor for the migration of adult females during the Romano-Christian period, it is not apparent from the $\delta^{18}O$ values. It would appear that a majority of the Kellis 2 females in this sample married locally in the Western Oases and did not move a great distance from the Nile, contesting previous mtDNA results (Parr 2002) and suggesting patrilocal residential organization. The migration of females into Dakhleh may have occurred at a much earlier time period, perhaps during the generations of the grandmothers or great-grandmothers of the females analyzed in this study. The $\delta^{18}O$ values support the nonmetric skeletal traits and nonmetric dental traits Molto (2001) and Haddow (2012) reported, suggesting that the sample population was homogenous and perhaps inbred, or at least that they intermarried. Adult females may have migrated from other settlements in Dakhleh such as Mut and Amheida and from Kharga Oasis and possibly Farafara Oasis for marriage.

Eight of the thirty-six females analyzed for bone apatite had $\delta^{18}O$ values bordering on being "foreign" (figure 4.3). These moderately high oxygen values indicate that these females were mobile within the last ten years before they died. No enamel was analyzed for these eight females, so it is impossible to de-

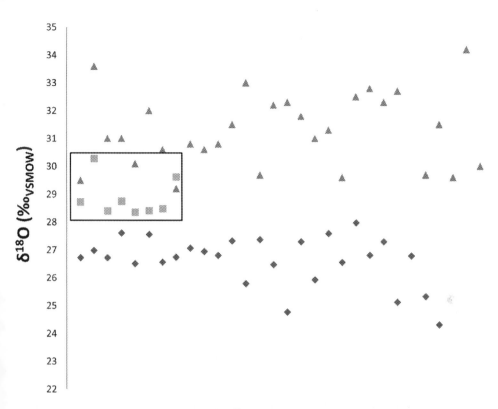

Figure 4.3. Scatterplot showing bone apatite δ¹⁸O values from eight females identified as possible foreigners plotted against the remaining Dakhleh Oasis adult females and Tombos (Sudan) δ¹⁸O values. ◆= all Dakhleh females; ▲=Tombos values; ■= possible foreign females.

termine whether they were born along the Nile or in the Dakhleh Oasis. Five of the eight adult females were older than 50 years at the time of death. Their moderately lower oxygen results may suggest that they had participated in slavery (and were possibly freed later in life) or domestic servitude. The three younger females (B105, B170, and B190) aged 19, 26, and 19, respectively, at the time of death may have relocated to marry or may have been slaves. Unfortunately, there are no enamel samples to indicate where they were born. Overall, results of oxygen isotope values from enamel and bone apatite indicate that females were not nearly as mobile as was previously thought. Thus, at least in the Kellis 2 population, the socioeconomic status of adult females may have been relegated to the household or private sphere. If these adult females were participating in apprenticeships, slavery, or patrilocal marriage, it was likely they were local to the Dakhleh Oasis or from other Western Desert Oases.

Adult Male Mobility

In males, the enamel of the third molar, which forms from 9.5 to 12 years of age, provides the best opportunity for documenting mobility associated with possible apprenticeships or training. Of the adult males analyzed, eight had the third molar available for testing. Four of these eight males (B124, B222, B392, B543) had third-molar oxygen values reflective of the Dakhleh Oasis. If these adult males participated in apprenticeships, it is likely that their travel was local within the Dakhleh Oasis or possibly to other nearby oases. Furthermore, four additional adult males (B107, B132, B281, B293) who only had values for the first and/or second molar also reflect values representative of the Dakhleh Oasis.

One adult male, B139, who was 29 years old at death, had oxygen isotope values that strongly support participation in an apprenticeship. The first-molar (26.0‰) and second-molar (25.3‰) oxygen values for B139 are reflective of birth, infancy, and early adolescence (up to 6 years of age) in the Dakhleh Oasis. Then, around the age of 9.5 to 12 years, there was a steep enrichment in the oxygen value for the third molar (31.8‰), indicating that B139 migrated to the Nile Valley. The fact that the timing for the development of the third molar (9.5 to 12 years) overlaps with the time period when a young child would be participating in an apprenticeship (10 to 13 years) provides support for the hypothesis that B139 left Dakhleh Oasis for training. Furthermore, $\delta^{18}O$ values from bone apatite of B139 (30.5‰) indicate that he continued to live in the Nile Valley or traveled between the Oasis and the Nile Valley during the years before his death. The slight decrease in $\delta^{18}O$ in the apatite of B139 indicates that he returned to Dakhleh Oasis long enough for his bone to begin remodeling.

Individuals B199, who was 35 years old, and B274, who was 20 years old, have $\delta^{18}O$ values that overlap with values from the Nile Valley. The bone apatite levels of B199 (31.2‰) and B274 (31.7‰) strongly indicate that they were traveling to or living in the Nile Valley just before death. Given the age of these two males and their $\delta^{18}O$ values, it is likely that they were living along the Nile River or frequently traveling back and forth. B293, who was 45 years old, provides strong evidence for a local Dakhleh male who perhaps joined a caravan, drove camels, or participated in military activities. The second molar enamel has a $\delta^{18}O$ value of 26.7‰, indicating an early life spent in the Dakhleh Oasis. The bone apatite $\delta^{18}O$ value (29.3‰) from this male, however, reveals an adult life of travel between the Oasis and the Valley.

The enamel $\delta^{18}O$ values of the first molar (32.0‰), second molar (31.9‰), and third molar (32.9‰) for B111, a 37-year-old male, strongly indicate birth and adolescence along the Nile. The bone apatite $\delta^{18}O$ value for B111 (29.7‰) is lower than his enamel values and falls just outside the range established for the Dakhleh Oasis and the Nile Valley. This indicates frequent travel between the two areas or residence in the Dakhleh Oasis long enough for bone remodeling to have occurred.

Illness may have also been a motivating factor for the migration of males to the Dakhleh Oasis. B6 and B116 show skeletal signs of leprosy (Molto 2002b). The enamel of B6's third molar (the only tooth available) shows a $\delta^{18}O$ value of 30.0‰, falling between ranges established for Dakhleh Oasis and the Nile Valley. Additionally, the bone apatite value of B6 shows a $\delta^{18}O$ value of 28.4‰, suggesting that B6 had moved to Dakhleh at least ten years before death and that he likely had been traveling most of his life between the two locations. B116 (a 23-year-old male) exhibited clear osteological evidence of pathology consistent with lepromatous leprosy. B116's first molar (31.9‰) and third molar (32.2‰) reflect Nile Valley $\delta^{18}O$ values. The bone apatite $\delta^{18}O$ value for B116 (32.5‰) indicates he was living along the Nile Valley not long before his death. Mito-

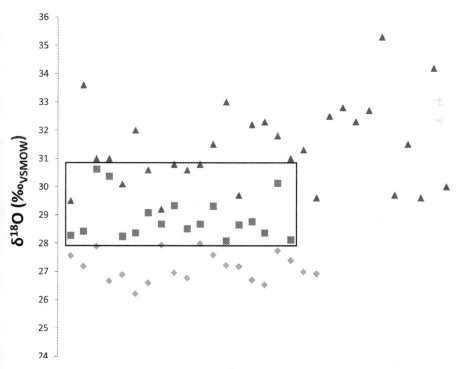

Figure 4.4. Scatterplot showing bone apatite $\delta^{18}O$ values from eighteen males identified as possible foreigners plotted against the remaining Dakhleh Oasis adult males and Tombos (Sudan) $\delta^{18}O$ values. ♦ = all Dakhleh males; ▲ =Tombos values; ■ = possible foreign males.

chondrial studies conducted by Parr (2002) indicate that B116 did not share any maternal genetic characteristics with any of the analyzed female burials. Dakhleh Oasis may have been a place of healing for individuals afflicted with leprosy, as the artesian waters are rich with alum (Groff et al. 2017).

Eighteen of the 45 adult males had apatite $\delta^{18}O$ values bordering on being "foreign" to the Dakhleh Oasis (figure 4.4). Moderately high $\delta^{18}O$ values in bone indicate that males were likely mobile within ten years before death. Because bone takes ten years to remodel, apatite values for males that fall in between the oxygen value ranges for the Dakhleh Oasis and for the Nile Valley indicate that they were moving between the two locations during the last ten years before death.

Conclusions

Stable oxygen isotope values from the Dakhleh Oasis are lower than the values found along the Nile Valley, allowing for the identification of individuals who originated from a less arid environment. Most tooth enamel and bone apatite $\delta^{18}O$ values for adult females fall within the average range documented in the Dakhleh Oasis, indicating that females functioned primarily in the private sphere or the household. One female, B437, who displayed classic signs of lepromatous leprosy, falls outside this range; her $\delta^{18}O$ values overlap with those from the Nile Valley. An additional eight adult females had $\delta^{18}O$ values that fell between those from the Dakhleh Oasis and those from the Nile Valley, suggesting movement. While long-distance migration was infrequent in the Dakhleh female population, it was likely linked to marriage, work (domestic servants), or slavery.

Oxygen isotope values for the adult male population revealed variable results. One adult male (B116) also showed signs of lepromatous leprosy and had $\delta^{18}O$ values that signified migration to Dakhleh right before death. Three additional adult males (B199, B274, and B293) also presented with high $\delta^{18}O$ values, indicating that they had lived outside the Dakhleh Oasis. Of particular interest is B139, whose $\delta^{18}O$ values indicate that he traveled away from his place of birth from the ages of 9.5 to 12 years and continued to live along the Nile until just before his death. Oxygen isotope values from tooth enamel reveal that nine of the twelve males were born and raised in Dakhleh Oasis. An additional eighteen adult males had $\delta^{18}O$ values that fell between $\delta^{18}O$ values from the Dakhleh Oasis and $\delta^{18}O$ values from the Nile Valley. It is hypothesized that these males were periodically moving between the two locations. Overall, the highest $\delta^{18}O$

values in the population at Dakhleh are found in adult males. This result is not surprising, as males were documented as participating in work parties, the military, camel driving, and caravans.

The examination of $\delta^{18}O$ values from the dentition and bone of individuals buried in Kellis 2 allows for an understanding of the social processes and frontier identity in the borderlands of Romano-Christian Egypt. The archaeological, historical, and ethnographic records were considered to provide a more complete view of the socioeconomic, labor, and kinship patterns and the mobility of individuals in this remote location. Although research indicated that females either married into families who lived in the Dakhleh Oasis or were slaves, this study indicates that they came from isotopically similar environments. Furthermore, male $\delta^{18}O$ results support previously held notions and documentation that describes males as migrating more frequently for work-related activities.

Acknowledgments

Data presented in this chapter are part of dissertation research submitted to the University of Florida under the supervision of Dr. John Krigbaum. The authors extend their thanks to the Egyptian Ministry of State of Antiquities and to all members of the Dakhleh Oasis Project for their support. We also thank Dr. J. Marla Toyne for use of her laboratory at the University of Central Florida and Dr. Jason Curtis for analysis of the oxygen isotopes at the Department of Geological Sciences at the University of Florida. We also thank Katie Whitmore for her assistance in processing samples and Dr. Paul Kucera for his assistance with figure 4.1.

References

Adams, C. 2007. *Land Transport in Roman Egypt: A Study of Economics and Administration in a Roman Province*. Oxford: Oxford University Press.

Alston, R. 1995. *Soldier and Society in Roman Egypt*. New York: Routledge.

Bagnall, R. S. 1985. "The Camel, the Wagon, and the Donkey in Later Roman Egypt." *Bulletin of the American Society of Papyrologists* 12: 1–6.

———. 1993. *Egypt in Late Antiquity*. Princeton, NJ: Princeton University Press.

———. 1997. *The Kellis Agricultural Account Book*. Oxford: Oxbow Books.

Bagnall, R. and B. Frier. 2006. *The Demography of Roman Egypt*. 2nd ed. Cambridge University Press: Cambridge.

Biezunska-Malowist, I. 1977. *The Slaves of Roman Egypt*. Wroclaw: Wroclaw University of Technology Press.

Birrell, M. 1999. "Excavations in the Cemeteries of Ismant el'Kharab." In *Dakhleh Oasis Project: Preliminary Reports on the 1992–1993 to 1993–1994 Field Seasons*, edited by Colin Hope and Anthony Milles, 29–41. Oxford: Oxbow Books.

Bowen, G. E. 2001. "Text and Textiles: A Study of the Textile Industry at Ancient Kellis." *The Artefact* 24: 18–24.

Bowen, G. J., and B. Wilkinson. 2002. "Spatial Distribution of 18O in Meteoric Precipitation." *Geology* 30: 315–318.

Bryant, J. D., and P. Froelich. 1995. "A Model of Oxygen Isotope Fractionation in Body Water of Large Mammals." *Geochimica et Cosmochimica Acta* 59: 4523–4537.

Buikstra, J. E., and D. H. Ubelaker. 1994. *Standards for Data Collections from Human Remains: Proceedings of a Seminar at the Field Museum of Natural History*. Research Series, no. 1. Fayetteville: Arkansas Archeological Survey.

Buzon, M., and G. J. Bowen. 2010. "Oxygen and Carbon Isotope Analysis of Human Tooth Enamel from the New Kingdom Site of Tombos in Nubia." *Archaeometry* 52: 855–868.

Dupras, T. L., and H. P. Schwarcz. 2001. "Strangers in a Strange Land: Stable Isotope Evidence for Human Migration in the Dakhleh Oasis, Egypt." *Journal of Archaeological Science* 28, 1199–1208.

Dupras, T. L., and M. Tocheri. 2007. "Reconstructing Infant Weaning Histories at Roman Period Kellis, Egypt Using Stable Isotope Analysis of Dentition." *American Journal of Physical Anthropology* 134: 63–74.

Emsley, J. 2001. *Nature's Building Blocks: An A–Z Guide to the Elements*. New York: Oxford University Press.

Gardner, I., A. Alcock, and W.-P. Funk. 1999. *Coptic Documentary Texts from Kellis*. Vol. 1. Dakhleh Oasis Project Monograph 9. Oxford: Oxbow Books.

Grenfell, B. P., and A. S. Hunt. 1899. *The Oxyrhynchus Papyri, Part II*. London: Egypt Exploration Fund.

Groff, A. T., T. L. Dupras, and J. Krigbaum. 2017. Banishment or Therapeutic Healing? Investigating the Relationship between Migration and Leprosy in the Dakhleh Oasis, Egypt. International Journal of Paleopathology. Unpublished manuscript.

Haddow, S. D. 2012. "Dental Morphological Analysis of Roman Era Burials from the Dakhleh Oasis, Egypt." PhD diss., University College, London.

Hedges, R., J. G. Clement, C. D. L. Thomas, and T. C. O'Connell. 2007. "Collagen Turnover in the Adult Femoral Mid-Shaft: Modeled from Anthropogenic Radiocarbon Tracer Measurements." *American Journal of Physical Anthropology* 133: 808–816.

Hedges, R., R. Stevens, and P. Koch. 2005. "Isotopes in Bones and Teeth." In *Isotopes in Paleoenvironmental Research*, edited by M. J. Leng, 117–138. New York: Springer.

Hope, C. 1988. "Three Seasons of Excavation at Ismant el'Kharab in Dakhleh Oasis, Egypt." *Mediterranean* 1: 160–178.

———. 2001. "Observations on the Dating of the Occupation at Ismant el'Kharab." In *The Oasis Papers 1: The Proceedings of the First International Symposium of the Dakhleh Oasis Project*, edited by M. Marlow, 43–59. Oxford: Oxbow Books.

Hope, C. A., P. Kucera, and J. Smith. 2009. "Alum Exploitation at Qasr el-Dakhleh in the Dakhleh Oasis." In *Beyond the Horizon: Studies in Egyptian Art and History in*

Honour of Barry J. Kemp, vol. 1, edited by S. Ikram and A. Dodson, 165–179. Cairo: American University of Cairo Press.

Iacumin, P., H. Bocherens, A. Mariotti, and A. Longinelli. 1996. "An Isotopic Palaeoenvironmental Study of Human Skeletal Remains from the Nile Valley." *Palaeogeography, Palaeoclimatology, Palaeoecology* 126: 15–30.

Kleindienst, M., C. Churcher, M. McDonald, and H. P. Schwarcz. 1999. "Geography, Geology, Geochronology, and Geoarchaeology of the Dakhleh Oasis Region: An Interim Report." In *Dakhleh Oasis Project: Reports from the Survey of the Dakhleh Oasis Western Desert of Egypt, 1977–1987*, edited by C. S. Churcher and A. J. Mills, 171–178. Oxford: Oxbow Press.

Kucera, P. 2010. "The Roman Military Presence in the Western Desert of Egypt." PhD diss., Monash University, Melbourne, Australia.

Lewis, N. 1999. *Life in Egypt under Roman Rule*. Atlanta: Scholars Press.

Longinelli, A. 1984. "Oxygen Isotopes in Mammal Bone Phosphate: A New Tool for Paleohydrological and Paleoclimatological Research." *Geochimica et Cosmochimica Acta* 48: 385–390.

Luz, B., and Y. Kolodny. 1989. "Oxygen Isotopic Variations In Bone Phosphate. IV. Mammal Teeth and Bones." *Applied Geochemistry* 4: 317–323.

Meier-Augenstein, W. 2010. *Stable Isotope Forensics: An Introduction to the Forensic Application of Stable Isotope Analysis*. Oxford: Wiley-Blackwell.

Mills, A. 1999. "Pharaonic Egyptians in the Dakhleh Oasis." In *Reports from the Survey of the Dakhleh Oasis Western Desert of Egypt, 1977–1987*, edited by C. S. Churcher and A. J. Mills, 171–178. Oxford: Oxbow Press.

Molto, J. E. 2001. "The Comparative Skeletal Biology and Paleoepidemiology of the People from Ein Tirghi and Kellis, Dakhleh, Egypt." In *The Oasis Papers 1: The Proceedings of the First International Symposium of the Dakhleh Oasis Project*, edited by M. Marlow, 81–100. Oxford: Oxbow Books.

———. 2002a. "Bio-Archaeological Research of Kellis 2: An Overview." In *Dakhleh Oasis Project: Preliminary Reports on the 1994–1995 to 1998–1999 Field Seasons*, edited by C. A. Hope and G. E. Bowen, 239–255. Oxford: Oxbow Books.

———. 2002b. "Leprosy in Roman Period Skeletons from Kellis 2, Dakhleh, Egypt." In *The Past and Present of Leprosy: Archaeological, Historical, Paleopathological, and Clinical Approaches*. edited by C. A. Roberts, M. E. Lewis, and K. Manchester, 179–192. Proceedings of the International Congress on the Evolution and Paleoepidemiology of Infectious Diseases 3. Oxford: Archaeopress.

Morkot, R. 1996. "The Darb el-Arbain, the Kharga Oasis and Its Forts, and Other Desert Routes." In *Archaeological Research in Roman Egypt: The Proceedings of the Seventeenth Classical Colloquium of the Department of Greek and Roman Antiquities*, edited by D. M. Bailey, 82–94. Ann Arbor, MI: Journal of Roman Archaeology.

Parr, R. 2002. "Mitochondrial DNA Sequence Analysis of Skeletal Remains from the Kellis 2 Cemetery." In *Dakhleh Oasis Project: Preliminary Reports on the 1994–1995 to 1998–1999 Field Seasons*, edited by C. A. Hope and G. E. Bowen, 257–261. Oxford: Oxbow Books.

Prowse, T. L., H. P. Schwarcz, P. Garnsey, M. Knyf, R. Macchiarelli, and L. Bondioli.

2007. "Isotopic Evidence for Age-Related Immigration to Imperial Rome." *American Journal of Physical Anthropology* 132: 510–519.

Roth, J. P. 1999. *The Logistics of the Roman Military at War (264 B.C.–A.D. 235)*. Columbia: Columbia University Press.

Rowlandson, J. 1998. *Women and Society in Greek and Roman Egypt*. Cambridge: Cambridge University Press.

Straus, J. A. 1988. "The Slaves of Roman Egypt." *Aufstieg und Niedergang der romishen Welt* 2(10): 841–911.

Stewart, J. D., J. E. Molto, and P. J. Reimer. 2003. "The Chronology of Kellis 2: The Interpretive Significance of Radiocarbon Dating of Human Remains." In *The Oasis Papers 3: The Proceedings of the Third International Symposium of the Dakhleh Oasis Project*, edited by C. A. Hope and G. E. Bowen, 373–382. Oxford: Oxbow Books.

Sullivan, C. H., and H. W. Krueger. 1983. "Carbon Isotope Ratios of Bone Apatite and Animal Diet Reconstruction." *Nature* 301(5896): 177–178.

Turner, B. L., J. L. Edwards, E. A. Quinn, J. D. Kingston, and D. P. Van Gerven. 2007. "Age-Related Variation in Isotopic Indicators of Diet at Medieval Kulubnarti, Sudanese Nubia." *International Journal of Osteoarchaeology* 17: 1–25.

Westermann, W. L. 1914. "Apprentice Contracts and the Apprentice System in Roman Egypt." *Classical Philology* 9: 295–315.

Wheeler, S. 2009. "Bioarchaeology of Infancy and Childhood at Kellis 2 Cemetery, Dakhleh Oasis, Egypt." PhD diss., University of Western Ontario, London, Ontario.

White, C., F. J. Longstaffe, and K. R. Law. 2004. "Exploring the Effects of Environment, Physiology and Diet on Oxygen Isotope Ratios in Ancient Nubian Bones and Teeth." *Journal of Archaeological Science* 31: 233–250.

White, C., M. Spence, and F. J. Longstaffe. 2000. "The Identification of Foreigners in Mortuary Contexts Using Oxygen Isotopes Ratios: Some Mesoamerican Examples (Abstract)." *American Journal of Physical Anthropology* supplement 30: 319.

White, C., M. Spence, H. L. Q. Stuart-Williams, and H. P. Schwarcz. 1998. "Oxygen Isotopes and the Identification of Geographical Origins: The Valley of Oaxaca versus the Valley of Mexico." *Journal of Archaeological Science* 25: 643–655.

Worp, K. 1995. *Greek Papyri from Kellis*. Vol. 1, *Nos. 1–90*. Oxford: Oxbow Books.

Wright, L. E., and H. P. Schwarcz. 1998. "Stable Carbon and Oxygen Isotopes in Human Tooth Enamel: Identifying Breastfeeding and Weaning in Prehistory." *American Journal of Physical Anthropology* 106: 1–18.

5

Temporal and Spatial Biological Kinship Variation at Campovalano and Alfedena in Iron Age Central Italy

EVAN MUZZALL AND ALFREDO COPPA

Frontiers and borderlands are difficult bioarchaeological concepts to define because they include overlapping physical, sociopolitical, economic, and ideological dimensions. While Barth (1969) insisted that we study culture in terms of dynamic interactions at the margins of societies, investigating relationships among past humans is challenging. Throughout antiquity, individuals and groups with dissimilar social adaptive strategies could have used different buffering mechanisms in local and regional crises. Evidence of such processes is potentially encoded in complex phenomena surrounding death and burial (Bentley and Maschner 2008; Hodder 1977, 1984). Biological kinship was often used as a structuring principle for the burial and social organization of past humans, although a variety of other nonbiological/social factors also were used (González-Ruibal 2006; Lévi-Strauss 1987; Paul et al. 2013; Pilloud and Larsen 2011).

Bioarchaeologists use static artifactual and biological remains to make inferences about the relationships between the social roles of the living and the dead—the corpse and spirit of the deceased and the mourners (Carr 1995; Goodenough 1956; Hertz 1960; Pearson 2000; Van Gennep 1960). The Saxe-Goldstein interpretive framework states that cemeteries were communal spaces where cultural definitions would have been ascribed, redefined, and/or abandoned relative to larger spiritual and socioeconomic systems. While ceremoniously burying the dead in specified areas is not a prerequisite for transmitting rights, inheritances, land, and other resources, formally organizing the dead in cemeteries and ritual affirmations of the dead was arguably one way to ensure proper transmission (Goldstein 1981, 2006; Meggit 1965; Morris 1991; Saxe 1970, 1971; van Rossenberg 2006). In death rituals, systematic patterns in burial location, sex, age, material culture, occupation, health, incidence of trauma, and rank were arguably some of the ways these relationships were expressed (Agarwal and Glencross 2011; Binford 1971; Braun 1984; Brown 1996; Buikstra 1981, 1991; Cook 1981; Hodder 1978; Pearson 1993; Peebles 1971; Peebles and Kus 1977; Shimada et al. 2004; Stodder 2008; Tainter 1978; van Rossenberg 2006). However, such categorizations are probably oversimplified when we project our own cultural biases onto the past. Furthermore, we are also poorly equipped to identify how and why the importance of past people, places, and things could have changed through time and across space (Hodder 1980; Robb 2015; Schmidt 2005; Ucko 1969; van Rossenberg 2001, 2005). These considerations make the investigation of cultural groupings and divisions difficult in bioarchaeological contexts. However, archaeological, geological, floral and faunal, spatial, and biological data and methods are often used to explore the relationships of past humans and their surroundings.

We used a biological distance (biodistance) approach to investigate the social borders of samples from Iron Age Central Italy (1000–27 BCE) and compare variation between two neighboring necropoles and across multiple time periods for one of them. Biodistance methods use data from skeletal and dental features to approximate the biological relatedness of archaeological skeletal populations when genetic information is not available (see Buikstra et al. 1990, 1, for a formal definition). We used cranial and dental metrics and the Arizona State University Dental Anthropology System (hereafter ASUDAS, Turner et al. 1991) morphological scoring system to obtain data on the morphology of tooth crowns and roots in three temporal Pretuzi samples from Campovalano and four Pentri Samnite samples from Alfedena. Our research tested three hypotheses.

Hypothesis 1: We tested the null hypothesis that there would be many cranial and dental differences over time at Campovalano and over space by comparing the Campovalano data to data collected from Alfedena. To do this, we investigated biological continuity at Campovalano using cranial (n = 278) and dental (n = 377) metrics and forty-seven ASUDAS (n = 492) crown and root traits (23 maxillary, 24 mandibular; Coppa et al. 1998). We used analyses of variance (ANOVA) and Tukey's Honest Significant Difference test to explore cranial and dental variation and plotted geometric means of dental metric data using multidimensional scaling. We compared ASUDAS data using neighbor-joining clustering.

Hypothesis 2: We tested the null hypothesis that there would be no differences between correlation strengths in the cranial and dental data for males and females and no statistical significance at Campovalano and Campo Consolino, an elite section of Alfedena. We did so using a novel method of measuring biodistance for the Campovalano (n = 29) and Alfedena Campo Consolino (n = 19 and n = 23) samples. While many studies interpret burial location as a way to discern social borders (see Stojanowski and Schillaci 2006), ours is the first study to quantify that idea by measuring distances between burials and correlating that data with data on cranial and dental biodistances via Mantel tests.

Hypothesis 3: We tested the null hypothesis that there would be no differences in the variations of the breadth of the maxillary distal premolar (P4) and the second molar (M2) by location or sex. To do this, we examined sex and location variation using the buccolingual breadths of P4 and M2 (n = 129) in logistic regression and analysis of covariance (ANCOVA) models.

Campovalano and Alfedena in Ancient Italy

The Adriatic region was the center of gene flow in the ancient Mediterranean due to its central geographic location between Europe and Africa and the Near East and the Iberian Peninsula (Calò et al. 2008; Coppa et al. 1997, 1998; Di Giacomo et al. 2003; Rodríguez et al. 2009; Rubini et al. 1997, 1999). Neolithic dental morphologies in Italy were similar to those from the Paleolithic and Mesolithic but then diverged phenotypically after Near East farming groups introduced agriculture to the region (Coppa et al. 2007; Fu et al. 2012; Perkins 2009). Peninsular Italy is bisected by the Apennine Mountains, which are characterized by peaks and rugged hills that slope down to fertile lands bordering the Tyrrhenian and Adriatic Seas (Bell et al. 2002; Peet 1907; Tavano 1996; Unger 1953). The practices of the transhumant agropastoralists who have inhabited this region since ancient times have shaped genetic, morphological, and environmental histories of the region. These groups built communities high above sea level in naturally defensible positions bolstered by ditches, moats, palisades, and stone walls (Bispham 2007; Bispham et al. 2000; D'Ercole 1987a; Oakley 1996; Riva 2007). The mortuary behavior and material culture of the people who inhabited peninsular Italy potentially originated from similar overarching traditions, but variation at the local level developed over time in aspects such as numbers and types of burials, how corpses were treated, and which grave goods were placed with the dead. The latter included pottery, jewelry, brooches, and weapons (Sestieri 1973, 1981, 1988; Sestieri and De Santis 2012). Genetic heterogeneity appears strongest in small mountainous communities and decreases in hilly and coastal areas (Cavalli-Sforza et al. 2004).

Origins of Social Differentiation

Italy has a long history of social differentiation. Gendered Neolithic (fourth millennium BCE) rock art may represent male power relationships and male mastery of the land and animals. Village inhumations may have expressed some gendered qualities depending on whether a body was buried on the left or right side, but these distinctions remain unclear. Common grave items generally consisted of ceramics, flint points and daggers, and stone axes, but their distributions relative to social differentiation also remain opaque (D'Ercole 1987b; Robb 1994a, 1994b, 1994c; 1997; 2007). The Copper Age (third millennium BCE) was characterized by the juxtaposition of isolated hillside burials with wealthy, intact grave items and communal tombs located in caves accompanied by purposely broken grave goods (Dolfini 2006).

Mortuary treatments during the Bronze Age (second millennium BCE) in Italy also show evidence of social differentiation. Cremation was the preferred way of disposing of the remains of elites during this period (Sestieri 1981, 2010; Sestieri and De Santis 2012). Evolving copper and bronze markets influenced the organization of settlements, community structures, and production hierarchies. Settlements began to nucleate into semi-autonomous, patrilocal communities that consisted of a core surrounded by networked peripheries of minor centers and agricultural outposts (Barker and Suano 1995; Bispham et al. 2000; Cianfarani 1972; Potter 1984). Burial of large amounts of metal objects in the countryside was common, but the relationship of this practice to concepts such as boundary definition and wealth remain unclear (Peroni 1979; van Rossenberg 2011).

By the Iron Age (1000–27 BCE), Central Italy was a vast conglomerate of state-level societies focused on agriculture, manufacturing, and marketing. This was a time of increasing social differentiation and warfare that ended with the founding of Augustinian Rome in 27 BCE. Iron Age groups subsisted on plants such as emmer wheat, barley, peas, beans, and olives and on meat sources such as sheep, cattle, pigs, boars, and deer (Bispham 2007; Coppa and Colarossi 1987; D'Alessandro et al. 2000; De Grossi Mazzorin 1987; Macchiarelli et al. 1988; Marchi et al. 2011).

The majority of Early and Middle Iron Age data come from burial rather than habitation sites. The burial rite at Campovalano and Alfedena consisted of placing the corpse supine in a pit or limestone box tomb, occasionally wrapped in a shroud. Male burials frequently contained weapons and armor, while female burials contained weaving equipment and items of personal adornment (Cianfarani 1972; Robb 1994b; Robb et al. 2001; Tagliamonte 1996; Navarro 1993). Ritual drinking and feasting wares were commonly placed with both sexes. Individuals were also sometimes buried tumulus-style, often encircled with stones, covered with an earthen mound, and arranged in circles or clusters. Some tombs contained niches and wooden boards that might have held food and drink necessary for burial rites and other activities pertaining to a cult of the dead (Chiaramonte Treré and D'Ercole 2003; Chiaramonte Treré et al. 2010; Badoni and Giove 1980; Tagliamonte 1996; Navarro 1993). These groups potentially worshiped Hercules, Mars, and Dioskouroi (Bispham 2007; Strazzulla 2013; Tagliamonte 2004; Tavano 1996; Whitehouse 1995). The locations of Campovalano and Alfedena are shown in figure 5.1.

Figure 5.1. Map showing locations of Campovalano and Alfedena in Central Italy. Source: Google Maps.

Campovalano

Campovalano is located 450 meters above sea level in the plains east of Montagne di Campania and Fiore, 20 kilometers west of the Adriatic coast near Campli (Cianfarani 1972; Coppa et al. 1987). Burials are clustered along an ancient road and in other areas of this necropolis (Chiaramonte Treré et al. 2010). The grave goods associated with Campovalano were more varied in quality than the grave goods at Alfedena. Many local items were generally of higher quality than was found at Alfedena and the Campovalano grave goods included more Greek wares and luxury items (Chiaramonte Treré and D'Ercole 2003; Chiaramonte Treré et al. 2010; D'Ercole 1987c). Pottery consisted of Etruscan black, brown, and red vessels and geometric painted Messapian and Apulian pottery from the southern Adriatic coast (Goethals et al. 2005; Naso 2000; Riva 2007). Weapons, belts, brooches, pendants, and other jewelry were also common items. No intracemetery kinship analyses have yet been conducted at Campovalano.

Alfedena

Alfedena is located 900 meters above sea level in the Sangro River Valley on the rugged eastern slopes of the Monti della Meta massif. The grave goods made locally at this location consisted of red-brown linear coarse pottery and fine Etruscan black wares and imitations. Other grave goods included belts, combs, razors, beads, brooches, pendants, and necklaces (Badoni and Giove 1980; Tagliamonte 1996). Alfedena Campo Consolino, which could have been the elite ritual core at Alfedena, is divided into three burial locations. The first location is a cluster of burials that includes personal ornaments but no weapons. The second and third burial locations are circular formations with hollow centers. The male burials in these locations contain weapons (Dench 1995; Badoni and Giove 1980). Previous research indicates that male phenotypic variation is homogeneous in each of the Alfedena three burial locations but is heterogeneous between them. This likely indicates that each location was reserved for a specific male biological lineage (Bondioli et al. 1986; Capasso 1985; Coppa et al. 1981; Coppa and Macchiarelli 1982; Mogliazza and Rubini 2003; Rubini 1996). Females do not express any identifiable biological pattern.

The burial population at Alfedena exhibits high frequencies of interpersonal trauma that includes fatal wounds to the head caused by blunt, sharp, and projectile blows that were likely suffered during battle (Macchiarelli et al. 1981; Paine et al. 2007; Sparacello et al. 2015). No such trauma has been noted at Campovalano. Aside from the evidence of trauma at Alfedena, individuals at both sites were generally healthy (Cucina et al. 1998, 2000; Macchiarelli 1988; Macchiarelli and Salvadei 1986; Mancinelli and Vargiu 2012; Mancinelli et al. 1993, 1997; Vargiu et al. 1993). The origins of Iron Age groups are difficult to identify, although myths state that individuals made spiritual migrations to *veris sacri* (sacred springs) in Pretuzi and Samnite homelands (Coppa et al. 1998; Krappe 1942; Rosivach 1983; Salmon 1967; Tagliamonte 1996).

Materials and Methods

The Campovalano samples originate from three locations in three time periods: (1) a necropolis that dates to the Iron Age (750–200 BCE); (2) St. Peter's Cathedral, a medieval church located near the Iron Age cemetery that dates to the ninth–eleventh centuries CE; and (3) a recent sample of individuals from the modern communal cemetery (twentieth century CE). The Iron Age sample consists of early (seventh–fifth centuries BCE) and late (fourth–third centuries BCE) time periods that we combined to address a numerical imbalance. However, we kept these two samples separate for the ASUDAS analysis.

The Alfedena samples (600–400 BCE) came from four locations in the necropolis: (1) individuals with known burial locations at Campo Consolino; (2) individuals without burial location information from the secondary elite section at Arboreto; (3) a series from the Sergi Museum; and (4) Scavi Mariani, excavations made at the turn of the twentieth century from the broader necropolis (Mariani 1901). The samples used in this study are listed in table 5.1. Six chord measurements were taken from between four landmarks on the cranial base, the cranial vault, and the face to encapsulate shape information from the main ontogenetic, functional, and heritable regions of the cranium for the purpose of estimating and comparing the degree of biological variation (Carson 2006; Devor 1987; Herrera et al. 2014; Martínez-Abadías et al. 2009; Sjøvold 1984; Strauss and Hubbe 2010; Weinberg et al. 2013). The definitions of the landmarks we used are listed in table 5.2. Individuals had to have at least one triangle of interconnected chord distances between landmarks to be included in analyses.

Dental metrics consisted of the maximum mesiodistal dimensions of the right maxillary canine (C) and the buccolingual breadths of the right mesial (P3) and distal (P4) premolars and the first (M1) and second (M2) molars (following Hillson et al. 2006). When a right-side tooth was absent, the corresponding left tooth

Table 5.1. Samples used in this study

| | | Cranial metric | | | | Dental metric | | | | ASUDAS |
Location	Dates	M	F	?	Total	M	F	?	Total	Pooled sex
CAMPOVALANO										
Iron Age	750–200 BCE	32	28	5	65	78	69	44	191	
Early Iron Age	700–400 BCE									74
Late Iron Age	400–200 BCE									162
St. Peter	9–11th C. CE	25	30	0	55	23	28	0	51	37
Recent	20th C. CE									84
ALFEDENA										135
Campo Consolino	600–400 BCE	40	13	0	53	45	12	0	57	
Arboreto	600–400 BCE	6	5	0	11	9	5	0	14	
Sergi Museum	600–400 BCE	19	13	0	32	17	11	0	28	
Scavi Mariani	600–400 BCE	34	17	11	62	9	5	22	36	
		156	106	16	278	181	130	66	377	492

M = male, F = female, ? = unknown sex.

was substituted when available. Raw dental metrics were further combined into a multivariate tooth row metric (Ortner and Corruccini 1976, 719) consisting of mesiodistal canine dimensions and buccolingual differences between the mesial and distal premolars (P3 minus P4) and between the first and second molars (M1 minus M2) transformed by a z-score. A maximum of twenty-four metrics could have been recorded from each individual (eighteen cranial, five raw dental, one tooth row). All of these variables were normally distributed according to Shapiro-Wilk tests for normality ($p > 0.05$) with the exception of cranial interlandmark distances from lambda to right asterion ($p = 0.0008$), nasion to basion ($p = 0.001$), and nasion to left porion ($p = 0.01$) for individuals from Alfedena and cranial interlandmark distances from nasion to left porion ($p = 0.03$) for individuals from Campovalano. Bartlett's tests for homoscedasticity indicated that all of the groups had similar variances ($p > 0.05$) except for cranial interlandmark distances from lambda to right asterion ($p = 0.04$) and nasion to left porion ($p =$

Table 5.2. Cranial landmarks used in this study

	Definition
FACE	
Nasion	The intersection of the nasofrontal suture in the midsagittal plane
Prosthion	The location of the anteriorly located portion of the anterior surface of the alveolar process at the most anterior point of the alveolar process
Right frontomalare orbitale	The location where the zygomaticofrontal suture intersects the orbital margin
Left zygomaxillare	The most inferior and anterior location on the zygomaticomaxillary suture
CRANIAL VAULT	
Bregma	The landmark where the sagittal and coronal sutures meet in the midsagittal plane. In cases where the sagittal suture deflects laterally, an estimation must be made of the location in the midsagittal plane.
Lambda	The landmark where the left and right lambdoid sutures intersect the sagittal suture. The landmark must be estimated when the suture intersection is obliterated or where strongly serrated sutures are present
Right asterion	The juncture of the lambdoid, parietomastoid, and occipitomastoid sutures
Left frontotemporale	The most medial and anterior point on the superior temporal line on the frontal bone
CRANIAL BASE	
Nasion	The intersection of the nasofrontal suture in the midsagittal plane.
Basion	The inner border where the anterior portion of the foramen magnum is intersected by the midsagittal plane
Hormion	The juncture of the sphenoid and vomer bones in the midsagittal plane
Left Porion	The most superior point on the external margin of the external auditory meatus

Sources: Howells 1973; Martin and Saller 1957; Moore-Jansen et al. 1994.

0.01) for the Alfedena group and right frontomalare orbitale to left zygomaxillare ($p = 0.006$) and nasion to basion ($p = 0.01$) for the Campovalano group.

To test our first hypothesis, we examined temporal variation in biological kinship at Campovalano and spatial variation in the Alfedena and Campovalano samples. We combined the metric data for the four Alfedena populations for the purpose of comparing those groups to the Iron Age and medieval samples from Campovalano. Although not ideal, we used univariate ANOVAs to compare the cranial (18), dental (5), and multivariate tooth row measurements among these samples. We used Tukey's Honest Significant Difference test to compute the pairwise differences among the three groups: we compared Alfedena to the Campovalano Iron Age and then to the Campovalano medieval sample and then we compared the Campovalano Iron Age sample to the Campovalano medieval sample. The standard cutoff was $p < 0.05$, but we applied Bonferroni-corrected p-values to account for family-wise error. We computed these values by dividing the standard cutoff ($p < 0.05$) by the number of measurements (six interlandmark distances from a given cranial region and measurements from five teeth). Thus, we used adjusted p-values of $0.05/6 = 0.0083$ for cranial measurements and $0.05/5 = 0.01$ for dental measurements. We used multidimensional scaling of scaled geometric means of dental data in an attempt to correct for gross size differences and data incompleteness. We analyzed the ASUDAS data by Euclidean distance neighbor-joining clustering with bootstrap resampling to compute p-values for each branching split in the dendrogram. This served as a complement to the metric analyses.

To test our second hypothesis, we investigated the strengths and significances of correlations between biological distance and burial distance at Campovalano and Alfedena Campo Consolino. Both of these samples contained individuals with known burial locations. We recorded distances between individual graves in meters using cemetery maps and the GNU Image Manipulation Program 2.8.14. We compared this data with cranial and dental biodistance data (including the tooth row metric) via Mantel tests (Pearson's r). We used this data to compare burial organization between the two sites using degree of biological relatedness as a structuring principle.

To test our third hypothesis, we used logistic regression and ANCOVA on a dental metric subset from all of the samples to examine distal premolar (P4) and second molar (M2) variation by location and sex. We chose these two teeth because the factor loadings from the multidimensional scaling's second coordinate of variation indicated that P3 and M2 contributed disproportionately to variation along this second coordinate (see the results section). Thus, we chose one less-influential tooth (P4) and one influential tooth (M2). Data incompleteness prevented more comprehensive modeling. We used ANCOVA to examine the interaction effect of sex on M2 variation for predicting the dimensions of P4. An ANOVA indicated that modeling the effects of the interaction term (sex) on M2 dimensions produced more interpretable results than the model that incorporated only main effects. Thus, the ANCOVA model that included the interaction term is the only one we report.

We sexed all of the individuals except for those in the Campovalano St. Peter sample (which EM estimated using cranial data) following traditional pelvic and cranial sex estimation methods compiled from the original research notes in Bondioli et al. (1986) and Coppa et al. (1987). All statistical analyses were performed using the R Program for Statistical Computing 3.2.2 and the "psych" and "vegan" packages.

Results

First hypothesis: many cranial and dental differences over time at Campovalano and over space between Campovalano and Alfedena. ANOVA and Tukey's Honest Significant Difference test indicate that there are few cranial differences and no dental differences between the Iron Age and medieval samples at Campovalano. However, the cranial metrics of the combined Alfedena sample differed considerably from both Campovalano samples. Table 5.3 shows the results of significant ANOVA and Tukey's Honest Significant Difference test for these three samples. The locations of the Iron Age and medieval samples differ significantly only between the interlandmark distances bregma to lambda, bregma to left frontotemporale, and lambda to left frontotemporale on the cranial vault. However, the Alfedena sample differs significantly from the Campovalano Iron Age sample in four face dimensions (nasion to prosthion, nasion to right frontomalare orbitale, prosthion to right frontomalare orbitale, and prosthion to left zygomaxillare) and two cranial vault dimensions (bregma to right asterion and lambda to right asterion). In addition, the Alfedena sample is significantly different from the Campovalano medieval sample in all six face dimensions (nasion to prosthion, nasion to right frontomalare orbitale, nasion to left zygomaxillare, prosthion to right frontomalare orbitale, prosthion to left zygomaxillare, and right frontomalare orbitale to left zygomaxillare), all six cranial vault dimensions (bregma to lambda, bregma to right asterion, bregma to left frontotemporale, lambda to right asterion, lambda to left frontotemporale, and right asterion to left frontotemporale), and three cranial base dimensions (nasion to basion, nasion to hormion, and basion to left porion). No significant dental differences were detected among the three groups.

Figure 5.2 shows multidimensional scaling of the scaled geometric mean dental metric data. The first coordinate accounts for 70 percent of observed variation and the second coordinate accounts for 15 percent. Loading scores for the first principal coordinate were all positive (C = 0.39, P3 = 0.49, P4 = 0.63, M1 = 0.34, M2 = 0.30), while scores for the second principal coordinate (C = -0.03, P3 = 0.70, P4 = -0.32, M1 = 0.18, M2 = 0.62) suggest that variation is strongly influenced by the mesial premolar (P3 = 0.70) and the second molar (M2 = 0.62). Figure 5.3, which illustrates ASUDAS neighbor-joining clustering, shows similarities among the Early Iron Age and Late Iron Age samples from Campovalano and the early twentieth-century sample from Campovalano. The St. Peter sample from Campovalano differs the most from

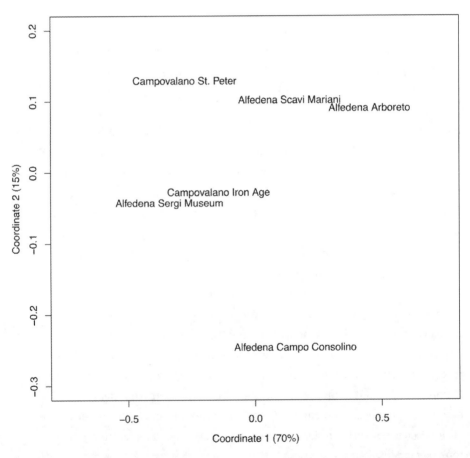

Figure 5.2. Multidimensional scaling scatterplot of geometric mean–scaled dental data showing the six metric samples from Campovalano and Alfedena.

Table 5.3. ANOVAs and Tukey HSDs for Iron Age Campovalano (IAC), Medieval Campovalano (MC), and Alfedena (ALF) populations

Metric	ANOVA p	Tukey HSD Group difference	Mean difference	p adjusted[a]
Nasion to prosthion	0.000	IAC and ALF	-4.35	0.003[b]
		MC and ALF	-3.87	0.000[b]
Nasion to right frontomalare orbitale	0.000	IAC and ALF	-2.22	0.007[b]
		MC and ALF	-1.53	0.002[b]
Nasion to left zygomaxillare	0.000	MC and ALF	-2.43	0.000[b]
Prosthion to right frontomalare orbitale	0.000	IAC and ALF	-4.34	0.000[b]
		MC and ALF	-3.71	0.000[b]
Prosthion to left zygomaxillare	0.000	IAC and ALF	-4.15	0.001[b]
		MC and ALF	-2.66	0.000[b]
Right frontomalare orbitale to left zygomaxillare	0.004	MC and ALF	-2.48	0.008[b]
Bregma to lambda	0.012	MC and ALF	-3.67	0.013[c]
		MC and IAC	-3.78	0.036[c]
Bregma to right asterion	0.000	IAC and ALF	-2.35	0.033[c]
		MC and ALF	-3.69	0.001[b]
Bregma to left frontotemporale	0.000	MC and ALF	-4.83	0.000[b]
		MC and IAC	-2.61	0.042[c]
Lambda to right asterion	0.000	IAC and ALF	-3.38	0.003[b]
		MC and ALF	-3.86	0.001[b]
Lambda to left frontotemporale	0.000	MC and ALF	-5.92	0.000[b]
		MC and IAC	-4.75	0.006[b]
Right asterion to left frontotemporale	0.004	MC and ALF	-3.13	0.005[b]
Nasion to basion	0.001	MC and ALF	-4.23	0.001[b]
Nasion to hormion	0.004	MC and ALF	-2.07	0.003[b]
Basion to left porion	0.012	MC and ALF	-1.72	0.008[b]

[a] P values were Bonferroni-adjusted by dividing $p < 0.05$ (standard cutoff value) by the number of measurements (six measurements for each cranial region and five tooth measurements). Adjusted p values of $0.05/6 = 0.0083$ for cranial measurements and $0.05/5 = 0.01$ for dental measurements were used.
[b] Significant at Bonferroni corrected $p < 0.0083$.
[c] Significant at $p < 0.05$.

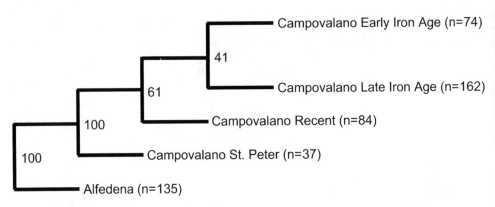

Figure 5.3. Neighbor-joining clustering of the five ASUDAS samples from Campovalano and Alfedena.

the other Campovalano samples. The Alfedena sample is the outlier. The p-values for each cluster are shown inside the clades in each division on the dendrogram.

Second hypothesis: no differences between correlation strengths for cranial metric data and dental data and burial distance data for males and females and no statistical significance for these metrics between the Campovalano and Alfedena Campo Consolino samples. We reported sex-specific differences in correlation strengths and statistical significance between biological and burial distances for the samples at Campovalano and Alfedena Campo Consolino. Mantel tests indicate that only the female tooth row metric (n = 29; r = 0.24, p = 0.021) correlates with burial distances at Campovalano and then only slightly. However, male face (n = 19; r = 0.21, p = 0.037) and cranial base (n = 23; r = 0.18, p = 0.046) biological distances correlate faintly with burial distances at Alfedena Campo Consolino.

Third hypothesis: no differences in the variations of the breadth of the maxillary distal premolar (P4) and the second molar (M2) by location or sex. Logistic regression on P4 and M2 data (n = 129) indicates that Alfedena Campo Consolino is the only significantly different location among the six samples. The sample from Alfedena Campo Consolino exhibits the only statistically significant coefficient for the actual data (estimate = 2.04, standard error = 1.00, z = 2.03, p = 0.043) and the bootstrapped data (estimate = 2.06, standard error = 1.00, z = 2.03, p = 0.040). In figure 5.4, which shows the ANCOVA scatterplot, the crossing regression lines illustrate the interaction effect of sex on M2 variation for predicting the dimensions of P4.

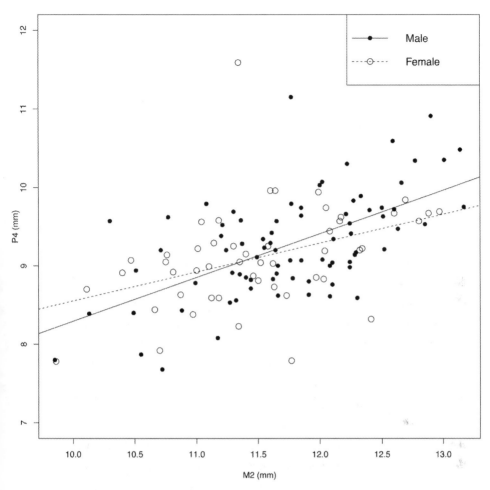

Figure 5.4. ANCOVA scatterplot of distal premolar (P4) and second molar (M2) data for females and males.

Discussion

All three null hypotheses were rejected. Results of metric ANOVAs, Tukey's Honest Significant Difference test, and multidimensional scaling indicate that the Campovalano Iron Age and medieval samples are more similar to each other than Alfedena is to either sample. ASUDAS neighbor-joining clustering supports this conclusion, with the exception that the early twentieth-century sample from Campovalano is more similar to the Iron Age samples than the St. Peter medieval sample is. Also, female tooth row biodistances correlate with burial distances at Campovalano for the Iron Age sample. This is interesting given that biodistances for male faces and cranial bases correlate with burial distances at Alfedena Campo Consolino. These results support previous research that burial organization at Alfedena Campo Consolino was strongly influenced by male biological lineage. We are hesitant to make more detailed interpretations based on logistic regression and ANCOVA results of P4 and M2 data. However, because the Alfedena Campo Consolino sample exhibited the only significant coefficient, logistic regression provided additional support for the idea that it was an exclusive burial site. The ANCOVA scatterplot could allude to divergent patterns in sex-specific morphogenetic variation in dentition. This suggests that variations in dental metrics among Iron Age populations from a regional perspective may be a promising line of study.

More specifically, the Iron Age and medieval samples from Campovalano differed only in one triangle of interlandmark distances of the cranial vault (bregma to lambda, bregma to left frontotemporale, and lambda to left frontotemporale), while the Alfedena sample differed noticeably from both of these samples. These results defied expectations not only because of the supposed history of gene flow in the region but also because of how incomplete the data were, which weakened our expectations. Why only these three vault distances differed in Campovalano Iron Age and medieval samples remains unclear, although variability in the left frontotemporale cranial landmark might help explain this variation due to its "floating" nature. If left frontotemporale was poorly estimated, then this variation is actually inflated. Such potentially inaccurate data recordation would actually have *increased* variation between the Iron Age and medieval samples at Campovalano. That is, variation around this landmark for these two samples might be even less than the small amount reported here. Regardless, our findings suggest remarkable continuity between the Iron Age and the medieval time period at Campovalano. The general dissimilarity of the Alfedena samples from the Campovalano samples supports the idea that endogamous practices could have persisted over large time spans in relatively small geographic areas at both locations, despite their close proximity. Rough agreement between the metric and ASUDAS data could also be interpreted to support this. Genetic evidence further supports the idea that neighboring communities can be genetically divergent and endogamous even though they are geographically close to each other and share aspects of language (Messina et al. 2010).

Moreover, three faint correlations between biological and burial distances were detected by Mantel tests for individuals with known burial locations at Campovalano and Alfedena Campo Consolino. While we are cautious about interpreting the significant correlation between the biodistance and burial distance using female multivariate tooth row data at Campovalano as new evidence of social organization in Iron Age Central Italy, our data does support the need for more emphasis on the role of women in the seemingly overarching male themes of the Italian metal ages (e.g., Sestieri 2008; Whitehouse 1998). Dichotomous descriptors such as patrilocal/matrilocal and biological/nonbiological organization are likely too exclusive to adequately describe variation in marriage rules and burial and social organization of many past human groups.

Our results also identify a few points about heritability. Some research has stated that the cranial base is a truer genetic signal than the face due to its phylogenetic preservation, as the face might generally be more variable due to functions of respiration, mastication, and sight (see discussion offered by Martínez-Abadías et al. 2009, 21). However, other research suggests that despite its variability, the face is still as useful as a basis for reconstructing populations (Taubadel 2009). This is interesting because both the cranial base and the face correlated with burial distances at Alfedena Campo Consolino.

Furthermore, Alfedena Campo Consolino was the only significantly different sample as identified by the logistic regression for location. The individuals buried there generally have larger cranial and dental dimensions than their counterparts from Campovalano (Table 5.3 reports the mean differences). Although many cranial differences were reported between Alfedena Campo Consolino and the other samples, the ANOVAs identified no statistically significant raw dental differences. However, when gross size is corrected for using geometric mean scaling, the relatively isolated position of Alfedena Campo Consolino along the second principal coordinate in figure 5.2 could lend support to the claim that it was biologically heterogeneous and/or more restricted in terms of who was allowed to be buried there.

While results of this study might be artifacts of small and imbalanced samples, our findings underscore the value of skeletal and dental data for investigating social borders of the past. Skeletal and dental data of multiple types should be investigated for covariation with other archaeological factors in creative and nested ways to provide broader definitions of the burial practices and social organization of past humans. Actually measuring distances between burials and other archaeological features should be considered as a means of constructing alternative meanings of space in the frontiers and borderlands of the past.

Acknowledgments

We thank Cristina Tica, Debra L. Martin, and Mark Toussaint for inviting us to participate in the Bioarchaeology of Frontiers and Borderlands symposium at the 81st annual meeting of the Society for American Archaeologists in Orlando, FL. We also thank the Soprintendenza Archeologica d'Abruzzo and the staffs of the Museo di Archeologico Nazionale di Campli, the Museo Antropologia de "Giuseppe Sergi"—Sapienza, the Museo Paludi di Celano, and the Museo Archeologico Nazionale d'Abruzzo di Chieti for granting us access to their collections. EM expresses sincere gratitude to the Southern Illinois University Carbondale Department of Anthropology and Center for Archaeological Investigations, the UC Berkeley D-Lab, Izumi Shimada, Robert S. Corruccini, Heather A. Lapham, Vitale Stefano Sparacello, Nicolino Farina, and Luca Bondioli. We also thank the copy editor for improving the quality of this chapter.

References

Agarwal, Sabrina C., and Bonnie A. Glencross, eds. 2011. *Social Bioarchaeology.* West Sussex: Blackwell Publishing.

Badoni, Franca Parise, and Maria Ruggeri Giove. 1980. *Alfedena: La necropoli di Campo Consolino, Scavi 1974–1979.* Chieti: Soprintendenza Archeologica dell'Abruzo.

Barker, Graeme, and Marlene Suano. 1995. "Iron Age Chiefdoms, c. 1000–500 BC." In *A Mediterranean Valley: Landscape Archaeology and Annales History in the Biferno Valley*, edited by Graeme Barker, 159–180. London: Leicester University Press.

Barth, Fredrik. 1969. *Ethnic Groups and Boundaries: The Social Organization of Culture Difference.* Oslo: Universitetsforlaget.

Bell, Tyler, Andrew Wilson, and Andrew Wickham. 2002. "Tracking the Samnites: Landscape and Communications Routes in the Sangro River Valley, Italy." *American Journal of Archaeology* 106: 169–186.

Bentley R. Alexander, and Herbert D. G. Maschner. 2008. "Complexity Theory." In *Handbook of Archaeological Theories*, edited by R. Alexander Bentley, Herbert Maschner, and Christopher Chippendale, 245–271. Lanham, MD: AltaMira Press.

Binford, Lewis. 1971. "Mortuary Practices: Their Study and Their Potential." *American Antiquity* 36: 6–29.

Bispham, Edward. 2007. "The Samnites." In *Ancient Italy: Regions without Boundaries*, edited by Guy Bradley, Elena Isayev, and Corinna Riva, 179–223. Exeter: University of Exeter Press.

Bispham, E. H., G. J. Bradley, J. W. J. Hawthorne, and S. Kane. 2000. "Toward a Phenomenology of Samnite Fortified Centers." *Antiquity* 74: 23–24.

Bondioli, Luca, Robert S. Corruccini, and Roberto Macchiarelli. 1986. "Familial Segregation in the Iron Age Community of Alfedena, Abruzzo, Italy, Based on Osteodental Trait Analysis." *American Journal of Physical Anthropology* 71: 393–400.

Braun, David P. 1984. "Burial Practices, Material Remains, and the Anthropological Record." In *The Archaeology of Death*, edited by Robert Chapman, Ian Kinnes, and Klavs Randsborg, 185–196. Cambridge: Cambridge University Press.

Brown, James A. 1996. *The Spiro Ceremonial Center: The Archaeology of Arkansas Valley Caddoan Culture in Eastern Oklahoma*. Memoirs of the Museum of Anthropology no. 29. Ann Arbor: University of Michigan Press.

Buikstra, Jane E. 1981. "Mortuary Practices, Palaeodemography and Palaeopathology: A Case Study from the Koster Site (Illinois)." In *The Archaeology of Death*, edited by Robert Chapman, Ian Kinnes, and Klavs Randsborg, 123–132. Cambridge: Cambridge University Press.

———. 1991. "Out of the Appendix and into the Dirt: Comments on Thirteen Years of Bioarchaeological Research." In *What Mean These Bones? Studies in Southeastern Bioarchaeology*, edited by Mary Lucas Powell, Patricia S. Bridges, and Ann Marie Wagner Mires, 172–189. Tuscaloosa: University of Alabama Press.

Buikstra, Jane E., Susan R. Frankenberg, and Lyle W. Konigsberg. 1990. "Skeletal Biological Distance Studies in American Physical Anthropology: Recent Trends." *American Journal of Physical Anthropology* 82: 1–7.

Calò, C. M., A. Melis, Giuseppe Vona, and I. S. Piras. 2008. "Sardinian Population (Italy): A Genetic Review." *International Journal of Modern Anthropology* 1: 39–64.

Capasso, Luigi. 1985. "Familiar Relationship Reconstruction in the Burial 'Circles' of the Alfedena Necropolis (Iron Age: L'Aquila, Italy) Using the Mobility and Topographic Distribution of Non-Malignant Osseous Neoplasm." *Ossa* 12: 3–7.

Carr, Christopher. 1995. "Mortuary Practices: Their Social, Philosophical-Religious, Circumstantial, and Physical Determinants." *Journal of Archaeological Method and Theory* 2: 105–200.

Carson, E. Ann. 2006. "Maximum Likelihood Estimation of Human Craniometric Heritabilities." *American Journal of Physical Anthropology* 131: 169–180.

Cavalli-Sforza, Luca L., Antonio Moroni, and Gianna Zei. 2004. *Consanguinity, Inbreeding, and Genetic Drift in Italy*. Princeton, NJ: Princeton University Press.

Chiaramonte Treré, Cristina, and Vincenzo d'Ercole, eds. 2003. *La Necropoli di Campovalano. Tombe orientalizzanti e arcaiche*. Vol. 1. BAR International Series 1177. Oxford: Archaeopress.

Chiaramonte Treré, Cristina, Vincenzo d'Ercole, and Cecilia Scotti, eds. 2010. *La Necropoli di Campovalano. Tombe orientalizzanti e arcaiche, II*. BAR International Series 2174. Oxford: Archaeopress.

Cianfarani, Valerio. 1972. "The Necropolis of Campovalano: Mysteries of Middle Adriatic Culture." *Expedition* 14: 27–32.

Cook, Della C. 1981. *Mortality, Age-Structure and Status in the Interpretation of Stress Indicators in Prehistoric Skeletons: A Dental Example from the Lower Illinois Valley*. In *The Archaeology of Death*, edited by Robert Chapman, Ian Kinnes, and Klavs Randsborg, 133–144. Cambridge: Cambridge University Press.

Coppa, Alfredo, and Patrizia Colarossi. 1987. "Study of Mortality." In *The Archaeological Museum of Campli*, edited by Vincenzo d'Ercole Walter Pellegrini, 76–78. Campli: Archaeological Service of the Abruzzi, Town Board of Campli.

Coppa, Alfredo, Andrea Cucina, M. Lucci, Domenico Mancinelli, and Rita Vargiu. 2007.

"Origins and Spread of Agriculture in Italy: A Nonmetric Dental Analysis." *American Journal of Physical Anthropology* 133: 918–930.

Coppa, Alfredo, Andrea Cucina, Domenico Mancinelli, and Rita Vargiu. 1997. "Biological Relationships of Etruscan-Culture Communities." *Etruscan Studies* 4: 86–102.

Coppa, Alfredo, Andrea Cucina, Domenico Mancinelli, Rita Vargiu, and James M. Calcagno. 1998. "Dental Anthropology of Central-Southern, Iron Age Italy: The Evidence of Metric versus Nonmetric Traits." *American Journal of Physical Anthropology* 107: 371–386.

Coppa, Alfredo, and Roberto Macchiarelli. 1982. "The Maxillary Dentition of the Iron-Age Population of Alfedena (Middle-Adriatic Area, Italy)." *Journal of Human Evolution* 11: 219–235.

Coppa, Alfredo, Roberto Macchiarelli, and Loretana Salvadei. 1981. "Craniologia della popolazione dell'età del Ferro di Alfedena (Abruzzo, Area Medio-Adriatica)." *Rivista di Antropologia* 61: 275–290.

Coppa, Alfredo, Domenico Mancinelli, Pier P. Petrone, and R. Priori. 1987. "Gli inumati dell'Eta del Ferro di Campovalano (Abruzzo, area medio-adriatica)." *Rivista di Antropologia* 65: 105–138.

Cucina, Andrea, Domenico Mancinelli, and Alfredo Coppa. 1998. "Stress and Mortality in Protohistoric Samples from Central Italy." *Science and Technology for Cultural Heritage* 7: 101–106.

———. 2000. "Life Span and Physiological Perturbations: Assessment of Demographic Parameters and Linear Enamel Hypoplasias in Past Populations." *Homo* 51: 56–67.

D'Alessandro, Aida, Luigi Capasso, and Fulvio Bartoli. 2000. "Indagni sulla paleodieta in due necropoli abruzzesi dell'Età del Ferro." *Rivista di Antropologia* 78: 151–158.

D'Ercole, Vincenzo. 1987a. "The Bronze Age." In *The Archaeological Museum of Campli*, edited by Vincenzo d'Ercole Walter Pellegrini, 17–19. Campli: Archaeological Service of the Abruzzi, Town Board of Campli.

———. 1987b. "From Prehistory to Protohistory." In *The Archaeological Museum of Campli*, edited by Vincenzo d'Ercole Walter Pellegrini, 11–13. Campli: Archaeological Service of the Abruzzi, Town Board of Campli.

———. 1987c. "A Mother's Outfit." In *The Archaeological Museum of Campli*, edited by Vincenzo d'Ercole Walter Pellegrini, 48–50. Campli: Archaeological Service of the Abruzzi, Town Board of Campli.

De Grossi Mazzorin, Jacopo. 1987. "From Animal Remains: Environment and Resources." In *The Archaeological Museum of Campli*, edited by Vincenzo d'Ercole Walter Pellegrini, 14–16. Campli: Archaeological Service of the Abruzzi, Town Board of Campli.

Dench, Emma. 1995. *From Barbarians to New Men: Greek, Roman, and Modern Perceptions of Peoples of the Central Apennines*. Oxford: Clarendon Press.

Devor, Eric J. 1987. "Transmission of Human Cranial Dimensions." *Journal of Craniofacial Genetics and Developmental Biology* 7: 95–106.

Di Giacomo, F., F. Luca, N. Anagnou, G. Ciavarella, R. M. Corbo, M. Cresta, F. Cucci, L. Di Stasi, V. Agostiano, M. Giparaki, A. Loutradis, C. Mammi, E. N. Michalodimitrakis, F. Papola, G. Pedicini, E. Plata, L. Terrenato, S. Tofanelli, P. Malaspina, and A. Novelletto. 2003. "Clinal Patterns of Y Chromosomal Diversity in Continental Italy and Greece are Dominated by Drift and Founder Effects." *Molecular Phylogenetics and Evolution* 28: 387–395.

Dolfini, Andrea. 2006. "Embodied Inequalities: Burial and Social Differentiation in Copper Age Central Italy." *Archaeology Review from Cambridge* 21: 58–77.

Fu, Qiaomei, Pavao Rudan, Svante Pääbo, and Johannes Krause. 2012. "Complete Mitochondrial Genomes Reveal Neolithic Expansion into Europe." *PLoS ONE* 7(3): e32473.

Goethals, Tanja, Morgan de Dapper, and Frank Vermeulen. 2005. "Geomorphology and Geoarchaeology of Three Sites in the Potenza Valley Survey Project (The Marches, Italy): Potentia, Montarice and Helvia Recina." *Revista de Geomorfologie* 7: 33–49.

Goldstein, Lynne. 1981. "One-Dimensional Archaeology and Multi-Dimensional People: Spatial Organization and Mortuary Analysis." In *The Archaeology of Death,* edited by Robert Chapman, Ian Kinnes, and Klavs Randsborg, 53–69. Cambridge: Cambridge University Press.

———. 2006. "Mortuary Analysis in Bioarchaeology." In *Bioarchaeology: A Contextual Approach*, edited by Jane E. Buikstra and Lane A. Beck, 375–387. New York: Academic Press.

González-Ruibal, Alfredo. 2006. "House Societies vs. Kinship-Based Societies: An Archaeological Case from Iron Age Europe." *Journal of Anthropological Archaeology* 25: 144–173.

Goodenough, Ward H. 1956. "Componential Analysis and the Study of Meaning." *Language* 32: 195–216.

Herrera, Brianne, Tsunehiko Hanihara, and Kanya Godde. 2014. "Comparability of Multiple Data Types from the Bering Strait Region: Cranial and Dental Metrics and Nonmetrics, mtDNA, and Y-Chromosome DNA." *American Journal of Physical Anthropology* 54: 334–348.

Hertz, Robert. 1960. "A Contribution to the Study of the Collective Representation of Death." In *Death and the Right Hand*, translated by Rodney and Claudia Needham, 29–88. London: Cohen and West.

Hillson, Simon, Charles FitzGerald, and Helen Flinn. 2006. "Alternative Dental Measurements: Proposals and Relationships with Other Measurements." *American Journal of Physical Anthropology* 126: 413–426.

Hodder, Ian. 1977. "Introduction." In *The Spatial Organisation of Culture,* edited by Ian Hodder, 1–3. Pittsburgh, Pa.: University of Pittsburgh Press.

———. 1978. "Social Organization and Human Interaction: The Development of Some Tentative Hypotheses in Terms of Material Culture." In *The Spatial Organisation of Culture*, edited by Ian Hodder, 199–270. Pittsburgh, Pa: University of Pittsburgh Press.

———. 1980. "Social Structures and Cemeteries: A Critical Appraisal." In *Anglo-Saxon Cemeteries: The Fourth Anglo-Saxon Symposium at Oxford*, edited by Philip A. Rahtz, Tania Marguerite Dickinson, and Lorna Watts, 161–169. British Archaeological Reports 82. Oxford: BAR.

———. 1984. "Burials, Houses, Women and Men in the European Neolithic." In *Ideology, Power and Prehistory*, edited by Daniel Miller and Christopher Tilley, 51–68. Cambridge: Cambridge University Press.

Howells, William W. 1973. *Cranial Variation in Man: A Study by Multivariate Analysis of*

Patterns of Difference among Recent Human Populations. Papers of the Peabody Museum of Archaeology and Ethnology vol. 67. Cambridge: Harvard University Press.

Krappe, Alexander H. 1942. "Guiding Animals." *Journal of American Folklore* 55: 228–246.

Lévi-Strauss, Claude. 1987. *Anthropology and Myth: Lectures 1951–1982.* Blackwell, Oxford

Macchiarelli, Roberto. 1988. "Age-Related Rates and Patterns of Cortical Bone Involution in Past Human Populations: A Protohistorical Example." *Rivista di Antropologia* 66: 55–76.

Macchiarelli, Roberto, and Loretana Salvadei. 1986. "Topographic Distribution of Maxillary Carious Lesions at Alfedena (VI–V Cent. B.C., Central Italy)." *Antropologia Contemporanea* 9: 201–206.

Macchiarelli, Roberto, Loretana Salvadei, and M. Dazzi. 1981. "Paleotraumatologia cranio-cerbrale nella comunità protostorica di Alfedena (VI–V sec. A.C., area medio-Adriatica)." *Antropologia Contemporanea* 4: 239–243.

Macchiarelli, Roberto, Loretana Salvadei, and Paola Catalano. 1988. "Biocultural Changes and Continuity throughout the First Millennium B.C. in Central Italy: Anthropological Evidence and Perspectives." *Supplemento del Rivista di Antropologia* 66: 249–272.

Mancinelli, D., A. Coppa, A. Cucina, and R. Vargiu. 1997. "Inquadramento paleodemografico di alcuni gruppi a cultural Etrusca nell'ambito della popolazioni dell'Italia centro-meridionale del I millennio a.C." In *Aspetti della xultura di Volterra Etrusca fra l'età ellenistica e contributi della ricerca antropologica alla conoscenza del popolo Etrusco. Atti del XIX Convegno di Studi Etruschi ed Italici Volterra, 15–19 ottobre 1995,* edited by G. Maetzke, 499–513. Firenze: Leo S. Olschki.

Mancinelli, Domenico, Alfredo Coppa, S. M. Damadio, and Rita Vargiu. 1993. "Continuità biologica delle comunità dell'Età del Ferro di Campovalano (X–III sec. A.C.)." *Antropologia Contemporanea* 16: 187–193.

Mancinelli, Domenico and Rita Vargiu. 2012. "The Trend of Stature in Pre-Protohistoric Central-Southern Italy." *Journal of Anthropological Sciences* 90: 239–242.

Marchi, Damiano, Vitale Sparacello, and Colin Shaw. 2011. "Mobility and Lower Limb Robusticity of a Pastoralist Neolithic Population from North-Western Italy." In *Human Bioarchaeology of the Transition to Agriculture,* edited by Ron Pinhasi and Jay T. Stock, 317–346. New York: John Wiley & Sons, Ltd.

Mariani, Lucio. 1901. *Aufidena: Ricerche archeologiche e storiche del Sannio settentrionale.* Roma: Accademia Nazionale dei Lincei.

Martin, Rudolph, and Karl Saller. 1957. *Lehrbuch der anthropologie.* Stuttgart: Fischer.

Martínez-Abadías, Neus, Mireia Esparza, Torstein Sjøvold, Rolando González-José, Mauro Santos, and Miquel Hernández. 2009. "Heritability of Human Cranial Dimensions: Comparing the Evolvability of Different Cranial Regions." *Journal of Anatomy* 214: 19–35.

Meggit, M. J. 1965. *The Lineage System of the Mae-Enga of New Guinea.* Edinburgh: Oliver and Boyd.

Messina, Francesco, Gabriele Scorrano, Christina Martínez Labarga, Mario Federico Rolfo, and Olga Rickards. 2010. "Mitochondrial DNA Variation in an Isolated Area of Central Italy." *Annals of Human Biology* 37: 385–402.

Mogliazza, Silvia, and Mauro Rubini. 2003. "Biological Relations in Ancient Populations: Use of Genetic Markers of the Skeleton." *Archivo per l'antropologia e la etnologia* 133: 119–137.

Moore-Jansen, Peer H., Richard L. Jantz, and Stephen D. Ousley. 1994. *Data Collection Procedures for Forensic Skeletal Material.* Report of Investigation no. 48. Knoxville: University of Tennessee Press.

Morris, Ian. 1991. "The Archaeology of Ancestors: The Saxe/Goldstein Hypothesis Revisited." *Cambridge Archaeological Journal* 1: 147–169.

Naso, Alessandro. 2000. *I Piceni: Storia e archeologia delle marche in epoca Preromana.* Milano: Longanesi & Co.

Navarro, M. Carmen Vida. 1993. "Warriors and Weavers: Sex and Gender in Early Iron Age Graves from Pontecagnano." *Journal of the Accordia Research Center* 3: 67–100.

Oakley, S. P. 1996. *The Hill-Forts of the Samnites.* BSR Archaeological Reports. London: British School at Rome.

Ortner, Donald J., and Robert S. Corruccini. 1976. "The Skeletal Biology of the Virginia Indians." *American Journal of Physical Anthropology* 45: 717–722.

Paine, R. R., Domenico Mancinelli, M. Ruggeri, and Alfredo Coppa. 2007. "Cranial Trauma in Iron Age Samnite Agriculturalists, Alfedena, Italy: Implications for Biocultural and Economic Stress." *American Journal of Physical Anthropology* 132: 48–58.

Paul, Kathleen S., Christopher M. Stojanowski, and Michelle M. Butler. 2013. "Biological and Spatial Structure of an Early Classic Period Cemetery at Charco Redondo, Oaxaca." *American Journal of Physical Anthropology* 152: 217–229.

Pearson, Mike Parker. 1993. "The Powerful Dead: Archaeological Relationships between the Living and the Dead." *Cambridge Archaeological Journal* 3: 203–229.

———. 2000. *The Archaeology of Death and Burial.* College Station: Texas A&M University Press.

Peebles, Christopher S. 1971. "Moundville and Surrounding Sites: Some Structural Considerations of Mortuary Practices." *Memoirs of the Society for American Archaeology* 25: 68–91.

Peebles, Christopher S., and Susan M. Kus. 1977. "Some Archaeological Correlates of Ranked Societies." *American Antiquity* 42: 421–448.

Peet, T. E. 1907. "The Early Iron Age in South Italy." *Papers of the British School at Rome* 4: 285–296.

Perkins, Philip. 2009. "DNA and Etruscan Identity." In *Etruscan by Definition: The Cultural, Regional and Personal Identity of the Etruscans. Papers in Honour of Sybille Haynes, MBE,* edited by Judith Swaddling and Philip Perkins, 95–111. London: The British Museum Press.

Peroni, Renato. 1979. "From Bronze Age to Iron Age: Economic, Historical and Social Considerations." In *Italy before the Romans: The Iron Age, Orientalizing and Etruscan Periods,* edited by David and Francesca Ridgway, 7–30. London: Academic Press.

Pilloud, Marin A., and Clark Spencer Larsen. 2011. "'Official' and 'Practical' Kin: Inferring Social and Community Structure from Dental Phenotype at Neolithic Çatalhöyük, Turkey." *American Journal of Physical Anthropology* 145: 519–530.

Potter, Tim. 1984. "Social Evolution in Iron Age and Roman Italy: An Appraisal." In *Eu-*

ropean Social Evolution: Archaeological Perspectives, edited by John Bintliff, 235–244. Bradford, West Yorkshire: Bradford University Press.

Riva, Corinna. 2007. "The Archaeology of Picenum: The Last Decade." In *Ancient Italy: Regions without Boundaries,* edited by Guy Bradley, Elena Isayev, and Corinna Riva, 79–113. Exeter: University of Exeter Press.

Robb, John. 1994a. "Skeletal Signs of Activity in the Italian Metal Ages: Methodological and Interpretive Notes." *Human Evolution* 9: 215–229.

———. 1994b. "Gender Contradictions: Moral Coalitions and Inequality in Prehistoric Italy." *Journal of European Archaeology* 2: 20–49.

———. 1994c. "Burial and Social Reproduction in the Peninsular Italian Neolithic." *Journal of Mediterranean Archaeology* 7: 29–75.

———. 1997. "Violence and Gender in Early Italy." In *Troubled Times: Violence and Warfare in the Past*, edited by Debra L. Martin and David W. Frayer, 111–144. Amsterdam: Gordon and Breach.

———. 2007. *The Early Mediterranean Village.* Cambridge: Cambridge University Press.

———. 2015. "What Do Things Want? Object Design as a Middle Range Theory of Material Culture." *Archaeological Papers of the American Anthropological Association* 26: 166–180.

Robb, John, Renzo Bigazzi, Luca Lazzarini, Caterina Scarsini, and Fiorenza Sonego. 2001. "Social 'Status' and Biological 'Status': A Comparison of Grave Goods and Skeletal Indicators from Pontecagnano." *American Journal of Physical Anthropology* 115: 213–222.

Rodríguez V., C. Tomàs, J. J. Sánchez, J. A. Castro, M. M. Ramon, A. Barbaro, N. Morling, and A. Picornell. 2009. "Genetic Sub-Structure in Western Mediterranean Populations Revealed by 12 Y-chromosome STR Loci." *International Journal of Legal Medicine* 123: 137–141.

Rosivach, V. T. 1983. "Mars, the Lustral God." *Latomus* 42: 509–521.

Rubini, Mauro. 1996. "Biological Homogeneity and Familial Segregation in the Iron Age Population of Alfedena (Abruzzo, Italy), Based on Cranial Discrete Traits Analysis." *International Journal of Osteoarchaeology* 6: 454–462.

Rubini, Mauro, E. Bonafede, and Silvia Mogliazza. 1999. "The Population of East Sicily during the Second and First Millennium B.C.: The Problem of the Greek Colonies." *International Journal of Osteoarchaeology* 9: 8–17.

Rubini, Mauro, E. Bonafede, Silvia Mogliazza, and L. Moreschini. 1997. "Etruscan Biology: The Tarquinian Population, Seventh to Second Century B.C. (Southern Etruria, Italy)." *International Journal of Osteoarchaeology* 7: 202–211.

Salmon, Edward T. 1967. *Samnium and the Samnites.* Cambridge: Cambridge University Press.

Saxe, Arthur A. 1970. "Social Dimensions of Mortuary Practices." PhD diss., University of Michigan, Ann Arbor.

———. 1971. "Social Dimensions of Mortuary Practices in a Mesolithic Population from Wadi Halfa, Sudan." *Memoirs of the Society for American Archaeology* 25: 39–57.

Schmidt, Robert A. 2005. "The Contribution of Gender to Personal Identity in the Southern Scandinavian Mesolithic." In *The Archaeology of Plural and Changing Identities: Beyond Identification*, edited by Eleanor Casella and Chris Fowler, 79–108. New York: Springer.

Sestieri, Anna Maria Bietti. 1973. "The Metal Industry of Continental Italy, 13th–11th Century, and Its Aegean Connections." *Proceedings of the Prehistoric Society* 39: 383–424.

———. 1981. "Economy and Society in Italy between the Late Bronze Age and Early Iron Age." In *Archaeology and Italian Society,* edited by Richard Hodges and Graeme Barker, 133–155. *BAR International Series* 102. British Archaeology Reports, Oxford.

———. 1988. "'The Mycenaean Connection' and Its Impact on the Central Mediterranean Societies." *Dialoghi di Archeologia* 6: 23–51.

———. 2008. "*Domi mansit, lanam fecit:* Was That All? Women's Social Status and Roles in the Early Latial Communities (11th–9th Centuries B.C.)." *Journal of Mediterranean Archaeology* 21: 133–159.

———. 2010. "Archeologia della morte fra età del bronzo finale ed età del ferro in Italia. Implicazioni delle scelte relative alla sepoltura in momenti di crisi o di trasformazione politico-organizzativa." In *Antropologia e Archeologia a Confronto, Atti dell'Incontro Internazionale di Studi in onore di Claude Lévi-Strauss,* edited by Valentino Nizzo, 397–417. Roma: ESS.

Sestieri, Anna Maria Bietti, and Anna De Santis. 2012. Elementi di continuità rituale in Etruria meridionale, Lazio e Campania fra l'età del bronzo finale e la prima età del ferro. In *L'Etruria dal Paleolitico al Primo Ferro: Lo stato delle ricerche,* edited by N. Negroni Catacchio, 635–650. Milan: Centro Studi di Preistoria e Archeologia.

Shimada, Izumi, Kenichi Shinoda, Julie Farnum, Robert S. Corruccini, and Hirokatsu Watanabe. 2004. "An Integrated Analysis of Pre-Hispanic Mortuary Practices: A Middle Sicán Case Study." *Current Anthropology* 45: 369–402.

Sjøvold, Torstein. 1984. "A Report on the Heritability of Some Cranial Measurements and Non-Metric Traits." In *Multivariate Statistical Methods in Physical Anthropology,* edited by G. N. Van Vark and William W. Howells, 223–246. Dordrecht: Reidel Publishing Company.

Sparacello, Vitale S., Vincenzo D'Ercole, and Alfredo Coppa. 2015. "A Bioarchaeological Approach to the Reconstruction of Changes in Military Organization among Iron Age Samnites (Vestini) from Abruzzo, Central Italy." *American Journal of Physical Anthropology* 156: 305–316.

Stodder, Ann L. W. 2008. "Taphonomy and the Nature of Archaeological Assemblages." In *Biological Anthropology of the Human Skeleton,* 2nd ed., edited by M. Anne Katzenberg and Shelley R. Saunders, 71–114. Hoboken, NJ: John Wiley and Sons.

Stojanowski, Christopher M., and Michael A. Schillaci. 2006. "Phenotypic Approaches for Understanding Patterns of Intracemetery Biological Variation." *American Journal of Physical Anthropology* 49: 49–88.

Strauss, André, and Mark Hubbe. 2010. "Craniometric Similarities within and between Human Populations in Comparison with Neutral Genetic Markers." *Human Biology* 82: 315–330.

Strazzulla, Josè M. 2013. "Forme di devozione nei luoghi di culto dell'Abruzzo antico." In *Sacrum facere: Atti del I Seminario di Archeologia del Sacro,* 41–94. Trieste: Edizioni Università di Trieste.

Tagliamonte, Gianluca. 1996. *I Sanniti: Caudini, Irpini, Pentri, Carricini, Frentani.* Milano: Longanesi & Co.

———. 2004. "Horsemen and Dioskouroi Worship in Samnite Sanctuaries." In *Samnium:*

Settlement and Cultural Change—The Third E. Togo Salmon Conference, edited by Howard Jones, 103–114. Providence, RI: Brown University Press.

Tainter, Joseph A. 1978. "Mortuary Practices and the Study of Prehistoric Social Systems." *Advances in Archaeological Method and Theory* 1: 105–141.

Taubadel, Noreen von Cramon. 2009. "Revisiting the Homoiology Hypothesis: The Impact of Phenotypic Plasticity on the Reconstruction of Human Population History from Craniometric Data." *Journal of Human Evolution* 57: 179–190.

Tavano, Giovanni. 1996. *Abruzzo—A Land to Discover.* Pescara: CARSA Edizioni.

Turner, Christy G., Christian R. Nichol, and G. Richard Scott. 1991. "Scoring Procedures for Key Morphological Traits of the Permanent Dentition: The Arizona State University Dental Anthropology System." In *Advances in Dental Anthropology*, edited by Mark A. Kelly and Clark Spencer Larsen, 13–31. New York: Wiley.

Ucko, Peter J. 1969. "Ethnography and the Archaeological Interpretation of Funerary Remains." *World Archaeology* 1: 262–290.

Unger, Leonard. 1953. "Rural Settlement in the Campania." *Geographical Review* 43: 506–524.

Van Gennep, Arnold. 1960. *The Rites of Passage.* Translated by M. B. Vizedom and G. L. Caffee. Chicago: University of Chicago Press.

van Rossenberg, Erik. 2001. "Discorsi coll'età del bronzo / Making Conversation with the Bronze Age." *Assemblage—The University of Sheffield Graduate Journal of Archaeology* 6: 1–3.

———. 2005. "Between Households and Communities: Layers of Social Life in the Later Bronze Age and Early Iron Age of Central Italy." In *Papers in Italian Archaeology VI: Communities and settlements from the Neolithic to the Early Medieval Period*, edited by Peter Attema, Albert Nijboer, and Andrea Zifferero, 84–91. Groningen: BAR International Series.

———. 2006. "Cemeteries as Central Places: A Nested Approach to Burial as a Locale for Community Formation." Paper presented at the 28th annual conference of the Theoretical Archaeology Group, Exeter.

———. 2011. "Making the Underground: Bronze Age Deposition as Flow of Substances and Cosmological Placemaking." Paper presented at the conference Gods in Ruins: The Archaeology of Religious Activity in Protohistoric, Archaic, and Republican Central Italy, Oxford.

Vargiu, Rita, Alfredo Coppa, and Michael L. Blakey. 1993. "L'ipoplasia dello smalto dei denti nelle necropolis di Campovalano di Campli (Teramo) e di San Marzano (Salerno)." *Antropologia Contemporanea* 16: 345–350.

Weinberg, Seth M., Trish E. Parsons, Mary L. Marazita, and Brion S. Maher. 2013. "Heritability of Face Shape in Twins: A Preliminary Study using 3D Stereophotogrammetry and Geometric Morphometrics." *Dentistry 3000* 1(1): 1–5.

Whitehouse, Ruth D. 1995. "From Secret Society to State Religion: Ritual and Social Organization in Pre- and Protohistoric Italy." In *Settlement and Economy in Italy 1500 B.C.–AD 1500, Papers of the Fifth Conference on Italian Archaeology,* edited by Neil Christie, 83–88. Oxford: Oxbow.

———, ed. 1998. *Gender and Italian Archaeology: Challenging the Stereotypes.* London: Accordia Research Institute of Archaeology, University College London.

III

Adaptability and Resilience on the Frontier

6

Living on the Border

Health and Identity during Egypt's Colonization of Nubia in the New Kingdom Period

KATIE MARIE WHITMORE, MICHELE R. BUZON,
AND STUART TYSON SMITH

Investigation into the modes and impacts of colonialism in past populations has been an integral part of the field of archaeology for several decades. A large portion of this research has focused on contact between European colonizers and New World indigenous groups (Cameron et al. 2015; Larsen 2001; Larsen and Milner 1994; Stojanowski 2015; Verano and Ubelaker 1992). To date, however, cultural interactions have been explored in archaeological contexts in the Old and New Worlds (Klaus et al. 2017; Murphy and Klaus 2016). Such studies include the colonial interactions in Central and South America, such as those that investigate the Wari (Schreiber 2005) and the Maya (Oland 2012). Examples from Europe include studies of Roman colonization (Wells 1998) and those from Asia include studies of colonization along China's frontier (Eng and Quanchao 2013). Comparatively less research has focused on colonization outside Europe and the New World. Many of the critiques of the acculturation and world-systems models have argued that the so-called universality of these models does not apply to ancient societies (Stein 1998). These issues can be addressed by examining examples from varied contexts. One example of the diverse and nuanced consequences of cultural interaction is that of Nubia and Egypt, which provides an example of colonialism in an ancient context and an alternative to perspectives based on research in Europe and the New World (Smith 1998).

Ancient Egypt and Nubia maintained a dynamic relationship for several thousands of years. Over time, the dominance oscillated between Egypt and Nubia (Edwards 2004; O'Connor 1993; Smith 1995, 2003b). Figure 6.1 provides a map of the changing boundaries between Egypt and Nubia and the location of the Cataracts of the Nile. Table 6.1 provides ancient chronologies of these two countries. The complex relationship between these two neighboring groups greatly impacted the movement of resources, goods, and technology (Edwards 2004) and the culture, food, religions, and funerary practices in the region (Buzon and Smith 2017; Smith 1995, 2003a, 2003b).

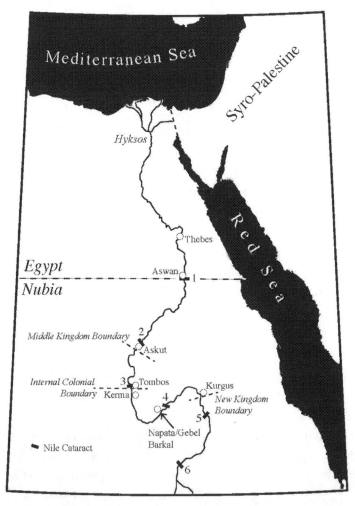

Figure 6.1. Map illustrating the changes in the border between Egypt and Nubia during the Middle and New Kingdom Periods, including the locations of the Nile Cataracts. Map by Stuart Tyson Smith.

Table 6.1. Chronologies of Ancient Egypt and Nubia

Date	Upper Nubia	Lower Nubia	Egypt
3500–2600 BCE	Neolithic	A Group	Predynastic/Early Dynastic
2600–2150 BCE	Old Kerma	?	Old Kingdom
2150–2050 BCE		C Group	First Intermediate period
2050–1650 BCE	Middle Kerma		Middle Kingdom
1650–1550 BCE	Classic Kerma		Second Intermediate period
1550–1050 BCE	Recent Kerma		New Kingdom
1050–750 BCE	Pre-Napatan	?	Third Intermediate period
750–332 BCE	Napatan	?	Late period

Sources: Smith 1995, 2003b.

Beginning in the Middle Kingdom period (ca. 2050–ca. 1650 BCE), the relationship between Nubia and Egypt became increasingly militaristic and violent. During this period, Egypt began imperialistic expansions into Lower Nubia that culminated in the construction of a series of fortresses at the Second Cataract of the Nile (Smith 2003b). These fortresses regulated trade and movement along the Nile and marked an important boundary: Egypt controlled the territory north of the Second Cataract. During the same period, the city of Kerma in Nubia was a powerful urban center that controlled the area between the Fourth Cataract and the Batn-el-Hajar (Trigger 1976a). Kerman religious ideology heavily influenced funerary practices of the time, which included burial with grave goods such as animal hides and funerary beds (Bonnet 1994). Animal burials also became more common during the Kerma periods (ca. 2500–ca. 1500 BCE). Kerma continued to grow in power and in the period circa 1650–circa 1550 BCE it unified all of Nubia, including a former Egyptian colony in the kingdom of Kush.

During this time, the Syro-Palestinian Hyksos disassembled the Egyptian Empire and took control of northern Egypt (Smith 2003b). After that, Kerma increased in size and its influence spread through the region and the Kerma state rose to the height of its power, posing a serious threat to the Egyptians (Bonnet 1994). After the reunification of Egypt during the New Kingdom period and in response to the growing threat of Kerma's power, Egypt mounted a number of military campaigns to conquer Nubia up to the Fourth Cataract (Morkot 2000;

O'Conner 1993; Smith 2003b). After centuries of shifting dominance during the Middle Kingdom and Second Intermediate periods, the increasingly tense relationship between Egypt and Nubia provided an intense backdrop for Egypt's colonization of Nubia in the New Kingdom period.

The New Kingdom Period

The New Kingdom period is marked by the Egyptian Empire's expansion into surrounding regions. In 1502 BCE, the Egyptian Pharaoh Thutmose I defeated the Kingdom of Kush in Nubia. For approximately the next 500 years, Egyptians maintained some form of colonial rule in Nubia, which today encompasses southern Egypt and northern Sudan. The Egyptian colonists established towns and temples in Nubia. The temples were centers for the spread and promotion of Egyptian religious beliefs (Trigger 1976b). The New Kingdom period was the pinnacle of Egypt's power and culture and a time of economic prosperity. An important goal of Egypt's imperial expansions was obtaining access to the goods and resources found throughout Nubia, of which one of the most significant and highly desired was gold. Nubian gold was highly sought after and was an important component of Nubia's annual tribute to Egypt (Smith 1995). There is some debate among scholars about the impact the demand for tribute and manufactured goods would have had on the native Nubians. Some have suggested that Egypt's expansion would have resulted in negative outcomes, including harsh manual labor and impoverishment (e.g., Trigger 1976b). However, others have suggested more positive interactions or interactions that had little impact on daily life (e.g., O'Conner 1993; Morkot 2001). We explore these questions by examining the health and identity of individuals living on the frontier of the Egyptian-Nubian border in the community of Tombos.

Tombos

While there are some temples further south, the site of Tombos is the southernmost colony Egypt established during the New Kingdom. This fact suggests that Tombos marked an important literal and figurative boundary between Egyptian and Nubian interaction. Tombos was founded on the eastern bank of the Nile River as an Egyptian colonial town (figure 6.2) and likely served as an administrative center for the empire (Smith 2003b). The cemetery at Tombos was used from the New Kingdom period through the Napatan period (ca. 1400–ca. 650 BCE). Along the Nile River there are six granite outcrops known as cataracts that create rapids that impede movement. Tombos, which was located at the headwaters of the Third Cataract, was perfectly situated to monitor and control trade and the movement of people along the Nile. Recent excavations at Tombos suggest evidence of the founding of a New Kingdom colony around 1450 BCE, including a defensive structure that consisted of a dry moat lined with mud brick walls. Smith and Buzon (2018) argue that the combination of the large size of the fortification system and the high rank of officials buried in the Tombos cemetery may indicate that Tombos is the location of the fortress Taroy. In his Semna inscription, Amenhotep III's viceroy Merymose mentioned recruiting soldiers for the colonial army for a campaign against Ibhet from the territory from "the *menenu* of Baki (Kuban) down to the *menenu* of Taroy, making 52 *iteru* of sailing" (quoted in Morris 2005).

Bioarchaeological evidence suggests that both Egyptian colonists and native Nubians lived at Tombos. Strontium isotope ratios ($^{87}Sr/^{86}Sr$) provide a means of identifying first-generation migrants and reconstructing population composition. Previous research by Buzon and colleagues determined that it may be possible to identify nonlocal individuals using strontium isotope ratios in the region (Buzon and Simonetti 2013; Buzon et al. 2007). Egyptian strontium values are statistically higher than Nubian values. Approximately one-third of the Tombos individuals had strontium values that were outside the local range and are more closely associated with Egyptian sites (figure 6.3). In fact, according to recent research by Buzon and colleagues (2016), it appears that over time Tombos formed a mixed community of Egyptians and Nubians. Based on in situ diagnostic pottery and the design of coffins and scarabs, we have categorized the burials of forty-eight individuals in Units 6 and 7 at Tombos into three broad phases of colonization in the New Kingdom period. The first phase encompasses the reign of Amenhotep II to that of Thutmose IV (from ca. 1427 to ca. 1390 BCE), the second phase encompasses the reign of Amenhotep III through the Amarna and Post-Amarna periods (ca. 1390 to ca. 1295 BCE), and the third phase encompasses the reign of Ramesses II through the late Ramesside period (ca. 1295 to ca. 1069 BCE). Both men and women moved to Tombos. The largest proportion of settlers (42 percent) arrived during the earliest phase of the cemetery. During the second phase, the number of first-generation immigrants dropped to 21 percent. The number of settlers increased again to 36 percent during the third phase, indicating that this region was still a focus for colonization late in the New Kingdom period (Buzon et al. 2016).

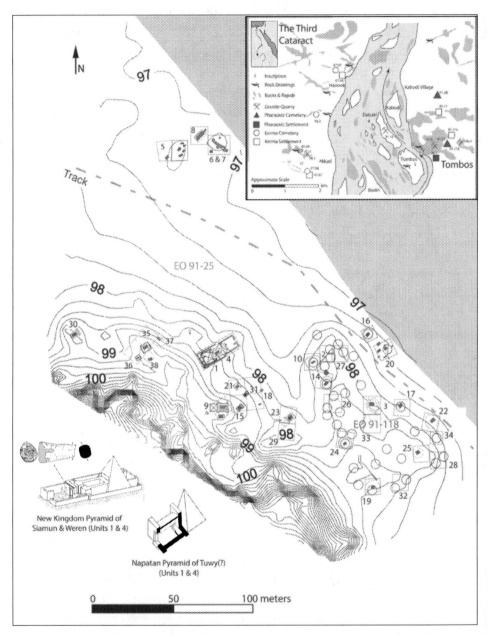

Figure 6.2. Map of the location and excavations at the Tombos cemetery. Map by Nadejda Reshetnikova and Stuart Tyson Smith.

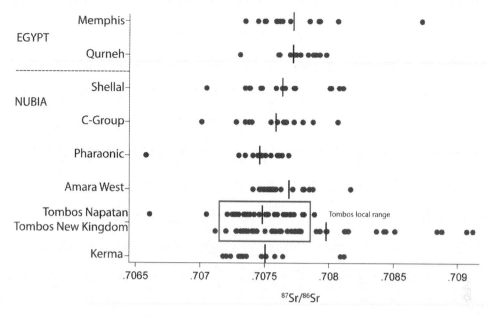

Figure 6.3. Scatter chart of $^{87}Sr/^{86}Sr$ values in the Nile Valley. While there is overlap between the sites, there is a statistically significant difference in the median between Egyptian and Nubian sites.

Archaeologically, the cemetery at Tombos provides strong evidence of Egyptian practices. During the New Kingdom period, pyramids were the most popular style of tomb among the elite. Following the colonization of Nubia, Egyptians and Egyptianized Nubian elites built large tombs that signaled their ties to Egypt. Additionally, the presence of funerary cones on at least two pyramids at Tombos represents a specific tie to Thebes (Smith and Buzon 2014). Funerary cones, which were stamped with the owner's name and titles, were placed across the façade of a tomb. Over 400 tombs in Thebes included funerary cones as decoration but very few tombs outside Thebes displayed them. There is only one other site in Nubia besides Tombos with funerary cones (Ryan 1988). This connection with Thebes signals an important tie to Egypt and Egyptian beliefs, as Thebes was both the religious and political capital of Egypt at the time and the seat of the viceroy of Kush (Smith and Buzon 2014). Recent excavations at Tombos revealed a large deposit of funerary cones that were stamped with a dedication to Siamun and his mother Weren. Some of these cones were much more intact and legible than funerary cones that had been found previously. In addition, they prompted a revision of Siamun's title, which now reads as Scribe-Reckoner of the Gold of Kush, indicating Siamun may have supervised the weighing and shipment of gold as the tribute to Kush was assembled (Smith and Buzon 2018).

Other burial practices indicative of Egyptianization and Egyptian culture are the inclusion of specialized grave goods, such as *ushabtis*, heart scarabs, and coffins (figure 6.4). *Ushabtis* are funerary figurines meant to do work in place of the deceased in the afterlife and are directly tied to Egyptian ideology and beliefs (Smith 2003b). Coffins and coffin decorations would have been particularly public displays and the use of coffins in funeral processions and related activities would have signaled strong ties to Egypt. Heart scarabs, which are rare and are indicative of elite status, are another type of grave good found at Tombos. Heart scarabs were inscribed with a spell from the Book of the Dead to ensure that the deceased's heart or soul would not betray the individual during final judgment (Smith and Buzon 2014). Egyptian burials were placed supine in coffins with head to the west, facing east toward the rising sun.

Figure 6.4. Examples of Egyptian-style burials and grave goods. *Clockwise from top left*: ushabti, heart scarab, supine and extended burial, decorated coffin, and chamber tombs. Photo by Stuart Tyson Smith.

In contrast, before the New Kingdom period, individuals in this part of Nubia were buried in the Kerma style, which included interment under tumuli, circular mounds that were often decorated with stones. Individuals were placed on a bed and/or on a cowskin in the flexed position on their side with the head to the east facing north. Animal sacrifices were often included, a practice that is nearly absent in Egyptian burials (figure 6.5; Buzon and Smith 2017; Edwards 2004). Not all of the individuals at Tombos were buried in the Egyptian style. Four individuals, all female, were placed in the traditional Nubian flexed position with the head to the east facing north instead of the extended burial in the Egyptian style. In one tomb, two females were found together in a semi-flexed position in association with Kerma-style ceramics and surrounded by wood framing, suggesting that these women were placed on a bed, another distinctly Nubian practice. A funeral in the Nubian style would have been a public affair and would have been visible to members of the community. The choice to be buried in the Nubian style these women and/or their families made would

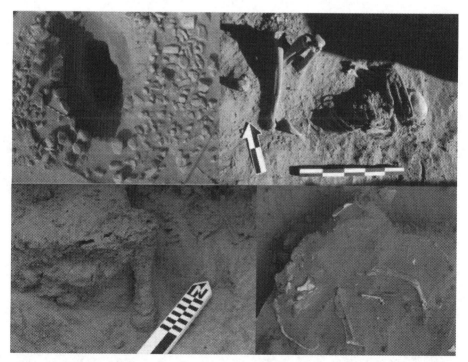

Figure 6.5. Examples of Kerma-style burial practices. *Clockwise from top left*: tumulus, flexed burial position, animal sacrifice, and funerary bed. Photo by Stuart Tyson Smith.

have made an important and influential statement about their affiliations and identity (Buzon and Smith 2017; Buzon et al. 2016; Smith and Buzon 2014). One of the women who was buried in the Nubian style was buried with a necklace that incorporated both Nubian and Egyptian jewelry styles. Some of the beads were made of glass and faience and included three Egyptian amulets of the god Bes. However, the necklace also had a Nerita shell bead, which is more typical of Nubian burials (Smith and Buzon 2014).

An Egyptocentric view of the period promotes the idea that complexity and progress was driven solely by the process of Egyptian acculturation and that the later rise of Napata is a result of influence from Egypt. This perspective has persisted in one form or another for almost a century (e.g. Breasted 1909; David 1988; Kendall 1999; Reisner 1919). However, the cultural interaction between Egypt and Nubia can be reevaluated in light of the increased criticisms of acculturation models and the more nuanced culture contact models that have arisen over the last two decades (Cusick 1998a, 1998b; Deagan 1998; Lightfoot 2005; Schortman and Urban 1998; Stein 2005). As Smith states, "The cultural entanglements and hybridity that appeared in the aftermath of empire allowed both for a strong Nubian revival and for a continuity of Egyptian colonial society, each of which blended Egyptian and Nubian elements" (2013, 96). At the end of the New Kingdom period there is evidence of both Egyptian-style burial practices and more Nubian practices at Tombos. The combination of Egyptian and Nubian practices is reflected in burial orientation, grave furniture, grave structure, and ceramics (Smith 2013). Another interpretation Smith (2013) has suggested is that Nubians co-opted and reinterpreted Egyptian elite ideology in order to gain power. Nubians were particular about which Egyptian practices they adopted. Smith (2013) provides the example of the ram god Khnum and the god Amun-Re, who also appears as a ram. Nubians selected the Egyptian god Khnum, his consort Satet, and their daughter Anukis because of their connection to Nubia as the patron gods of Aswan, which marked the border between ancient Egypt and Nubia and retained Nubian associations. Khnum's ram imagery also resonated with long-standing Nubian religious iconography. Nubians likely syncretized Amun-Re, the patron god of Egypt's southern capital at Thebes, and Amani, a Nubian god. A new myth of the god's Nubian origin was created around the sacred mountain at Gebel Barkal, where a series of New Kingdom and Napatan period temples were built. Additionally, the New Kingdom ram form of Amun-Re was probably borrowed from Nubia.

Health Indicators

Frontiers and borderlands can often be contentious zones where individuals from different cultures, perspectives, goals, and positions find their lives intertwined. Colonialism brings to mind ideas of dominance, oppression, control, sickness, and malnutrition of local peoples. For example, some scholars working in the New Kingdom Nile Valley describe Nubians being forced into harsh manual labor and impoverishment (e.g., Trigger 1976b). However, archaeological and bioarchaeological evidence from Tombos reflects a town where Egyptians and Nubians were integrated into each other's daily lives. The unique location of Tombos on the border between direct Egyptian colonization and a more indirect mode of control in Nubia provides a compelling context for exploring the health impacts of Egyptian colonialism on Egyptian colonialists and native Nubians. Given evidence that Tombos was a mixed community of Egyptian colonialists and native Nubians, how did living in a community on the frontier of Egyptian and Nubian interaction affect individuals' health? This question can be addressed by examining skeletal indicators of nutritional deficiency, infection, traumatic injury, and activity patterns. Such data can provide insight into the relationship between Nubians and Egyptians at Tombos. In this study, we used linear enamel hypoplasia, cribra orbitalia/porotic hyperostosis, femur length, oral health, osteoperiostitis, traumatic injury, and evidence of activity patterns to assess health.

Linear Enamel Hypoplasia

Linear enamel hypoplasia (LEH) is associated with systemic metabolic problems caused by nutritional deficiencies, infectious pathogens, and traumatic physical or psychological circumstances during the period of tooth development. LEH are developmental enamel defects and/or disturbances in dental development (Goodman and Martin 2002; Ortner 2003). According to Aufderheide and Rodríguez-Martin (1998), such defects in the structure of the tooth are indicative of bodywide metabolic insults and can be used to discern metabolic stress. LEH develops in early childhood, from before birth to approximately seven years of age, and corresponds to discrete periods of stress (Goodman and Martin 2002). Identifying the etiology of these dental defects is extremely difficult as their development is influenced by over 100 different factors. Thus, they are used only as an indication of nonspecific stress. These defects are visually apparent transverse deficiencies in enamel thickness and can be present

Table 6.2. Number of individuals exhibiting linear enamel hypoplasia (LEH), cribra orbitalia, and osteoperiostitis by sex and age category

	LEH	Cribra Orbitalia	Osteoperiostitis
Female	8/31	2/40	4/17
Male	2/17	1/27	1/10
Young Adult	8/20	2/24	0/6
Middle Adult	2/14	0/16	3/8
Old Adult	2/7	1/11	2/9

singularly or in multiples (Goodman and Martin 2002). They are considered to be present when the indentation can be felt with a fingernail.

Among the Tombos sample, 12 of 52 individuals that could be examined from the New Kingdom portion of the cemetery displayed LEH in at least one anterior tooth. Eight of 31 females exhibited LEH, as did two of 17 males (table 6.2). Our examination of the prevalence of LEH by age groups revealed that 8 of 20 young adults (aged 18 to 29), 2 of 14 middle adults (aged 30 to 45), and 2 of 7 old adults (aged 46+ years) exhibited LEH (table 6.2; Buzon 2006, 2014).

Cribra Orbitalia and Porotic Hyperostosis

Porotic hyperostosis is commonly associated with anemia and is frequently found on the cranial bones and on the roof of the eye orbits. It consists of lesions that are caused by bone marrow proliferation. Porotic hyperostosis on the roof of the eye orbits is more commonly referred to as cribra orbitalia. Anemia can be a result of a number of factors, including hereditary conditions, discrete genetic traits, or nutritional disorders (Goodman and Martin 2002). The exact etiology of cribra orbitalia has been widely discussed and debated in bioarchaeological circles (e.g., Walker et al. 2009). However, it is often associated with anemia and/or deficiencies of iron, vitamin B_{12}, vitamin C, and vitamin D and with infection during childhood. Iron deficiency, infectious disease, and parasites can all cause anemia, and researchers should exercise caution when interpreting rates of porotic hyperostosis, especially as very different cultural, biological, and ecological conditions can cause the same lesions (Goodman and Martin 2002). Despite the multiple etiologies of porotic hyperostosis/cribra orbitalia, these skeletal manifestations are useful indicators of nonspecific stress and nutritional deficiencies.

All recorded instances of cribra orbitalia in the Tombos New Kingdom sample showed evidence of remodeling. Three of 69 individuals that could be examined from the New Kingdom portion of the cemetery displayed cribra orbitalia: 2 of 40 females and 1 of 27 males (table 6.2). Our examination by age groups revealed that 2 of 24 young adults (aged 18 to 29), 0 of 16 middle adults (aged 30 to 45) and 1 of 11 old adults (aged 46+) exhibited cribra orbitalia (table 6.2; Buzon 2006, 2014). We also examined individuals for the presence of lesions on the cranial vault, but in the Tombos New Kingdom sample, porotic hyperostosis on the cranial vault is nearly nonexistent.

Growth Disruption

Many researchers consider growth in stature and weight to be sensitive and powerful indicators of nutritional status (Goodman and Martin 2002). Long-bone length is used to assess growth. Due to the state of preservation and the commingling of the Tombos sample, we used femur length. New Kingdom females had an average maximum femur length of 41.93 centimeters (n = 12), and males had an average maximum femur length of 43.82 centimeters (n = 7) (Buzon 2006, 2014).

Oral Health

Dentition is among the most frequently recovered elements in the archaeological record and can be used to provide information on dietary choices and other behavior. Goodman and Martin state that dentition provides a direct record of individual conditions, specifically "the state of [an individual's] health, [an individual's] diet, age, and certain aspects of his [or her] material culture are indicated by the appearance of the teeth and the supporting bone" (2002, 44). Dental caries is a disease process that causes demineralization due to the presence of acidogenic bacteria (e.g. *Streptococcus mutans*) on the surfaces of dentition. However, several intrinsic and extrinsic factors are related to the development of carious lesions, including individual resistance and hygiene, pathogenic agents, environment, and diet (Goodman and Martin 2002). The expression of carious lesions are also related to other dental conditions. For example, dental attrition and tooth loss can obscure the presence of caries. Additionally, dental attrition can promote the expression of caries through exposing the underlying dentin (Goodman and Martin 2002). Another oral health disorder used in studies of health and stress is antemortem tooth loss. It is frequently associated with other dental conditions including abscesses, extreme alveolar resorption, excess attrition, and caries (Goodman and Martin 2002). Extensive tooth loss

Table 6.3. Number of individuals exhibiting abscesses, antemortem tooth loss (AMTL), and carious lesion by tooth (total number of individual teeth observed) and by individual (with at least one tooth observable)

	By Tooth			By Individual		
	Total	Female	Male	Total	Female	Male
Abscesses	82/821	54/495	21/216	31/65	19/38	11/23
AMTL	296/821	154/495	126/216	46/64	23/37	21/23
Carious lesion	53/821	41/985	10/216	16/76	10/37	6/21

can have a deleterious effect on the nutritional and health status of an individual as foods become difficult to chew (Goodman and Martin 2002).

Table 6.3 displays the results of our examination of oral health from individuals in the Tombos cemetery by number of teeth affected and by individuals with at least one observable tooth. Individuals in the Tombos sample have high rates of abscesses (48 percent) and antemortem tooth loss (72 percent) and comparatively low instances of carious lesions (24 percent) (Buzon and Bombak 2010). Our examination of the sample by sex revealed that 19 of 38 of females (50 percent) had abscesses, 23 of 37 of females (62 percent) had antemortem tooth loss, and 10 of 37 females (27 percent) had caries. For males, 11 of 23 (48 percent) had abscesses, 21 of 23 (91 percent) had antemortem tooth loss, and six of 21 (29 percent) had caries (Buzon and Bombak 2010).

Osteoperiostitis

Osteoperiostitis, or periosteal lesions on the outer layer of bone, can be caused by both infections and inflammatory conditions. While particular patterns of osteoperiostitis can be associated with specific diseases, most lesions cannot be linked to an identifiable pathogen. Osteoperiostitis is the process of reactive periosteal bone deposition. This can result from an injury to the periosteum or from infection of the bone (Goodman and Martin 2002; Roberts and Manchester 2005; Steckel et al. 2002). Since osteoperiostitis refers to the inflammation of the periosteum rather than to the bone itself, some scholars use the more appropriate term periostosis, which refers to the bone the periosteum produces

(Weston 2012). In Steckel et al. (2011), the authors use the umbrella term "osteo-periostitis" to refer to periostitis (the result of infection) and to periostosis (the result of noninfectious agents). According to Steckel et al. (2002), periosteal lesions that are distributed bisymmetrically indicate hematogenous infection, where blood distributes the infections throughout the body. In contrast, osteoperiostitis can be caused by injury. Thus, when such lesions are found near fractures, traumatic injury is likely the cause. It is important to note that not all scholars are in agreement regarding the incorporation of osteoperiostitis in the examination of stress in past populations. For example, Weston critiques the incorporation of osteoperiostitis in stress models in general and argues "the interpretation of proliferative periosteal reactions as a stress indicator is inherently flawed. . . . Stress results in the stimulation of glucocoricoid secretion, which in turn inhibits bone formation, and therefore inhibits periosteal new bone production" (2012, 506).

With these limitations in mind, we counted only individuals that displayed bilateral lesions on one or more long bone types and excluded small, localized reactions that could be caused by injury. In the Tombos sample, six of 31 individuals that could be examined from the New Kingdom portion of the cemetery displayed osteoperiostitis. Four of seventeen of these individuals were female and one of ten was male (table 6.2). Examining the prevalence of osteoperiostitis by age groups reveals that zero of six young adults (aged 18 to 29 years), three of eight middle adults (aged 30 to 45 years), and two of nine old adults (aged 46+ years) exhibited osteoperiostitis (table 6.2; Buzon 2006, 2014).

Traumatic Injury

Traumatic lesions resulting from physical force are caused by a number of types of injuries, including fractures, dislocations, wounds caused by weapons, and crushing injuries (Goodman and Martin 2002). The evidence on the bone of the intensity and direction of the force can provide information about the process and timing of the injury. If a periosteal reaction occurs with the traumatic injury, then both bone and soft tissue were involved (Goodman and Martin 2002). Traumatic injuries can provide insight into societal and environmental relationships through evidence of accidents, violence, and medical treatment. Specific environments, such as those with rocky terrains, can produce different patterns of traumatic lesions. Evidence of interpersonal violence can provide important insight into a social and political milieu (Larsen and Milner 1994; Martin and Frayer 1997; Steckel et al. 2002).

Both cranial injuries and parry fracture injuries to the forearms have been used as measures of interpersonal violence in archaeological contexts. Archaeological and documentary evidence of conflict between Egypt and Nubia can be identified in the presence of fortifications, political documents, victory monuments, and other artistic representations. At Kerma, a Nubian site just 10 kilometers south of Tombos that dates to the Kerma Classic period (ca. 1750–ca. 1550 BCE), the rate of traumatic injury was investigated. The study found that 21 of 187 individuals (11.2 percent) had traumatic injuries to the cranium and 43 of 1,771 (2.4 percent) had traumatic injuries to the limb bones (Judd 2004). These injuries may be reflective of interpersonal violence. At Tombos, individuals had very low rates of injuries. Only 1 of 72 (1.4 percent) of the crania and 19 of 923 (2.3 percent) of the limb bones displayed evidence of injury (Buzon and Richman 2007).

Evidence of Activity Patterns

The demand for Egyptian tribute may have increased the need to mine gold, to manufacture trade goods, and to produce agricultural products, resulting in increased manual labor. Questions regarding physical activities can be addressed through examining entheseal remodeling and osteoarthritis. Such evidence can provide information about who performed strenuous physical activity and who did not. Entheses, also referred to as musculoskeletal stress markers, allow for physical movement. Entheseal remodeling provides broad evidence of physical activity. Osteoarthritis refers to lesions that result from primary inflammatory processes. Most commonly, lesions present as marginal (osteophytic) lipping; in more severe forms it presents as eburnation (pitting and/or polishing of the articular surface).

Schrader (2012) examined sixteen fibrocartilaginous attachment sites for entheseal remodeling using the Hawkey and Merbs (1995) scoring system for the Tombos sample. All individuals had all mean entheseal scores below the Hawkey and Merbs (1995) score of 1. Entheseal remodeling was most severe at the elbow and least severe at the shoulder. Composite groups for the wrist and knee produced scores that were significantly higher in bones of males than in bones of females. However, this correlation might reflect body size rather than sexual differences (Schrader 2012). Osteoarthritis was scored using the standardized scoring system presented in Buikstra and Ubelaker (1994). A very small portion of the bones in the Tombos sample exhibited indications of osteoarthritis. Sex was not significantly correlated with osteoarthritic lipping at any composite site. There was only one case of severe osteoarthritis in the Tombos sample (Schrader 2012).

Discussion

Much of the early research on colonialism focused on European or New World contexts. Many of these contexts are associated with negative interactions, especially related to health outcomes, particularly for local peoples. While this pattern holds true in many contexts, colonialist polices are not universal, and modern examples should not be used uncritically as models for prehistoric or ancient contexts. The rich archaeological and bioarchaeological data available at Tombos depict a community where Nubian and Egyptian identity was entangled in the context of an ancient Egyptian colonial center. The setting at Tombos is a good context for investigating issues related to the impact of Egyptian colonialism on health in Nubia.

Monuments describe overt rebellion by the Nubians who attempted to overthrow the Egyptian colonial regime. These acts of resistance were unsuccessful, however, in part due to the close geographic proximity of the two societies. A small contingent of Egyptians could attack or respond to Nubian rebels quite quickly, and a larger Egyptian military force could reach a Nubian population center within a month (Smith 2013). Based on archaeological evidence of assimilative acculturation in northern Nubia, Egyptologists have assumed that Nubians assimilated to Egyptian cultural norms in the face of Egyptian dominance. However, the reality was more complex. During the first years of occupation, Nubian burial practices were largely replaced by Egyptian practices, perhaps due to an Egyptian policy of forced assimilation. Smith (1998, 2013) argues that the pattern of Egyptianized burials throughout the colonial New Kingdom period suggests that this assimilation began with the wealthy and the elite. The general lack of specialized grave goods such as inscribed *ushabti* figurines and heart scarabs in the New Kingdom has led others to argue that the Egyptianization of burials was superficial. However, Smith (2013) contends that this pattern is more reflective of social status than of cultural affinity, as these types of specialized grave goods were quite expensive and were beyond the means of most individuals at the time. Furthermore, there is no archaeological evidence for the widespread adoption of Egyptianized cultural practices in the Nubian heartland south of Tombos. In fact, at some sites there is evidence that Nubian cultural practices continued long after the Egyptian conquest, even in the zone of Egyptian territorial control and colonization below the Third Cataract. Evidence from the sites of Askut and Tombos also suggest that women played an integral role in maintaining elements of Nubian culture during these time periods through foodways, ceramics, and burial practices (Smith 2013).

Within the field of Egyptology, the interaction between Nubia and Egypt has generally been viewed as that of a dominant core and a subordinate periphery. This view has either not considered how Nubians influenced Egyptians or has considered such influence to be nonexistent. Additionally, this view of Egyptian-Nubian interactions assumes that Egyptians required harsh manual labor and that the native Nubians became impoverished. However, more recently, scholars have adopted perspectives that emphasize native agency and recognize the complexity of internal dynamics that led to different outcomes for different groups within both native and colonial society. These more recent models incorporate indigenous frameworks and more nuanced models of interaction that suggest limited changes for some aspects of Nubian lifeways and an incorporation of Nubian elite and others into the Egyptian colonial social and political structure. Archaeological and biological evidence from Tombos support these more nuanced models of Nubian and Egyptian interaction and provide evidence of complexity in the interactions between these groups that led to cultural and biological entanglements between Egyptian colonists and Nubians rather than a straightforward assimilation and/or oppression of the local population (Buzon et al. 2016).

The frequencies of LEH, cribra orbitalia, and osteoperiostitis in the Tombos adults are rather low. Only 23 percent of adults with anterior teeth that could be examined for LEH had these lesions. Additionally, there is no statistically significant difference between males and females. The frequency of osteoperiostitis is similarly low; only 19 percent of the Tombos sample displayed bilateral lesions. Osteoperiostitis is found almost exclusively on the lower limbs and porotic hyperostosis is nearly absent from all periods of Tombos. The frequency of cribra orbitalia in the New Kingdom period adults is extremely low at 4 percent. All lesions displayed evidence of remodeling and there was no statistically significant difference between males and females. Growth stunting, as reflected in long-bone length, can be a result of exposure to disease and inadequate nutrition during childhood, and indeed we found that the average femur length in the New Kingdom period sample from Tombos was shorter than that of adults from comparative sites in the Nile Valley (Buzon 2006) and from individuals from the Third Intermediate/Napatan periods at Tombos (Buzon 2014). While the low frequencies of skeletal indicators of nonspecific stress and infection paint a picture of relative health at Tombos, the relatively short adult femur length indicates that individuals at Tombos might have been exposed to physiological stress. Further analysis of juveniles is needed to fully understand the timing and impact of stress and disease in the Tombos population.

Oral health can provide insight into the diet and lifestyles of individuals. The Tombos sample reveals levels of dental disease that were similar to those of contemporaneous Nile Valley populations (Buzon and Bombak 2010). However, the rates of dental attrition and antemortem tooth loss are higher, possibly a result of physiological and mental stress associated with the sociopolitical changes of colonialism during the period. Males had significantly higher rates of antemortem tooth loss than females in the Tombos New Kingdom sample. These rates may be a reflection of the fact that there are more older males than females in this sample or of differences in labor patterns by which males were engaged in activities that exposed them to higher levels of grit in the environment, such as quarrying (Buzon and Bombak 2010). However, oral health indicators and LEH frequencies in this sample may have been influenced by the high levels of postmortem damage, especially on the anterior teeth.

The rate of traumatic injury in the Tombos New Kingdom sample was considerably lower than that found at Kerma, which may suggest that the relationship between the native Nubians and Egyptian colonists living at Tombos was relatively peaceful in terms of physical violence. The lower proportion of traumatic injuries suggested by these data may indicate that the Egyptians changed their strategy, relying more on diplomacy and inclusion and less on military action after Thutmose I's initial conquest of Nubia (Buzon and Richman 2007). They may also reflect the cultural and political dynamics of earlier Kerman versus later Egyptian rule or the benefits conveyed by living at an important colony. The very low frequency and low severity of entheseal changes and osteoarthritis suggests that individuals at Tombos were likely not engaging in intensive labor (Schrader 2012). This supports the assertion that the Tombos population included members of the middle to upper socioeconomic classes and that Tombos may have served as an administrative center. The near-absence of bioarchaeological evidence of strenuous activity suggests that those that lived at Tombos were professionals, bureaucrats, and tradespeople (Schrader 2012). This analysis is also supported by archaeological evidence such as grave structures and grave goods. Skeletal indicators of osteoarthritis and entheseal changes also point to a community that had a prosperous lifestyle even though it was located on the frontier of Egyptian colonization. The archaeological and bioarchaeological evidence suggests that at Tombos, a mixed community of individuals coexisted in peace in terms of physical violence and that this extended into the Third Intermediate period, a time of supposed collapse and hostility between Egyptians and Nubians (Buzon and Richman 2007; Smith 2013). Furthermore, skeletal indicators of nonspecific stress and nutritional deficiencies suggest that individuals in this community had relatively low levels of disease and nutritional deficiency.

Conclusions

Examples of negative colonial encounters are prolific in the historical and archaeological record, especially for the native inhabitants of a region. Traditionally, it was thought that during Egypt's colonization of Nubia in the New Kingdom period, Egyptians used aggression to force native Nubians to perform harsh labor and imposed policies that impoverished them. However, it appears that at the frontier community of Tombos, biological and/or ethnic identity was more integrated and fluid and individuals enjoyed high social status and position. Archaeological and bioarchaeological evidence suggest that the individuals living at Tombos incorporated both Egyptian and Nubian practices, resulting in a biologically and culturally entangled community. Those who lived in the Tombos community were not subjected to the physically demanding activities or aggression that are sometimes associated with imperial subjugation. Additionally, the population at Tombos exhibited little skeletal evidence of nutritional deficiencies or infection. This is not to suggest that all Nubians benefited equally from Egyptian rule. Historical sources suggest that those who openly rebelled were harshly suppressed. But for those who collaborated, there was a degree of cultural accommodation and real benefits reflected in the health and prosperity of the mixed population at Tombos.

The investigation into health at Tombos is by no means complete. Until recently, excavations at Tombos had produced very few young individuals. In addition, recent excavations have revealed several individuals with severe impairments. Future analyses of juveniles and individuals with impairments will illustrate a more complete picture of health in the Tombos community and will provide additional insight into the impacts of colonialist activities on a broader range of the community. Examination of individuals of all ages can illuminate perceptions of personhood, childhood, and adulthood. Moreover, such study will provide crucial information about health and disease risk by detangling the social and cultural factors that contribute to stress and poor health. While the individuals at Tombos show little evidence of traumatic injury, strenuous activity, nutritional deficiencies, or nonspecific stress, this pattern might not be reflective of other communities on the frontier during the New Kingdom period. However, our data provide a foundation for understanding the health impacts of Egyptian colonialism in Nubia.

Acknowledgments

We would like to acknowledge the support of the National Science Foundation (BCS-0917824, 0907815, 0313247); the National Geographic Society; James and Louise Bradbury; Nancy Delgado; Francis and Jim Cahill; Jan Bacchi; and Connie Swanson Travel; the Schiff-Giorgini Foundation; the Brennan Foundation; the American Philosophical Society; the American Association of Physical Anthropologists; the Killam Trust; the Institute for Bioarchaeology; the Academic Senate and Institute for Social, Behavioral and Economic Research at the University of California, Santa Barbara; and the Purdue University Office of the Executive Vice President for Research and Partnerships. Additionally, we would like to thank the National Corporation for Antiquities and Museums in Sudan and the Tombos community for their support for our excavations. Last but not least, we are grateful to Professors Ali Osman M. Salih (University of Khartoum) and David Edwards (University of Leicester) for their generous suggestions and encouragement and their kindness in allowing our initial work to overlap with the University of Khartoum concession.

References

Aufderheide, Arthur C., and C. Rodríguez-Martin. 1998. *The Cambridge Encyclopedia of Human Paleopathology*. Cambridge: Cambridge University Press.

Bonnet, Charles 1994. "Archaeological Mission of the University of Geneva at Kerma (Sudan): Report on the 1992–1993 Campaign." *Nyame Akuma* 41: 61–63.

Breasted, James H. 1909. *A History of Egypt from the Earliest Times to the Persian Conquest*. New York: Scribner's.

Buikstra, Jane, and Douglas Ubelaker, eds. 1994. *Standards for Data Collection from Human Skeletal Remains*. Arkansas Archaeological Survey Research Series no. 44. Fayetteville: Arkansas Archaeological Survey.

Buzon, Michele R. 2006. "Health of the Non-Elites at Tombos: Nutritional and Disease Stress in New Kingdom Nubia." *American Journal of Physical Anthropology* 130: 26–37.

———. 2014. "Tombos during the Napatan Period (~ 750–660 BC): Exploring the Consequences of Sociopolitical Transitions in Ancient Nubia." *International Journal of Paleopathology* 7: 1–7.

Buzon, Michele R., and Andrea Bombak. 2010. "Dental Disease in the Nile Valley during the New Kingdom." *International Journal of Osteoarchaeology* 20: 371–387.

Buzon, Michele R., and Rebecca Richman. 2007. "Traumatic Injuries and Imperialism: The Effects of Egyptian Colonial Strategies at Tombos in Upper Nubia." *American Journal of Physical Anthropology* 133(2): 783–791.

Buzon, Michele R., and Antonio Simonetti. 2013. "Strontium Isotope (^{87}Sr/^{86}Sr) Variability in The Nile Valley: Identifying Residential Mobility during Ancient Egyptian and Nubian Sociopolitical Changes in the New Kingdom and Napatan Periods." *American Journal of Physical Anthropology* 151: 1–9.

Buzon, Michele R., Antonio Simonetti, and Robert A. Creaser. 2007. "Migration in the Nile Valley during the New Kingdom Period: A Preliminary Strontium Isotope Study." *Journal of Archaeological Science* 34: 1391–1401.

Buzon, Michele R., and Stuart T. Smith. 2017. "New Kingdom Egyptian Colonialism in Nubia at the Third Cataract: A Diachronic Examination of Sociopolitical Transition (1750–650 BC)." In *Colonized Bodies, Worlds Transformed: Toward a Global Bioarchaeology of Contact and Colonialism,* edited by Melissa S. Murphy and Haagen D. Klaus, 70–94. Gainesville: University Press of Florida.

Buzon, Michele R., Stuart T. Smith, and Antonio Simonetti. 2016. "Entanglement and the Formation of the Ancient Nubian Napatan State." *American Anthropologist* 118: 284–300.

Cameron, Catherine, Paul Kelton, and Alan Swedlund. 2015. *Beyond Germs: Native Depopulation in North America*. Tucson: University of Arizona Press.

Cusick, James. 1998a. "Historiography of Acculturation: An Evaluation of Concepts and their Application in Archaeology." In *Studies in Culture Contact: Interaction, Culture Change, and Archaeology,* edited by James Cusick, 126–145. Carbondale: Center for Archaeological Investigations, Southern Illinois University.

———. 1998b. "Introduction." In *Studies in Culture Contact: Interaction, Culture Change, and Archaeology,* edited by James Cusick, 1–22. Carbondale: Center for Archaeological Investigations, Southern Illinois University.

David, A. Rosalie. 1988. *Ancient Egypt*. Oxford: Phaidon.

Deagan, Kathleen. 1998. "Transculturation and Spanish American Ethnogenesis: the Archaeological Legacy of the Quincentenary." In *Studies in Culture Contact: Interaction, Culture Change, and Archaeology,* edited by James Cusick, 236–243. Carbondale: Center for Archaeological Investigations, Southern Illinois University.

Edwards, David N. 2004. *The Nubian Past: An Archaeology of the Sudan*. New York: Routledge.

Eng, Jacqueline T., and Z. Quanchao. 2013. "Conflict and Trauma Among Nomadic Pastoralists on China's Northern Frontier." In *Bioarchaeology of East Asia: Movement, Contact, Health*, edited by Kate Pechenkina and Marc Oxenham, 213–245. Gainesville: University Press of Florida.

Goodman, Alan H., and Debra L. Martin. 2002. "Reconstructing Health Profiles from Skeletal Remains." In *The Backbone of History: Health and Nutrition in the Western Hemisphere,* edited by Richard H. Steckel and Jerome C. Rose, 11–60. Cambridge: Cambridge University Press.

Hawkey, Diane E., and Charles F. Merbs. 1995. "Activity-Induced Musculoskeletal Stress Markers (MSM) and Subsistence Strategy Changes among Ancient Hudson Bay Eskimos." *International Journal of Osteoarchaeology* 5: 324–338.

Judd, Margaret A. 2004. "Trauma in the City of Kerma: Ancient and Modern Injury Patterns." *International Journal of Osteoarchaeology* 14: 3 4–51.

Kendall, Timothy 1999. "The Origin of the Napatan State: El-Kurru and the Evidence for the Royal Ancestors." In *Meroitica 15: Studienzum Antiken Sudan,* edited by Dietrich Wildung, 3–117. Berlin: Harrasowitz.

Klaus, Haagen D., Amanda R. Harvey, and Mark Nathan Cohen. 2017. *Bones of Complexity.* Gainesville: University Press of Florida.

Larsen, Clark Spencer. 2001. *Bioarchaeology of Spanish Florida: The Impact of Colonialism.* Gainesville: University Press of Florida.

Larsen, Clark Spencer, and George R. Milner. 1994. *In the Wake of Contact: Biological Responses to Conquest.* New York: Wiley-Liss.

Lightfoot, Kent G. 2005. "The Archaeology of Colonization: California in Cross-Cultural Perspective." In *The Archaeology of Colonial Encounters*, edited Gil J. Stein, 207–236. Santa Fe, NM: School of American Research Press.

Martin, Debra L., and David W. Frayer. 1997. *Troubled Times: Violence and Warfare in the Past.* Amsterdam: Gordon and Breach Publishers.

Morkot, Robert G. 2000. *The Black Pharaohs: Egypt's Nubian Rulers.* Rubicon Press, London.

———. 2001. "Egypt and Nubia." In *Empires: Perspectives from Archaeology and History*, edited by Susan E. Alcock, Terrance N. D'Altroy, Kathleen D. Morrison, Carla M. Sinopoli, 227–251. Cambridge: Cambridge University Press.

Morris, Ellen F. 2005. *The Architecture of Imperialism: Military Bases and the Evolution of Foreign Policy in Egypt's New Kingdom.* Leiden: Brill.

Murphy, Melissa S., and Haagen D. Klaus. 2016. *Colonized Bodies, Worlds Transformed: Toward a Global Bioarchaeology of Contact and Colonialism.* Gainesville: University Press of Florida.

O'Connor, David 1993. *Ancient Nubia: Egypt's Rival in Africa.* Philadelphia: University Museum of Archaeology and Anthropology, University of Pennsylvania.

Oland, Maxine. 2012. "Lost among the Colonial Maya: Engaging Indigenous Maya History at Progresso Lagoon, Belize." In *Decolonizing Indigenous Histories: Exploring Prehistoric Colonial Transitions in Archaeology*, edited by Melanie Oland, Siobhan M. Hart, and Liam Frink, 178–200. Tucson: University of Arizona Press.

Ortner, Donald J. 2003. *Identification of Pathological Conditions in Human Skeletal Remains.* San Diego: Academic Press.

Reisner, George A. 1919. "Discovery of the Tombs of the Egyptian XXVth Dynasty." *Sudan Notes and Records* 2: 237–254.

Roberts, Charlotte A., and Keith Manchester. 2005. *The Archaeology of Disease.* 3rd ed. Ithaca, NY: Cornell University Press.

Ryan, Donald P. 1988. "The Archaeological Analysis of Inscribed Egyptian Funerary Cones." *Varia Egyptiaca* 4: 165–170.

Schortman Edward M., and Patricia A. Urban. 1998. "Culture Contact Structure and Process." In *Studies in Culture Contact: Interaction, Culture Change, and Archaeology,* edited by James Cusick, 102–125. Carbondale: Center for Archaeological Investigations, Southern Illinois University.

Schrader, Sarah A. 2012. "Activity Patterns in New Kingdom Nubia: An Examination of

Entheseal Remodeling and Osteoarthritis at Tombos." *American Journal of Physical Anthropology* 149: 60–70.

Schreiber, Katharina J. 2005. "Imperial Agendas and Local Agency: Wari Colonial Strategies." In *The Archaeology of Colonial Encounters*, edited by Gil J. Stein, 237–262. Santa Fe: School of American Research Press.

Smith, Stuart T. 1995. *Askut in Nubia: The Economics and Ideology of Egyptian Imperialism in the Second Millennium BC*. New York: Keegan Paul International.

———. 1998. "Nubia and Egypt: Interaction, Acculturation, and Secondary State Formation from the Third to First Millennium B.C." In *Studies in Culture Contact: Interaction, Culture Change and Archaeology*, edited by James G. Cusick, 256–287. Carbondale: Center for Archaeological Investigations, Southern Illinois University.

———. 2003a. "Pharaohs, Feast, And Foreigners: Cooking, Foodways, and Agency on Ancient Egypt's Southern Frontier." In *The Archaeology and Politics of Food and Feasting in Early States and Empires*, edited by Tamara Bray, 39–64. New York: Kluwer Academic/Plenum Publishers.

———. 2003b. *Wretched Kush: Ethnic Identities and Boundaries in Egypt's Nubian Empire*. London: Routledge.

———. 2013. "Revenge of the Kushites: Assimilation and Resistance in Egypt's New Kingdom Empire and Nubian Ascendancy over Egypt." In *Empires and Complexity: On the Crossroads of Archaeology*, edited by Gregory Areshian, 84–107. Los Angeles: Cotsen Institute of Archaeology at UCLA.

Smith, Stuart T., and Michele R. Buzon. 2014. "Identity, Commemoration and Remembrance in Colonial Encounters: Burials at Tombos during the Egyptian New Kingdom Empire and its Aftermath." In *Remembering and Commemorating the Dead: Recent Contributions in Bioarchaeology and Mortuary Analysis from the Ancient Near East*, edited by Benjamin Porter, and Alexis Boutin, 187–217. Boulder: University Press of Colorado.

———. 2018. "The Fortified Settlement at Tombos and Egyptian Colonial Strategy in New Kingdom Nubia." In *From Microcosm to Macrocosm: Individual Households and Cities in Ancient Egypt and Nubia*, edited by Julia Budka and Johannes Auenmüller, 205–225. Leiden: Sidestone Press.

Steckel, Richard H., Paul W. Sciulli, and Jerome C. Rose. 2002. "A Health Index from Skeletal Remains." In *The Backbone of History: Health and Nutrition in the Western Hemisphere*, edited by Richard H. Steckel, and Jerome C. Rose, 11–61. Cambridge: Cambridge University Press.

Stein, Gil J. 1998. "World System Theory and Alternative Modes of Interaction in the Archaeology of Culture Contact." In *Studies in Culture Contact: Interaction, Culture Change, and Archaeology*, edited by James G. Cusick, 220–255. Carbondale: Center for Archaeological Investigations, Southern Illinois University.

———. 2005. "Introduction: The Comparative Archaeology of Colonial Encounters." In *The Archaeology of Colonial Encounters*, edited by Gil J. Stein, 3–31. Santa Fe, NM: School of American Research Press.

Stojanowski, Christopher M. 2015. *Mission Cemeteries, Mission Peoples: Historical and Evolutionary Dimensions of Intracemetery Bioarchaeology in Spanish Florida*. Gainesville: University Press of Florida.

Trigger, Bruce 1976a. "Kerma: The Rise of an African Civilization." *The International Journal of African Historical Studies* 9(1): 1–21.

———. 1976b. *Nubia under the Pharaohs*. Boulder, CO: Westview Press.

Verano, John W., and Douglas H. Ubelaker. 1992. *Health and Disease in the Southwest before and after Spanish Contact*. Washington DC: Smithsonian Institution Press.

Walker Phillip L., Rhonda R. Bathurst, Rebecca Richman, Thor Gjerdrum, and Valerie A. Andrushko. 2009. "The Causes of Porotic Hyperostosis and Cribra Orbitalia: A Reappraisal of the Iron-Deficiency-Anemia Hypothesis." *American Journal of Physical Anthropology* 139: 109–125.

Wells, Patricia S. 1998. "Culture Contact, Identity, and Change in the European Provinces of the Roman Empire." In *Studies in Culture Contact: Interaction, Culture Change and Archaeology*, edited by Gil J. Cusick, 316–334. Carbondale: Center for Archaeological Investigations, Southern Illinois University.

Weston, Darlene A. 2012. "Nonspecific Infection in Paleopathology: Interpreting Periosteal Reactions." In *A Companion to Paleopathology*, edited by Anne L. Grauer, 492–512. Chichester: Blackwell Publishing Ltd.

7

Life on the Northern Frontier

Bioarchaeological Reconstructions of Eleventh-Century Households in North Iceland

GUÐNÝ ZOËGA AND KIMMARIE MURPHY

In the ninth century, the previously uninhabited North Atlantic island of Iceland was colonized by settlers who were predominantly from Norway but were also from other Scandinavian countries and northern Britain. The island's position at the margins of the Viking world created a fluid frontier space that presented a wide variety of environmental and behavioral challenges that, in turn, impacted the settlers' political, economic, and ideological structures. When Iceland was first settled, it represented the western geographical frontier of the Viking world. By the eleventh century, this geographic frontier was evolving as Norse settlements expanded into Greenland and, for a very short period, Newfoundland (Byock 2001; Karlsson 2000). The adoption of Christianity in the early eleventh century wrought important social and ideological changes that are reflected in the proliferation of farm-based churches and cemeteries that individual households owned and operated. Excavations of a number of these cemeteries are offering an important glimpse of the nature and makeup of medieval Icelandic households and how the population was affected by and reacted to the physical environment and changing social and ideological realities (Zoëga 2014).

By the eleventh century, the Skagafjörður region of northern Iceland was home to hundreds of independent households that formed core social units in a country that had no king or central government. This chapter will focus on the archaeological and osteological evidence obtained from two early Christian cemeteries excavated in Skagafjörður, Keldudalur, in the Hegranes region and Seyla in the Langholt region (see figure 7.1). We will explore how the advent of a new

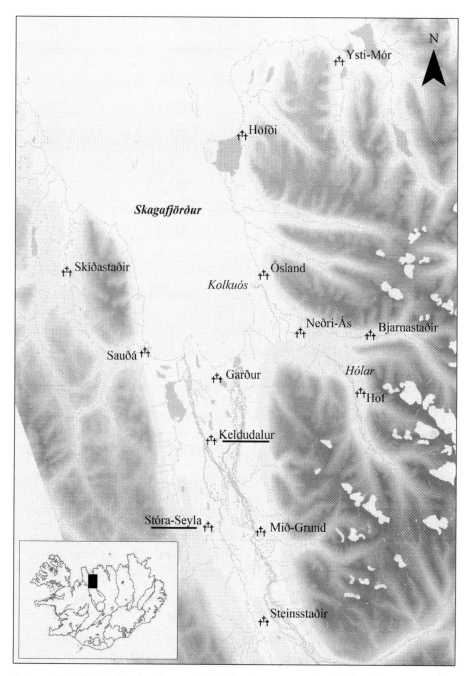

Figure 7.1. Map showing location of cemeteries that have been excavated in the Skagafjörður area. Keldudalur and Seyla are underlined. Map by Bryndís Zoëga.

religious reality is present in the archaeological record and discuss the impacts of frontiers and borderland spaces on the settlers' biology and culture.

Frontiers and Borderlands

The *Oxford English Dictionary* defines frontier as "the part of a country that borders on another country" or as "the part of country held to form the border or furthest limit of its settled or inhabited regions" and borderland as "a land or district on or near the border between two countries or districts." Numerous overviews of the history of frontier studies can be found in the archaeological literature. For a more thorough discussion and critique of this research one should consult works by Parker (2006) and Naum (2010). A large body of work regarding the various frontiers associated with the medieval period in Europe also exists, and many of these studies extend definitions of frontiers and boundaries to include political, religious, economic and cultural aspects of different societies (e.g., Abulafia and Berend 2002; Merisalo 2006).

Naum (2010) views the terms "frontiers" and "borderlands" as synonymous, although this perspective is not unanimous (for an alternative perspective, see Parker 2006; Ylimaunu et al. 2014). Frontiers and borderlands, according to Naum, "are physically present wherever two or more groups come into contact with each other, where people of different cultural backgrounds occupy the same territory and where the space between them grows intimate" (Naum 2010, 101). Most migrations in colonial contexts also involve the interaction of the colonizers with indigenous populations and many frontier and borderland studies in archaeology have focused on the subsequent clashes or means of coexisting that result from these encounters (Lightfoot and Martinez 1995). However, Parker's discussion of frontiers and borderland processes argues that "such zones may also be made up of empty areas where no such units exist or where they do not come into direct physical contact" (Parker 2006, 79). In other words, it is not necessary for two or more culture groups to come into contact in order for a context to be considered a frontier.

Oram and Adderley's ideas about "Norse frontiers" (Oram and Adderley 2011) are also of interest for framing our use of the term "frontier" in an Icelandic context. In their discussion of Innse Gall, one of the Western Isles of Scotland that was originally settled by Norse and Celts, Oram and Adderley take the concept of frontiers further by discussing how environmental historians view the term "frontier" as implying "a limit to the viable or sustainable pursuit of a specific exploitation regime" (2011, 125). They argue that the physical geography of Innse Gall constrained the viability of the subsistence strategies the original Norse and Celtic settlers on Innse Gall brought with them and limited their ability to succeed in the new frontier context. Naum also expands on the other dimensions of a frontier; she argues that "frontiers and borderlands imply the existence of limits confining the territorial scope of one's domain, settlement, or known world. A frontier seen as a limit of possession or settlement means that borderlands are ultimately also politically, socially, ideologically, and culturally charged spaces" (Naum 2010, 102). Ylimaunu and colleagues (2014) applied many of Naum's ideas about frontiers and borderlands in their recent research in medieval northern Finland. In addition to interactions between indigenous populations and subsequent settlers, the work in Finland also looks at the role of ideology as a factor in frontier and borderland interactions. Citing the work of Siikala and Siikala (2005), they argue that "sacred spaces, especially churches and cemeteries, were particularly important sites" (Ylimaunu et al. 2014, 4) for negotiating social relationships, identities, and power in northern Ostrobothnia during the Middle Ages.

The first wave of settlement in Iceland would have provided the inhabitants with a unique set of possibilities and problems. The first settlers had the luxury of choosing their own properties, the climate was relatively mild, and there was an abundance of wild birds, freshwater fish, and marine life (Karlsson 2016). However, the settlers' unfamiliarity with the landscape and the climate, and a lack of social infrastructure would have meant a precarious existence and a need to be resourceful in the first decades. By the eleventh century, a judicial infrastructure was in place and regional municipalities (*hreppr*) had been constructed for dealing with social issues such as providing for the poor or unfortunate and for overseeing various communal enterprises (Sigurðsson 2008). The country lacked a centralized power structure; the fact that there were no villages or towns meant that individual farms and households were the essential building blocks of society and were largely dependent on their own production (Byock 2001).

We argue that the settlers of Iceland operated in numerous frontiers and borderlands. This argument is idiosyncratic in some ways. The settlement of Iceland is one of the few colonizing events in which there were no earlier inhabitants and as an island, Iceland does not have close physical borders with another country. But at one time, it was the farthest limit of settlement for the European medieval world. The early settlers of Iceland faced very real environmental and climatic limitations and challenges to their subsistence and survival strategies when they first arrived, and these constraints and limitations continually modified and changed their behavioral responses over time. In this context, Icelandic settlers were interacting with a new environment while maintaining contact with their homelands, all of which likely resulted in a landscape "with power to unsettle conventional cultural practices, identities, and political orders" (Ylimaunu et al. 2014, 5).

The settlement and social history of Iceland has been widely discussed and debated as it relates to archaeology and to the written sources (see for instance Karlsson 2000; Karlsson 2016; McGovern et al. 2007; Miller 1990; Sigurðsson 1999; Smith 1995; Vésteinsson and McGovern 2012). However, until now, the frontier realities of Icelandic society have not been examined using bioarchaeological methods. Here we want to present a bioarchaeological interpretation of two eleventh-century household cemeteries, Keldudalur and Seyla, and examine how the data may add to analyses of social and environmental frontiers. Burials from both sites will be discussed to explore the impacts of frontier existence on biology and culture.

Icelandic Frontiers and Borderlands

Environmental Challenges

The climatic and environmental conditions of Iceland presented numerous challenges for the early settlers. Iceland's rocky central plateau dotted with glaciers limited most settlement to the coasts and inland valleys of the island. Settlements were established in highland valleys, but most of them were abandoned in later centuries (Karlsson 2016; Sveinbjarnardóttir 1992). Although the climate was relatively mild during the first couple of centuries after initial settlement (Ogilvie et al. 2000; Ogilvie and Jónsson 2001), there is evidence for deterioration as early as the late tenth century (Patterson et al. 2010) and it is becoming increasingly evident that there were frequent fluctuations and regional variations in weather patterns (Axford et al. 2011; Axford et al. 2009). The effects of these fluctuations are occasionally mentioned in the medieval Icelandic vernacular literature (sagas) and in later annals, where they are often referred to as "bad years" but also as cold summers, hard winters, and so forth. At times, these episodes resulted in countrywide famines and social upheavals (Finnsson 1970).

The early settlers of Iceland brought a Scandinavian agricultural subsistence way of life that relied heavily on animal husbandry, haying, and, when possible, cultivating domestic cereals such as barley (Edwards et al. 2005). The growing season was very short and even minor fluctuations in temperature and rainfall could adversely impact barley and fodder production. Iceland straddles temperate and subarctic climatic zones and the variability from one season to the next can be extremely challenging for human, plant, and animal survival (Patterson et al. 2010). The environmental stressor of prolonged exposure to cold can lead to hypothermia, increased risks for trauma, increased exposure to domestic pollutants, infectious diseases, and seasonal dietary deficiencies for both humans and their domestic animals (Martens 1998; Young and Mäkinen 2010).

Iceland sits at the boundary between opposing atmospheric pressures and oceanic currents in the Atlantic and the Arctic (Patterson et al. 2010). Seasonal variations in this region can result in the formation of sea ice, which can dramatically lower land temperatures, negatively impact the growth of forage for livestock, limit access to fishing grounds, and prevent trade ships from landing. However, sea ice can also result in the increased beaching of whales and other large marine mammals that can serve as dietary supplements and can bring driftwood onshore for use by inhabitants (Ogilvie et al. 2009). Marine resources would have been an important component of the diet from the onset (Ogilvie and Jónsdóttir 2000), but analysis of C^{13} and C^{12} isotope ratios at the site of Keldudalur suggests that the marine element of the diet was around only 20 percent, pointing to a reliance on terrestrial food items. This low number is surprising, as the site is not situated far inland. However, a similar pattern has been suggested for other sites in the North Atlantic and greater reliance on marine foodstuffs was not evident until later, during the later Middle Ages (Sveinbjörnsdóttir et al. 2010; Zoëga 2009).

Last but not least, we must consider the impacts of volcanic eruptions. Based on written and/or geologic evidence, it is estimated there have been somewhere between 200 and 300 volcanic eruptions since settlement. Local immediate impacts from volcanic activity include danger from lava flows, melting glaciers, ash and pyroclastic fallout, and inhalation of poisonous gases. Eruptions can result in disruptions to the climate that have long-term, negative consequences for surviving flora and fauna (Dugmore and Vésteinsson 2012, 67–69).

Social Reactions

Beyond the physical, environmental, and economic stressors and constraints described above, the first settlers also experienced changes in and challenges to their social, political, and ideological realms. During the settlement period, Icelanders would have owned a number of seaworthy ships that they used to transport people and livestock to the island. The Icelandic sagas also tell of Viking raids, of trade missions to Europe, and of a mission of ships deployed to Greenland in the late tenth century. Connections to the Norwegian homeworld and to Europe would have been relatively frequent in the beginning but the number of ships may have been decreasing as early as the eleventh century due to the lack of suitable wood for ship construction (Jóhannesson 1956; Líndal 1974).

Archaeological investigations have identified distinctive shifts in the size, structure, and complexity of early medieval farmsteads in Skagafjörður (Bolender et al. 2011, 9). Initial settlements consisted of large, stratified households that consisted of a landowner, his family, his servants, and possibly his slaves. From the tenth through the early eleventh centuries, there is evidence that original farmstead properties were divided and that smaller, subsidiary farmsteads emerged (Steinberg et al. 2016) Demographic pressures, gradual environmental degradation, and decreased interseasonal predictability associated with climate shifts are likely contributors to social, political and economic changes in this period (Dugmore et al. 2007; McGovern et al. 2007; Vésteinsson et al. 2002), but see Geirsdóttir and colleagues (2009, 95) for an alternative interpretation of environmental degradation.

A major catalyst of social change in eleventh-century Iceland was the advent of Christianity. This major ideological shift brought about changes in burial customs that allow for a detailed bioarchaeological analysis of individual households. While the ideological beliefs of the original settlers were likely a mixture of paganism and Christianity, the country was essentially pagan until the official adoption of Christianity at the National Assembly in the year 999/1000 CE (Jóhannesson 1956; Sigurðsson 1999; Vésteinsson 2000). The burial landscape before people converted is markedly different from the Christian cemeteries that featured burials placed outside the homefield, often near roads or the boundaries of farms (Friðriksson and Vésteinsson 2011). The early burials are not representative of the farmstead population, since the majority of individuals are adult males; few women are present in early burials and children are almost absent (Friðriksson 2000; Zoëga 2014).

After conversion, farmstead churches arose and isolated burials were replaced with Christian cemeteries where numerous individuals from across the population began to be interred (Friðriksson 2000; Zoëga 2014). Individual farmsteads established their own churches and cemeteries where they buried their dead. How services were held and who performed them in these small household churches is unknown, but it has been suggested that their primary function would have been funerary (Vésteinsson 2000). This individualistic response to the new religion is different than what happened in Scandinavia, where the first churches that were built seem to have been mostly communal efforts (Gjerland and Keller 2009). This household management of cemeteries seems to suggest that individual farms had a certain degree of autonomy, but the widespread discontinuation of these cemeteries in the late eleventh and early twelfth centuries suggests that this autonomy was changing, perhaps as the church started to gain ground and power as an institution (Zoëga 2014). Since these cemeteries are temporally well defined—they were established around the time of the conversion and came out of use in the late eleventh and early twelfth centuries—the skeletal population represents about 100 years of a household. This potential that skeletal populations in each cemetery represent all members of a household over time, that these cemeteries are an excellent source for bioarchaeological study.

A regionwide archaeological survey, the Skagafjörður Church Project, has revealed the presence of over 130 possible early household churches/cemeteries in the Skagafjörður region. Fifteen of these have been investigated archaeologically (Sigurðardóttir 2012; Zoëga and Sigurðarson 2010). The research has shown that early Christian cemeteries in Skagafjörður are stylistically similar. They consist of round or oval turf-wall enclosures approximately 15–25 meters in diameter with a church in the center of the enclosure. Graves are predominantly found north, east, and south of the churches. The churches are firmly associated with a dwelling that was often only a few meters away. Excavation and analysis of the human remains from a number of these churches has revealed Christian-style inhumations oriented east to west with supine bodies. The individuals are typically buried without grave goods, though some individuals were interred in wooden coffins.

The sites of Keldudalur and Seyla are of interest to this study because they may reflect different experiences in the frontier space. Seyla, one of the larger farms in the area, was situated on a fertile slope. It retained its independent status up to modern times. Keldudalur is located on Hegranes, a rocky outcrop subject to environmental degradation. Although the farm was initially affluent, it was considerably smaller than Seyla and by the thirteenth century it had become a tenant farm. Both farms established Christian cemeteries around or just after 1000 CE. The Keldudalur cemetery was abandoned around 1100 CE and has yielded a relatively complete skeletal sample. In contrast, the church at Seyla and the occupants of half the graves were relocated to a new cemetery on the farm sometime in the eleventh century (Zoëga and Bolender 2017). The selective removal of some skeletons at Seyla differs from the pattern of interment seen at Keldudalur and may provide an intriguing glimpse into different responses by households on the frontier. What can the skeletal and mortuary data tell us about these two households on the frontier?

Materials and Methods

In this study, only relatively complete skeletons from discrete graves were included. The Keldudalur sample, which includes fifty-three individuals available for study (twenty-seven adults and twenty-six subadults), was more complete than the Seyla sample. Because of the selective removal of many of the burials at Seyla, only twelve individuals were available for study (three adults and nine subadults). Data from skeletal remains were collected for the following health status indicators: developmental perturbations (stature estimation, defects of dental enamel), porotic hyperostosis, infectious disease, trauma, degenerative joint disease, dental caries, and tooth loss (Goodman and Martin 2002, 18). Dental and skeletal pathology was observed and scored using criteria Ortner (2003) and Buikstra and Ubelaker (1994) have outlined. Age and sex estimations were based on the various methods Buikstra and Ubelaker (1994) have outlined. Additional criteria were followed for estimating the age of subadult skeletons based on epiphyseal fusion (Scheuer and Black 2000). Individuals were evaluated for skeletal and dental changes associated with (1) environmental stressors that impacted growth and development during childhood; (2) exposure to infectious pathogens; (3) evidence of impacts related to diet and behavior; and (4) traumatic and/or changes related to activity. More detailed discussion of these results as they pertain to Keldudalur can be found in Zoëga and Murphy (2016).

A variety of environmental stressors can disrupt an individual's skeletal growth and development during childhood. Impacts on linear growth were evaluated by collecting data on femoral length, calculating stature estimates, and comparing these data to appropriate referent populations (Zoëga and Murphy 2016). Defects of dental enamel (DDE) are also a reflection of health and dietary stressors during an individual's growth and development. Dentition was evaluated macroscopically in accordance with various methods (Goodman and Rose 1990; Hillson 1996) to identify evidence of DDE in either population.

The potential for health impacts due to diet and infectious diseases was also evaluated. Gastrointestinal infections, chronic dietary deficiencies and deficiencies of vitamin B_{12} and/or folic acid can result in an increase in the size of the diploic space and in cortical porosities of the cranial vault and orbits known as porotic hyperostosis and cribra orbitalia (Gowland and Western 2012; Walker et al. 2009). Similar skull porosities linked with forces associated with the masticatory process can be attributable to deficiencies of vitamin C or ascorbic acid—that is, scurvy insults (Ortner 2003; Stark 2014; Zuckerman et al. 2014).

Skeletal elements were observed for the presence of periostitis (proliferative and/or resorptive skeletal pathology). Other lesions were noted following methods in Buikstra and Ubelaker (1994; figure 3). Periostitis can result from primary exposure to pathogens such as tuberculosis, syphilis, actinomycosis, hydatidosis, and brucellosis (Aufderheide and Rodríguez-Martin 1998; Ortner 2003) or as a secondary response to traumatic injuries. Finally, degenerative joint disease can lead to changes in the joint surfaces of the skeleton. All skeletal material was examined for the presence or absence of degenerative joint changes and results were recorded using criteria from Buikstra and Ubelaker (1994).

Social Analyses of the Burial Data

The skeletal assemblage and burial data from these cemeteries offer a unique view of household-based actions and of possible social differentiation. The facts that early Christian graves tend to be simple in form and lack grave goods have prompted the assumption that they lack the potential for interpreting social status. In recent years, however, various scholars have pointed out the interpretive possibilities of early Christian cemeteries (Andrén 2000; Gilchrist and Sloane 2005; Jonsson 2009b). Even though both Keldudalur and Seyla contain simple inhumations without grave goods, social analysis may be attempted through a combination of osteological and archaeological analysis. Factors such as the age, sex, stature, paleopathology, burial furnishings, and location of burials in a cemetery may also offer important clues about a society (Arcini 1999; Gilchrist and Sloane 2005; Jonsson 2009b).

Patterns Associated with Age

Demographic profiles for each cemetery reveal roughly equal proportions of adults and subadults (figure 7.2; figure 7.3). For both sites, the majority of the

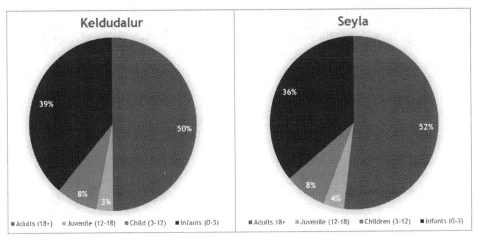

Figure 7.2. Pie graphs showing the distribution of age at the Keldudalur and Seyla cemeteries.

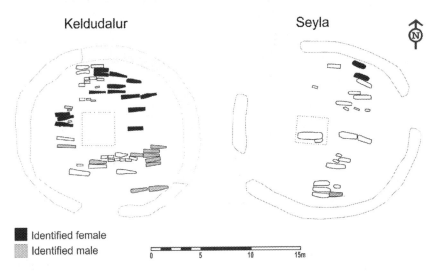

Figure 7.3. Drawing showing sex distribution of the burials at the Keldudalur and Seyla cemeteries. Drawing by Guðný Zoëga.

subadults consisted of infants less than 3 years old. At Keldudalur this group accounted for 39 percent of subadults and at Seyla it accounted for 36 percent. The proportion of individuals in the category of child (3–12 years) and juvenile (12–18 years) was identical, accounting for 8 percent of each population. Within the adult categories at Keldudalur, 12 of 27 adults were 45+ years of age, 7 were 30–44 years, and 4 were 18–30 years. At Seyla, only four adults remained in the cemetery. One was 45+ years, two were 30–44 years, and one was too fragmentary to assign an age range. Skeletal pathologies can vary by age and/or sex (Hollimon 2011; Martin et al. 2013; Soafer 2011). Growth and development perturbations impact the skeletons of subadults and can remain present in adults, while degenerative changes are typically evidenced among adults. In addition, dietary deficiencies and infectious disease have the potential to pattern based on age and sex.

Evidence that suggests that environmental stressors impacted growth and development are present at both sites (table 7.1). At Keldudalur, average adult male stature (n = 9) was 166.4 centimeters, shorter than comparative samples from the British Isles and Northern Europe but similar to the early medieval site of Hrísbrú in Iceland (167.32cm) (Walker et al. 2004). Interestingly, the earlier settlers in eastern Greenland were taller on average (173.5 centimeters) than the adult males at Keldudalur. Later settlers in western Greenland seem to have been shorter than early settlers at the eastern Greenland sites and the individuals from Keldudalur. The average height of adult females from Keldudalur did not vary as much from the average heights at sites in Greenland and Iceland, but they are shorter than those of populations from Northern Europe and the British Isles. Stature at Seyla was more ambiguous because of the small sample size. Adult females (n = 2) seem to have been shorter on average (149.9 centimeters) than females at all the other North Atlantic sites in table 7.1 and the height of the sole adult male (171.2 centimeters) was more similar to estimates from sites outside Iceland except for sites in western Greenland (162) (Lynnerup 1998).

DDE are often the result of nutritional deficiency, infection, and/or other environmental stressors that occur during childhood when enamel is forming. At Keldudalur, 33.3 percent of the individuals (7 of 21) had evidence of DDE (see figure 7.4 for an example). DDE was not as common among the adults; this is most likely due to the loss of evidence of DDE associated with underrepresentation of DDE-affected teeth in adults due to effects of increasing tooth wear and tooth loss during the life course. At Seyla, four of six individuals (66.6 percent) had evidence of DDE (figure 7.4). While the sample size for Seyla was much smaller, the pattern of DDE among subadults and adults was similar to that of Keldudalur. Given the potential for disturbances to growth and development at each site and the high rate of infant mortality as evidenced by the high proportion of infants under 3 years of age at Keldudalur (39 percent) and Seyla (36 percent), childhood seems to have been a stressful time in this region.

Table 7.1. Comparison of the stature of human remains in medieval cemeteries in the North Atlantic

Site	Female				Male				Source
	N	Max. Femur Length (mm)	T and G[a] (cm)	Boldsen[b] (cm)	N	Max. Femur Length (mm)	T and G[a] (cm)	Boldsen[b] (cm)	
Keldudalur	11	415.9	156.6	155.9	9	434.7	166.4	162.4	Zoëga and Murphy 2016
Seyla	2	385.5	149.9	148.3	1	447	171.2	165.5	
Hrisbrú, Iceland	-	-	-	-	-	438.7	167.3	163.4	Walker et al. 2004
Skeljastadir, Iceland	24	421.1	158.1	157.2	27	458.5	171.9	168.5	Gestsdóttir 2004
Early Eastern Greenland	2	402.8	153.6	152.6	11	467.0	173.5	171.5	Lynnerup 1998
Late Western Greenland	16	411.3	154.8	154.7	5	425.0	162.0	159.34	Lynnerup 1998
St. Mary's, Bergen, Norway	10	428.7	160.0	159.2	8	457.6	171.7	168.2	Lorvik 2009
Trondheim, Norway	48	421.1	157.2	158.1	42	457.3	171.6	168.0	Hanson 1992
Hamar, Norway	-	427.5	159.7	159.0	-	473.1	175.3	172.0	Sellevold 2001
St. Peter's Waterford, Ireland	23	430.4	160.4	159.5	36	451.2	170.2	166.5	Power 1994
Medieval Scotland	58	427.5	159.7	159.0	60	445.6	168.9	165.2	Jennings 2010

[a] Stature calculated using stature formulae from Trotter and Gleser (1952).
[b] Stature calculated using stature formulae from Boldsen (1984).

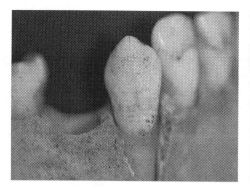
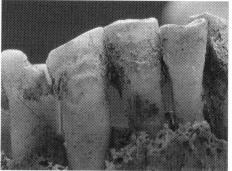

Figure 7.4. Defects of dental enamel at Keldudalur (*l*) and Seyla (*r*). Photographs by Kimmarie Murphy.

Table 7.2. Summary of pathologies at Keldudalur and Seyla by frequency and percent

	Defects of Dental Enamel		Porotic Hyperostosis		Degenerative Joint Disease		Periostitis/ Trauma	
	N	%	N	%	N	%	N	%
KELDUDALUR								
Infants and subadults	5/21	24.0	7/22	32.0	0/22	0.0	3/22	13.6
Females	2/7	29.0	4/14	29.0	10/14	71.4	4/14	29.0
Males	1/9	11.1	8/11	73.0	9/11	82.0	8/11	73.0
Total	7/21	33.3	19/47	19.1	19/47	19.1	15/47	32.0
SEYLA								
Infants and subadults	2/3	66.6	3/6	50.0	0/6	0.0	1/6	16.7
Females	1/2	50.0	0/2	0.0	2/2	100.0	1/2	50.0
Males	1/1	100.0	1/1	100.0	1/1	100.0	1/1	100.0
Total	4/6	66.6	4/9	44.4	3/9	33.3	3/9	33.3

A review of other pathologies (see table 7.2) shows that degenerative joint disease and periostitis/trauma increased with age at both Keldudalur and Seyla. In an early analysis of the pathologies at Keldudalur, Zoëga and Murphy found that both abscessing and antemortem tooth loss increased with age (2016). Unfortunately, the sample size at Seyla is too small to draw any real conclusions about age-related dental pathologies, although two of the three adults exhibit both abscesses and antemortem tooth loss.

Patterns Associated with Sex Differences

At both Keldudalur and Seyla, the sexes were segregated in the cemetery: women were buried to the north of the church, men to the south. Such sex segregation is known in other early Christian cemeteries in Iceland and Greenland and Scandinavia and is described in one instance in the Christianity section of the medieval Norwegian provincial laws (Jonsson 2009a; Kieffer-Olsen 1993; Lynnerup 1998; Nilsson 1994; Steffensen 1943). Although it was not possible to estimate sex for the subadults, they seem to have been equally distributed in the male and female halves of the cemetery at both sites. The presence of periostitis and trauma at Keldudalur was less for females (29 percent) and greater for males (73 percent). At Seyla, one male adult showed evidence of trauma to the arm and an adult of indeterminate sex found on the south side of the chapel had evidence of trauma to the lower leg. No evidence for trauma was found on the northern side of the church in the female burials. DDE were common among both females (2 of 7) and males (1 of 9) at Keldudalur. Similarly, at Seyla both adult females showed evidence of DDE, as did the one adult male with dentition. Possible scurvy was identified in one juvenile skeleton at Keldudalur (Zoëga and Murphy, 2016). At Seyla, an estimated female had lesion patterning on the greater wings of the sphenoid consistent with scurvy, as did the single adult male (Ortner 2003; Stark 2014; Zuckerman et al. 2014). Porotic hyperostosis was more common in the males at Keldudalur (8 of 11) than in the females (4 of 14) at the site. At Seyla, porotic hyperostosis was found in the one adult male and in three of the subadults located on the female side of the chapel. Finally, degenerative joint disease was found in similar proportions at Keldudalur, occurring in 71.4 percent of females and 82 percent of males. Both male and female adults at Seyla had evidence of degenerative joint disease.

Patterns Associated with Status Differences

The oldest Christianity section of early Norwegian provincial laws detail where certain social groups are to be placed in a cemetery: church owners next to the church and slaves out by the churchyard wall (Halvorsen and Rindal 2008). Without the presence of grave goods at either site, status differences are difficult to ascertain. While there was evidence for coffins in about 70 percent of the graves at both cemeteries, no coffins were associated with graves near the cemetery wall (see figure 7.5). At Seyla, those who were left behind were subadults and adults buried by the cemetery wall. If the selective removal at Seyla and the lack of coffins in the outer cemetery are interpreted

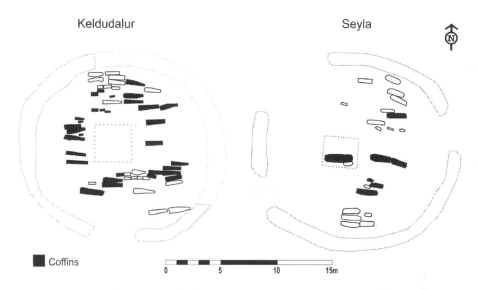

Figure 7.5. Drawing of the location of coffin graves in the Keldudalur and Seyla cemeteries. Drawing by Guðný Zoëga.

as indicators of social status, a similar form of social division may have been practiced in the two cemeteries.

Pathology has also been associated with social status and position in early Christian cemeteries. Differential location for the sick or the socially distinctive has been reported and in some cases these seem to have been located by the cemetery wall (Andrén 2000; Arcini 1999; Hadley 2010). At Keldudalur, there was little that pointed to pathology patterning based on position in the cemetery—in other words, individuals closer to walls did not have more pathology than those nearer to the chapel. At Seyla, three adult individuals who were located closer to turf walls did have a number of pathologies indicative of a variety of environmental stressors. More detailed work at other household cemeteries is needed to establish whether there is evidence for patterning of pathology based on status.

Discussion

At the outset of this chapter we argued that early settlement in Iceland represented a frontier space where environmental constraints placed settlers at the limits of sustainable subsistence practices and the balancing of older traditions and behaviors with new responses to the frontier space could lead to flux in political, economic, and ideological realms of practice. The case studies of the Keldudalur and Seyla cemeteries give us an intriguing view of two households that were to some degree culturally, ideologically, and socially connected to the outside world but at the same time had a physical existence that can only be termed precarious. Viking Age households existed in many shapes and sizes in Iceland, from only a single individual to complex households where more than one family shared a dwelling. Add to that slaves, servants, dependent relatives, children, and possible foster children (Miller 1988, 1990; Sigurðsson 2008). The bioarchaeological interpretation of both households suggests that the numbers of men and women were roughly equal and that there would have likely been approximately eight to ten people in the household at any given time. Infant mortality was high, but after the first year chances for survival increased dramatically. Taking infant death into account, average life expectancy would have come to about 20 years; if only adults are considered, the average life expectancy was about 40 (Zoëga 2015).

The skeletal evidence at the two sites points to members of households living in and adapting to a subarctic environment that was harsh and periodically resource scarce. The analysis reveals a number of skeletal pathologies that are indicative of nonspecific environmental stressors, such as potentially shorter stature, DDE, and porotic hyperostosis. Individuals from both households have lesions that may be attributable to scurvy, indicating the possibility of seasonal shortages. Many years of hard agricultural work and treacherous weather conditions may have contributed to the common occurrence of degenerative joint disease and periostitis and trauma in both households. Unlike previous reports from the site of Hrísbrú in Iceland (Walker et al. 2004), there is no distinctive diagnostic evidence for infectious diseases such as brucellosis or tuberculosis, although they cannot be ruled out. There is little to indicate differences in mortality between men and women, but the high rates of infant death support the interpretation that numerous environmental and/or social stressors existed (Zoëga and Murphy 2016).

The funerary data indicate a population that was well versed in Christian traditions from early on and the few finds that have been retrieved show that there was a cross-Atlantic transmission of both ideology and goods (Zoëga and Traustadóttir 2007). According to the written sources, some of the original settlers were Christian and many would have come in contact with Christianity on trading voyages or raids. The knowledge of traditions may also have spread by word of mouth and through the activities of foreign missionary priests. The advent of Christianity had a profound effect on burial traditions. Even if it is impossible to estimate whether all individuals in the cemetery viewed themselves as Christian, it seems evident that the cemeteries were meant to represent the notion of a Christian household, a bounded individual social unit that also belonged to the wider Christian community (Zoëga and Bolender 2017). Belonging to the Christian community potentially meant that all individuals had a place in the household cemetery, irrespective of social status.

However, all were not equal in the household, as the cemeteries seem to show evidence of social stratification including different treatment of the dead in the outlying areas of the cemetery and selective removal of bodies when cemeteries were discontinued. The cemeteries were thus not only a bounded sacred area in the farmstead but also, to a certain degree, an avenue of expression of social boundaries and possibly exclusion (Gilchrist and Sloane 2005; Hadley 2001; Lucy and Reynolds 2002; Williams 2006).

The life of the pioneer was likely difficult, both in terms of physical exertion and the social uncertainty those who settled in an unknown and uninhabited landscape experienced. None of the individuals lying in the cemeteries are likely to have belonged to the original group of ninth-century settlers, but they definitely included individuals born in the tenth century, the first century of settlement. The obvious signs of stress markers in the Keldudalur and Seyla skeletal material suggests that even after 100 years of settlement, living conditions were still demanding and that periodic shortages were a way of life for the population. It is known from the written sources that there was a widespread famine in the late tenth century that coincided with a reported famine in Norway. Another such episode is reported in the middle of the eleventh century, a countrywide event that, according to the sources, prompted the king of Norway to send four ships to Iceland to provide aid and to transport poor and displaced people back to Norway (Finnsson 1970). A number of isolated "bad" years are also reported. Data are not likely to exist for all such episodes, not least when they would have happened at a more regional level. Thus, even if the climate was generally mild, the recurring "bad" years or epochs would have seriously impacted people's livelihood and chances of survival and made a mark on the household for some time after conditions had improved. It would have taken some time to repopulate livestock that had died and nutritional deficiency would have impacted the health and survival rate of infants. Hence, eleventh-century Skagafjörður was still very much on the edge of what could be termed sustainable or viable for survival, evoking the frontier environment suggested by Oram and Adderley (2011, 125).

That being said, the number of "older" individuals also suggests remarkable tenacity of a section of the population. This may reflect the reality that even if the recurring "bad" periods were taxing or in some instances even devastating, the overall long-term living conditions were sustainable and the population was able to use countermeasures that would have increased the likelihood of survival through successful management of resources (Jesch 2015). Social ties of both kinship and friendship were also an important part of the support system and the communally organized *hreppr* municipality system was in place to aid those who fell upon hard times (Miller 1990; Sigurðsson 2008). So although each household was largely responsible for its own economic success, it was effectively a part of a larger, interconnected community.

Conclusion

In conclusion, the osteological analyses from both sites support the interpretations that the frontier landscape subjected settlers to periodically harsh and demanding living conditions. They also highlight the fact that people managed to survive and counteract these conditions, indicating a high level of social adaptation and the implementation of successful survival strategies. The comparison of bioarchaeological features from the sites of Keldudalur and Seyla in the Skagafjörður region of northern Iceland reveals the constant state of flux the early Christians in the area experienced. The geographically and environmentally marginal conditions in the north meant that settlers had to strive to maintain a precarious balance between success and failure. Unlike many frontier lands that were eventually transformed into stable, permanent settlements, the northern Icelanders occupied a liminal space on the landscape and were continually forced to adjust and adapt to environmental instability.

Acknowledgments

This preliminary analysis is part of a large ongoing multidisciplinary archaeological project funded by the National Science Foundation (PLR 1417772) aimed at systematically researching Viking Age and medieval settlement patterns in relation to the early Christian cemeteries in Skagafjörður. Additional funding was also obtained from internal grants at Kenyon College.

References

Abulafia D., and N. Berend. 2002. *Medieval Frontiers: Concepts and Practices.* Aldershot: Ashgate.

Andrén, A. 2000. "Ad sanctos—de dödas plats under medeltiden." *Hikuin* 27: 7–26.

Arcini, C. 1999. *Health and Disease in Early Lund: Osteopathologic Studies of 3,305 Individuals Buried in the First Cemetery Area of Lund, 990–1536.* Lund: Medical Faculty Lund University.

Aufderheide, A. C., and C. Rodríguez-Martin. 1998. *The Cambridge Encyclopedia of Human Palaeopathology.* Cambridge: Cambridge University Press.

Axford, Y., C. S. Andresen, J. T. Andrews, S. T. Belt, Á. Geirsdóttir, G. Massé, G. H. Miller, S. Ólafsdóttir, and L. L. Vare. 2011. "Do Paleoclimate Proxies Agree? A Test Comparing 19 Late Holocene Climate and Sea-Ice Reconstructions from Icelandic Marine and Lake Sediments." *Journal of Quaternary Science* 26(6): 645–656.

Axford, Y., Á. Geirsdóttir, G. Miller, and P. Langdon. 2009. "Climate of the Little Ice Age and the Past 2000 Years in Northeast Iceland Inferred from Chironomids and Other Lake Sediment Proxies." *Journal of Paleolimnology* 41(1): 7–24.

Boldsen, J. 1984. "A Statistical Evaluation of the Basis for Predicting Stature from Lengths of Long Bones in European Populations." *American Journal of Physical Anthropology* 65(3): 305–311.

Bolender, D. J., J. M. Steinberg, and B. N. Damiata. 2011. "Farmstead Relocation at the End of the Viking Age, Results of the Skagafjörður Archaeological Settlement Survey." *Archaeologia Islandica Rit Fornleifastofnunar* Íslands 9: 77–99.

Buikstra, J. E., and D. H. Ubelaker. 1994. *Standards for Data Collection from Human Skeletal Remains.* Arkansas Archeological Survey Research Series no. 44. Fayetteville: Arkansas Archeological Survey.

Byock, J. 2001. *Viking Age Iceland.* London: Penguin.

Dugmore, A., D. Borthwick, M. Church, A. Dawson, K. Edwards, C. Keller, P. Mayewski, T. McGovern, K.-A. Mairs, and G. Sveinbjarnardóttir. 2007. "The Role of Climate in Settlement and Landscape Change in the North Atlantic Islands: An Assessment of Cumulative Deviations in High-Resolution Proxy Climate Records." *Human Ecology: An Interdisciplinary Journal* 35(2): 169–178.

Dugmore, A., and O. Vésteinsson. 2012. "Black Sun, High Flame, and Flood: Volcanic Hazards in Iceland." In *Surviving Sudden Environmental Change: Understanding Hazards, Mitigating Impacts, Avoiding Disasters,* edited by J. Cooper and P. Sheets, 67–90. Boulder: University Press of Colorado.

Edwards, K. J., I. T. Lawson, E. Erlendsson, and A. J. Dugmore. 2005. "Landscapes of Contrast in Viking Age Iceland and the Faroe Islands." *Landscapes* 6(2): 63–81.

Finnsson, H. 1970. *Mannfækkun af hallærum.* Reykjavík: Almenna bókafélagið.

Friðriksson, A. 2000. "Viking Burial Practices in Iceland." In *Kuml og haugfé,* edited by A. Friðriksson, 549–610. Reykjavík: Mál og menning.

Friðriksson, A., and O. Vésteinsson. 2011. "Landscapes of Burial: Contrasting the Pagan and Christian Paradigms of Burial in Viking Age and Medieval Iceland." *Archaeologia Islandica Rit Fornleifastofnunar* Íslands 9: 50–64.

Geirsdóttir, Á., G. Mille, T. Thordarson, and K. Ólafsdóttir. 2009. "A 2000 Year Record of Climate Variations Reconstructed from Haukadalsvatn, West Iceland." *Journal of Paleolimnology* 41(1): 95–115.

Gestsdóttir, H. 2004. *The Palaeopathology of Iceland: Preliminary Report 2003*. Reykjavík: Fornleifastofnun Íslands.

Gilchrist, R., and B. Sloane. 2005. *Requiem. The Medieval Monastic Cemetery in Britain*. London: Museum of London Archaeology Service.

Gjerland, B., and C. Keller. 2009. "Graves and Churches of the Norse in the North Atlantic: A Pilot Study." *Journal of the North Atlantic* 2(Sp2): 161–177.

Goodman, A., and D. Martin. 2002. "Reconstruction of Health Profiles from Skeletal Remains." In *The Backbone of History: Health and Nutrition in the Western Hemisphere*, edited by R. H. Stecke and J. C. Rose, 11–60. Cambridge: Cambridge University Press.

Goodman, A., and J. C. Rose. 1990. "Assessment of Systemic Physiological Perturbations from Dental Enamel Hypoplasia and Associated Histological Structures." *Yearbook of Physical Anthropology* 33: 59–110.

Gowland, R. L., and A. G. Western. 2012. "Morbidity in the Marshes: Using Spatial Epidemiology to Investigate Skeletal Evidence for Malaria in Anglo-Saxon England (AD 410–1050." *American Journal of Physical Anthropology* 147(2): 301–311.

Hadley, D. M. 2001. *Death in Medieval England*. Stroud: Tempus.

———. 2010. "Burying the Socially and Physically Distinctive in Later Anglo-Saxon England." In *Burial in Later Anglo-Saxon England, c. 650–1100 AD*, edited by J. L. Buckberry, and A. Cherryson, 93–115. Oxford: Oxbow Books.

Halvorsen, E. F., and M. Rindal. 2008. *De eldste Østlandske kristenrettene. Riksarkivet Norrøne tekster*. Oslo: Riksarkivet.

Hanson, C. L. 1992. "Population-Specific Stature Reconstruction for Medieval Trondheim, Norway." *International Journal of Osteoarchaeology* 2(4): 289–295.

Hillson, S. 1996. *Dental Anthropology*. Cambridge: University Press.

Hollimon, S. E. 2011. "Sex and Gender in Bioarchaeological Research." In *Social Bioarchaeology*, edited by S. C. Agarwal, 149–182. Chichester: Wiley-Blackwell.

Jennings, J. D. 2010. "Stress along the Medieval Anglo Scottish Border? Skeletal Indicators of Conflict-Zone Health." PhD diss., University of Durham.

Jesch, J. 2015. *The Viking Diaspora*. London: Routledge.

Jóhannesson, J. 1956. Íslendinga *saga I*. Þjóðveldisöld. Reykjavík: Almenna bókafélagið.

Jonsson, K. 2009a. "Bodily Dimensions in Medieval Burials: On Age and Gender Structures in Socially Stratified Churchyards." In *From Ephesos to Dalecarlia: Reflections on Body, Space and Time in Medieval and Early Modern Europe*, edited by E. Regner, C. von Heijne, Åhfeldt L. Kitzler, and A. Kjellström, 119–144. Stockholm: Museum of National Antiquities.

———. 2009b. *Practices for the Living and the Dead*. Stockholm: Stockholm University.

Karlsson, G. 2000. *Iceland's 1100 Years: History of a Marginal Society*. London: C. Hurst.

———. 2016. *Landnám* Íslands. Reykjavík: Háskólaútgáfan.

Kieffer-Olsen, J. 1993. *Grav og gravskik i det middelalderlige Danmark—8 kirkegårdsudgravninger*. Højbjerg: University of Aarhus.

Lightfoot, K. G., and A. Martinez. 1995. "Frontiers and Boundaries in Archaeological Perspective." *Annual Review of Anthropology* 24: 471.

Lorvik, K. 2009. "Life and Death in the Early Town: An Osteoarchaeological Study of the

Human Skeletal Remains from St Mary´s Churchyard, Bergen." In *Osteoarchaeological Analyses From Medieval Bergen* edited by I. Øye, 19–116. Bergen: Fagbokforlaget.

Líndal, S. 1974. Ísland og umheimurinn." In *Saga Íslands*, vol. 1, edited by S. Líndal, 199–223. Reykjavík: Hið íslenzka bókmenntafélag.

Lucy, S., and A. J. Reynolds, eds. 2002. *The Anglo-Saxon Way of Death: Burial Rites in Early England*. Stroud: Stroud-Sutton.

Lynnerup, N. 1998. *The Greenland Norse. A Biological-Anthropological Study*. Copenhagen: Museum Tusculanum Press.

Martens, W. J. M. 1998. "Climate Change, Thermal Stress and Mortality Changes." *Social Science and Medicine* 46(3): 331–344.

Martin, D. L., R. P. Harrod, and V. R. Pérez. 2013. *Bioarchaeology: An Integrated Approach to Working with Human Remains*. New York: Springer.

McGovern, T. H., R. Edvarsson, O. Vésteinsson, G. Lucas, A. Fridriksson, O. Aldred, M. Church, A. Dugmore, A. Newton, I. Lawson et al. 2007. "Landscapes of Settlement in Northern Iceland: Historical Ecology of Human Impact and Climate Fluctuation on the Millennial Scale." *American Anthropologist* 109(1): 27–51.

Merisalo, O., ed. 2006. *Frontiers in the Middle Ages: Proceedings of the Third European Congress of Medieval studies (Jyväskylä, 10–14 June 2003). The Third European Congress of the Medieval Studies*. Louvain-la-Neuve: Brepols.

Miller, W. I. 1988. "Some Aspects of Householding in the Medieval Icelandic Commonwealth." *Continuity and Change* 3(3): 321–355.

———. 1990. *Bloodtaking and Peacemaking: Feud, Law, and Society in Saga Iceland*. Chicago: University of Chicago Press.

Naum, M. 2010. "Re-Emerging Frontiers: Postcolonial Theory and Historical Archaeology of the Borderlands." *Journal of Archaeological Method and Theory* 17(2): 101–131.

Nilsson, B. 1994. *Kvinnor, män och barn på medeltida begravningsplatser*. Uppsala: Lunne böcker.

Ogilvie, A. E. J., L. K. Barlow, and A. E. Jennings. 2000. "North Atlantic Climate c. AD 1000: Millennial Reflections on the Viking Discoveries of Iceland, Greenland and North America." *Weather* 55(2): 34–45.

Ogilvie, A. E. J., and J. Jónsdóttir. 2000. "Sea Ice, Climate, and Icelandic Fisheries in the Eighteenth and Nineteenth Century." *Arctic* 53(4): 383–394.

Ogilvie, A. E. J., and T. Jónsson. 2001. "'Little Ice Age' Research: A Perspective from Iceland." *Climatic Change* 48(1): 9–52.

Ogilvie, A. E. J., J. M. Woollett, K. Smiarowski, J. Arneborg, S. Troelstra, A. Kuijpers, A. Pálsdóttir, and T. H. McGovern. 2009. "Seals and Sea Ice in Medieval Greenland." *Journal of the North Atlantic* 2: 60–80.

Oram, R., and P. Adderley. 2011. "Innse Gall: Culture and Environment on a Norse Frontier in the Scottish Western Isles." In *The Norwegian Domination and the Norse World c. 1100–c. 1400*, edited by S. Imsen 125–148. Trondheim: Rostra Books.

Ortner, D. J. 2003. *Identification of Pathological Conditions in Human Skeletal Remains*. San Diego: Academic Press.

Parker, B. J. 2006. "Toward an Understanding of Borderland Processes." *American Antiquity* 71(1): 77–100.

Patterson, W. P., K. Dietrich, C. Holmden, and J. Andrews. 2010. "Two Millennia of

North Atlantic Seasonality and Implications for Norse Colonies." *Proceedings of the National Academy of Sciences* 107(12): 5306–5310.

Power, C. 1994. "A Demographic Study of Human Skeletal Populations from Historic Munster." *Ulster Journal of Archaeology* 23(1): 67–79.

Scheuer, L., and S. M. Black. 2000. *Developmental Juvenile Osteology*. San Diego, CA: Academic Press.

Sellevold, B. J. 2001. "From Death to Life in Medieval Hamar: Skeletons and Graves as Historical Source Material." PhD diss., University of Oslo.

Sigurðardóttir, S. 2012. *Skagfirska kirkjurannsóknin. Miðaldakirkjur 1000–1300*. Akureyri: Byggðasafn Skagfirðinga.

Sigurðsson, J. V. 1999. *Chieftains and Power in the Icelandic Commonwealth*. Odense: Odense University Press.

———. 2008. "Becoming 'Old': Ageism and Taking Care of the Elderly in Iceland, c. 933–1300." In *Youth and Age in the Medieval North*, edited by S. Lewis-Simpson, 227–242. Leiden: Brill.

Siikala, A.-L., and J. Siikala. 2005. *Return to Culture: Oral Tradition and Society in the Southern Cook Islands*. Helsinki: Suomalainen tiedeakatemia.

Smith, K. 1995. "Landnám: The Settlement of Iceland in Archaeological and Historical Perspective." *World Archaeology* 26(3): 319–347.

Soafer, J. R. 2011. "Towards a Social Bioarchaeology of Age." In *Social Bioarchaeology*, edited by S. C. Agarwal and B. A. Glencross 285–311. Chichester: Wiley-Blackwell.

Stark, R. J. 2014. "A Proposed Framework for the Study of Paleopathological Cases of Subadult Scurvy." *International Journal of Paleopathology* 5: 18–26.

Steffensen, J. 1943. "Knoglerne fra Skeljastaðir i Þjórsárdalur." In *Forntida gårdar i Island: meddelanden från den nordiska arkeologiska undersökningen i Island sommaren 1939*, edited by M. Stenberger and A. Roussell, 227–260. Copenhagen: Munksgaard.

Steinberg, J. M., D. J. Bolender, and B. N. Damiata. 2016. "Viking Age Settlement Patterns in Northern Iceland: Initial Results of the Skagafjörður Archaeological Settlement Survey." *Journal of Field Archaeology* 41(4): 389–412.

Sveinbjarnardóttir, G. 1992. *Farm Abandonment in Medieval and Post-Medieval Iceland: An Interdisciplinary Study*. Oxford: Oxbow Books.

Sveinbjörnsdóttir, Á. E., J. Heinemeier, J. Arneborg, N. Lynnerup, G. Ólafsson, and G. Zoëga. 2010. "Dietary Reconstructions and Reservoir Correction of 14C Dates on Bones from Pagan and Early Christian Graves in Iceland." *Radiocarbon* 52(2–3): 682–696.

Trotter, M., and G. C. Gleser. 1952. "Estimation of Stature from Long Bones of American Whites and Negroes." *American Journal of Physical Anthropology* 10: 463–514.

Vésteinsson, O. 2000. *The Christianization of Iceland: Priests, Power and Social Change 1000–1300*. Oxford: Oxford University Press.

Vésteinsson, O., and T. H. McGovern. 2012. "The Peopling of Iceland." *Norwegian Archaeological Review* 45(2): 206–218.

Vésteinsson, O., T. H. McGovern, and C. Keller. 2002. "Enduring Impacts: Social and Environmental Aspects of Viking Age Settlement in Iceland and Greenland." *Archaeologia Islandica* 2: 98–136.

Walker, P. L., R. R. Bathurst, R. Richman, T. Gjerdrum, and V. A. Andrushko. 2009.

"The Causes of Porotic Hyperostosis and Cribra Orbitalia: A Reappraisal of the Iron-Deficiency-Anemia Hypothesis." *American Journal of Physical Anthropology* 139(2): 109–125.

Walker, P. L., J. Byock, J. T. Eng, J. M. Erlandson, P. Holck, K. Prizer, and M. A. Tveskov. 2004. "Bioarchaeological Evidence for the Health Status of an Early Icelandic Population." *American Journal of Physical Anthropology* supplement 38: 204.

Williams, H. 2006. *Death and Memory in Early Medieval Britain.* Cambridge: Cambridge University Press.

Ylimaunu, T., S. Lakomäki, T. Kallio-Seppä, P. R. Mullins, R. Nurmi, and M. Kuorilehto. 2014. "Borderlands as Spaces: Creating Third Spaces and Fractured Landscapes in Medieval Northern Finland." *Journal of Social Archaeology* 14(2): 244–267.

Young, T. K., and T. M. Mäkinen. 2010. "The Health of Arctic Populations: Does Cold Matter?" *American Journal of Human Biology* 22(1): 129–133.

Zoëga, G. 2009. "Fólkið í Keldudal." In *Endurfundir Fornleifarannsóknir styrktar af Kristnihátíðarsjóði 2001–2005,* edited by G. Ólafsson and S. Kristjánsdóttir, 30–43. Reykjavík: Þjóðminjasafn Íslands.

———. 2014. "Early Church Organization of Skagafjörður, North Iceland: The Results of the Skagafjörður Church Project." *Collegium Medievale* 27: 23–62.

———. 2015. "A Family Revisited: The Medieval Household Cemetery of Keldudalur, North Iceland." *Norwegian Archaeological Review* 48(2): 1–20.

Zoëga, G., and D. J. Bolender. 2017. "An Archaeology of Moments: Christian Conversion and Practice in a Medieval Household Cemetery." *Journal of Social Archaeology* 17(1): 69–91.

Zoëga, G., and K. Murphy. 2016. "Life on the Edge of the Arctic: The Bioarchaeology of the Keldudalur Cemetery in Skagafjörður, Iceland." *International Journal of Osteoarchaeology* 26(4): 574–584.

Zoëga, G., and G. S. Sigurðarson. 2010. "Skagfirska kirkjurannsóknin." In Árbók *hinz* íslenska *fornleifafélags, 2010,* edited by S. Sigmundsson, 95–116. Reykjavík: Hinz Íslenska Fornleifafélags

Zoëga, G., and R. Traustadóttir. 2007. "Keldudalur: A Sacred Place in Pagan and Christian Times in Iceland." In *Cultural Interaction between East and West: Archaeology, Artefacts and Human Contacts in Northern Europe,* edited by U. Fransson, M. Svedin, S. Bergerbrant, and F. Androshchuk, 225–230. Stockholm: University of Stockholm.

Zuckerman, M. K., E. M. Garofalo, B. Frohlich, and D. J. Ortner. 2014. "Anemia or Scurvy: A Pilot Study on Differential Diagnosis of Porous and Hyperostotic Lesions Using Differential Cranial Vault Thickness in Subadult Humans." *International Journal of Paleopathology* 5: 27–33.

IV

Violence on the Frontier

8

A Mass Grave outside the Walls

The Commingled Assemblage from Ibida

ANDREI SOFICARU, CLAUDIA RADU,
AND CRISTINA I. TICA

The Lower Danube Frontier in the Later Roman Empire

During the later empire, Romans came to see the concept of imperial frontiers as significant, and by the later fourth century its inhabitants saw the empire as a bounded territory and themselves separated not only culturally but also physically from the different groups outside the empire (Graham 2006). As imperial political boundaries collapsed or shifted, increased news from and about the peripheries cemented the frontiers as a key topic of discussion and an important indicator of the coherence of the empire. In other words, "frontier consciousness reached its zenith" (Graham 2006, 121), a situation similar to what we are seeing today in our society.

Even if Romans from the third century onward started to think about their territories more in terms of bounded holdings and not just as partitions between people that were enclosed by natural frontiers such as rivers, deserts, and mountains (Graham 2006, 45), the frontier was a fluid series of overlapping zones, not a line or a simple zone (Elton 1996, 4). However, perceiving the Danube, for example, as a border marker did not preclude the frontier from becoming a mixture of political, social, ethnic, religious, linguistic, economic, and military boundaries. In addition, different groups defined their own boundaries of different types. Sometimes these coincided with the boundaries of other groups, but they did not have to. Together, these overlapping boundaries constituted the frontier (Elton 1996, 4–5). Far from being natural lines, frontiers are and always have been "ethnically confused" (Whittaker 1994, 62). The frontier has cultural and intellectual significance since it is a site where entire societies negotiate and transform their identities. Thus, it becomes a "vital force" in shaping a society, as the American historian Frederick Jackson Turner asserted (Graham 2006, 165).

This chapter focuses on the Roman frontier province of Scythia Minor during the fourth–sixth centuries CE in an attempt to get a glimpse of how life on the frontier might have worked. Scythia Minor (modern Dobrudja in southeastern Romania), which encompassed over 400 years of history, covered the strip of land between the lower Danube and the Black Sea (see figure 8.1). At that time, the lower Danube was a key frontier for the empire (Whittaker 1994, 173).

Over the duration of the Romano-Byzantine period, the region was divided into overlapping indigenous, Greek, and Roman political and cultural domains. The interior hinterland was occupied by indigenous Iron Age populations that the Romans colonized. The Roman imperial administration also took over the well-established Greek cities on the coast of the Black Sea, and the Roman army and navy established military bases along the Danube, a land-based porous frontier.

Rome created Scythia Minor as a buffer zone with provincial *limes* (Ellis 2011, 242). In the Roman eyes, *limes* was more than just a term that referred to a border that divided Roman-controlled territory from non-Roman territory; it was a psychological frontier between "us" and "them," the border of civilization itself. The epithets "barbarian" and "*barbaricum*" (the land beyond the *limes*, beyond Roman administrative control) are thus symbolic of "cultural *limes*" (Ellis 2011, 245, 246). In the mid-sixth century, Prokopios of Caesarea viewed the Danube as the "strongest possible line of defense" against barbarians, a frontier that separated the "territory of the Romans, which is on the right" bank from the barbarians living on the northern or left bank of the river (Curta 2006, 39).

The communities of Scythia Minor were very diverse. In the early second century, numerous villages appeared in Dobrudja under Latin names that featured a mixed community of Roman citizens and natives (Poulter 2004, 228). In the western half there was a strongly Romanized native Getae population, while the eastern area had a Greek-speaking population. Dacians from the left bank of the Danube, freshly colonized Thracians, or foreign communities such as the Sarmatians, found a common area where the Roman seal and a refined Greek culture blended languages and cultures to create a society of Latin and Greek culture and civilization. The epigraphic monuments in Scythia bear exclusively Latin and Greek inscriptions. Although in the interior, the majority of the pop-

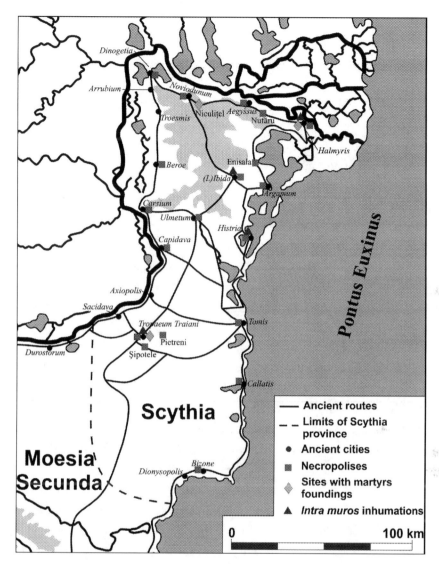

Figure 8.1. Map of the Roman province of Scythia Minor showing the site of Ibida. Map by Mihai Constantinescu.

ulation was Romano-Thracian (Getae) in culture and language, the society was becoming very cosmopolitan in the fourth to sixth centuries, especially on the Black Sea coast. Scythia maintained stable large-scale relations with provinces in the Balkans, Asia Minor, and the Near East (Zahariade 2006, 127).

Many groups desired to move into the empire. Before the arrival of the Romans, migration was much less constrained and regulated. Creating fixed military boundaries transformed tribal migration into war against Rome, which became a constant feature of the frontier (Elton 1996, 107). In the fourth century, Goths occupied center stage on the lower Danube frontier and its delta. Pressed by the Huns and Alans who were moving off the Russian steppe, they were forced to cross into the Roman provinces. At Adrianople in 378, they served the Roman army one of its most memorable defeats (Whittaker 1994, 133).

Historical sources such as Ammianus Marcellinus most likely exaggerated the political and military organization of the Goths; their main activity was probably petty raids and infiltration (Whittaker 1994, 173). The term "Goths" means "men," a generic term that gives the false impression of unity. Actually, the Goths were many groups, a fragmented society that typically split up after rare shows of unity and victory (Whittaker 1994, 213). With other intruding groups such as the Huns, the Alans, the Slavs, the Bulgars, and the Avars, they put pressure on the frontier. The individual groups were probably small, but the combination of this increase in population and lack of resources led to food shortages in the lower Danube region. Because of these stresses, the lower Danube had more recorded cases of voluntary "surrender" and *receptio* into the Roman Empire than any other frontier of the empire (Whittaker 1994, 220).

There is abundant literary evidence that the Romans imported labor, not just foreign army auxiliaries but also "barbarian" immigrant workers. Most of these immigrants disappeared into the mass of provincial poor (Burns 2003, 29; Whittaker 2004, 17, 203). After numerous Goth groups settled in the empire during the fourth century (Elton 1996, 109), these settlements became an instrument of frontier policy for local authorities (Whittaker 1994, 189). But the Roman upper class, exemplified by writers such as Ammianus Marcellinus, had an attitude of contempt toward the Goths, whom Romans often saw as savage beasts who were trying to take over the empire (Whittaker 1994, 188–189) and who brought about "the destruction of the Roman world" (Ammianus Marcellinus 1986, 31.4, 417). It is no surprise that the starving Goth refugees who were granted asylum in the empire when they were allowed to legally cross the Danube in 376 were brutally mistreated because of lack of planning and the greed and incompetence of officials (Ammianus Marcellinus 1986, 31.4, 417–418).

The Site of Ibida

In the fourth century, Ibida, a major urban center in the northern part of Scythia Minor that occupied 24 hectares, was the largest settlement after the capital Tomis (Zahariade 2006, 17, 95; see also chapter 1). Located in the Slava Rusă River valley, Ibida was the only town in the province that was transected by a river course. This was a highly privileged situation, since it made it possible to build special systems to distribute drinking water throughout the residential areas and likely water mills also. Large areas of the surrounding forested hills were gradually included into the town and served as sustainable defense features (Zahariade 2006, 95, 113). Ibida was included in Justinian's extensive building program. Its transformation into one of the most important urban (and probably military) centers of northern Scythia implied a dramatic reorganization of its own territory and that of neighboring towns in the second to third centuries CE (Zahariade 2006, 118).

Archaeological work at the site has been ongoing since 2001, and large areas of the fortification system, the west gate, a bridge, houses and workshops have been excavated (Iacob et al. 2015, 559–573). The mortuary discoveries are represented by 174 burials, most of which date to the Late Roman period (Aparaschivei et al. 2012; Rubel and Soficaru 2012; Soficaru 2011, 107–113; Soficaru 2014).

A nonspecific mortuary assemblage known as feature M141 was identified in 2008 when scattered human remains were discovered during the archaeological investigation of the foundation of the tenth tower of the walled enclosure (Iacob et al. 2009, 197). Following this initial discovery, new excavations were organized in the area in 2011, 2012, and 2013 that sought to better understand the presence of human remains in this unusual place. The excavated surface was structured in three squares measuring 9 square meters each with a maximum depth of 2.5 meters from ground level (Iacob et al. 2012, 133; Iacob et al. 2013, 120; Iacob et al. 2014, 125). The overall size of feature M141 is unknown, as the ends have not been reached yet.

From a stratigraphic point of view, the west profile of feature M141 is illustrative. The first level from the bottom contained human and animal bones, a small quantity of pottery fragments, construction material (tiles and bricks), stones, one glass fragment, and two iron pieces. The second level was composed exclusively of construction material and stones, in higher numbers and larger dimensions than those in the first level. The third and last level (on the surface) contained contemporary discoveries. Levels one and two are deeper due north, suggesting that this feature had an initial bell shape. The human osteological material was located in the southeast corner of this peculiar feature. All the bones are fragmented and only a handful were identified in anatomical position.

The chronology of M141 has been established based on the stratigraphy of the complex and on the relative dating of the pottery fragments. This has been corroborated by radiocarbon dating, which provided two absolute dates: one for 304–406 CE (1700±30 BP) and one for 244–398 CE (1715±35 BP). Both samples for radiocarbon dating were taken from human osteological material identified in this pit.

The way these human remains were processed and treated in a mortuary context fundamentally differs from the other two burial assemblages found at the site. Thus, this treatment might be considered "deviant" according to the expected norms, which are amply illustrated by the other mortuary assemblages from the site, the town necropolis, and a family vault (see figure 8.2; also mentioned in chapter 1). The aim of this chapter, therefore, is to explore and offer a preliminary analysis of these "deviant" skeletal remains. The fragmentary state of the bones, the place of disposal, and their scattered distribution in feature M141 argue for a detailed investigation of the complex. The osteological material was transferred to the Institute of Anthropology at the Romanian Academy in Bucharest, where further macroscopic assessment of the bones was undertaken. Here we present the first results of this analysis, including a preliminary discussion of the assemblage and the individuals whose bones constitute it.

Materials and Methods

Due to the high number of osteological fragments (n = 2,566), the present analysis targeted the cranial and femoral fragments, since they were better preserved and could offer more information on both trauma and pathology. (A previous cursory inspection of the bones revealed that the cranial and femoral fragments had what appeared to be the highest incidence of cut marks). The osteological material was commingled and unevenly distributed at various depths in the 20-square-meter excavated area. Thus, each fragment was given an identification number based on year of excavation and place of discovery. The macroscopic analysis was undertaken using the manual of White and colleagues (2012).

Each fragment was assigned to a category: frontal, parietal, occipital, and temporal bone, for cranial fragments and proximal epiphysis, diaphysis, and distal epiphysis for femoral fragments. All the fragments were verified for conjoins. Estimates of age at death (adult and subadult), metric measurements, and assessment for pathological changes and different potential signs of traumatic injuries were undertaken according to the guidelines in Aufderheide and Rodríguez-Martín (1998), Buikstra and Ubelaker (1994), Karr and Outram (2012), Ortner (2003), Outram (2001), Outram and colleagues (2005), Villa

Figure 8.2. Google Earth map showing location of funeral discoveries at Ibida. Map by Andrei Soficaru.

and Mahieu (1991), and White and colleagues (2012). Sex estimation for cranial fragments was done by visually assessing traits as described in Soficaru and colleagues (2014).

For the purpose of comparison, we selected four other contemporary archaeological groups: Callatis, Histria, the vault at Ibida, and the necropolis at Ibida. Callatis (Mangalia) and Histria were major contemporaneous urban centers in Dobrudja, while the last two samples were retrieved from Ibida. The sample from the Ibida vault includes the remains of thirty-nine individuals in a family vault situated at the periphery of the necropolis (Mirițoiu and Soficaru 2003; figure 8.2). To date, the skeletonized remains of 136 individuals have been analyzed by the first author from the necropolis at Ibida located in the Late Roman cemetery (Soficaru et al. 2004; Soficaru 2014; figure 8.2).

Results

Given the fragmentary state of the bones, we attempted to estimate the minimum number of individuals by using the duplication of certain skeletal elements, in this case the temporal bone and femoral head. The highest value, twenty-eight, was achieved by counting the right temporal bone.

The cranial fragments offered limited but valuable information regarding the age at death and sex of the individuals. A total number of 220 cranial fragments were analyzed, distributed by element and side and, where possible, by age at death (see table 8.1). The frontal and occipital bones were the most frequently encountered elements (21.81 percent and 20.00 percent, respectively). However, the frontal and temporal bones were the most important for the purpose of sex estimation, although most of the fragments could not be assigned to male or female individuals. The distribution of the M141 sample by age at death is 70.59 percent adults and 20.36 percent subadults. The proportion of adults is similar to the proportion in the vault at Ibida (74.36 percent) but quite different from populations in the necropolis at Ibida (65.15 percent), at Histria (61.11 percent), and at Callatis (81.18 percent). The proportion of subadults also varies from three of the comparison sites: at the necropolis at Ibida it was 25.64 percent, at Callatis it was 18.82 percent, and at Histria it was 38.89 percent. There were no children buried in the family vault.

We organized a number of the 141 femoral fragments by anatomical side and two age-at-death categories (adult and subadult). Most of the fragments came from the diaphysis and the proximal epiphysis. For a better comparison

Table 8.1. Distribution of the identified cranial fragments from feature M141 by age group and sex

	Frontal	Parietal left	Parietal right	Temporal left	Temporal right	Occipital
Percent of total assemblage	21.81	16.81	16.36	12.27	12.72	20
Adult	68.75	62.16	72.22	85.19	89.29	70.45
Subadult	22.92	32.43	13.89	3.70	3.57	20.45
Not assigned	8.33	5.41	13.89	11.11	7.14	9.09
N	48	37	36	27	28	44
Males	22.92	0.00	0.00	18.52	7.14	9.09
Females	12.50	2.70	0.00	22.22	21.43	2.27
Not assigned	64.58	94.59	100.00	48.15	71.43	88.64
N	48	37	36	27	28	44

between population groups, we attempted to estimate the sex of each individual based on metric measurements by comparing the values obtained for M141 to the values available for individuals from the vault at Ibida and the necropolis at Ibida. For the latter groups, where the sex of the individuals was estimated from whole-skeleton analysis, we calculated the minimum, average, and maximum values for the sagittal and transverse diameters of both the femoral head and diaphysis. Each fragment of interest from M141 was categorized using these limits and assigned to the male, female, or the indeterminate group. This resulted in an interesting picture when we compared the five population groups. The female individuals from M141 displayed the smallest values for the femoral diaphysis, while the male individuals from M141 showed the highest values for both the femoral shaft and the femoral head (see table 8.2).

We did preliminary documentation of surface modifications, taking into consideration the extreme fragmentation of the bones. We recorded each skeletal mark using standard protocols (Buikstra and Ubelaker 1994). At this point in our analysis, we focused on assessing the nature of the modifications, particularly with regard to taphonomy and age at death. We acknowledge the challenge of discerning between perimortem and postmortem bone modifications, given the fact that in the case of M141, the postmortem intervention took place when the bodies were not completely skeletonized. The degree of ossification for these remains can be inferred from two sources.

Table 8.2. Sagittal and transverse diameter (in millimeters) of femoral shaft and head for the five groups included in this study

| | Femoral shaft | | | | Femoral head | | | |
| | Females | | Males | | Females | | Males | |
	SD[a]	TD[b]	SD	TD	SD	TD	SD	TD
Ibida M141	23.67	23.98	32.64	33.89	41.70	41.72	49.87	49.89
Ibida vault	26.09	25.72	30.53	28.36	41.74	41.00	47.44	46.75
Ibida necropolis	25.93	24.4	29.86	28.55	—	41.06	—	48.48
Callatis	26.32	26.09	29.37	28.84	—	41.85	—	48.00
Histria	26.04	24.31	29.00	28.85	—	41.36	—	48.92

[a] Sagittal diameter is anteroposterior diameter.
[b] Transverse diameter is mediolateral diameter.

First, only a small number of fragments were identified in anatomical connection. Second, the macroscopic morphological assessment of the surface modifications in some instances indicated dry bone while in others it indicated fresh tissue. For the macroscopic morphological evaluation, we used a distinction between ancient breakage, trauma and fractures, and animal activity. These categories were evaluated using the guidelines Outram (2001) has described (see also Karr and Outram 2012; Outram et al. 2005; Villa and Mahieu 1991).

Using the criteria Outram used to calculate the Fracture Freshness Index, we tried to discern between green and mineralized bone fractures. Outram used three classifications: dry, fresh, and mixed specimen (Outram 2001). The first type is represented in our analysis by the "ancient breakage" category, which refers to postmortem breakage characterized by right-angle fractures, transverse fracture outlines, and rough edges (Villa and Mahieu 1991). Virtually all the fragments identified in M141 display this type of breakage. Both the fresh and the mixed specimens from Outram (2001) were included in the second category, "trauma and fractures," which is characterized by obtuse angles, smooth fracture surface and helical breaks. Some fragments from M141 potentially showed mixed attributes. The "animal activity" category clearly indicates scavenging before the interment of the remains. A more detailed analysis of bone surface modifications will be done in the future, when feature M141 has been completely excavated.

Andrei Soficaru, Claudia Radu, and Cristina I. Tica

In the category of trauma and fractures, we distinguished between three types of bone modifications: cut marks, chop marks, and scrape marks. For greater accuracy in our analysis of femur fragments, we used five categories: shaft, condyle, head and neck, proximal third, and distal third. We also added another category, "unassigned fragments." This division allowed for a more accurate understanding of the distribution of bone surface modifications. In total, ninety-one bone modifications were identified on femoral fragments, of which three were seen on subadult bones. Cut marks occurred most often, followed by chop marks and animal activity in the form of canid punctiform holes. The extremities of the femurs were most affected by animal activity, while cut marks and chop marks were most often seen on the diaphysis (see table 8.3). In twenty-

Table 8.3. Distribution of modifications to bone surface

	Cut Mark		Chop Mark		Scrape Mark		Animal Activity		Total
	N	%	N	%	N	%	N	%	
FEMUR									
Shaft	25	59.25	17	54.83	0	0.00	0	0.00	42
Condyle	1	2.38	0	0.00	0	0.00	7	58.33	8
Head and Neck	6	14.28	5	16.12	0	0.00	3	25	14
Proximal Third	1	2.38	9	29.03	0	0.00	0	0.00	10
Distal Third	8	19.04	0	0.00	1	33.33	1	8.33	10
Unassigned Fragments	1	2.38	0	0.00	2	66.66	1	8.33	4
Total	42	100.00	31	100.00	3	100.00	12	100.00	88

	Cut Mark		Blow/Fracture		Animal Activity		Total
	N	%	N	%	N	%	
SKULL							
Frontal	5	38.5	3	75	0	0.00	8
Parietal	8	61.5	0	0.00	0	0.00	8
Occipital	0	0.00	1	25	0	0.00	1
Temporal	0	0.00	0	0.00	0	0.00	0
Total	13	100.00	4	100.00	0	0.00	17

one cases, it was possible to join two, three, or four fragments. These fragments were scattered inside or between sections, suggesting that they were broken before they became part of feature M141.

We identified seventeen cut marks and blows or fractures on the cranial fragments. The temporal bone was not affected. No traces of animal teeth were seen on cranial fragments. In fourteen cases, conjoining was possible.

Some of the adult individuals also suffered from antemortem trauma, as was evidenced by healed cranial depression fractures (CDFs). There is evidence of healed shallow CDFs on two adult parietal fragments, a left and a right, that could not be conjoined; they might or might not belong to different individuals. On the right parietal fragment, one CDF that was close to the sagittal suture was 27.99 millimeters long and 3.45 millimeters deep. This bone fragment also had signs of porotic hyperostosis. On the left parietal fragment, the CDF was 13.69 millimeters long × 10.14 millimeters wide and 1.12 millimeters deep.

During this preliminary analysis, we also looked for evidence of stress indicators on bone fragments and saw signs of cribra orbitalia, porotic hyperostosis, and periosteal reaction. However, since most fragments cannot be attributed to specific individuals, all we can infer is that some individuals suffered from nutritional stress, vitamin deficiency, inadequate levels of iron, infection, metabolic diseases, or comorbidity with other diseases (Klaus 2014, 296; Oxenham and Cavill 2010; Pētersone-Gordina et al. 2013; Walker et al. 2009; Weston 2009, 186).

Our analysis showed signs of periosteal reaction only in adults and young adults; we did not see any in subadults. Both males and females were affected. Adult males and subadults showed signs of cribra orbitalia; we cannot say anything about females. Adult males, adult females, and subadults showed signs of porotic hyperostosis. We were able to incompletely reassemble three crania. One of them, an adult male, showed signs of both cribra orbitalia and porotic hyperostosis.

Discussion

As seen from this analysis, feature M141 exhibits a series of attributes that suggest it was special. In this section we will consider the formation process of the deposit, a theoretical interpretation of the findings, and the historical events that could have led to the formation of this assemblage. We used a *chaîne-opératoire*-type diagram to plot the properties of M141 (figure 8.3). The diagram allows us to discern three events that led to the formation of M141: death of the indi-

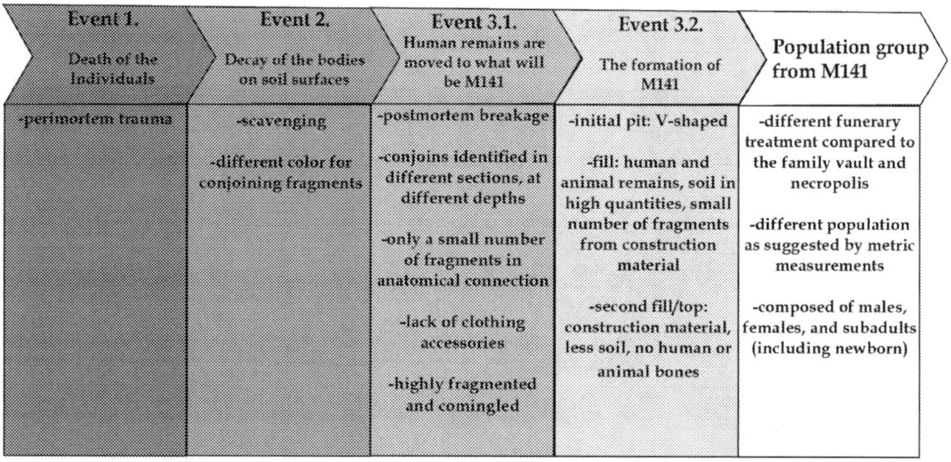

Event 1.	Event 2.	Event 3.1.	Event 3.2.	Population group from M141
Death of the individuals	Decay of the bodies on soil surfaces	Human remains are moved to what will be M141	The formation of M141	
-perimortem trauma	-scavenging	-postmortem breakage	-initial pit: V-shaped	-different funerary treatment compared to the family vault and necropolis
	-different color for conjoining fragments	-conjoins identified in different sections, at different depths	-fill: human and animal remains, soil in high quantities, small number of fragments from construction material	-different population as suggested by metric measurements
		-only a small number of fragments in anatomical connection		
		-lack of clothing accessories	-second fill/top: construction material, less soil, no human or animal bones	-composed of males, females, and subadults (including newborn)
		-highly fragmented and comingled		

Figure 8.3. Diagram illustrating the multistage process that led to the formation of the M141 deposit.

viduals, decay of the bodies, and the transport of the bodies to a deposit that we named M141. Each event is inferred based on findings from the osteological material and the archaeological data.

The first event—the death of the individuals—is characterized by the presence of perimortem trauma (as exemplified in figure 8.4). This group included both sexes and all ages. The high frequency of cut marks and other trauma strongly suggests a violent death. The second event, the decay of the bodies, is inferred through the presence of animal activity and different colors for some of the fragments. The puncture marks suggest that the bodies were exposed on the surface of the soil to scavengers (dogs) for some time. The different color of some of the fragments could also be due to exposure to the elements. The third event consists of the formation of M141, which is structured as an initial cut, the fill, and a top or cover composed of construction material.

Within the first level or the fill, lack of clothing accessories suggests that there were no clothes with the human remains. Moreover, only a small number of fragments were in anatomical connection, which suggests that the remains were in an advanced state of decay when they were moved to this pit. The fact that conjoining fragments were identified in different parts of the fill indicates that they may have been separated before interment. Last but not least, the postmortem breakage (as exemplified in figure 8.5 and figure 8.6) seen on the majority of the bones could be linked with this event, or more specifically with the process of

Figure 8.4. Cranial fragment with perimortem bone modification from the M141 deposit. Photo by Andrei Soficaru.

transferring the remains to the pit, which resulted in extensive disarticulation, high fragmentation, and erratic commingling.

This chain of events highlights the fact that the treatment these individuals were subjected to differs from the experiences of other contemporary population groups, particularly the ones from the vault and the necropolis at Ibida. In the Roman province of Scythia Minor, three types of mortuary assemblages were identified: a cemetery, which was always located outside the settlement; a crypt (in the case of martyrs) or family vault; and graves located inside the settlement (for newborns or for deceased individuals who were buried near or inside the church) (Rubel and Soficaru 2012; Soficaru 2011, 136–141). Feature M141 is located 12 meters north of the city walls and does not fit the expected pattern for funerary contexts. Moreover, the osteological material represents only a small part of the human remains belonging to at least twenty-eight individuals, including subadults and male and female adults who presented with perimortem trauma and for whom the metric measurements suggest a foreign origin compared to the inhabiting population. It should also be mentioned that

Figure 8.5. (*left*) Femur fragment with postmortem bone modification from the M141 deposit. Photo by Andrei Soficaru.

Figure 8.6. (*below*) Femur fragment with postmortem bone modification from the M141 deposit. Photo by Andrei Soficaru.

among these commingled remains we found a cranial fragment belonging to a newborn: it is a frontal bone fragment that includes the left supraorbital margin and orbit (see figure 8.7).

There is compelling evidence that the remains of these individuals were subjected to a violent, irreverent, and unceremonious treatment instead of the pre-

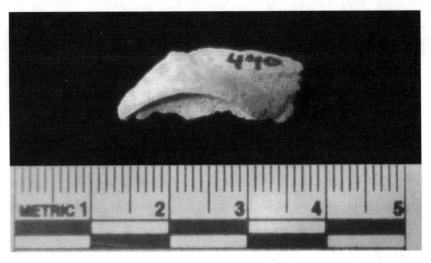

Figure 8.7. Fragment of frontal bone of newborn with left orbit from the M141 deposit. Photo courtesy of Mihai Constantinescu.

scribed funerary ceremony and interment that was common in Scythia Minor during the Late Roman Empire. Although the human long bones show traces of scavenging, the animal bones in the same pit do not. The faunal assemblage, which includes 256 osseous fragments, contained remains from cow, sheep/goat, pig, horse, camel, hedgehog, and fox (Soficaru et al. 2015). For the domestic species, most of the remains show cut marks that are specific for meat removal but no traces of carnivore activity, indicating that they represent discard from meat consumption. The presence of these animal remains along with the human bones in the same context suggests that the community assigned a low status to these individuals.

A better understanding of this assemblage can be achieved by discussing its attributes in the explanatory frameworks Komar (2008) and Osterholtz and colleagues (2014) provide for analyzing commingled human remains. Osterholtz and colleagues (2014) propose a typology for deposits that contain human remains in fragmentary and commingled states based on how long the deposit was used and based on the presence of several subtypes, accounting for the degree of commingling, the representation of various skeletal elements, or the demography of the group. Drawing upon these characteristics, M141 could represent the final phase of a multistage process that involved highly commingled and fragmentary remains that decomposed elsewhere. The idea that they were moved from an initial place of decomposition is suggested by the underrepresentation of some skeletal elements and the presence of postmortem breakage. However, the model Osterholtz and colleagues propose suggests a long-term usage of the assemblage, which is not the case for M141. This deposit displays an episodic usage and its demography reflects the process that led to its formation. The presence of traumatic perimortem injuries in combination with the demographic profile of the group is highly suggestive of a massacre (Osterholtz et al. 2014).

Komar (2008) provides a thorough discussion of commingled assemblages, with particular emphasis on the archaeological identification of massacres. She distinguishes massacres from other causes of death through the recognition of the intent of the perpetrator to destroy a targeted group. This intent is determined in the archaeological record through a detailed analysis of mortuary practices that looks for a specific set of variables.

At this stage in our research we can already infer several characteristics of M141. For example, we have concluded that the minimum number of individuals is twenty-eight; we also know that sex and age-at-death distribution includes both males and females and all age groups. No grave marker has been found. The deposit used a preexisting feature that likely was used as a trash pit. M141 is located in a nonfunerary area and the feature has no traces of coffins, clothing or body coverings, and adornments and no evidence of bindings or burning.

Finally, the deposit is a secondary interment that involved erratic commingling and high degrees of fragmentation and disarticulation. Komar distinguishes three types of creators of deposits containing human remains: the self (a well-intentioned person or group), the other (an ill-intentioned person or group), and a neutral (a third-party agent) (2008). The properties of M141 suggest that this deposit is an other-created burial of a nonfunerary character and a presumed function of disposing of bodies. This treatment of the remains is suggestive of the attitudes of the agents involved, which fit the description of the genocidal self that Hinton provided (1996, cited in Komar 2008, 125). This self allows individuals to dehumanize their victims so they can kill them and not face the burden of responsibility. The presence of human and discarded animal remains in the same assemblage is indicative of such a dehumanization of the deceased.

In ancient times, these types of acts of violation would have been sanctioned by society in specific contexts. Several written documents provide a description of similar events. For example, Ammianus Marcellinus describes instances where Romans and Goths were involved in this type of behavior toward each other and the extreme violence seen in their conflicts:

Everything was consumed in an orgy of killing and burning that paid no regard to age or sex. Infants were snatched from the very breast and put to death, mothers ravished, and married women widowed by seeing their husbands killed before their eyes. Boys of tender years or past adolescence were dragged away over the corpses of their parents. (Ammianus Marcellinus 1986, 31.6, 422, 376 CE during battles around Adrianople, Thrace)

Some of the dead who were men of note received such burial as time and place allowed. The bodies of the rest were devoured by birds of prey, which were accustomed to feast on corpses at that period; the proof of this is that the battlefield is still white with bones. (Ammianus Marcellinus 1986, 31.7, 425, 377 CE, battle near Salices, Thrace)

At this time Julius, who commanded beyond the Taurus, distinguished himself by a swift and salutary deed. Learning of the disasters in Thrace, he sent secret orders to those in charge of Goths who had been transferred earlier to Asia, and dispersed in various cities and fortresses. These commanders were all Romans, an unusual thing at the present time. The Goths were to be collected quite unsuspecting outside the walls in the expectation of receiving the pay that they had been promised, and at a given signal all put to death on one and the same day. This wise plan was carried out without fuss or delay, and the provinces of the East saved from serious danger. (Ammianus Marcellinus 1986, 31.16, 443, 378 CE, events in Thrace)

The events described in these paragraphs present good analogies to the M141 deposit, from both a chronological and a geographical point of view. Both of the radiocarbon dates obtained from the M141 human skeletal materials cover a period for which we have written records attesting to various conflicts between the Romans and the Goths in the lower Danube region: the event of 367–368 at Vicus Carporum—the Carpi's Village, the winter camp of the Emperor Valens (Ammianus Marcellinus 1986, 27.5, 336–337); the Roman military episode against the Greuthungi in 369 at Noviodunum (Ammianus Marcellinus 1986, 27.5, 336–337); the battle with the Goths at Salices in 377 (Ammianus Marcellinus 1986, 31.7, 422–425); the military conflict of 386 at Tomis, where Gerontius, the Roman commander of the local garrison, fought Goth soldiers from his garrison (Zosimus 1837, 40). Another example is the Goths' crossing of the Danube in 376 CE as they ran from the incoming Huns. When the Goths begged the emperor for asylum, Valens granted one group asylum (but not another, as that group's request was not "in the public interest") and the refugees ended up being badly mistreated by his generals (Ammianus Marcellinus 1986, 31.4, 416–418; event also mentioned in chapter 1).

Although these types of acts of violence seem to not have been a rare encounter, when we searched the archaeological literature for similar discoveries, we could identify only five possible cases in the Roman Empire. In the United Kingdom, at Maiden Castle, a mass grave was uncovered near the eastern entrance in the fortress. The burial is dated to 43 CE, during the Roman conquest of Britain. The deposit contained fifty-nine skeletons, mostly young adult males that exhibited perimortem injuries indicating decapitation, blunt and sharp force trauma, and fractures (Redfern 2013). Also in the United Kingdom, in Gloucester at London Road, a mass grave dated to 70–240 CE, during the time of the Antonine plague, was discovered in a cemetery. The deceased group from the mass grave consisted of fifteen subadults and seventy-six adults. The overall population included fifteen females (including one adolescent), thirty-eight males (including three adolescents), and twenty-seven individuals for which sex could not be estimated. A small number of objects (such as brooches, bracelets, rings, some footwear, an iron buckle, and two bone pins) was identified with the deceased, suggesting that at least some of them were clothed when they were unceremoniously dumped into this grave. These skeletonized human remains, however, display no traces of violence, as no perimortem fractures were identified (Simmonds et al. 2008, 14–18, 34–66).

In Germany, two unusual deposits were identified at Regensburg-Harting (Bavaria) and Mundelsheim (Baden-Württemberg). The first was a well from the fourth century that contained thirteen skeletons. The second included two skeletons, an older man and a teenage girl, that showed signs of burning and scavenging (Lee 2007, 139). Finally, a case that best resembles the situation seen in feature M141 was discovered at Hradisko (Mušov, Czech Republic). The assemblage is an inhumation burial in a ditch outside a Roman fortification that dates to 170–180 CE, the period of the Marcomannic Wars. The assemblage contained thirty-four skeletons: six subadults, six males, twenty females, and eight adults of unknown sex. In addition to the human remains, the fill contained animal bones, stones, charcoal, gravel, pottery fragments, a bronze clip, silver S-shaped clasps, and two iron keys. Traces of violence in the form of perimortem cut marks, stab wounds, and fracturing were evident in the bones of seventeen individuals, especially on the crania. All the osteological remains were commingled and canid gnaw marks were evident on some of the fragments (Dočkalová 2005).

Social Theory: Political Violence

The contemporary word "territory," according to the *Oxford English Dictionary*, is derived from *terra*, meaning earth, land, soil, nourishment. However, "territory" also derives from *terrere*, which means to terrorize, to frighten, to exclude (Connolly 1995, xxii). These meanings support Connolly's (1995, xxii) argument that "territory is sustaining land occupied and bounded by violence." Borders and boundaries can protect against violence, but they can also divide and violate. They are preconditions for the development of identity, individual agency, and collective action, but they simultaneously close off possibilities. Borders both promote and constrain freedom (Connolly 1995, 163). Thus, borders and frontiers are the perfect theater for political violence.

Political violence often includes the annihilation of the dead, a complete destruction of human remains in order to signal the success of the victors and a transition from war to total victory (Pérez 2012, 15). Desecration and mutilation of the conquered underlines total surrender and the triumph of the victors' ideology (Pérez 2012, 20). This is one way that stress placed on regional spheres of interaction manifests itself (Pérez 2012, 23). Whitehead (2004, 55) reminds us that violence is "pervasive, ancient, infinitely various, and a central fact of human life" and is "poorly understood in general." That is why as anthropologists we have a responsibility to reconstruct the past without reducing it to a simplistic understanding of deviant behavior that we name and label without attempting to explain or make sense of it in the bigger scheme of events (Pérez 2012, 15).

Because violence and violent acts are not the result of a single event or a static entity, the type of violence used should always be understood in larger political, social, economic, and ecological contexts (Pérez 2012, 17). Pérez (20) suggests that the presence in the osteological record of individuals with nonlethal injuries or individuals with health problems demonstrates that violence can play out in different ways since violence occurs on a spectrum.

Political violence is about making a statement. And since borderlands and frontiers and the act of bordering are violent, the purpose of violence on the frontier is to amplify and broadly disseminate that statement, whatever it may be. As Verdery (1999, 33) argues, dead bodies have unique characteristics that make them powerful political symbols. Annihilation of the dead body is designed to create a spectacle, induce anxiety, and disrupt the normal mourning process (Pérez 2012, 15). When older people, young men, young women, and children are reduced to an unrecognizable mass, the aggressors make a substantial psychological impact on the regional interaction sphere in which they operate (Pérez 2012, 17). As a form of political violence, massacres create a powerful symbolic imagery in the form of two groups pitted against each other: the in-group (those doing the killing) creates a second group, the "less than human" group, the one to be killed without compunction (Pérez 2012, 17). The death and annihilation of the individuals excavated from feature M141 must have sent a powerful message in the frontier province of Scythia Minor.

Conclusion

The archaeological feature described in this chapter provides a significant example of a mass grave from the Roman Empire. Only a handful of comparable cases from the empire have been described before. The identified human remains represent individuals who most likely suffered a violent death and underwent a postmortem treatment intended to humiliate. The bodies were probably left on the surface, exposed to scavengers and to the elements. At a later point, some of these remains, which by that point were in an advanced state of decay, were transported to and discarded in a previously existing feature. This process led to the extreme fragmentation and commingling of these remains. They were tossed in a trash pit along with discarded animal bones and were covered with construction material.

The individuals who were deposited in M141 either set themselves apart from the rest of Ibida's inhabitants or were set apart as an "other" group. And because they were different, they were targeted. The dehumanizing treatment of their remains tells us something about those who "buried" them and who might have also been involved in their death. The combination of a high frequency of perimortem trauma and a degrading postmortem treatment is highly suggestive of political violence toward this group of people and the will to completely eradicate their presence from the collective memory. There was no commemorative sign or consecrated ground for the deceased. Instead, they were tossed into a trash pit.

Written documents from the same period provide examples of similar situations in which groups were mass murdered. We argue that feature M141 is telling a similar story. However, more in-depth osteological, biogeochemical, and biomolecular analyses need to be undertaken before a definitive conclusion can be reached. We plan to continue the bioarchaeological analysis and conduct isotope and aDNA research on this commingled assemblage in order to see if multiple lines of evidence will support our preliminary analysis.

Acknowledgments

This work was supported by a grant from the Romanian National Authority for Scientific Research (CNCS-UEFISCDI), project number PNII-ID-PCCE-2011-2-0013. We are thankful to Dr. M. Iacob, Dr. D. Paraschiv, Dr. L. Mihăilescu-Bârliba, and Dr. G. Nuțu and to various students who joined us during the excavation process. We would also like to thank Mihai Constantinescu for his assistance with figures 8.1 and 8.7 and Trent Skinner and Aaron Woods for their assistance with figure 8.3.

References

Ammianus Marcellinus. 1986. *The Later Roman Empire (A.D. 354–378)*. Translated by Walter Hamilton. Introduction by Andrew Wallace-Hadrill. New York: Penguin Books.

Aparaschivei, D., M. Iacob, A. D. Soficaru, and D. Paraschiv. 2012. "Aspects of Everyday Life in Scythia Minor Reflected in Some Funerary Discoveries from Ibida (Slava Rusă, Tulcea County)." In *Homines, Funera, Astra. Proceedings of the International Symposium on Funerary Anthropology. 5–8 June 2011. '1 Decembrie 1918' University (Alba Iulia, Romania)*, edited by R. Kogălniceanu, R.-G. Curcă, M. Gligor and S. Stratton, 169–182. Oxford: Archaeopress.

Aufderheide, A. C. and C. Rodríguez-Martín. 1998. *The Cambridge Encyclopedia of Human Paleopathology*. Cambridge: Cambridge University Press.

Buikstra, J. E. and D. H. Ubelaker. 1994. *Standards for Data Collection from Human Skeletal Remains*. Arkansas Archaeological Survey Research Series no. 44. Fayetteville: Arkansas Archaeological Survey.

Burns, T. S. 2003. *Rome and the Barbarians: 100B.C.–A.D. 400*. Baltimore: John Hopkins University Press.

Connolly, W. E. 1995. *The Ethos of Pluralization*. Borderlines, vol. 1. Minneapolis: University of Minnesota Press.

Curta, F. 2006. *Southeastern Europe in the Middle Ages, 500–1250*. Cambridge: Cambridge University Press.

Dočkalová, M. 2005. "A Mass Grave from the Roman Period in Moravia (Czech Republic)." *Anthropologie* 43(1): 23–43.

Ellis, L. 2011. "Elusive Places: A Chronological Approach to Identity and Territory in Scythia Minor (Second–Seventh Centuries)." In *Romans, Barbarians, and the Transformation of the Roman World: Cultural Interaction and the Creation of Identity in Late Antiquity*, edited by R. W. Mathisen and D. Shanzer, 241–251. Surrey, England: Ashgate Publishing.

Elton, H. 1996. *Frontiers of the Roman Empire*. Bloomington: Indiana University Press.

Graham, M. W. 2006. *News and Frontier Consciousness in the Late Roman Empire*. Ann Arbor: University of Michigan Press.

Iacob, M., A. Ibba, D. Paraschiv, and A. Teatini. 2015. "La citta romana di (L)Ibida, in Scythia Minor. Le ricerche recenti e l'accordo di collaborazione tra l'Istituto di Ricerche Eco-Museali di Tulcea e l'Universita di Sassari." In *Culti e religiosità nelle province danubiane*, edited by L. Zerbini. Bologna: I libri di Emil. Bologna: I libri di Emil.

Iacob, M., D. Paraschiv, M. Mocanu, G. Nuțu, L. Marcu, C. Chiriac, D. Aparaschivei, A. Rubel, L. Mihăilescu-Bîrliba, A. Doboș, A. Soficaru, and S. Stanc. 2009. 83. *Slava Rusă, com. Slava Cercheză, jud. Tulcea, (L)Ibida*, 196–201. Cronica Cercetărilor Arheologice din România. Târgoviște: Campania 2008.

Iacob, M., D. Paraschiv, G. Nuțu, M. Mocanu, D. Chiriac, D. Aparaschivei, A. Rubel, A. Opaiț, L. Mihăilescu-Bîrliba, S. Stanc, A. Soficaru, and D. Nedu. 2012. 72. *Slava Rusă, com. Slava Cercheză, jud. Tulcea, (L)Ibida*, edited by M. V. Angelescu, 131–134. Cronica Cercetărilor Arheologice din România. Bucharest: Campania 2011.

Iacob, M., D. Paraschiv, G. Nuțu, M. Mocanu, C. Chiriac, D. Aparaschivei, A. Rubel, A. Opaiț, L. Mihăilescu-Bîrliba, S. Stanc, A. Soficaru, and N. Mateevici. 2013. 60. *Slava Rusă, com. Slava Cercheză, jud. Tulcea (L)Ibida*, edited by M. V. Angelescu, A. Pescaru, I. Opriș, Z. K. Pinter, and R. Iosipescu, 119–121. Cronica Cercetărilor Arheologice din România. Iași: Campania 2012.

Iacob, M., D. Paraschiv, G. Nuțu, M. Mocanu, C. Chiriac, D. Aparaschivei, A. Rubel, A. Opaiț, L. Mihăilescu-Bîrliba, S. Stanc, A. Soficaru, N. Mateevici, and D. Nedu. 2014. 83. *Slava Rusă, com. Slava Cercheză, jud. Tulcea [(L), Ibida]*, edited by M. V. Angelescu, D. Mihai, A. Pescaru, I. Opriș, Z. K. Pinter, and R. Iosipescu, 130–134. Cronica Cercetărilor Arheologice din România. Oradea: Campania 2013.

Karr, L. P., and A. K. Outram. 2012. "Tracking Changes in Bone Fracture Morphology over Time: Environment, Taphonomy, and the Archaeological Record." *Journal of Archaeological Science* 39: 555–559.

Klaus, H. D. 2014. "Frontiers in the Bioarchaeology of Stress and Disease: Cross-Disciplinary Perspectives from Pathophysiology, Human Biology, and Epidemiology." *American Journal of Physical Anthropology* 155: 294–308.

Komar, D. 2008. "Patterns of Mortuary Practice Associated with Genocide: Implications for Archaeological Research." *Current Anthropology* 49(1): 123–133.

Lee, A. D. 2007. *War in Late Antiquity: A Social History*. Malden, MA: Blackwell Publishing.

Mirițoiu, N., and A. D. Soficaru. 2003. "Studiul antropologic al osemintelor din cavoul Romano-Bizantin "Tudorca" de la Slava Rusă (antica Ibida)." *PEUCE* s.n. 1(14): 511–530.

Ortner, D. J. 2003. *Identification of Pathological Conditions in Human Skeletal Remains*. San Diego: Academic Press.

Osterholtz, A., K. M. Baustian, and D. L. Martin. 2014. "Introduction." In *Commingled and Disarticulated Human Remains: Working toward Improved Theory, Method, and Data*, edited by A. Osterholtz, K. M. Baustian, and D. L. Martin, 1–13. New York: Springer.

Outram, A. K. 2001. "A New Approach to Identifying Bone Marrow and Grease Exploitation: Why the 'Intermediate' Fragments Should Not Be ignored." *Journal of Archaeological Science* 28: 401–410.

Outram, A. K., C. J. Knüsel, S. Knight, and A. F. Harding. 2005. "Understanding Complex Fragmented Assemblages of Human and Animal Remains: A Fully Integrated Approach." *Journal of Archaeological Science* 32: 1699–1710.

Oxenham, M. F., and I. Cavill. 2010. "Porotic Hyperostosis and Cribra Orbitalia: The Erythropoietic Response to Iron-Deficiency Anaemia." *Anthropological Science* 118(3): 199–200.

Pérez, V. R. 2012. "The Politicization of the Dead: Violence as Performance, Politics as Usual." In *The Bioarchaeology of Violence*, edited by D. L. Martin, R. P. Harrod, and V. R. Pérez, 13–28. Gainesville: University Press of Florida.

Pētersone-Gordina, E., G. Gerhards, and T. Jakob. 2013. "Nutrition-Related Health Problems in a Wealthy 17–18th Century German Community in Jelgava, Latvia." *International Journal of Paleopathology* 3: 30–38.

Poulter, A. 2004. "Cataclysm on the Lower Danube: The Destruction of a Complex Roman Landscape." In *Landscapes of Change: Rural Evolutions In Late Antiquity and the Early Middle Ages*, edited by N. Christie, 223–255. Aldershot: Ashgate Publishing.

Redfern, R. 2013. "A Bioarchaeological Study of Violence in the Roman World." In *The Routledge Handbook of the Bioarchaeology of Human Conflict*, edited by C. Knüsel and M. Smith, 203–212. London: Routledge.

Rubel, A., and A. D. Soficaru. 2012. "Infant Burials in Roman Dobrudja: A Report of Work in Progress: The Case of Ibida (Slava Rusă)." In *Homines, Funera, Astra. Proceedings of the International Symposium on Funerary Anthropology. 5–8 June 2011. '1 Decembrie 1918' University (Alba Iulia, Romania)*, edited by R. Kogălniceanu, R.-G. Curcă, M. Gligor and S. Stratton, 163–168. Oxford: Archaeopress.

Simmonds, A., N. Marquez-Grant, and L. Loe. 2008. *Life and Death in a Roman City: Excavation of a Roman Cemetery with a Mass Grave at 120–122, London Road, Gloucester*. Oxford Archaeology Monograph No. 6. Oxfordshire: Alden Group.

Soficaru, A. D. 2011. *Populația provinciei Scythia în perioada Romano-Bizantină (sf. Sec. III–înc. Sec. VII)*. Iași, Romania: Editura Universității "Alexandru Ioan Cuza."

———. 2014. "Anthropological Data about the Funeral Discoveries from Slava Rusă, Tulcea County, Romania." *PEUCE* s.n. 12: 307–340.

Soficaru, A. D., N. Mirițoiu, N. M. Sultana, M. M. Gătej, and M. D. Constantinescu. 2004. "Analiza antropologică a osemintelor descoperite în campania din 2002, în necropola Romano-Bizantină de la Slava Rusă (Jud. Tulcea)." *PEUCE* s.n. 2: 329–386.

Soficaru, A., M. Constantinescu, M. Culea, and C. Ionică. 2014. "Evaluation of Discriminant Functions for Sexing Skulls from Visually Assessed Traits Applied in the Rainer Osteological Collection (Bucharest, Romania)." *HOMO: Journal of Comparative Human Biology* 65: 464–475.

Soficaru, A., C. Radu, M. Prociuc, and Ş. Honcu. 2015. "Humans and Animals in the Same Pit: Preliminary Results Regarding the Burial M 141 from Slava Rusă." Paper presented at the International Symposium on Funerary Anthropology, "Homines, Funera, Astra," October 18–21, Alba Iulia, Romania.

Verdery, K. 1999. *The Political Lives of Dead Bodies: Reburial and Postsocialist Change*. New York: Columbia University Press.

Villa, P. and E. Mahieu. 1991. "Breakage Patterns of Human Long Bones." *Journal of Human Evolution* 21: 27–48.

Walker, P. L., R. R. Bathurst, R. Richman, T. Gjerdrum, and V. A. Andrushko. 2009. "The Causes of Porotic Hyperostosis and Cribra Orbitalia: A Reappraisal of the Iron-Deficiency-Anemia Hypothesis." *American Journal of Physical Anthropology* 139: 109–125.

Weston, D. A. 2009. "Brief Communication: Paleohistopathological Analysis of Pathology Museum Specimens: Can Periosteal Reaction Microstructure Explain Lesion Etiology?" *American Journal of Physical Anthropology* 140: 186–193.

White, T. D., M. T. Black, and P. A. Folkens. 2012. *Human Osteology.* 3rd ed. Boston: Elsevier Academic Press.

Whitehead, N. L. 2004. "On the Poetics of Violence." In *Violence,* edited by N. L. Whitehead, 55–77. Santa Fe, NM: School of American Research Press.

Whittaker, C. R. 1994. *Frontiers of the Roman Empire: A Social and Economic Study.* Baltimore, MD: John Hopkins University Press.

———. 2004. *Rome and Its Frontiers: The Dynamics of Empire.* New York: Routledge.

Zahariade, M. 2006. *Scythia Minor: A History of a Later Roman Province (284–681).* Amsterdam: Adolf M. Hakkert Publisher.

Zosimus. 1837. *Istoria Nea: Corpus Scriptorum Historiae Byzantinae.* Vol. 50. Edited by I. Bekker. Bonn: E. Weber.

9

A Line in the Sand

Bioarchaeological Interpretations of Life along the Borders of the Great Basin and the American Southwest

AARON R. WOODS AND RYAN P. HARROD

The notion of conflict along the frontiers or borderlands of neighboring regions, territories, or areas is a topic of interest for anthropologists studying both modern and past cultures (Adelman and Aron 1999; Alvarez 2016; Hämäläinen and Truett 2011; Lightfoot and Martinez 1995; Parker 2006). To identify and understand groups living along the frontier we must first define these populations. In the past, we used things like habitation, material remains, and subsistence to characterize a culture (Bernardini 2005). A prime example of this tradition was the creation of distinct temporal periods in the Pecos Classification System such as Basketmaker II or Pueblo II, which were defined by distinct cultural traits (Kidder 1927a, 1927b). Charles Riggs (2005, 342) suggests that "discrete suites of material traits represent different cultural traditions as much in the past as they continue to do today."

In North America, the Smithsonian Institute published a series of edited volumes called the *Handbook of the North American Indians*. These volumes focused on living groups and used ethnographic and archaeological data to organize native groups into regions by using a concept know as a "culture area" (Smith 1929). The creation and delineation of cultural areas in the Smithsonian handbooks served to increase our understanding of existing and late prehistoric precontact groups. The delineation of cultural areas is also a useful tool for attempting to improve our understanding of more prehistoric populations by following a similar strategy and recognizing shared cultural similarities based on geographic regions, subsistence, and material culture (Kroeber 1931, 1939; Smith 1929; Wissler 1917, 1927). Two cultural areas explored in the Smithsonian handbooks are the Great Basin and the American Southwest. The culture area defined as the Great Basin covers part of the states of Colorado, Idaho, Nevada, Oregon, Utah, and Wyoming (D'Azevedo 1986). It is an arid region that is in the rain shadow of the Sierra Nevada Mountains and bordered on the east by the Rocky Mountains. The culture area known as the American Southwest covers all of the states of Arizona and New Mexico; part of the states of Colorado, Nevada, and Utah; and portions of northern Mexico (Ortiz 1979, 1983). Within these two culture areas, we will look at two archaeologically defined cultures: the Fremont and the Ancestral Puebloans. The Fremont and Ancestral Puebloans share borders along the southern portions of Utah and Nevada (figure 9.1). The Fremont and Puebloan borders considered in this chapter include the boundary between Parowan Valley and the St. George Basin, and the Canyons of the Escalante River and the Kaiparowits Plateau, all in the state of Utah. Additional Ancestral Puebloan bioarchaeological data will be discussed from southern Nevada to help illustrate differences between Fremont and Ancestral Puebloan skeletons.

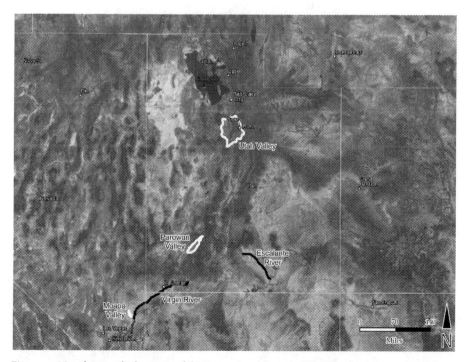

Figure 9.1. Map showing the locations of the Fremont and Ancestral Puebloan border areas in southern Utah and southern Nevada. Map by Aaron Woods.

Violence along Borders: Archaeological Evidence of Fremont and Pueblo Interactions

We were inspired to explore Fremont and Pueblo relations after reading a chapter on conflict in the prehistoric Puebloan Southwest by Polly Schaafsma (2007). In that chapter, Schaafsma proposed that the Fremont practiced trophy head collection based on her interpretation that objects in the hands of some of the rock art anthropomorphs represented severed heads. The role of violence among the Fremont was a topic that was not widely discussed or well understood because until very recently, the bulk of Fremont research was focused on behavioral ecology (Jennings 1956, 1960, 1978; Madsen and Simms 1998).

In order to expand our understanding of the role of violence among the Fremont and more accurately explore the differences and similarities between Fremont and Ancestral Puebloan violence, we conducted several literature reviews focused on Fremont violence. However, we found only sparse results on the subject. Some researchers have discussed the role of violence among the Fremont (Lambert 2002; Novak and Kollmann 2000; Owsley et al. 1998; Rood 2001; Schaafsma 1971, 2007), but they have all focused on very specific sites and regions. (We include brief summaries below.) Julie Howard and Joel Janetski (1992) discussed the presence of scalps recovered from a dry cave with cross-dates contemporary to the Fremont era, but they may also be associated with the Puebloans who lived in the area during the Basketmaker periods. Other researchers noted the presence of possible trophy skulls from excavations of one pit house in central Utah (Novak and Kollmann 2000; Owsley et al. 1998; Rood 2001). These skulls were found in a context that suggests they were hung from the ceiling rafters of a pit house. Patricia Lambert (2002) noted a partial cranial fragment with indications of scalp marks from the Great Salt Lake area. Schaafsma (2000) has also discussed the presence of shield imagery in Fremont and Puebloan rock art.

Examinations of violence among Ancestral Puebloan groups are much more extensive and have a longer history. Discussions of violence among Ancestral Puebloan groups in the Southwest were first started by Richard Wetherill, who first explored places such as Chaco Canyon and Canyon del Muerto in the 1890s (McNitt 1957). Beginning in the mid-nineteenth century, there was an increased interest in violence in this region that led to publications on scalping, dismemberment, warfare, and even anthropophagy, or cannibalism (Billman et al. 2000; Crown and Nichols 2008; Haas 1990; LeBlanc 1999; Lekson 2002; Ogilvie and Hilton 2000; Osterholtz 2012; Pérez 2012; Potter and Chuipka 2010;

Rice and LeBlanc 2001; Turner 1983; Turner and Turner 1999; Wilcox and Haas 1994; Woodbury 1959).

In this chapter we investigate and reassess the elements of daily life among the Fremont compared to that of their neighbors to the south, using skeletal remains. The purpose of this presentation is to outline additional methods for highlighting the individual and social identity of the Fremont. We discuss bioarchaeological methods and present them as an often-overlooked tool for evaluating differences and similarities among Fremont individuals.

Using an archaeological and bioarchaeological approach, this chapter evaluates the interactions between these two cultures and attempts to answer the following questions:

Does living on the "frontier" have an impact on the overall health of a
    population? (e.g., nutritional deficiencies and pathological conditions)
Are there differences in the frequency and pattern of violence among the
    Fremont, the Virgin Branch Puebloans, and the Kayenta Puebloans?
Are there regional patterns of violence based on proximity to another
    culture?

Cultural Context of the Fremont

The Fremont, who in prehistory were located almost entirely in the modern state of Utah, were originally considered to be part of a northern periphery of the southwestern agricultural traditions (Kidder 1927a, 1927b; Judd 1926). Judd and Kidder viewed the Fremont as part of the greater pan-southwestern agricultural tradition, but their presence on the border of what was considered the Southwest and their halting or region-specific adoption of agriculture placed them in a marginal position. Later, the human behavioral ecology research agenda Jesse Jennings (1956, 1960, 1978) and others pushed redefined the Fremont as hunter-gatherer groups that adopted or abandoned agriculture when it was advantageous in terms of caloric intake. This shift in focus further marginalized and separated the Fremont from the greater pan-southwestern tradition in the thinking of researchers.

However, the reality is that researchers continue to struggle with clear definitions of the Fremont. Researchers freely admit that the Fremont are complex and that their subsistence practices varied by geographic location. David Madsen (1989, 2–3), one of the foremost Fremont researchers, has stated that the Fremont are "characterized by variation and diversity and are neither readily defined nor easily encapsulated within a single description."

Researchers now generally accept that while the Fremont possessed elements of southwestern culture, they are their own distinct group and are not well suited to being defined as peripheral to the Southwest, merely influenced by southwestern material culture and perhaps ideology (Janetski et al. 2011; Madsen and Simms 1998; Searcy and Talbot 2016). Some of the most recent research is promoting the term "Fremont regional system" (Allison 2015), which allows us to consider Fremont mortuary remains in the context of the greater Fremont region, regardless of the variables of subsistence strategy, interactions with external groups, and other factors that initially led Madsen and Simms (1998) to gerrymander the Fremont into regional pockets focused heavily on subsistence strategies and ecological models. The traits that define the Fremont cultural tradition are one-rod-and-bundle basketry, "Fremont" hock-style moccasins, trapezoidal anthropomorphs depicted in rock art and clay figurines, and distinctive grayware pottery. The Utah-style metate is considered an additional material culture marker of the Fremont culture.

Cultural Context of the Ancestral Puebloans

The Ancestral Puebloans, also known as the Anasazi (Geib 1996), are even less homogeneous than the Fremont. Four major branches have been identified: the Virgin Branch, the Kayenta Branch, the Mesa Verde Branch, and the Chaco Branch. The differences used to identify Virgin, Kayenta, and Chacoan Puebloans are based on variations in ceramic style, architecture, and settlement patterns. In the Pueblo II period (900–1150 CE) large sites develop in the San Juan Basin and the Kayenta Region. The Pueblo III period (1150–1285 CE) has been characterized as a time of disturbance when population centers shifted and whole communities were abandoned (Dean 2002; Haas and Creamer 1993).

Virgin Branch Puebloans

An examination of the development of the Virgin Branch Puebloans suggests that they developed between the Basketmaker III period and the Pueblo II period, as evidenced in changes in architecture (from pit houses to pueblos) and ceramics.

Some have argued that the Virgin Branch Ancestral Puebloans are different from the Kayenta and Chacoan Puebloans. This is based on the facts that they are relatively isolated from other Ancestral Puebloan groups in terms of trade and architectural style and that although the color or style of the ceramics resembles those of other Ancestral Puebloan groups, it is not quite the same. The Virgin Branch Puebloans are also arguably the least migratory of the Puebloan groups, but there is evidence of village abandonment. For example, at some sites in the Virgin Branch Puebloan Region there is migration away from the river, which some researchers have argued is a sign of environmental change (Larson and Michaelsen 1990; Lyneis 1996). The theory is that changes in climate may have caused periodic flooding that made farming unreliable. At the end of the Pueblo II period, the Virgin Branch Puebloans abandoned the region. Some researchers suggest that they disbanded and joined the neighboring Paiute or Fremont, while others argue that they went south and joined the Kayenta (see Lyneis [1996] for a discussion of the fate of the Virgin River Brach Pueblo). While the fate of the Virgin Anasazi may not be clear, there is strong evidence to support the idea that the abandonment of the region was associated with climate change, specifically flooding. Through time, Virgin Branch Puebloan site locations changed and moved away from the river and back and above the river, which may indicate flood avoidance strategies (Anderson and Neff 2011).

Kayenta Branch Puebloans

To the west, a branch of Puebloans called the Kayenta developed transitioning from the architecture focused on pit houses of the Basketmaker III period to the more aggregated village sites of the Pueblo I and Pueblo II periods. Between the Pueblo I and Pueblo II periods, a shift to smaller Prudden unit pueblos occurred and these small pueblos spread throughout the region. Researchers have noted that toward the end of the Pueblo II period, the architecture of specific Kayenta sites such as Whitehouse Pueblo exhibit similarities to Chacoan architecture, suggesting that Chacoan Puebloans established communities among the Kayenta (LeBlanc 1999; Lekson 1999, 2015). The evidence of Chacoan settlers or regional interlopers, however, is not entirely convincing, especially since during the late Pueblo II, Kayenta and Northern San Juan groups migrated away from open sites to more defensible locations, suggesting a turning away from Chacoan Puebloans. By the Pueblo III period, there was a large-scale migration away from the Kayenta region. Recent research by Charles Riggs (2005) and Julia Lowell (2007, 2010) suggests that some of Kayenta migrated to the south and joined large multiethnic Mogollon pueblos, such as Grasshopper Pueblo and Point of Pines.

In order to examine the differences and similarities related to health, violence markers, and overall patterns of violence among Fremont and Ancestral Puebloans along their borders, we analyzed skeletal remains of these groups.

Materials and Methods

The human skeletal remains analyzed included forty individuals associated with the Fremont culture and forty-one individuals identified as Ancestral Puebloans. While differences among the Fremont by site are noted, they are not as significant as the differences noted between the Virgin Branch and Kayenta Branch Puebloans. The Ancestral Puebloan sample included twenty-one Kayenta Branch and twenty Virgin Branch individuals. The samples used in this study were based solely on remains that were complete enough for analysis and could be identified as individual burials. Commingled remains in a poor state of preservation were often not included.

The methodological approach taken in this study is bioarchaeological because analyzing human skeletal remains in a regional context allows us to identify and compare markers of identity among the Fremont living in areas adjacent to Ancestral Puebloan groups. Reconstruction of Fremont and Ancestral Pueblo individuals is accomplished by recording indicators of health, nutrition, activity, and trauma injury.

Providing a baseline demographic profile for a sample is the foundation for understanding any population. This is accomplished by identifying the approximate age and estimating the sex for each individual. The methods used to estimate age and sex rely on established osteological techniques (Brooks and Suchey 1990; Lovejoy et al. 1985; Meindl and Lovejoy 1985; Phenice 1969; Todd 1920) that are summarized in Bass (2005), Buikstra and Ubelaker (1994), and White et al. (2012).

Entheses, formerly known as musculoskeletal stress markers, are an important aspect of this research because changes to the sites where tendons and ligaments attach to the bone can provide insight into variations in activity among different sample populations. The muscle stress markers most pertinent to this research are those that involve the major extremities, which are associated with carrying heavy loads and squatting. However, it should be noted that entheses cannot reveal specific activities; they can only illuminate large patterns of activity, such as variation in subsistence. The method used to describe differences among the entheses is based on work by Mariotti and colleagues (2007), who provide a means of describing the degree of development of many more entheseal sites based on a ranking system of slight (1) to severe (3) buildup.

In order to identify the quality of the overall health of the samples, we recorded cranial and postcranial pathological conditions and indicators of nutritional deficiency. The pathological conditions of most interest are generalized physiological responses to stress such as periosteal reactions and diseases such as tuberculosis. We scored nutritional deficiencies by looking at cribra orbitalia, porotic hyperostosis, and enamel hypoplasias. We recorded pathological conditions and nutritional deficiencies following diagnostic criteria outlined by Ortner (2003) and Aufderheide and Rodríguez-Martin (1998).

Analysis of trauma involved identifying descriptions of antemortem or nonlethal injuries or trauma that occurs during an individual's lifetime. We have focused on the head because the presence or absence of trauma to the head can enable a researcher to assess the quality of the person's life, similar to what can be gleaned by looking at entheses. Walker (1989) notes that cranial depression fractures and broken noses are more likely to be the result of interpersonal conflict, so repeated trauma to the head tends to indicate that the person either held a lower status in the society or was engaged in active conflict (e.g., raiding, feuding, ritual combat). Furthermore, injuries involving the head are also usually of more interest because a blow to the head tends to be associated with neurological and behavioral changes, whereas injury to the body is solely physical. The method for recording trauma includes describing, measuring (length, width, and depth), and photographing the injured area.

Results

We compared the estimated biological sex and approximate age at death of individuals across three samples. Each individual was assigned one of two categories of sex estimation: (1) female or probable female; or (2) male or probable male. The categories are simplified in the analysis to female and male (see figure 9.2). Overall, all three groups had nearly equal distributions of both female and male individuals, but the Fremont group had a slightly higher percentage of males.

The estimation of age at death was broken down into three categories: young adult, middle adult, and old adult (see figure 9.3). Of the forty Fremont individuals, sixteen were in the young adult category (18–34), fourteen were in the middle adult category (35–54), and ten were in the old adult category (55+). In the Kayenta Branch, eighteen individuals were complete enough to estimate biological age and sex. These individuals included six young adults, eight middle adults, and four old adults. In the Virgin Branch, eighteen individuals were complete enough to estimate biological sex and age. Of these individuals, five were young adults, ten were middle adults, and three were old adults.

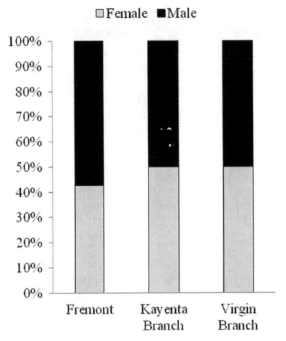

Figure 9.2. Histogram showing sex ratios of Fremont, Kayenta Branch, and Virgin Branch samples.

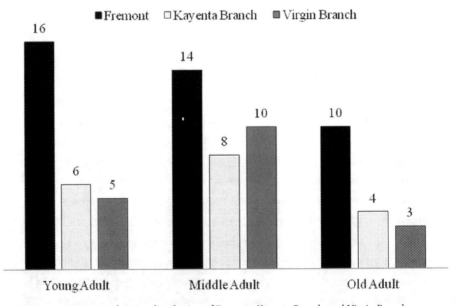

Figure 9.3. Histogram showing distribution of Fremont, Kayenta Branch, and Virgin Branch samples by age groups.

Markers of Activity and Stress

Analysis of the morphological change of the entheses for all three populations indicates that among the Fremont sample, when age was controlled for, both males and females scored higher in entheseal development (Mariotti et al. 2007) than individuals from either the Virgin Branch or Kayenta Branch Ancestral Puebloans. A possible implication is that Fremont individuals were engaged in more activities that resulted in traumatic injuries or performed more activities that remodeled their bones, but the small sample size limits our interpretation.

Analysis of porotic hyperostosis and cribra orbitalia (see table 9.1) is useful for determining if an individual was at risk for nutritional or "physiological stress in early childhood" (Yaussy and DeWitte 2018, 3). The etiology for these two conditions is debated, but it is generally linked to vitamin B_{12} deficiency or anemia. However, they may also be caused by infectious disease or a specific

Table 9.1. Indications of nutritional stress among the Fremont, Kayenta Branch, and Virgin Branch groups

Sex	N	Slight	Moderate	Severe	Cribra Orbitalia/ Porotic Hyperostosis	
					N	%
FREMONT						
Female	17	6	2	2	10/17	41.20
Male	23	9	6	1	16/23	69.57
Total	40	15	8	3	26/40	65.00
KAYENTA						
Female	9	2	3	—	5/9	55.55
Male	9	—	2	—	2/9	22.22
Indeterminate	3	—	1	—	1/3	33.33
VIRGIN BRANCH						
Female	7	3	—	—	4/7	42.86
Male	9	—	4	—	3/9	44.44
Indeterminate	4	2	2	—	4/4	100.00
Total	41	7	12	0	19/41	46.34

The Fremont population shows a slightly higher rate (65.00%) than the two Puebloan groups (46.34%) but this difference is not statistically significant (Fisher's exact, $p = 0.1188$ two-tailed; $p = 0.0711$ one-tailed).

disease such as scurvy (Oxenham and Cavill 2010; Walker et al. 2009). In this analysis, both conditions were counted together as an indicator of nonspecific stress in childhood. The results suggest that individuals in all three societies suffered periods of stress as young children.

Traumatic Injuries Associated with Intergroup Conflict

An examination of nonlethal violence indicates that the frequency of traumatic injuries within the Fremont sample is noticeably higher than in the Ancestral Puebloan sample, particularly compared to the Virgin Branch Puebloans (see table 9.2). Of the forty Fremont individuals, nine females and eleven males (20) had a cranial depression fracture (CDF), three females and five males (8) had fractured nasal bones, and one female had both a CDF and nasal fracture. Of the forty Kayenta Branch individuals, only two males had a CDF, while one female and two males in the Virgin Branch had a CDF. In both Ancestral Puebloan

Table 9.2. Nonlethal trauma among the Fremont, Kayenta Branch, and Virgin Branch groups

Sex	N	CDF[a]	Nasal[a]	Both	Trauma	
					N	%
FREMONT						
Female	17	9	3	1	13/17	76.47
Male	23	11	5	—	16/23	69.57
Sample total	40	20	8	1	29/40	72.50
KAYENTA BRANCH						
Female	9	—	—	—	0/7	0.00
Male	9	2	—	—	2/9	22.22
Indeterminate	3	—	—	—	0/9	00.00
VIRGIN BRANCH						
Female	7	1	1	—	2/7	28.57
Male	9	2	—	—	2/9	22.22
Indeterminate	4	—	—	—	0/4	0.00
Sample Total	41	5	1	—	6/41	14.63

[a] CDF = cranial depression fracture; Nasal = fracture of the nasal bones.

branches, only one individual had a nasal fracture and she was female. The Fremont population shows a noticeably higher rate (72.50 percent) than the two Puebloan groups (14.63 percent). This difference is statistically significant (Fisher's exact test, $p = 0.0001$ two-tailed; $p = 0.0001$ one-tailed). While a CDF or a nasal bone fracture can be the result of an accident, injuries in these areas are also often the result of violent encounters (Brink 2009; Brink et al. 1998; Walker 1989).

Discussion

Analysis of Fremont and Ancestral Puebloan skeletal remains provides us with some insights into the daily lives of these groups beyond what we can learn from items of material culture. Specifically, it enables us to glimpse at what life was like along the frontiers or borders that existed between these groups. Our first question regarding the impacts of overall health of a population living on the border can be answered by comparing pathological conditions among the three groups.

Pathological conditions indicate that nutrition was not always reliable among the Fremont and the Puebloans during the important years of human growth and development. These conditions were particularly noticeable among the Fremont of Parowan Valley, which might suggest that children living along the frontier were more likely to have a stressful childhood. Additionally, the data regarding activity markers on the bones bolster archaeological evidence that the Fremont were involved in more diverse or mixed subsistence strategies in the Fremont regional system. While both sexes show an increase in entheseal development with age, males seem to be more robust than age-matched females. In an unpublished senior thesis, Nicole Raymond et al. (2014) noted that Fremont subadults from the same archaeological sites discussed in this chapter had more severe cases of nutritional deficiency at sites in the Parowan Valley, which are closer to the frontier between the Fremont and Puebloan culture areas. Puebloan populations, at least in our sample, do not indicate that living along a border adversely affected their overall health and that perhaps a more focused subsistence strategy was less impactful, leading to minimal remodeling of their bones.

A comparison of the Fremont to the Virgin and Kayenta branches of Ancestral Puebloans in frequencies and patterns of violence revealed a higher rate of trauma among the Fremont. Cranial trauma in particular was higher among the

Fremont in both male and female skeletons. While cranial trauma can be accidental, it is often associated with interpersonal violence and may provide additional evidence that depictions of trophy heads and shields Schaafsma noted (2007) were inspired by a reality in which violence played a role.

These data bolster evidence presented in previous Fremont violence studies and rock art depictions. Analysis of traumatic injuries through the lens of sociopolitical interactions along the border between Fremont and other populations requires thorough consideration of archaeological data. Rock art motifs throughout the Fremont cultural area depict shield-bearing anthropomorphs, some of which are holding heads (Schaafsma 2007). Phil Geib, who did research in Glen Canyon, Utah (1996), noted distinct differences in Fremont and Kayenta anthropomorphs. The Fremont generally depicted themselves as trapezoidal in shape with square heads. Kayenta tended to depict themselves with rounded heads and more anatomically correct bodies. In his research, Geib was able to clearly distinguish Fremont and Puebloan rock art figures (Geib 1996, 9). These differences in self-depiction are worth noting as they serve to demonstrate borders. The depiction of violence in these rock art panels may identify the penalties or warnings for encroachment into culturally delineated borders. During the Escalante Drainage Survey: Escalante Valley II of 2003, researchers and field school students from Brigham Young University noted one scene depicting perceived violence between clearly depicted Fremont and Kayenta rock art figures at site 42GA5814 (Talbot 2003). In addition to rock-art motifs, archaeological sites in the Fremont cultural area resemble massacre site or extreme processing sites among the population in Mesa Verde. These events are identified when skeletal collections are recovered from the US Southwest that have evidence of intentional modification indicating the bodies were disarticulated, chopped, and burned (Osterholtz et al. 2014, 8, table 1). However, there are far fewer cases of extreme processing events among the Fremont and when they do occur they are at sites near the frontier.

Conclusions

Overall, there was a much higher rate of trauma and pathology among the Fremont. The implications of these data suggest that despite the close proximity of the Fremont to Virgin and Kayenta Puebloans, there was something different about the Fremont lifeway and culture compared to either Puebloan group. The skeletal evidence allows us to infer that the borders between the Fremont and

Virgin Branch Puebloans and the Fremont and the Kayenta Puebloans were very distinct. This inference improves our understanding of the behavior of three groups situated in close proximity to each other in a way that mere examination of material culture items cannot.

Acknowledgments

We thank Michelle Knoll, assistant curator at the Natural History Museum of Utah; Paul Stavast, director of the Museum of Peoples and Cultures, Brigham Young University; and Barbara Frank, curator of the Archaeological Repository, Southern Utah University, for granting us access to the human skeletal remains. Additionally, we thank Debra Martin and Jennifer Thompson for granting permission to use their original data on some of the human remains recovered from the Lost City site in Nevada.

References

Adelman, Jeremy, and Stephen Aron. 1999. "From Borderlands to Borders: Empires, Nation-States, and the Peoples in between in North American History." *American Historical Review* 104(3): 814–841.

Allison, James R. 2015. "Introducing the Fremont." *Archaeology Southwest Magazine* 29(4): 3–5.

Alvarez, Alex. 2016. "Borderlands, Climate Change, and the Genocidal Impulse." *Genocide Studies International* 10(1): 27–36.

Anderson, Kirk C., and Ted Neff. 2011. "The Influence of Paleofloods on Archaeological Settlement Patterns during A.D. 1050–1170 along the Colorado River in the Grand Canyon, Arizona, USA." *Catena* 85: 168–186.

Aufderheide, Arthur C., and Conrado Rodríguez-Martin. 1998. *The Cambridge Encyclopedia of Human Paleopathology*. Cambridge: Cambridge University Press.

Bass, William M. 2005. *Human Osteology: A Laboratory and Field Manual*. 5th ed. Columbia: Missouri Archaeological Society.

Bernardini, Wesley. 2005. "Reconsidering Spatial and Temporal Aspects of Prehistoric Cultural Identity: A Case Study from the American Southwest." *American Antiquity* 70(1): 31–54.

Billman, Brian R., Patricia M. Lambert, and Banks L. Leonard. 2000. "Cannibalism, Warfare, and Drought in the Mesa Verde Region in the Twelfth Century AD." *American Antiquity* 65(1): 145–178.

Brink, Ole. 2009. "When Violence Strikes the Head, Neck, and Face." *Journal of Trauma* 67 (1): 147–151.

Brink, Ole, Annie Vesterby, and Jørn Jensen. 1998. "Patterns of Injuries Due to Interpersonal Violence." *Injury: International Journal of the Care of the Injured* 29(9): 705–709.

Brooks, Sheilagh, and Judy Suchey. 1990. "Skeletal Age Determination Based on the Os

Pubis: A Comparison of the Acsadi-Nemskeri and Suchey-Brooks Methods." *Human Evolution* 5(3): 227–238.

Buikstra, Jane E., and Douglas H. Ubelaker. 1994. *Standards for Data Collection from Human Skeletal Remains.* Research Series no. 44. Fayetteville: Arkansas Archaeological Survey.

Crown, Patricia L., and Deborah L. Nichols, eds. 2008. *Social Violence in the Prehispanic American Southwest.* Tucson: University of Arizona Press.

D'Azevedo, Warren L., ed. 1986. *Handbook of North American Indians.* Vol. 11, *Great Basin.* Washington, DC: Smithsonian Institution Press.

Dean, Jeffrey S. 2002. "Late Pueblo II-Pueblo III in Kayenta-Branch Prehistory." In *Prehistoric Culture Change on the Colorado Plateau: Ten Thousand Years on Black Mesa,* edited by Shirley Powell and Francis E. Smiley, 121–158. Tucson: University of Arizona Press.

Geib, Phil R. 1996. "Formative Cultures and Boundaries: Reconsideration of the Fremont and Anasazi." In *Glen Canyon Revisited,* edited by P. R. Geib, 98–114. Anthropological Papers no. 119. Salt Lake City: University of Utah.

Haas, Jonathan. 1990. "Warfare and the Evolution of Tribal Polities in the Prehistoric Southwest." In *The Anthropology of War,* edited by J. Haas, 171–189. Cambridge: Cambridge University Press.

Haas, Jonathan, and Winifred Creamer. 1993. *Stress and Warfare Among the Kayenta Anasazi of the Thirteenth Century A.D.* Chicago: Field Museum of Natural History.

Hämäläinen, Pekka, and Samuel Truett. 2011. "On Borderlands." *Journal of American History* 98(2): 338–361.

Howard, Julie, and Joel C. Janetski. 1992. "Human Scalps from Eastern Utah." *Utah Archaeology* 5(1): 125–132.

Janetski, Joel C., Lane D. Richens, and Richard K. Talbot 2011. "Fremont-Anasazi Boundary Maintenance and Permeability in the Escalante Drainage." In *Meetings at the Margins,* edited by D. Rhode, 191–210. Salt Lake City: University of Utah Press.

Jennings, J. D. 1956. "The American Southwest: A Problem in Cultural Isolation." In *Seminars in Archaeology,* edited by R. Wauchope, 59–127. Society for American Archaeology Memoirs 11. Washington, DC: Society for American Archaeology.

———. 1960. "Early Man in Utah." *Utah Historical Quarterly* 28(1): 3–27.

———. 1978. *Prehistory of Utah and the Eastern Great Basin: A Review.* University of Utah Anthropological Papers 98. Salt Lake City: University of Utah Press.

Judd, N. M. 1926. *Archaeological Observations North of the Rio Colorado.* Bureau of American Ethnology Bulletin 82. Washington, DC: Government Printing Office.

Kidder, Alfred V. 1927a. "Southwestern Archaeological Conference." *El Palacio* 27(22): 554–561.

———. 1927b. "Southwestern Archaeological Conference." *Science* 66(1716): 489–491.

Kroeber, Alfred L. 1931. "The Culture-Area and Age-Area Concepts of Clark Wissler." In *Methods in Social Science, A Case Book,* edited by S. Rice, 248–265. Chicago: University of Chicago Press.

———. 1939. *Cultural and Natural Areas of Native North America.* Berkeley: University of California Press.

Lambert, Patricia M. 2002. "The Archaeology of War: A North American Perspective." *Journal of Archaeological Research* 10(3): 207–241.

Larson, Daniel O., and Joel Michaelsen. 1990. "Impacts of Climatic Variability and Population Growth on Virgin Branch Anasazi Cultural Developments." *American Antiquity* 55(2): 227–249.

LeBlanc, Steven A. 1999. *Prehistoric Warfare in the American Southwest*. Salt Lake City: University of Utah Press.

Lekson, Stephen H. 1999. *The Chaco Meridian: Centers of Political Power in the Ancient Southwest*. Walnut Creek, CA: AltaMira Press.

———. 2002. "War in the Southwest, War in the World." *American Antiquity* 67(4): 607–624.

———. 2015. *The Chaco Meridian: Centers of Political Power in the Ancient Southwest*. 2nd ed. Lanham, MD: Rowman and Littlefield.

Lightfoot, Kent G., and Antoinette Martinez. 1995. "Frontiers and Boundaries in Archaeological Perspective." *Annual Review of Anthropology* 24: 471–492.

Lovejoy, C. Owen, Richard S. Meindl, Thomas R. Pryzbeck, and Robert P. Mensforth. 1985. "Chronological Metamorphosis of the Auricular Surface of the Ilium: A New Method for the Determination of Adult Skeletal Age at Death." *American Journal of Physical Anthropology* 68(1): 15–28.

Lowell, Julia C. 2007. "Women and Men in Warfare and Migration: Implications of Gender Imbalance in the Grasshopper Region of Arizona." *American Antiquity* 72(1): 95–123.

———. 2010. "Survival Strategies of Gender-Imbalanced Migrant Households in the Grasshopper Region of Arizona." In *Engendering Households in the Prehistoric Southwest*, edited by B. J. Roth. Tucson: University of Arizona Press.

Lyneis, Margaret M. 1996. "Pueblo II-Pueblo III Change in Southwestern Utah, the Arizona strip, and Southern Nevada." In *The Prehistoric Pueblo World, A.D. 1150–1350*, edited by Michael A. Adler, 11–28. Tucson: University of Arizona Press.

Madsen, David B. 1989. *Exploring the Fremont*. Salt Lake City: Utah Museum of Natural History.

Madsen, David B., and Steven R. Simms. 1998. "The Fremont Complex: A Behavioral Perspective." *Journal of World Prehistory* 12(3): 255–337.

Mariotti, Valentina, Fiorenzo Facchini, and Maria Giovanna Belcastro. 2007. "The Study of Entheses: Proposal of a Standardised Scoring Method for Twenty-Three Entheses of the Postcranial Skeleton." *Collegium Antropologicum* 31(1): 291–313.

McNitt, Frank. 1957. *Richard Wetherill: Anasazi: Pioneer Explorer of Southwestern Ruins*. Albuquerque: University of New Mexico Press.

Meindl, Richard S., and C. Owen Lovejoy. 1985. "Ectocranial Suture Closure: A Revised Method for the Determination of Skeletal Age at Death Based on the Lateral-Anterior Sutures." *American Journal of Physical Anthropology* 68(1): 57–66.

Novak, Shannon A., and Dana D. Kollmann. 2000. "Perimortem Processing of Human Remains among the Great Basin Fremont." *International Journal of Osteoarchaeology* 10: 65–75.

Ogilvie, Marsha D., and Charles E. Hilton. 2000. "Ritualized Violence in the Prehistoric American Southwest." *International Journal of Osteoarchaeology* 10: 27–48.

Ortiz, Alfonso, ed. 1979. *Handbook of North American Indians*. Vol. 9, *Southwest*. Washington, DC: Smithsonian Institution Press.

———. 1983. *Handbook of North American Indians*, Vol. 10, *Southwest*. Washington, DC: Smithsonian Institution Press.

Ortner, D J. 2003. *Identification of Pathological Conditions in Human Skeletal Remains*. London: Academic Press.

Osterholtz, Anna J. 2012. "The Social Role of Hobbling and Torture: Violence in the Prehistoric Southwest." *International Journal of Paleopathology* 2(2–3): 148–155.

Osterholtz, Anna J., Kathryn M. Baustian and Debra L. Martin. 2014. "Introduction." In *Commingled and Disarticulated Human Remains: Working toward Improved Theory, Method, and Data*, edited by A. J. Osterholtz, K. M. Baustian, and D. L. Martin, 1–16. New York: Springer.

Owsley, Douglas W., Shannon A. Novak, Lee Jantz, and Chip Clark. 1998. *Preliminary Report: Examination of the Utah State Antiquity Skeletal Collection*. Washington, DC: National Museum of Natural History, Smithsonian Institution.

Oxenham, Marc F., and Ivor Cavill. 2010. "Porotic Hyperostosis and Cribra Orbitalia: The Erythropoietic Response to Iron-Deficiency Anaemia." *Anthropological Science* 118 (3): 199–200.

Parker, Bradley J. 2006. "Toward an Understanding of Borderland Processes." *American Antiquity* 71(1): 77–100.

Pérez, Ventura R. 2012. "The Politicization of the Dead: Violence as Performance, Politics as Usual." In *The Bioarchaeology of Violence*, edited by D. L. Martin and R. P. Harrod, 13–28. Gainesville: University of Florida Press.

Phenice, T. W. 1969. "A Newly Developed Visual Method of Sexing the Os Pubis." *American Journal of Physical Anthropology* 30(2): 297–301.

Potter, James M., and Jason P. Chuipka. 2010. "Perimortem Mutilation of Human Remains in an Early Village in the American Southwest: A Case for Ethnic Violence." *Journal of Anthropological Archaeology* 29(4): 507–523.

Raymond, Nicole M., Ryan P. Harrod, and Aaron R. Woods. 2014. "Childhood in a Marginal Environment: Analyzing Health, Nutrition, and Demographic Characteristics of Two Populations of Children living in the Pre-Contact U.S. Southwest." Paper presented at the 41st Annual Meeting of the Alaska Anthropological Association, Fairbanks, Alaska.

Rice, Glen E., and Steven A. LeBlanc. 2001. *Deadly Landscapes: Case Studies in Prehistoric Southwestern Warfare*. Salt Lake City: University of Utah Press.

Riggs, Charles R. 2005. "Late Ancestral Pueblo or Mogollon Pueblo? An Architectural Perspective on Identity." *Kiva* 70: 323–348.

Rood, Ronald J. 2001. *Preliminary Report: Archaeological Investigations at the Hysell Site, 42Sv2443*. Salt Lake City: Antiquities Section, Utah Division of State History.

Schaafsma, Polly. 1971. *Rock Art of Utah*. Cambridge: Peabody Museum of Archaeology and Ethnology Harvard University.

———. 2000. *Warrior, Shield, and Star: Imagery and Ideology of Pueblo Warfare*. Santa Fe, NM: Western Edge Press.

———. 2007. "Head Trophies and Scalping: Images in Southwest Rock Art." In *The Tak-*

ing and Displaying of Human Body Parts as Trophies by Amerindians, edited by R. J. Chacon and D. H. Dye, 90–123. New York: Springer.

Searcy, Michael T., and Richard K. Talbot. 2016. "Late Fremont Cultural Identities and Borderland Processes" In *Late Holocene Research on Foragers and Early Farmers in the Desert West*, edited by Barbara Roth and Maxine McBrinn, 234–264. Salt Lake City: University of Utah Press.

Smith, Russell Gordon. 1929. "The Concept of the Culture-Area." *Social Forces* 7(3): 421–432.

Talbot, Richard. 2003. "Intermountain Antiquities Computer System (IMACS) Archaeological Site Form for Site 42GA5814." Document on file at the Division of State History, Utah State Historic Preservation Office, Salt lake City, Utah.

Todd, T. W. 1920. "Age Changes in the Pubic Bone. I. The Male White Pubis." *American Journal of Physical Anthropology* 3: 285–334.

Turner, Christy G., II. 1983. "Taphonomic Reconstructions of Human Violence and Cannibalism Based on Mass Burials in the American Southwest." In *Carnivores, Human Scavengers, and Predators: A Question of Bone Technology*, edited by G. M. LeMoine and A. S. MacEachern, 219–240. Calgary: Archaeological Association of the University of Calgary.

Turner, Christy G., II, and Jacqueline A. Turner. 1999. *Man Corn: Cannibalism and Violence in the Prehistoric American Southwest*. Salt Lake City: University of Utah Press.

Walker, Phillip L. 1989. "Cranial Injuries as Evidence of Violence in Prehistoric Southern California." *American Journal of Physical Anthropology* 80 (3): 313–323.

Walker, Phillip L., Rhonda R. Bathurst, Rebecca Richman, Thor Gjerdrum, and Valerie A. Andrushko. 2009. "The Causes of Porotic Hyperstosis and Cribra Orbitalia: A Reappraisal of the Iron-Deficiency-Anemia Hypothesis." *American Journal of Physical Anthropology* 139(2): 109–125.

White, Tim D., Pieter A. Folkens and Michael T. Black. 2012. *Human Osteology*. 3rd ed. Boston: Academic Press.

Wilcox, David R., and Jonathan Haas. 1994. "The Scream of the Butterfly: Competition and Conflict in the Prehistoric Southwest." In *Themes in Southwest Prehistory*, edited by G. J. Gumerman, 211–238. Santa Fe, NM: School of American Research Press.

Wissler, Clark. 1917. *The American Indian: An Introduction to the Anthropology of the New World*. New York: Douglas C. McMurtrie.

———. 1927. "The Culture-Area Concept in Social Anthropology." *American Journal of Sociology* 32(6): 881–891.

Woodbury, Richard B. 1959. "A Reconsideration of Pueblo Warfare in the Southwestern United States." In *Actas del XXXIII Congreso Internacional de Americanistas*, Tomo II, 124–133. San Jose, CA: Lehmann.

Yaussy, Samantha, and Sharon N. DeWitte. 2018. "Patterns of Frailty in Non-Adults from Medieval London." *International Journal of Paleopathology* 22(September): 1–7.

V

Challenges and Limitations
of Bioarchaeological Methods and Theory

10

Mortuary Practices in the First Iron Age Romanian Frontier

The Commingled Assemblages of the Măgura Uroiului

ANNA J. OSTERHOLTZ, VIRGINIA LUCAS, CLAIRA
RALSTON, ANDRE GONCIAR, AND ANGELICA BĂLOS

In this chapter, we present the analysis of the human remains from the Măgura Uroiului, an Iron Age mortuary monument located on the Uroi Hill. This is the first of its kind to combine archaeological, bioarchaeological, and zooarchaeological analyses into a single interpretive framework for this region. It thus presents a different approach than previous work in which specialists were brought in to examine their own piles of bones at different times. For the current analysis, zooarchaeologists (such as Virginia Lucas) and bioarchaeologists (such as Anna Osterholtz) were both involved in the excavations and were able to make in-field observations. These researchers along with multiple students (including Claira Ralston, who later completed the zooarchaeological analysis of the 2015 materials) then completed analysis of both human and faunal remains in the same lab space at the same time, which facilitated a more synergistic approach to the project.

The Frontier of Context

Little archaeological work has been conducted in Iron Age deposits in the region of Transylvania. Although this region is part of Romania, it has a distinct cultural identity from the rest of the country. The majority of archaeological work that has been conducted is of good quality and has been headed by regional museum officials who produce reports of their work. However, these reports are published in Romanian. They are not typically published in peer-reviewed journals or widely disseminated.

Because the primary reporting mechanism is through gray literature, the extent of the reports varies. In general, they are completed close to the time of the excavations and present only preliminary results and usually lack correlated dates of the sites. The scant literature on Iron Age publications for Măgura Uroiului provides no calibrated dates for any of the excavations. Material culture places the Măgura Uroiului within the First (or Early) Iron Age (ca. 1200 –500 BCE). Martian (1921) described a fortified settlement during the Dacian period. In 1957, Floca described a medieval fortress on top of the hill but could not identify earlier settlements at the top of the hill. Andritoiu (1992) noted Bronze Age artifacts, but their location is not securely identified. The terrace where the mortuary monument is located was the subject of excavations and nondestructive resistivity surveys in 2004 and 2015 (Crandell and Bălos n.d.). There are no published calibrated dates for the construction or use of the monument.

During World War II, the Uroi Hill was used as a platform to hold a gun battery because of the excellent viewshed the top of the hill provides (Hansen and Oltean 2000). Numerous craters are present on the hill as a consequence of shelling activities during World War II.

When we expanded the scope of the search to the Iron Age in Romania, a question emerged. Could we expect the Iron Age in Romania to look the same as the Iron Age in Slovenia or Cyprus or the UK? There is no reason to expect cultural expressions to be consistent across geographic regions. The applicability of research conducted in any one area when examining another area is very open to debate. Also, if the definition is based on the presence of a particular artifact class (i.e., iron), dates will vary by region.

Very few publications are available for Iron Age Romania and the majority of these are reproductions of presentations at regional conferences that have been published in English on websites such as ResearchGate (e.g., Crandell and Bălos n.d.) or have been published in foreign languages translatable via Google Translate. The expectation of widely available peer-reviewed publications in English is indicative of western privilege. Despite the acknowledgment of this privilege, having publications regarding archaeological work in Romania in more readily available formats and languages would greatly assist studies such as our exploration of a little-known but important time frame.

Given the difficulties of examining published literature for the area surrounding the site and for the Iron Age in general, the current project is to a certain extent operating in an unknown space on the frontier of bioarchaeology in Transylvania. Drawing population-level conclusions about mortuary processes is not appropriate based on this single assemblage, but without the description of a single assemblage such as this one we will never build a basis for discussing mortuary processes during the Iron Age in Transylvania. The goal of this chapter is to provide such a description.

The Măgura Uroiului

Geography of the Măgura Uroiului

The funerary monument known as the Măgura Uroiului sits on the Uroi Hill at the confluence of the Mureș and Strei Valleys (figure 10.1). The Mureș and Strei Rivers run through these valleys and serve as access routes between the center of Transylvania and the Orăștie Mountains. Geologically, the hill is made up of andesites, augite, magnetite, and microlites of feldspar. All of these have been continuously quarried from prehistoric to modern times (Crandell and Bălos n.d.).

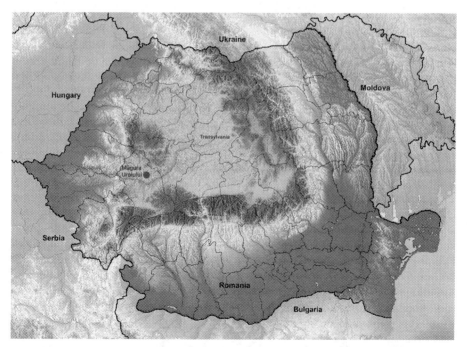

Figure 10.1. Map of Romania showing location of the Măgura Uroiului monument. Map adapted from Google Maps by Anna Osterholtz.

This area has always had a significant cultural role. It was the political and administrative center of the Dacian kingdoms in approximately 1 BCE or 1 CE. The terraces below the monument described in this chapter host Dacian reenactments multiple times each year, including the widely known DacFest put on by the Terra Dacica Aeterna (2013), whose website states that their goal is to "bring the general public closer to ancient history through experimental archaeology and reenactment. With the aid of experimental archaeology, the members of the association have recreated ancient equipment, tools, and buildings by using, as much as possible, the working methods and tools available during that period." Many archaeologists, including Angelica Bălos, are involved with these reenactments, which rely heavily on archaeological findings. These reenactments are a primary method of involving the public with their own history and disseminating archaeological findings to the public and to other researchers.

Excavation of the Mortuary Monument

Excavation of the funerary monument was conducted in block units in 2014 and 2015 under the direction of Angelica Bălos through the auspices of the Hunedoara County Ministry of Culture. The excavations uncovered the remains of a large mortuary monument that consisted of a rubble wall and an associated trench. The 2015 season was conducted as an intensive bioarchaeological and zooarchaeological workshop through ArchaeoTek. Analyses of recovered materials from all seasons was conducted in 2015 and completed in 2016.

Bălos developed a model for the construction of the mortuary monument. Based on information from her excavations, she theorizes that construction of the mortuary monument was a multistage process. First, a large trench at least 1 meter wide was dug. Into this trench human remains and animal sacrifices were deposited. Large natural stones in the form of a rubble wall were placed on top of these remains. Large ceramic vessels have been found along the sides of the rubble wall and the remains of feasting activities can be seen in the rubble fill of the wall itself. This suggests that feasting at the monument occurred after it was constructed and that the remnants of the feast were deposited on site. The ceramics were left in place. The overall size of the monument is unknown, as the ends have not been found, but it extends for at least 15 meters along the escarpment. The monument was later disturbed by Dacians and Romans but has remained in local memory.

Human Remains

Demography

During excavations from 2004 to 2010, only adult females and children between the ages of 6 and 10 years were recovered from the monument. During the 2015 season, commingled elements from a single adult male were recovered along with the remains of an additional adult female and four children. Two of the children were less than 3 years old at death and one was between of 3 and 7 years. The fourth child's age could not be more finely estimated than between 2 and 12 years (table 10.1). The discrepancy between the assemblages recovered in 2004–2010 and those recovered in 2015 is not likely a methodological one or related to excavation bias, since the excavation team was led by the same director and the analysis was conducted using the same researchers, techniques, and database. The differences reflect a different depositional history for this section of the monument than the other sections of the monument that were excavated in previous years.

The demography is intriguing, but given the small sample sizes, it is difficult to use these data to begin to understand larger cultural practices in Iron Age Romania. All of these individuals were placed in similar contexts—under the fill for a large mortuary monument. The assemblage is not large enough to contain all individuals from the nearby settlement (on the top of the escarpment). It is likely, therefore, that these individuals are a subset of the population and were given distinct mortuary treatment. Without discovery and excavation of additional materials and remains, though, this remains a hypothetical assertion.

Table 10.1. Demography of the human Măgura Uroiului assemblages

| Year Excavated | Unit | Subadult | | Adult | | |
		Child	Adolescent	Female	Male	Totals
2004	S3	2		1		3
2005	S4	1		1		2
2006	S6	1	1	1		3
2006	S7	1		2		3
2010	S15	2		1		3
2015	S18	4		1	1	6
Totals		11	1	7	1	20

Trauma

All elements were scored for antemortem and perimortem trauma, but the only instances of interpersonal trauma were healed cranial depression fractures. Table 10.2 presents the overall results. Figure 10.2A gives the overall distribution visually. Of the twenty individuals recovered, four (20 percent) exhibited healed cranial trauma. In particular, of the eleven children present, two (18 percent) had healed trauma. The only adolescent identified had healed trauma. Cranial depression fractures were recorded on both the parietals and the frontal bone in the two children, the frontal bone of the adolescent, and the frontal bone of the only adult to exhibit healed trauma (figure 10.2B). All of the fractures were located either at or above the hat-brim line (HBL). This line is a visual marker on the skull that is used to describe the location of traumatic injuries based on modern forensic science. Through an examination of modern traumatic injury, researchers have defined this area on the skull to be a useful interpretive aid in both forensic and bioarchaeological contexts. Essentially, injuries that occur superior to the HBL are more likely to be the result of interpersonal trauma, while those inferior to the HBL are more likely to be the result of accidents (Guyomarc'h et al. 2010; Kremer et al. 2008; Maxeiner and Ehrlich 2000).

One individual, a child between the ages of 6 and 10 years at death, exhibited two cranial depression fractures—an indicator of violence recidivism. Multiple

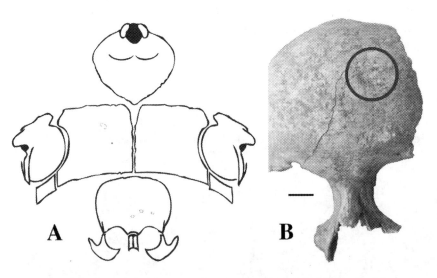

Figure 10.2. Distribution of cranial trauma (*A*) and an example of a large healed cranial depression fracture on an adult female (*B*) at the Măgura Uroiului. Photos by Anna Osterholtz.

Table 10.2. Cranial depression fractures by demography, size, location, and depth

| | | Subadult | | | | | | | | Adult | | | |
| | | Child | | | | Adolescent | | | | Female | | | |
Year excavated	Unit	N	Location	Area	Depth	N	Location	Area	Depth	N	Location	Area	Depth
2005	S4	1	Parietal	90.52	0.44								
2006	S6		Midline frontal	24.43	0.2								
		2	Parietal	2.265	0.1								
						1	Left frontal	34.45	0.4				
2010	S15									1	Midline frontal	46.56	0.27

traumas put an individual at increased risk of neurological and behavior problems, including cognitive changes that, in turn, put an individual at risk for future injury and additional cranial depression fractures (Blackmer and Marshall 1999; Caufield et al. 2004; Centers for Disease Control 2010; Hedges et al. 1995). The indications of multiple traumas on an individual of such young age suggests that violence had a significant social function and was commonplace in this society.

Pathology

We recorded pathological changes for each fragment. Two areas are of interest: the cranium and the lower limb. In the cranium, we scored two areas: the vault was scored for porotic hyperostosis and the orbits were scored for cribra orbitalia. Both porotic hyperostosis and cribra orbitalia are characterized by the expansion of the diplöe through the outer table of the parietals and frontal, creating a porous appearance in the outer surface of the bone. Porotic hyperostosis occurs on the external vault of the skull (figure 10.3A), while cribra orbitalia occurs on the superior surface of the orbit (figure 10.3B). Both have been linked to iron-deficiency anemia; some researchers assert that this is the most common cause of these disorders worldwide (Stuart-Macadam 1992; Stuart-Macadam and Kent 1992). Martin and colleagues (1985), however, note that individuals with anemia are more susceptible to infections. Porotic hyperostosis and cribra orbitalia may, in fact, be the result of opportunistic infections associated with larger health issues.

Furthermore, several studies have argued for separate but related etiological pathways for the development of porotic hyperostosis and cribra orbitalia lesions (Walker 2009; Oxenham and Cavill 2010). A recent study by Rivera and Lahr (2017) provides further evidence that porotic hyperostosis and cribra orbitalia may be produced by different underlying hematopoietic conditions. For example, porotic hyperostosis, which is associated with diplöic expansion of the cranial vault, Rivera and Lahr (2017) suggest that it is caused by nutritional stress (e.g., iron deficiency, vitamin B12 deficiency) and infectious disease. They suggest that cribra orbitalia has a more complicated etiology. When it co-occurs with porotic hyperostosis, the lesions are produced by similar disease processes as porotic hyperostosis; when it is not associated with porotic hyperostosis, it is likely the result of anemia due to chronic infectious disease or scurvy.

Regardless of the actual etiology of these disorders, they are general indicators of stress, either as the primogenitors of the lesions or as a precursor to the

Figure 10.3. Porotic hyperostosis in a juvenile cranium (A) and cribra orbitalia in an adult female cranium (B) at the Măgura Uroiului. Photos by Anna Osterholtz.

opportunistic infections that possibly create the lesions. We chose these two indicators for this study for several reasons. First, they are easily recognizable and scorable on a sliding scale of both presence and degree using the methodology set forth in Buikstra and Ubelaker (1994). Second, they can be recorded on fragmentary remains.

The Telekfalva church assemblage (detailed in chapter 11) that dates to the medieval period shows that nutritional deficiency was not uncommon in Transylvania. Ongoing paleopathological analyses indicate that both scurvy and rickets were present in the church population. Given the findings of the Telekfalva church, one specific pathological process of interest to us is scurvy (vitamin C deficiency). Though the Telekfalva church assemblage dates to a much later period and is farther to the east than the Măgura Uroiului (Bethard et al. 2014; Osterholtz et al. 2014; chapter 11, this volume), the presence of multiple scorbutic individuals suggests that these diseases may have been present in other parts of Transylvania. The presence of a single individual with changes that are pathognomonic for scurvy, including porotic hyperostosis on the cranial vault, increased porosity on the greater wings of the sphenoid, and bilateral cribra orbitalia indicates that vitamin C deficiency was a reality for at least some of the population.

The long bones, particularly the tibia and fibula, were scored for the presence of periosteal reactions. Periosteal reactions are frequently interpreted to be caused by generalized inflammatory responses at the periosteum of bone surfaces in response to prolonged or chronic infection (Martin et al. 2013; Ortner 2003). Thus, these lesions are often identified and used in conjunction with other skeletal indicators of stress to identify individuals who experienced disproportionate morbidity throughout their lives or at the time of their death (Martin et al. 2013).

Faunal Remains

Faunal material was excavated along with human skeletal remains from trenches in all years. As noted above, zooarchaeological research is a relatively recent newcomer to the archaeological canon of Transylvania. Because of this, comparative materials and published sources were even rarer for zooarchaeological materials than for bioarchaeological materials. Despite this, Lucas and Ralston were able to identify elements from multiple genera and species, including rabbits, carnivores, horse, pig, deer, bison, cattle, sheep, goat, numerous birds, catfish, and gastropods (table 10.3; Lucas et al. 2017; Osterholtz et al. 2016). Some of the faunal material was located in close proximity to human burials while other material was distributed throughout the trench, indicating multiple depositional histories for the fauna. This suggests that animals were important to mortuary ritual in more than one way, both as animal sacrifices and as remnants of feasting activity.

Animal Sacrifice

The presence of mostly complete and articulated skeletons suggests that the animals were placed whole into the funerary monument, which is indicative of sacrifice. Furthermore, elements present in articulation suggest that the respective limb or trunk would have been fleshed as it was placed in the monument. Russell (2012) has stated that identifying sacrifice in the archaeological record

Table 10.3. Nonhuman species represented at the Măgura Uroiului

Taxon	Common Name	Taxon	Common Name
Mammalia	Mammals	cf. *Bison bonasus*	cf. European bison
Mammalia, sm.	Small mammal	*Bos primigenius*	Aurochs
Mammalia, sm.–med.	Small–medium mammal	*Bos taurus*	Domestic Cattle
Mammalia, med	Medium mammal	*Capra* spp.	Goat
Mammalia, med-lg.	Medium–large mammal	*Ovis* spp.	Sheep
Mammalia, lg.	Large mammal	*Ovis* or *Capra* spp.	Sheep or goat
Talpus spp.	European mole	Aves	Bird
Leporidae	Rabbit	Aves, sm.	Small bird
Lepus europaeus	European hare	Aves, med.	Medium bird
Rodentia	Rodent	Aves, med.–lg.	Medium–large bird
Sciurus spp.	Squirrel	Aves, lg.	Large bird
Sciurus vulgaris	Red squirrel	Anatidae	Duck
Muridae	Old World mice and rats	cf. Ciconiidae	cf. Stork
Mus sp.	Mouse	Passeriformes	Perching birds
Rattus spp.	Rat	Emydidae	Pond or marsh turtle
Carnivora	Carnivore	Siluriformes	Catfish
Canis sp.	Wolf, dog, etc.	Bivalvia	Bivalve
Canis lupus	Gray wolf	Unionidae	Freshwater bivalve
Equus caballus	Domestic horse	*Unio* spp.	Freshwater mussel
Artiodactyla	Even-toed ungulate	Gastropoda	Gastropods
Sus scrofa	Pig	*Helix* spp.	Land snail
Cervidae	Deer	*Helix lutescens*	True land snail
Cervus elaphus	Red deer	*Alopia livida*	Land snail
Dama dama	Fallow deer	*Alopia maciana*	Land snail
Bovidae	Cloven-hoofed mammal	*Cepaea vindobonensis*	Grove Snail
Bison bonasus	European bison		

can be complicated. However, several analyses have been completed that identify animal sacrifice and inclusion of faunal remains in human funerary contexts. Croft (2003) indicates that complete, unbutchered carcasses of immature sheep and goat were excavated from human burial contexts at the Pre-Pottery Neolithic B site of Kissonerga-Mylouthkia on Cyprus. In addition, the Iron Age site of La Tène in northern France yielded animal remains in human burial contexts that exhibited processing marks, suggesting sacrificial and feasting activity (Russell 2012). Furthermore, ethnographic accounts in Africa indicate that animal sacrifice is an important element of funerary rites (de Heusch 1985; Russell 2012).

In the Măgura excavations, the articulated left forelimb of a horse, including the carpals; a metacarpal; and proximal, intermediate, and distal phalanges were excavated from trench S6. Excavation photos from 2010 portray a mostly intact domestic cow skeleton in close proximity to a human mandible. The presence of these articulated skeletal elements in the monument and in proximity to a human mandible suggests that at least part of the animal was placed in the monument still fleshed at or around the same time as the human remains. A mostly complete and articulated sheep or goat skeleton was excavated during the 2015 field season, indicating that the animal was whole and fleshed when placed in the monument.

Ritual Animal Use

The 2010 and 2015 field seasons yielded three relatively intact crania: one gray wolf cranium in 2010 and domestic horse and goat in 2015. The gray wolf cranium (*Canis lupus*) will be discussed below. The other two crania, including a single horse (*Equus caballus*) and a single goat (*Capra* sp.) were particularly interesting as this was the only skeletal element of these individuals recovered from these contexts. The domestic horse (*Equus caballus*) cranium appears to have been balanced between two rocks in close proximity to human remains. The goat cranium was located in close proximity to a mostly complete sheep or goat skeleton. However, this cranium did not articulate with that skeleton.

The gray wolf cranium from 2010, which was located near human skeletal remains, was relatively intact with the exception of the left frontal orbit and other smaller fragments of the left parietal (figure 10.4). Additionally, a single gray wolf metacarpal was uncovered resting atop human remains excavated during the 2010 field season (figure 10.5). A sheep or goat metacarpal and proximal

Figure 10.4. Gray wolf (*Canis lupus*) skull in situ at the Măgura Uroiului. Photo by Angelica Bălos.

Figure 10.5. Gray wolf (*Canis lupus*) metacarpal in close proximity to human remains at the Măgura Uroiului. Photo by Angelica Bălos.

Figure 10.6. Carving of a Dacian dragon at the Măgura Uroiului site. Photo by Virginia Lucas.

phalanges were also located under both the human remains and the gray wolf metacarpal.

The presence of these relatively intact and isolated crania and the single gray wolf metacarpal in association with human remains suggests the preferential selection or status of these animals (Croft 2003). In addition to the aforementioned elements, approximately thirty-three elements and fragments were identified as gray wolf. The presence of the wolf in this funerary monument is indicative of the importance of this species to the community who built and used the monument. The gray wolf is prevalent in the mythology of the Hallstatt period and among Dacian peoples who inhabited this region. While this site predates the Hallstatt time period, the syncretism of a wolf (head) and dragon body (figure 10.6), embodied by the Dacian Dragon, was a prevalent motif in the religious views of the local population (Pârvan 1928).

Feasting

The faunal remains from Măgura also exhibit evidence of feasting activity. Several long-bone elements from horse, red deer, fallow deer, domestic cow, and sheep or goat display cut marks near joint articulation sites. Perimortem fracture patterns are also evident on the diaphyses of marrow-rich long bones, and many elements exhibit charring consistent with burning. All are features consistent with human butchering, processing, and preparation of elements for consumption (Binford 1981). The presence of numerous unfused elements and epiphyses suggests the butchery of young animals, a practice consistent with feasting activities (Sandefur 2002). Finally, the inclusion of several articulated hind limbs and forelimbs of sheep or goat in the same depositional context is also consistent with butchering behavior and is thus evocative of feasting activity (Lev-Tov and McGeough 2007). In sheep and lamb, for example, the forelimb is often selected for the lamb shank, a tender cut of meat (Lev-Tov and McGeough 2007). Cut marks on the distal humerus of a horse and the inclusion of a proximal femur of a juvenile horse, indicated by the incomplete fusion of the greater trochanter and head, suggest the consumption of horse, which is a common food staple in this area of Romania today. Feasting often coincided with the type of ritual activity this funerary monument denotes (Stocker and Davis 2004). Funerary feasting continues to occur throughout the world. Different rituals occur depending on the geographic location of the community, but a feast will typically coincide with funerary mores (Wilson 2011).

Identifying ritualized feasting in the archaeological record can be problematic, as a number of factors must be considered when evaluating this activity. These factors include identifying activity patterns that reflect how different foodstuffs were used than those used in daily practice and evidence of ritualization that sets these foods apart from commonly used foods (Clarke 2001; Dietler 2001; Hamilakis 2008; Hayden 2001; Russell 2012; Twiss 2008, 2012; Wright 2004). The presence of wild game, such as the red deer and fallow deer (the only Cervids in the assemblage), suggests a deviation from the daily meat products consumed by the community, providing evidence of ritualistic feasting episodes. The represented elements of the red deer include antlers, an unfused calcaneus, and femora; the represented elements of the fallow deer include tarsals, metatarsals, metacarpals, and antlers. The calcaneus exhibits cut marks, suggestive of skinning and thus of processing activity.

In addition to the long-bone fragments, several freshwater mussels and land snails are present in the faunal assemblage. Land snails and bivalves are occasionally disregarded as intrusive in an archaeological context. In this case, however, the species present in the assemblage are edible snails. Fifty-one fragments of freshwater bivalves are present, including six that form a complete shell. In total, 568 complete or relatively complete gastropods are present, representing four identified species, including true land snail (*Helix lutescens*), land snail (*Alopia livida, Alopia maciana*), and grove snail (*Cepaea vindobonensis*). Because several of the gastropods and bivalves exhibit signs of heat alteration, we can infer that these likely were used in a feasting activity. Although gastropods and bivalves are often discounted as having little to no nutritional value and consequently are overlooked as evidence of subsistence practices in archaeological analyses, we posit that at this site they were used in a ritual feasting context, as many complete bivalves were present in the assemblage. The invertebrates represent the majority of the burned elements of the faunal assemblage. Many of the vertebrate remains have not been altered by heat, suggesting the meat was cooked without affecting the bone.

Conclusion

The majority of human remains have been found under the platform structure in a deep trench dug in preparation for the platform. Based on the presence of multiple small human hand and foot bones, the burials appear to be primary in nature. They seem to have been laid under the platform before it was constructed and the platform appears to have been built on top of them. It is likely that the commingling that has occurred since their deposition is due to normal postdepositional processes, normal moving and shifting of earth, and movement of earth caused by heavy machinery and modern warfare.[1]

The majority of the processed animal bone appears to have come from the fill of the platform, along the top of the platform, or in the trench to the sides of the platform. Both animal sacrifice and feasting can be identified based on the faunal assemblages.

Taken together, data gathered from the Măgura Uroiului monument indicate that mortuary activity of the First Iron Age in Transylvania was complex. The burials described here were likely deposited intentionally as a part of the construction of the monument. One male was recovered in the presence of multiple female and child skeletons. It is unclear how these individuals relate to other Iron Age assemblages, as very little archaeological or osteological work has been performed in the area. Given the small sample sizes and lack of comparative burials, it is unclear whether the individuals included in this monument represent a unique portion of the population or are similar to the rest of Iron Age Romanian society. These assemblages, however, give us a glimpse into at least one part of the Romanian frontier.

Note

1. At least one large impact crater from World War II is visible on the hillside. The impact destroyed part of the funerary platform.

References

Andritoiu, I. 1992. *Civilizatia tracilor din sud: Estul Transilvaniei in epoca bronzului.* Bucharest: Bibliotheca Thracologica.

Bethard, Jonathan D., Anna J. Osterholtz, Andre Gonciar, and Z. Nyaradi. 2014. "Of Infants and Elderly: A Bioarchaeological Analysis of a 17th Century Mortuary Context from Transylvania, Romania." Paper presented at the 79th Annual Meeting of the Society for American Archaeology, Austin, TX.

Binford, L. R. 1981. *Bones: ancient men and modern myths.* Academic Press, New York.

Blackmer, J., and S. C. Marshall. 1999. A Comparison of Traumatic Brain Injury in the Saskatchewan Native North American and Non-native North American Populations. *Brain Injury* 13(8):627–635.

Buikstra, Jane E., and Douglas H. Ubelaker, eds. 1994. *Standards for Data Collection from Human Skeletal Remains: Proceedings of a Seminar at the Field Museum of Natural History, Organized by Jonathan Haas.* Fayetteville: Arkansas Archaeological Survey.

Caufield, J., A. Singhal, R. Moulton, F. Brenneman, D. Redelmeier, and A. J. Baker. 2004. "Trauma Recidivism in a Large Urban Canadian Population." *Journal of Trauma, Injury, Infection, and Critical Care* 57(4): 872–876.

Centers for Disease Control. 2010. "Traumatic Brain Injury in Prisons and Jails: An Unrecognized Problem." https://www.cdc.gov/traumaticbraininjury/pdf/prisoner_tbi_prof-a.pdf.

Clarke, Michael J. 2001. "Akha Feasting: An Ethnoarchaeological Perspective." In *Feasts: Archaeological and Ethnographic Perspectives on Food, Politics, and Power*, edited by M. Dietler and B. Hayden, 144–167. Washington, DC: Smithsonian Institution.

Crandell, Otis and Angelica Bălos. N.d. "Non-Destructive Research at Măgura Uroiului. Resistivity Surveys during 2006–2007." https://www.researchgate.net/publication/256253987_Non-Destructive_Research_at_Magura_Uroiului_Resistivity_Surveys_During_2006-2007.

Croft, Paul. 2003. "The Animal Bones." In *The Colonisation and Settlement of Cyprus: Investigations at Kissonerga-Mylouthkia, 1976–1996*, edited by Edgar J. Peltenburg, 49–58. Savedalen: Paul Astroms Forlag.

De Heusch, Luc. 1985. *Sacrifice in Africa: A Structural Approach.* Manchester: Manchester University Press.

Dietler, Michael. 2001. "Theorizing the Feast: Rituals of Consumption, Commensal Politics, and Power in African Contexts." In *Feasts: Archaeological and Ethnographic Perspectives on Food, Politics, and Power*, edited by M. Dietler and B. Hayden, 65–114. Washington, DC: Smithsonian Institution.

Floca, O. 1957. *Regiunea Hunedoara.* Deva: Ghid Turistic.

Guyomarc'h, P., M. Campagna-Vailancourt, C. Kremer, and A. Sauvageau. 2010. "Discrimination of Falls and Blows in Blunt Head Trauma: A Multi-Criteria Approach." *Journal of Forensic Sciences* 55(2): 423–427.

Hamilakis, Yannis. 2008. "Time, Performance, and the Production of Mnemonic Record: From Feasting to an Archaeology of Eating and Drinking." In *Dais: The Aegean Feast*, edited by L. Hitchcock, R. Laffineur, and J. I. Crowley, 3–20. Liège: Université de Liège.

Hansen, W. S., and I. A. Oltean. 2000. "A Multi-Period Site on Uroi Hill, Hunedoara: An Aerial Perspective." *Acta Musei Napocensis* 37(1): 43–50.

Hayden, Brian. 2001. "Fabulous Feasts: A Prolegomenon to the Importance of Feasting." In *Feasts: Archaeological and Ethnographic Perspectives on Food, Politics, and Power*, edited by M. Dietler and B. Hayden, 23–64. Washington, DC: Smithsonian Institution.

Hedges, Bruce E., Joel E. Dimsdale, David B. Hoyt, Charles Berry and Karsten Leitz. 1995. "Characteristics of Repeat Trauma Patients, San Diego County." *American Journal of Public Health* 85(7): 1008–1010.

Kremer, Célia, Stéphanie Racette, Charles-Antoine Dionne, and Anny Sauvageau. 2008. "Discrimination of Falls and Blows in Blunt Head Trauma: Systematic Study of the Hat Brim Line Rule in Relation to Skull Fractures." *Journal of Forensic Sciences* 53(3): 716–719.

Lev-Tov, Justin, and Kevin McGeough. 2007. "Examining Feasting in Late Bronze Age Syro-Palestine through Ancient Texts and Bones." In *The Archaeology of Food and Identity*, edited by K. C. Twiss, 85–111. Center for Archaeological Investigations Occasional Paper no. 34. Carbondale: Southern Illinois University.

Lucas, Virginia, Claira Ralston, Anna J. Osterholtz, Andre Gonciar, and Angelica Bălos. 2017. "Sacrifice or Feasting: Fauna Interpretations of the First Iron Age Romanian Commingled Assemblages at Măgura Uroiului." Paper presented at the 82nd annual meeting of the Society for American Archaeology, Vancouver, BC.

Martian, I. 1921. *Urme din razboaiele romanilor cu dacii.* Publicatiile Comisiunii Monumentelor Istorice. Cluj: Krafft & Drotleff.

Martin, Debra L., Alan H. Goodman, and George J. Armelagos. 1985. "Skeletal Pathologies as Indicators of Quality and Quantity of Diet." In *The Analysis of Prehistoric Diets*, edited by R. I. Gilbert Jr. and J. H. Mielke, 227–279. Orlando, FL: Academic Press.

Martin, Debra L., Ryan P. Harrod, and Ventura R. Pérez. 2013. *Bioarchaeology: An Integrated Approach to Working with Human Remains.* New York: Springer.

Maxeiner, H., and E. Ehrlich. 2000. "Uber die Lokalisation, Anzahl und Länge von Wunden der Kopfhaut bei Sturz und Schlag—ein Beitrag zur Anwendbarkeit der sogenannten Hutkrempenregel" (Site, Number and Depth of Wounds of the Scalp in Falls and Blows: A Contribution to the Validity of the So-Called Hat Brim Rule). *Archiv für Kriminologie* 205(3–4): 82.

Ortner, Donald J. 2003. *Identification of Pathological Conditions in Human Skeletal Remains.* Los Angeles: Academic Press.

Osterholtz, Anna J., Jonathan D. Bethard, Andre Gonciar and Z. Nyaradi. 2014. "Possible Prenatal and Perinatal Scurvy at Telekfalva, Romania." Paper presented at the Annual Meeting of the American Association of Physical Anthropologists, Calgary, Alberta.

Osterholtz, Anna J., Virginia Lucas, Andre Gonciar, and Angelica Bălos. 2016. "Mortuary Practices in the First Iron Age Romanian Frontier: The Commingled Assemblages of the Magura Uroiului." Paper presented at the 81st annual meeting of the Society for American Archaeology, Orlando, FL.

Oxenham, Marc Fredrick, and Ivor Cavill. 2010. "Porotic Hyperostosis and Cribra Orbitalia: The Erythropoietic Response to Iron-Deficiency Anaemia." *Anthropological Science* 118(3): 199–200.

Pârvan, Vasile. 1928. *Dacia: An Outline of the Early Civilization of the Carpatho-Danubian Countries.* Cambridge: Cambridge University Press.

Rivera, Frances, and Marta Mirazón Lahr. 2017. "New Evidence Suggesting a Dissociated Etiology for Cribra Orbitalia and Porotic Hyperostosis." *American Journal of Physical Anthropology* 164(1): 76–96.

Russell, Nerissa. 2012. *Social Zooarchaeology: Humans and Animals in Prehistory.* New York: Cambridge University Press.

Sandefur, Elsie. 2002. "Animal Husbandry and Meat Consumption." In *Empire and Domestic Economy*, edited by T. N. D'Altroy and C. A. Hastdorf, 179–202. New York: Springer.

Stocker, S. R., and J. L. Davis. 2004. "Animal Sacrifice, Archives, and Feasting at the Palace of Nestor." In *The Mycenaean Feast*, edited by J. C. Wright, 179–195. Princeton, NJ: American School of Classical Studies at Athens.

Stuart-Macadam, Patricia. 1992. "Anemia in Past Human Populations." In *Diet, Demography and Disease*, edited by P. Stuart-Macadam and S. Kent, 151–172. New York: Aldine de Gruyter.

Stuart-Macadam, Patricia, and Susan Kent, eds. 1992. *Diet, Demography, and Disease.* New York: Aldine de Gruyter.

Terra Dacica Aeterna. 2013. "What We Do." http://terradacica.ro/ce-facem/?lang=en.

Twiss, Katheryn C. 2008. "Transformations in an Early Agricultural Society: Feasting in the Southern Levantine Pre-Pottery Neolithic." *Journal of Anthropological Archaeology* 27: 418–442.

———. 2012. "The Archaeology of Food and Social Diversity." *Journal of Archaeological Research* 20(4): 357–395.

Walker, P. L., R. R. Bathurst, R. Richman, T. Gjerdum, and V. A. Andrushko. 2009. "The Causes of Porotic Hyperostosis and Cribra Orbitalia: A Reappraisal of the Iron-Deficiency Anemia Hypothesis." *American Journal of Physical Anthropology* 139(2): 109–125.

Wilson, R. J. A. 2011. "Funerary Feasting in Early Byzantine Sicily: New Evidence from Kaukana." *Journal of Archaeology* 115(2): 263–302.

Wright, James C. 2004. "A Survey of Evidence for Feasting in Mycenaean Society." In *The Mycenaean Feast*, edited by J. C. Wright, 13–58. Princeton, NJ: American School of Classical Studies.

11

Marginalized Motherhood

Infant Burial in Seventeenth-Century Transylvania

JONATHAN D. BETHARD, ANNA J. OSTERHOLTZ,
ZSOLT NYÁRÁDI, AND ANDRE GONCIAR

The Concept of Frontier

This volume takes the term "frontier" out of a static understanding and urges us to examine more aspects of bioarchaeological analysis. Contributions have posted questions such as What is a frontier? How do we conceptualize it? and How can bioarchaeologists contribute to our understanding of frontier? We argue that a broadly construed notion of frontier has the potential to answer each of these questions and we attempt to do so in this chapter.

To begin, we provide some basic definitions. The Merriam-Webster dictionary defines "frontier" as:

a border between two countries
a distant area where few people live
the limits of knowledge in a particular field

We argue that a flexible application of this definition that includes the sense of both a geographic boundary and innovative, boundary-bending bioarchaeological scholarship has potential to enhance what we know about the past. In this chapter, we examine the bioarchaeology of the frontier from these two perspectives with a case study from seventeenth-century Transylvania.

First, we address the notion of frontier by presenting our work in Telekfalva, a Hungarian-speaking Székely community located at the eastern edge of Transylvania.[1] Because few bioarchaeologists are familiar with the Székely population, virtually all lines of bioarchaeological inquiry are at the frontier of knowledge production in this area. While our local colleagues working across this region have a rich, multidisciplinary, and nuanced understanding of Székely history, political events of the twentieth century isolated the region from international scholars, including bioarchaeologists (chapter 10, this volume). Thus, this chapter can be seen as an introduction of Székely bioarchaeology to a wider audience and the beginning of a conversation that we anticipate will take many forms.

Second, our work contributes to the bioarchaeology of the frontier by addressing questions that are somewhat new for bioarchaeological scholars: those related to maternal health and infant death and to mortuary practices related to the burial of newborn infants in a post-Reformation Calvinist mortuary context in Transylvania. We will introduce what we consider to be a frontier of bioarchaeological research on Hungarian-speaking Székely communities in Transylvania by combining archaeological data with archival documentation and new bioarchaeological literature on the subject of maternal and infant stress.

Transylvania and the Székelyföld

We begin our discussion by introducing the history of the region of Eastern Europe widely known as Transylvania.[2] A recent study of mitochondrial DNA variation for different portions of present-day Romania exemplifies the complexity of population movement in this part of Europe through time (Cocoş et al. 2017). In a study of over 700 individuals from the historically Romanian territories of Wallachia, Dobrudja, Moldavia, and Transylvania, mitochondrial DNA haplotypes show much greater similarity for individuals from Wallachia, Dobrudja, and Moldavia with the Balkan states.[3] Transylvanian individuals, in contrast, are more closely related to individuals from Central Europe. Cocoş and colleagues (2017) attribute this primarily to topography and the fact that the Carpathian Arch would have limited movement from the Balkans into Transylvania.

While the political history of this region is remarkably complex, we provide a brief sketch here. The kingdom of Hungary existed in some form or another for nearly 1,000 years (Marczali 1971; Molnár 2001; Murdock 2000a; Rady 2000). Due to the rise of the Ottoman Empire, beginning in the second half of the sixteenth century, the kingdom of Hungary split into three parts: Royal Hungary (ruled by the Habsburgs), Ottoman Hungary, and the semi-independent Principality of Transylvania (Molnár 2001). Though semi-independent, the Principality of Transylvania functioned as a vassal state of the Ottoman Empire until 1711, when Habsburg authority over Transylvania was consolidated. During this period, Transylvania was a multiethnic, multi-religious landscape. Magyars and Szeklers constituted the majority of the population, followed by Romanians, Saxons, Serbians, and Roma (Molnár 2001).[4] As was the case throughout Europe, the mid-sixteenth-century Reformation transformed the social landscape as people exchanged Catholicism for Protestant denominations (Murdock 2000a). According to Molnár (2001), many historians see the seventeenth century as Transylvania's "golden age" because this is when the population reached its apex of some 955,000 people.

While bioarchaeologists and historians have contributed to the study of medieval and early modern Transylvanian Saxon populations (e.g., Istrate et al. 2015; Morgan 2009), our work focuses on the Székely region at the geographic frontier of eastern Transylvania, which for centuries has stayed relatively constant in terms of a Hungarian-speaking majority. According to numerous scholars, the Székely arrived in this region of Transylvania sometime in the fifth to ninth centuries, although the specific date remains unknown (Brandstätter et al. 2007; Molnár 2001). While the exact timing of the arrival of the Székely remains elusive, scholars agree that they have inhabited this region since the thirteenth century, and they are still there today (Bíró et al. 2015; Brandstätter et al. 2007; Molnár 2001). This predominately Hungarian-speaking Székely region of northeastern Transylvania changed hands twice in the twentieth century and was not finally incorporated into present-day Romania until after World War II. Living people today can recall a time when they or their parents or grandparents experienced a shift in international borders and national identity.

Although bioarchaeologists have contributed a great deal to what is known about medieval and early modern Europeans through carefully contextualizing their analysis of human skeletal remains archaeologically and historically, such studies have been rare in the Székelyföld. Few researchers have used bioarchaeological data to answer questions about the daily life, mortuary customs, and population structure of Hungarian-speaking Székely communities despite their centuries-long presence in the eastern Carpathian Basin of Transylvania. Though analyses of skeletal remains are rare, contemporary Székely communities have been the focus of several genetic population studies (Bíró et al. 2015; Brandstätter et al. 2007). However, biological distance analysis and ancient DNA (aDNA) has not been used to investigate broad questions about Transylvanian population structure or more specific questions about particular Székely communities.

In addition to reconstructing site-specific demography, dietary practices, and patterns of stress and disease and interpreting mortuary customs, bio-archaeology is uniquely positioned to provide direct evidence of population structure through the analysis of aDNA (Hassan et al. 2014; Bolnick and Smith 2007; Hagelberg et al. 2015; Stone and Stoneking 1993; Stone et al. 1999). Molecular anthropologists have used aDNA obtained from archaeologically derived human skeletons to answer broad questions such as when the first farmers arrived in Neolithic Europe and when the New World was colonized by its first inhabitants (Bramanti et al. 2009; Stone and Stoneking 1993; Stone et al. 1999). Studies of both the mitochondrial and nuclear genomes have ushered in a multidisciplinary approach to understanding population structure and have elucidated answers to numerous questions about the origins of contemporary human groups around the globe. Indeed, as is the case in Transylvania, aDNA has the potential to serve as a primary tool for answering long-standing debates about when particular populations arrived in specific geographic regions and what degree of isolation or migration has occurred across generations. Our novel ongoing work, described in the conclusion of this chapter, aims to contribute to this line of inquiry.

Outside anthropological and other scholarly discourse, the question of when the Székely arrived in Transylvania has important implications for contemporary politics of memory and place-making, as evidenced by the debates surrounding the publication of Ilie Ceaușescu's well-known book *Transylvania: An Ancient Romanian Land* (Ceaușescu 1983). Ceaușescu's work served to solidify the post–World War II Romanian state's claim over the territory of Transylvania by suggesting that Romanian people had occupied the region since time immemorial. This perspective has been at odds with Székely oral tradition for decades and has continued to be a divisive issue in contemporary Romanian society. As discussed above, recent genetic research shows that modern Transylvanian populations have greater affinities with central European states while other parts of Romania are more closely related to the Balkan states (Cocoș et al. 2017). These results are more consistent with Székely oral history.

A growing area of research in bioarchaeological scholarship involves the analysis and interpretation of non-adult individuals, including infants and preterm individuals. Recent book-length treatments of the bioarchaeology of children have contributed to a discussion of a population that bioarchaeological scholars have often overlooked. The archaeology of children and childhood was initiated by the pioneering work of Lillehammer (1989, 2010, 2015a, 2015b) and further synthesized by Perry (2006) and Baxter (2008). Numerous scholars have renewed and expanded scholarly interest in both archaeological and bio-archaeological contexts involving an array of questions about the juvenile life course (Bacvarov 2008; Halcrow and Tayles 2011; Lally and Moore 2011; Lewis 2007; Thompson et al. 2014). Recent literature has addressed diverse topics, including the language bioarchaeologists use to refer to non-adult individuals. For example, Lewis (2011) suggests that the term "subadult" is problematic because it implies that younger individuals are somehow less important than their adult contemporaries. Other recent discussions have called attention to the wide number of terms used to describe the age of juvenile individuals (Scheuer and Black 2000; Lewis 2007; Lewis 2011). These scholars have pointed out the importance of finding a standardized, explicit terminology, a theme that is highlighted in other areas of recent bioarchaeological work (Appleby et al. 2015; Klaus 2017). Other works have interpreted the social role of juveniles and have considered the interaction of children with adults, particularly as children transition from infancy to childhood to adolescence and finally to adulthood (Halcrow and Tayles 2011; Penny-Mason and Gowland 2014). However, few studies from Transylvania on the bioarchaeology of infants and children and virtually none related to Székely populations have been reported. In the following section, we seek to add Transylvanian Székely communities to a broader bioarchaeological conversation.

Case Study: The Reformed Church in Telekfalva

The case study presented in the remainder of this chapter focuses on the Székely community of Telekfalva (Teleac in Romanian), which is located approximately 12 kilometers from the modern-day city of Székelyudvarhely (Odorheiu Secuiesc in Romanian) (see figure 11.1).

Salvage archaeological excavations were conducted in 2007 inside the Reformed Church in this community in order to mitigate flood damage and install a new drainage system. Excavations were conducted by personnel from the Haáz Rezső Múzeum and were directed by a co-author of this chapter, Zsolt Nyárádi. To the surprise of the archaeologists who excavated inside the church, well-preserved human remains were recovered. The vast majority of human remains were dated to the seventeenth century based on the presence of material culture, including coins that were recovered in direct association with several burials (see figure 11.2).

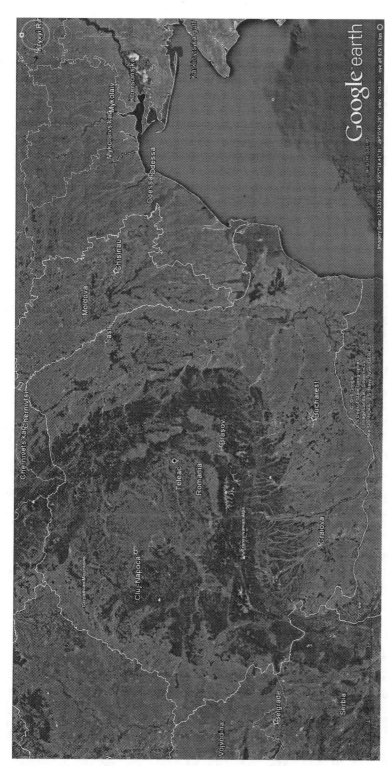

Figure 11.1. Google Earth map of Eastern Europe depicting how the Carpathian Arch formed the eastern borderland of the Principality of Transylvania. Teleac (the Romanian name for Telekfalva) is marked with a pin.

Figure 11.2. Photograph of Burial 54 at the Telekfalva Reformed Church excavation. A coin in the individual's right hand is dated to 1625 CE. Photos by Zsolt Nyárádi.

These coins provide a relatively narrow date range of 1616 to 1625. In addition, the cornerstone of the south wall of the church is inscribed with a date of 1694. Architectural evidence suggests that the footprint of the church was modified in the seventeenth century and again in the eighteenth century (for an original plan of the church, see figure 11.3).

Bioarchaeological Analysis

A total of seventy individuals were present in this mortuary context. Seventy percent (n = 49) of the burials were estimated to be newborn infants or preterm individuals (Bethard et al. 2014a; Bethard et al. 2014b; Osterholtz et al. 2014). Age-at-death estimates were derived from "The London Atlas of Human Tooth Development and Eruption" (AlQahtani et al. 2010), long-bone lengths, and/or ossification of skeletal elements following Scheuer and Black (2000). Fifty percent of the juvenile assemblage was assigned to the perinatal age cohort (36–40 weeks gestation) and 20 percent of the assemblage was allocated a preterm age

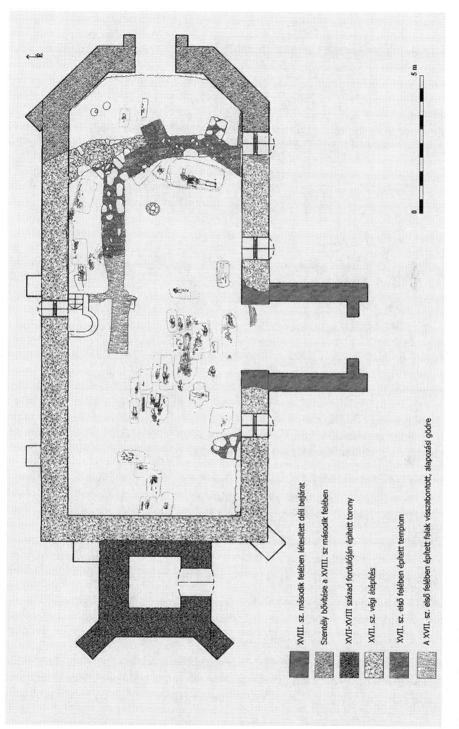

Figure 11.3. Original plan view of the Telekfalva Reformed Church excavation (text in Hungarian). Map by Zsolt Nyárádi.

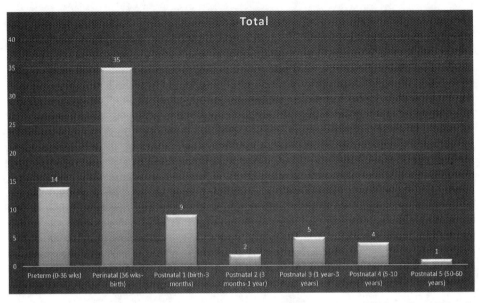

Figure 11.4. Histogram showing age distribution of all individuals recovered from the Telekfalva Reformed Church.

cohort (< 36 weeks gestation). The remaining juvenile individuals were all aged between birth to 10 years (see figure 11.4). A single elderly adult female was documented (Stuck et al. 2014).

In addition to estimating age at death, thorough paleopathological analyses were conducted. Every individual exhibited extreme levels of pathological changes and the more severe expressions occurred in the youngest individuals. These remains were compared with published examples and diagnostic criteria for both scurvy (vitamin C deficiency) and rickets (vitamin D deficiency). Our identification of pathological changes typical of scurvy and rickets is based on the co-occurrence of skeletal indicators of both diseases. Pathognomonic lesions for scurvy are easier to identify based on criteria developed by Ortner et al. (2001) and others (Armelagos et al. 2014; Brickley and Ives 2006; Klaus 2014; Ortner and Ericksen 1997; Stark 2014). These include increased porosity (holes measuring less than 1 millimeter in diameter) on the greater wing of the sphenoid (Ortner et al. 2001; Ortner and Ericksen 1997), the roof and lateral margin of the orbits, the hard palate (Brickley and Ives 2006) and the supraspinatus fossae and infraspinatus fossae of the scapulae (Klaus 2017). Additionally, pronounced vascular channeling was recorded. This was scored as present when the normal vessel tracks were deeply defined and surrounded by deposition of abnormal bone. This abnormal bone is poorly organized and is likely due to hemorrhaging of the associated blood vessels (Klaus 2014, 43).

Pinhasi and colleagues (2006) provide macroscopic criteria for identifying rickets in the skeleton. These include porosity at the metaphyses, bowing of the long bones, superior flattening of the femoral shaft, flaring and porosity of the costochondral rib, concavity of the ilium, cribra orbitalia, porotic hyperostosis, and deformity of the mandibular ramus. Flaring of the costochondral rib can also be present in scorbutic individuals. In scurvy there is a sharper angle of junction between the rib and cartilage than is seen in rickets. In rickets, this angle is less likely to be present because of the interposition of the rachitic intermediate zone between the proliferative cartilage and the shaft (Brickley and Ives 2008).

Bowing of the long bones can occur only during development of the affected elements. If an individual does not have sufficient vitamin D during growth but is still putting loading force on the legs (i.e., standing, walking, and so on), the long bones may bow due to improperly ossified bony matrix. This deformity may become permanent and will be a lasting sign of rickets, even if the individual ultimately has sufficient vitamin D intake as an adult. Because of the skeletal effects, it is simpler to identify rickets in individuals of specific age groups, primarily relating to locomotion. The most obvious signs of rickets, the bowing of the long bones, occurs when an individual is old enough to crawl or walk. This deformation only occurs with weight bearing, so individuals who die in utero or shortly after birth will not exhibit this deformation. Pinhasi and colleagues (2006) found that curvature of the long bones is well pronounced in individuals 1–5 years of age. This is in line with Mughal's (2011) note that skeletal manifestation of rickets will depend on the amount and method of locomotion used. Crawling children will develop deformities in the forearms and ambulatory children will develop bowed femora.

To our knowledge, this bioarchaeological context is an exceptionally rare type of Székely mortuary program due to the unique demographic structure of the sample. Ongoing work from other Székely sites present an entirely different pattern, where adult and non-adult individuals do not appear to have been segregated (Bailey et al. 2016; Peschel et al. 2017; Rothwell et al. 2015; Voas et al. 2018). While the age distribution of this mortuary sample provides insight into a segregated space for the burial of newborn infants and preterm individuals and older children, sex-specific mortality cannot be inferred because it is not possible to estimate sex from the skeletons of newborn infants without DNA.

This is unfortunate because sex-specific mortality data are potentially useful, as neonatal males have a higher mortality risk than neonatal females (Pakot 2015).

Reconstructing infant mortality is a complex and difficult task for bioarchaeologists. One vexing question concerns the representativeness of our samples.: How do isolated mortuary assemblages such as this population from Telekfalva reflect broad temporal phenomena? Although having some sense of regionally specific infant mortality is quite useful, the majority of available data comes from other areas of Europe (Appleby 1973; Orme 2003). Recognizing the dearth of data from Transylvania, Pakot (2015) examined maternal health and infant mortality in two eighteenth- and nineteenth-century communities approximately 30 kilometers from Telekfalva. Although this instance postdates our case study, it provides a useful baseline for better understanding maternal health and infant mortality in Transylvanian Székely communities, as Pakot's study is likely the first to use parish registers to make such inferences. The two villages Pakot studied, Szentegyházasfalva and Kápolnásfalva (Vlăhița and Căpâlnița in Romanian), were inhabited by people who engaged in small-scale farming, lumbering, and animal husbandry. Fertility rates were high, emigration was low, and infant and child mortality was relatively high (Pakot 2015). Pakot analyzed parish registers dating from 1776 to 1943, focusing on children born from 1850 to 1939. Ultimately, Pakot (2015) concluded that 79 percent of infants stayed alive at least through their first birthday and that survivorship beyond 30 days was strongly dependent on maternal health and numerous endogenous variables. Although this study involves Székely communities that were inhabited over two centuries after the period when infants were buried in the Reform Church in Telekfalva, it provides a small snapshot for beginning to consider the context in which Székely women managed their pregnancies and experienced infant loss. Unfortunately, as Murdock notes, "invasions and revolutions have taken a heavy toll on historical records in Hungary and Transylvania. There are almost no surviving parish records from [the seventeenth century]" (2000a, 9). Despite this gap in historical sources, bioarchaeological work centered on medieval and early modern Transylvania can certainly benefit from a multidisciplinary perspective that incorporates work produced by historians and demographers.

The Social Context of Burial at Telekfalva

The questions of the social role of infant death and the interactions of adult members of the Telekfalva community with deceased infants generated a great number of discussions during the months of our fieldwork in Transylvania. Given the unique pattern of the Telekfalva assemblage, we drew on examples from other bioarchaeological contexts in Europe for comparison. For example, Finlay (2000) and Murphy (2011) describe the presence of *cillíni* (separate burial grounds for infants and older children) throughout Ireland. Finlay (2000) argues that these burial grounds functioned to isolate young individuals from baptized adults. Finlay (2000) also suggests that a separate burial space for infants was an indication of the Roman Catholic belief in Limbo. Unlike Roman Catholic contexts, Reformed Church belief systems did not include Purgatory or Limbo. Murdock describes Hungarian Reformed Church funeral services as "simple affairs directed more towards the needs of surviving relatives and the congregation than towards the deceased" (2000b, 209). Reformed church ministers had the ability to grant permission to bury in sanctified church burial grounds, both inside and outside physical structures. Notably, ministers maintained the authority to deny burial in church spaces to any individual who did not repent before their death (Murdock 2000b). The bodies of these individuals were oftentimes deposited in unsanctified spaces (i.e., at the foot of local gallows). The fact that infants are buried inside the Reformed Church in Telekfalva suggests that members of the clergy approved the practice. The inclusion of infants and older children in this sacred space affirms that they were not categorized in the same way as socially deviant adults.

We argue that burial inside the church may also indicate that these infants were baptized shortly after birth. Karen Spierling (2005) has extensively documented the role of infant baptism in sixteenth-century Reformed Churches and argues that parents would have wanted their sickly newborn infants baptized as quickly as possible, even though typical Reformed Church doctrine called for baptism to occur on a "preaching day" in front of the entire congregation. Todd writes that parents "feared for the souls of sickly infants likely to die before baptism" (2002, 122). Although we cannot be sure about the timing of the baptism of the infants interred inside the church, it is clear that parents in this community did not bury their infants in the same way that their Catholic contemporaries did in Ireland. What remains unclear is how Telekfalva community members interacted with the Reformed Church outside times when infant inhumations were taking place. We also do not know where other members of this community were buried. No other archaeological excavations have taken place in Telekfalva and thus we do not know if other infants were buried elsewhere in the village or if adults and non-adults were interred in some other unknown community cemetery. Ongoing excavations in the collapsed church in the village of Patakfalva, located approximately 3 kilometers from Telekfalva, suggest that non-adults, including infants, and adults were buried together there (Zejdlik 2015).

As Osterholtz and colleagues (2014) have described, nonspecific periosteal reactions were present in 100 percent of the perinatal and preterm skeletons analyzed in this sample. Vitamin C deficiency (scurvy) is likely, but rickets (vitamin D deficiency) is probably also present. The comorbidity of scurvy and rickets is likely and has been identified for other early modern European assemblages. In their analysis of sixteenth- and eighteenth-century France, Schattmann and colleagues (2016) note that the co-occurrence can change the expression of both deficiencies, with one (usually scurvy) appearing to be more prominent.

But why should multiple nutritional deficiencies be present in so many perinatal and preterm individuals? The presence of pathological conditions so severe in this sample is indicative of maternal insufficiency during pregnancy, possibly leading to premature labor or miscarriage. Few documented records from the historical archive are available to help us better understand why a vitamin C deficiency may have affected the pregnancies of women in the Telekfalva community. However, recent work by Transylvanian historian Andrea Fehér (2011) has shed some light on the dietary practices of pregnant women in eighteenth-century Transylvania. Although this example postdates the period of our study, Fehér's work is helpful. She writes:

> Pregnant women also had a severe diet, they were prohibited to eat food hard to digest such as beef or rabbit; then milk, cabbage, rice, chestnuts, etc. . . . Instead they should eat prunes, figs, chicken, ginger, apple with honey, but it was strictly forbidden to drink, especially dry wines. (2011, 137)

Fehér (2011) notes that these prohibitions and recommendations were observed in every family and that many families seemed to have special recipes for pregnant women.

Fehér's work with the documentary record provides a glimpse into other aspects of pregnancy in Transylvania. She describes the high frequency of miscarriages, which seemed to affect a majority of Transylvanian women in the eighteenth century. She also describes the emotional toll on the women who experienced miscarriages. For example, she recounts correspondence between a mother and daughter in 1777. The mother, Kata Csáky, wrote:

I've written you before, that certain letters that I received from you remind me of my own life, in which all the joy was mixed with sadness. Great was my joy that we will soon meet, but I became more upset when you wrote that nature has been on you. Worse news I cannot imagine, because believe me, I am writing with respect, but in these things I am very experienced, because I had myself gone through this eight times. . . . The biggest was three months old, the rest were so small that no midwife could notice . . . but me, with watery eyes, roving through the coagulated blood and so I found and showed them to the midwives. And because they are so small, you will not feel anything, they will go without pain. . . . I did not do anything, just treat myself with white tea (Albis Essentia dulcis) and I was lying down for two weeks. (2011, 138)

What emerges from this brief look at one documentary source is a recognition of the difficult realities of carrying a fetus to term during this time period. It is also clear that women experienced grief at the loss of their infant children. Contrary to the notions of historian Philip Ariès (1962), parents in early modern Europe were attached to their children from a very early age and were gravely concerned about the salvation of children who passed away before their lives began.

In a recent contribution, Cannon and Cook (2015) draw on perspectives from the psychological literature, namely John Bowlby's (1980) attachment theory and Margaret Stroebe and Henk Schut's (1999) dual process model of bereavement to provide a framework for how archaeologists might use infant death to make inferences about the human emotion of grief. They provide examples of reactions to infant death that range from detachment and ambivalence to intense distress. In the case of infant burials from Telekfalva, we argue that this archaeological context and documentation from Transylvanian historical sources indicate that Székely parents, and perhaps especially mothers, likely experienced significant grief at the loss of their infant children, despite the high risk of mortality around the time of birth. This area of archaeological inquiry is in its nascent stage and we are interested to know how other scholars will apply the model Cannon and Cook (2015) have developed.

Continuing Research

Our work with the interpretation of this bioarchaeological assemblage is ongoing. We would like to further understand the role of Reformed Church theology in shaping perceptions about infant baptism and burial practices in Transylvania. We are optimistic that this work will add to the growing literature on the bioarchaeology of infants and children and the archaeology of the Reformation (Gaimster and Gilchrist 2003). We argue that these data cannot be interpreted to their fullest extent without a thorough understanding of the historical and cultural context and recognize the importance of engaging with colleagues and literature outside the field of bioarchaeology. While surviving primary sources from Transylvania are scarce (Papahagi 2015), continued dialogues with historians of this region are imperative. Historians of medieval Europe have already initiated this multidisciplinary approach to the past and have used bioarchaeological literature to bolster their interpretations (Fleming 2006). It is our hope that bioarchaeologists will practice reciprocal scholarship and consider incorporating the work of researchers outside the discipline.

In addition to further understanding the patterning and etiology of skeletal pathologies, we are interested in exploring the spatial patterning of all burials recovered from inside the Telekfalva Reformed Church. Moreover, we hope to include data from analyses of material culture (e.g., textiles) in the future. We would like to continue genetic sex typing to better understand this sample's overall demographic composition. In addition, histological analysis of dental enamel may provide useful information about the presence or absence of neonatal lines. Neonatal line data may help elucidate a pattern of postnatal survivorship and/or provide information on the number of stillborn individuals in the sample.

Bethard and colleagues (2018) have conducted a pilot project using molecular anthropological methods to produce genetic sex estimates and reconstruct familial relationships. Initial results have yielded genetic sex estimates for eight Telekfalva infants and have suggested that at least two individuals are related matrilineally. While several bioarchaeological studies have used aDNA to investigate sex-specific infanticide in Roman Ashkelon (Faerman et al. 1998) and Roman Britain (Mays and Faerman 2001), the intentional pattern of infant and preterm burial inside the Reformed Church in Telekfalva differs markedly from those expected in infanticide contexts (Mays 2014). We hope that the results of the aDNA project will provide clearer insight into what kind of sex-specific mortality pattern, if any, is present in this Székely mortuary context.

In the future, we would like to address novel ways that our work fits into exciting new developments at the frontier of bioarchaeological scholarship. We call attention to the work of Beaumont and colleagues (2015), who have provided a framework for understanding infant stress, maternal health, and weaning. These scholars suggest that isotopic data from mother/fetus pairs can provide some insight into stress events that take place during pregnancy. Although this approach cannot be tested at Telekfalva because of the lack of associated female skeletons, we suggest that this approach holds promise for the continued investigation of maternal stress during pregnancy. We have, however, produced preliminary isotopic data on a sample of individuals from the neighboring Székely community of Bögöz (in Romanian: Mugeni) (Peschel et al. 2017; Voas et al. 2018). These data are generated from both adult and non-adult individuals and we are beginning to get a sense of overall dietary practices in at least one Székely community.

To conclude, we would like to return to the concepts that we introduced at the beginning of this chapter. We argue that our flexible understanding of the concept of the frontier has enriched our work in interpreting the bioarchaeology of Transylvanian Székely communities. Besides geographic boundaries, our investigation of infant burials at the Reformed Church in Telekfalva has pushed us to better understand an array of topics at the forefront of bioarchaeological scholarship. Embedded in a remarkable seventeenth-century context are questions related to the bioarchaeology of fetuses, infants, and children; maternal health and physiological stress during pregnancy; mortuary practices and religious ideology related to infant burial in the Reformed Church; and notions about infant death and the archaeology of grief. We argue that rich bioarchaeological data recovered from Székely mortuary contexts cannot be interpreted to their fullest extent without a thorough understanding of the biohistorical and biocultural context and we look forward to continued synthesis of the bioarchaeological record and the historical archive in the future.

Notes

1. Székely people are an ethnic group of people who live in a particular region of Transylvania. They speak Hungarian as opposed to Romanian and they have lived in this region for centuries.

2. The Székelyföld is the term used to refer to the particular region in Transylvania where Székely communities are located.

3. Wallachia, Dobrudja, and Moldavia are regions that make up the part of Romania that existed prior to World War I.

4. Magyars are Hungarians from Hungary and Székely people live in Transylvania.

References

AlQahtani, S. J., M. P. Hector, and H. M. Liversidge. 2010. "Brief Communication: The London Atlas of Human Tooth Development and Eruption." *American Journal of Physical Anthropology* 142(3): 481–490.

Appleby, A. B. 1973. "Disease or Famine? Mortality in Cumberland and Westmorland 1580–1640." *Economic History Review* 26(3): 403–432.

Appleby, J., R. Thomas, and J. Buikstra. 2015. "Increasing Confidence in Paleopathological Diagnosis: Application of the Istanbul Terminological Framework." *International Journal of Paleopathology* 8: 19–21.

Ariès, P. 1962. *Centuries of Childhood: A Social History of Family Life*. New York: Vintage Books.

Armelagos, G. J., K. Sirak, T. Werkema, and B. L. Turner. 2014. "Analysis of Nutritional Disease in Prehistory: The Search for Scurvy in Antiquity and Today." *International Journal of Paleopathology* 5: 9–17.

Bacvarov, K. 2008. *Babies Reborn: Infant/Child Burials in Pre- and Protohistory*. Oxford: Archaeopress.

Bailey, S. L., S. B. Kondor, J. D. Bethard, Z. Nyaradi, and A. Gonciar. 2016. "A Probable Case of Rheumatoid Arthritis from Medieval Transylvania." Paper presented at the 85th Annual Meeting of the American Association of Physical Anthropologists, Atlanta, GA.

Baxter, J. E. 2008. "The Archaeology of Childhood." *Annual Review of Anthropology* 37: 159–175.

Beaumont, J., J. Montgomery, J. Buckberry, and M. Jay. 2015. "Infant Mortality and Isotopic Complexity: New Approaches to Stress, Maternal Health, and Weaning." *American Journal of Physical Anthropology* 157(3): 441–457.

Bethard, J. D., A. J. Osterholtz, A. Gonciar, and Z. Nyaradi. 2014a. "A Bioarchaeological Study of Childhood Mortality in 17th Century Transylvania." Paper presented at the 83rd Annual Meeting of the American Association of Physical Anthropologists, Calgary, Alberta.

———. 2014b. "Of Infants and Elderly: A Bioarchaeological Analysis of a 17th-Century Mortuary Context from Transylvania, Romania." Paper presented at the 79th Annual Meeting of the Society for American Archaeology, Austin, TX.

Bethard, J. D., A. Nyaradi, A. Gonciar, C. Monroe, and C. Hoffman. 2018. "Molecular Approaches to Understanding the Past: A Case Study from 17th Century Transylvania." Paper presented at the 24th Annual Meeting of the European Association of Archaeologists, Barcelona, Spain.

Bíró, A., T. Fehér, G. Bárány, and H. Pamjav. 2015. "Testing Central and Inner Asian Admixture among Contemporary Hungarians." *Forensic Science International: Genetics* 15: 121–126.

Bolnick, D. A., and D. G. Smith. 2007. "Migration and Social Structure among the Hopewell: Evidence from Ancient DNA." *American Antiquity* 72(4): 627–644.

Bowlby, J. 1980. *Attachment and Loss*. New York: Basic Books.

Bramanti, B., M. G. Thomas, W. Haak, M. Unterlaender, P. Jores, K. Tambets, I. Antanaitis-Jacobs, M. N. Haidle, R. Jankauskas, C.-J. Kind et al. 2009. "Genetic Discontinuity between Local Hunter-Gatherers and Central Europe's First Farmers." *Science* 326(5949): 137–140.

Brandstätter, A., B. Egyed, B. Zimmermann, N. Duftner, Z. Padar, and W. Parson. 2007. "Migration Rates and Genetic Structure of Two Hungarian Ethnic Groups in Transylvania, Romania." *Annals of Human Genetics* 71(6): 791–803.

Brickley, M., and R. Ives. 2006. "Skeletal Manifestations of Infantile Scurvy." *American Journal of Physical Anthropology* 129: 168–172.

———. 2008. *The Bioarchaeology of Metabolic Bone Disease*. London: Academic Press.

Cannon, A., and K. Cook. 2015. "Infant Death and the Archaeology of Grief." *Cambridge Archaeological Journal* 25(2): 399–416.

Ceauşescu, I. 1983. *Transylvania: An Ancient Romanian Land*. Bucharest: Military Publishing House.

Cocoş, R., S. Schipor, M. Hervella, P. Cianga, R. Popescu, C. Bănescu, M. Constantinescu, A. Martinescu, and F. Raicu. 2017. "Genetic Affinities among the Historical Provinces of Romania and Central Europe as Revealed by an mtDNA Analysis." *BMC Genetics* 18(20): 1–11.

Faerman, M., G. K. Bar-Gal, D. Filon, C. L. Greenblatt, L. Stager, A. Oppenheim, and P. Smith. 1998. "Determining the Sex of Infanticide Victims from the Late Roman Era through Ancient DNA Analysis." *Journal of Archaeological Science* 25(9): 861–865.

Fehér, A. 2011. "When the time is coming . . . Childbirth in Eighteenth Century Transylvania." *Studia Universitatis Babes-Bolyai-Historia* 56(1): 135–148.

Finlay, N. 2000. "Outside of Life: Traditions of Infant Burial in Ireland from Cillin to Cist." *World Archaeology* 31(3): 407–422.

Fleming, R. 2006." Bones for Historians: Putting the Body Back into Biography." In *Writing Medieval Biography, 750–1250: Essays in Honour of Frank Barlow*, edited by D. Bates, J. Crick, and S. Hamilton, 29–48. Woodbridge: Boydell & Brewer.

Gaimster, D. R., and R. Gilchrist. 2003. *The Archaeology of Reformation, 1480–1580*. Leeds, UK: Maney Leeds.

Hagelberg, E., M. Hofreiter, and C. Keyser. 2015. "Ancient DNA: The First Three Decades." *Philosophical Transactions of the Royal Society B: Biological Sciences* 370(1660): 20130371.

Halcrow, S. E., and N. Tayles. 2011. "The Bioarchaeological Investigation of Children and Childhood." In *Social Bioarchaeology*, edited by Sabrina C. Agarwal and Bonnie A. Glencross, 333–360. New York: Wiley-Blackwell.

Hassan, N. Abu-Mandil, K. A. Brown, J. Eyers, T. A. Brown, and S. Mays. 2014. "Ancient DNA Study of the Remains of Putative Infanticide Victims from the Yewden Roman Villa Site at Hambleden, England." *Journal of Archaeological Science* 43: 192–197.

Istrate, D. M., M. Constantinescu, and A. Soficaru. 2015. *The Medieval Cemetery from Sibiu (Hermannstadt) Huet Square: Archaeology, Anthropology, History*. Tübinger Forschungen zur historischen Archäologie 6. Büchenbach: Verlag Dr. Faustus.

Klaus, H. D. 2014. "Subadult Scurvy in Andean South America: Evidence of Vitamin C Deficiency in the Late Pre-Hispanic and Colonial Lambayeque Valley, Peru." *International Journal of Paleopathology* 5: 34–45.

———. 2017. "Paleopathological Rigor and Differential Diagnosis: Case Studies Involving Terminology, Description, and Diagnostic Frameworks for Scurvy in Skeletal Remains." *International Journal of Paleopathology* 19: 96–110.

Lally, M., and A. Moore. 2011. *(Re)thinking the Little Ancestor: New Perspectives on the Archaeology of Infancy and Childhood.* Oxford: Archaeopress.

Lewis, M. E. 2007. *The Bioarchaeology of Children: Perspectives from Biological and Forensic Anthropology.* Cambridge, UK: Cambridge University Press.

———. 2011. "The Osteology of Infancy and Childhood: Misconceptions and Potential." In *(Re)Thinking the Little Ancestor: New Perspectives on the Archaeology of Infancy and Childhood,* edited by M. Lally and A. Moore, 1–13. Oxford: Archaeopress.

Lillehammer, G. 1989. "A Child Is Born: The Child's World in an Archaeological Perspective." *Norwegian Archaeological Review* 22(2): 89–105.

———. 2010. "Archaeology of Children/Arqueología de la infancia." *Complutum* 21(2): 15–45.

———. 2015a. "25 Years with the 'Child' and the Archaeology of Childhood." *Childhood in the Past* 8: 78–86.

———. 2015b. "Steps to Children's Living Spaces." In *Children, Spaces, and Identity,* edited by M. Sánchez Romero, E. Alarcón García, and G. Aranda Jiménez, 10–24. Oxford: Oxbow.

Marczali, H. 1971. *Hungary in the Eighteenth Century.* New York: Arno Press.

Mays, S. 2014. "The Bioarchaeology of the Homicide of Infants and Children." In *Tracing Childhood: Bioarchaeological Investigations of Early Lives in Antiquity,* edited by J. L. Thompson, M. P. Alfonso-Durruty, and J. J. Crandall, 99–122. Gainesville: University Press of Florida.

Mays, S., and M. Faerman. 2001. "Sex Identification in Some Putative Infanticide Victims from Roman Britain Using Ancient DNA." *Journal of Archaeological Science* 28(5): 555–559.

Molnár, M. 2001. *A Concise History of Hungary.* Cambridge: Cambridge University Press.

Morgan, D. 2009. "Examining Transylvanian Saxon Fortified Churches from the 13th to the 16th Centuries: The History and Archaeology of the Saxon Rural Church in Romania: Roles and Identities." PhD thesis, University of Leicester.

Mughal, M. Z. 2011. "Rickets." *Current Osteoporosis Reports* 9: 291–299.

Murdock, G. 2000a. *Calvinism on the Frontier, 1600–1660: International Calvinism and the Reformed Church in Hungary and Transylvania.* Oxford: Oxford University Press.

———. 2000b. "Death, Prophecy and Judgement in Transylvania." In *The Place of the Dead: Death and Remembrance in Late Medieval and Early Modern Europe,* edited by B. Gordon and P. Marshall, 206–223. Cambridge: Cambridge University Press.

Murphy, E. M. 2011. "Children's Burial Grounds in Ireland (Cillini) and Parental Emotions toward Infant Death." *International Journal of Historical Archaeology* 15(3): 409.

Orme, N. 2003. *Medieval Children.* New Haven, CT: Yale University Press.

Ortner, D. J., W. Butler, J. Carafella, and L. Milligan. 2001. "Evidence of Probable Scurvy from Archaeological Sites in North America." *American Journal of Physical Anthropology* 114: 343–351.

Ortner, D. J., and M. F. Ericksen. 1997. "Bone Changes in the Human Skull Probably Resulting from Scurvy in Infancy and Childhood." *International Journal of Osteoarchaeology* 7: 212–220.

Osterholtz, A. J., J. D. Bethard, A. Gonciar, and Z. Nyaradi. 2014. "Possible Prenatal and Perinatal Scurvy at Telekfalva, Romania." Paper presented at the 83rd Annual Meeting of the American Association of Physical Anthropologists, Calgary, Alberta.

Pakot, L. 2015. "Maternal Health and Infant Mortality in Rural Transylvania: A Case Study of Vlăhiţa and Căpâlniţa, 1850–1939." *Romanian Journal of Population Studies* 9(1): 5–24.

Papahagi, A. 2015. "Lost Libraries and Surviving Manuscripts: The Case of Medieval Transylvania." *Library and Information History* 31(1): 35–53.

Penny-Mason, B. J., and R. L. Gowland. 2014. "The Children of the Reformation: Childhood Palaeoepidemiology in Britain, AD 1000–1700." *Medieval Archaeology* 58(1): 162–194.

Perry, M. A. 2006. "Redefining Childhood through Bioarchaeology: Toward an Archaeological and Biological Understanding of Children in Antiquity." *Archeological Papers of the American Anthropological Association* 15(1): 89–111.

Peschel, E. M., T. E. Dunn, J. D. Bethard, Z. Nyaradi, A. Gonciar, M. A. Katzenberg, and S. H. Ambrose. 2017. "Reconstructing Székely Subsistence: Stable Isotope Evidence for Medieval Diet in Eastern Transylvania." Paper presented at the 86th Annual Meeting of the American Association of Physical Anthropologists, New Orleans, Louisiana.

Pinhasi, R., P. Shaw, B. White, and A. R. Ogden. 2006. "Morbidity, Rickets and Long-Bone Growth in Post-Medieval Britain: A Cross-Population Analysis." *Annals of Human Biology* 33(3): 372–389.

Rady, M. 2000. *Nobility, Land and Service in Medieval Hungary*. New York: Palgrave.

Rothwell, J., D. Hansen III, J. D. Bethard, A. Gonciar, and Z. Nyaradi. 2015. "Legions of Lesions: An Examination of the Severity and Prevalence of Dental Caries in Medieval Bögöz." Paper presented at the 84th Annual Meeting of the American Association of Physical Anthropologists, St. Louis, Missouri.

Schattmann, A., B. Bertrand, S. Vatteoni, and M. Brickley. 2016. "Approaches to Co-Occurrence: Scurvy and Rickets in Infants and Young Children of 16–18th Century Douai, France." *International Journal of Paleopathology* 12: 63–75.

Scheuer L., and S. M. Black. 2000. *Developmental Juvenile Osteology*. Bath: Elsevier Academic Press.

Spierling, K. E. 2005. *Infant Baptism in Reformation Geneva: The Shaping of a Community, 1536–1564*. Louisville, KY: Westminster John Knox Press.

Stark, R. J. 2014. "A Proposed Framework for the Study of Paleopathological Cases of Subadult Scurvy." *International Journal of Paleopathology* 5: 18–26.

Stone, A. C., and M. Stoneking. 1993. "Ancient DNA from a Pre-Columbian Amerindian Population." *American Journal of Physical Anthropology* 92(4): 463–471.

Stone, A. C., M. Stoneking, A. J. Davidson, A. Millard, J. Bada, and R. Evershed. 1999. "Analysis of Ancient DNA from a Prehistoric Amerindian Cemetery." *Philosophical Transactions of the Royal Society of London B: Biological Sciences* 354(1379): 153–159.

Stroebe, M., and H. Schut. 1999. "The Dual Process Model of Coping with Bereavement: Rationale and Description." *Death Studies* 23(3): 197–224.

Stuck, J., S. Wallace, J. D. Bethard, A. Gonciar, and Z. Nyaradi. 2014. "The Mysterious Elder: A Bioarchaeological Analysis of Burial 61 at Telekfalva, Harghita County, Romania." Paper presented at the 41st Annual North American Meeting of the Paleopathology Association, Calgary, Alberta.

Thompson, J. L., M. P. Alfonso-Durruty, and J. J. Crandall. 2014. *Tracing Childhood: Bioarchaeological Investigations of Early Lives in Antiquity*. Gainesville: University Press of Florida.

Todd, M. 2002. *The Culture of Protestantism in Early Modern Scotland*. New Haven, CT: Yale University Press.

Voas, M. R., K. Killgrove, J. D. Bethard, R. H. Tykot, A. Gonciar, and Z. Nyaradi. 2018. "Milk and Honey: Isotopic Reconstruction of Infant Weaning in Medieval Transylvania." Paper presented at the 87th Annual Meeting of the American Association of Physical Anthropologists, Austin, Texas.

Zejdlik, K. 2015. ArchaeoTek Summer Field Season 2015: Medieval Funerary Excavations at Papdomb, Patakfalva. 23 pp. Unpublished report in authors' possession.

Conclusion

The Future of Bioarchaeology and Studies at the Edges

CRISTINA I. TICA

Today, among the 194 independent states in the world, there are more than 100 active border disputes, without taking into consideration the disputed islands (Diener and Hagen 2010, 3). Frontiers and borders are likely to remain significant in the twenty-first century in the political, economic, and sociocultural affairs of almost every nation-state. Frontiers and borders are also not likely to retain a fixed function or meaning (Diener and Hagen 2010, 14). According to Anderson (1996, 8), politics would be inconceivable and international relations would not exist without frontiers and there would be no friends, foes, or allies without borders. "The value of borders may well be in the bordering of values, but not in an essentialist way that assumes community is somehow fixed and immune from alteration through interaction with outsiders," states Williams (2006, 114). Thus, borders both shape what they enclose and are also shaped by it; they need to be continually sustained and socially reproduced (Anderson and O'Dowd 1999, 602).

Frontiers are dynamic areas where identities are created, contested, maintained, negotiated, or manipulated in a context of continually changing micro-level processes and shifting alliances. Frontier zones and borderlands are sites and symbols of power (Donnan and Wilson 1999, 1), as some of the chapters in this volume have illustrated (see chapters 2, and 8). Frontiers and borders are also sites of counter-power (Amilhat Szary and Giraut 2015, 13), as several chapters have argued (see chapters 2, 3, 6, and 7). For example, in chapter 6, Whitmore and colleagues illustrate how archaeological and bioarchaeological data available at Tombos depict a community where Nubian and Egyptian identity was entangled in the context of an ancient Egyptian colonial center. They demonstrated that those living in the Tombos community were not subjected to physically demanding activities or aggression, as is sometimes the case with imperial subjugation. While the historical sources suggest that those who openly rebelled were harshly suppressed, Whitmore and colleagues showed that those who collaborated were the recipients of a degree of cultural accommodation and other benefits. This was reflected in the health and prosperity of the mixed population at Tombos. Chapter 7 also deals with adaptability and resilience on the frontier. Iceland is one of the few cases in history when colonizing events happened in a place where there were no earlier inhabitants. As an island, Iceland does not have close physical borders with another country, and at one time it represented the farthest limit of settlement for Europe. Zoëga and Murphy emphasize how people managed to survive and counteract these conditions by implementing successful survival strategies and making adjustments in their social spheres. The geographically and environmentally marginal conditions in the north meant that settlers strove to maintain a precarious balance between success and failure.

Frontiers are dynamic areas that are conducive to the creation, syncretization, and transformation of new cultural constructs and new cultural identities. Since they cut across multiple social networks, frontiers are interaction zones where identities are actively constructed, manipulated, and negotiated (Lightfoot and Martinez 1995, 474). Groups living on the border are in a constant state of shifting and renegotiating their identity, often adopting multiple identities (Alvarez 1995, 452), as illustrated in one form or another in chapters 1, 2, 3, 4, and 6.

Frontiers and border regions are at once prison and refuge; they can enable persecution and violence or they can help people escape it (Anderson and O'Dowd 1999, 596). This point has been argued in chapters 1, 8, 9 (for violence and persecution), and 6 (for resilience and escape). Paradoxically, building fences acknowledges plurality while respecting a community's decision to be different, to adopt alternative ways to work out their social needs (Williams 2006, 120). However, building walls to shut out the world as security measures when migratory tensions are at their highest has proven to be ineffective (Anderson and O'Dowd 1999, 596; Lambert and Clochard 2015, 131–132). In the words of Lambert and Clochard (2015, 132), "these walls are often disaster zones where human tragedy takes place."

This volume is not just about territorial frontiers and borderlands. It addresses different aspects of frontiers and borders, as variously illustrated in chapters 3, 5, 9, 10, and 11. For example, in chapter 3, Toussaint uses gender as a lens for examining how frontiers can be places where power is stringently enforced and conformity is policed or places where individual agency, creativity, and hybridity flourish. His preliminary study suggests a multitude of ways that identity was negotiated to the north of the Carpathian Mountains. He argues that Mierzanowice Culture populations provide a unique opportunity to study the interactions between gender and the frontier. In chapter 5, Muzzall and Coppa investigate social borders of the past. Their results indicate that Campovalano Iron Age and Medieval samples are more similar to each other than Alfedena is to either. They show that the Campovalano group increased endogamy through exclusive marriage practices that were negotiated in social interactions at territorial and ideological and cultural borders. In chapter 9, Woods and Harrod explore borders at the skeletal level. The authors look at the boundaries between the Fremont and Virgin Branch and Kayenta Puebloans. Their analysis seeks to outline additional methods that highlight the individual and social identity of the Fremont. Their findings lead them to suggest that despite the close proximity of the Fremont to Virgin and Kayenta Puebloans, there is something distinct about the Fremont lifeway and culture. In chapter 11, Bethard and colleagues also go beyond investigating geographic boundaries: their work addresses infant burials at the Reformed Church in the community of Telekfalva in the seventeenth century. They note that their approach has pushed them to seek a better understanding of an array of topics at the forefront of bioarchaeological scholarship.

While the chapters have been grouped into five parts organized around themes, these themes crisscross each other. For example, the chapters by Tica (chapter 1), Nugent (chapter 2), Groff and Dupras (chapter 4), and Soficaru and colleagues (chapter 8) all adopt various approaches to "frontiers and borders" at the edge of the Roman world. In chapter 1, Tica shows that the differences in poor health indicators between the two samples from Romania can be explained by looking at the historical context of the Lower Danube frontier in late antiquity. However, no single or simple explanation can account for the complexity of these peoples' lives on the frontier and their health differences. In chapter 2, Nugent develops the idea that new and hybrid identities may have been shaped by interactions between military personnel and the locals living in the frontier zones of Azerbaijan. Although Groff and Dupras' research in chapter 4 indicated that females either married into families who lived in the Dakhleh Oasis in Egypt or were slaves, they demonstrate that both groups of women came from isotopically similar environments. Furthermore, the $\delta^{18}O$ results for males in their sample support previously held notions and documentation that describes males as migrating more frequently for work-related activities. Finally, in chapter 8, Soficaru and colleagues present a case where the death and annihilation of the individuals excavated from feature M141 must have sent a powerful message in the frontier province of Scythia Minor.

Many chapters show similarities in terms of geographic focus and time periods addressed. One of our goals has been to look at the development and transformation of frontiers and borders through time and we hope we have at least scratched the surface by encompassing a large swath of time, including the Early Bronze Age in Central Europe (chapter 3), the New Kingdom period in North Africa (chapter 6), and the seventeenth century in Transylvania (chapter 11). The Iron Age is covered in Southern and Eastern Europe in chapters 5 and 10. Several chapters focus on the Roman period in Eastern Europe, the South Caucasus, and North Africa (chapters 1, 2, 4, and 8). The medieval period is covered in chapters 5, 7, and 11 in Southern Europe, the North Atlantic, and Eastern Europe, respectively. While most of the chapters focus on the Old World, chapter 9 examines the prehistoric American Southwest. Regardless of the time period or geographic region researchers are interested in, we hope we have succeeded in persuading the reader that the theoretical perspectives highlighted in this work hold explanatory power and could be applicable to different geographic and temporal contexts.

Perhaps now more than ever, frontiers and borders are imperative demarcations for a highly interconnected and interdependent global society. Nowadays, borders are politically and internationally reified and are considered to be stable and secure. Yet many who study borders know that they are anything but static and safe. Many borders have been toppled overnight with pressure from social movements or political powers. Thus, borders and frontiers are both formulations of historic demarcations and dialectics that embody both resistance and subordination. It can take just one second or one vote to bring back the old boundaries, the lines in the sand, the real or metaphorical walls.

By taking the border and the frontier as a point of departure, this collection of studies shifts the analytical focus from the center to someplace else, from the locus of power to places of contested power, and from places with presumed stability to places of presumed disorder, tension, and instability.

We hope we have shown that while frontiers and borderlands can be violent places they do not have to be, that they are not always unstable or completely marked by tension. Like Diener and Hagen (2010, 9), we have realized that it would be impossible to come up with one border and frontier theory that can explain and be applicable to all borders at all times. However, this should not detract us from attempting to understand how frontiers and borderlands shape societies. Border research is not in any danger of becoming redundant; it has become even more important and more revealing of wider social change (Anderson and O'Dowd 1999, 603).

Scholars agree that a world entirely without borders is unlikely in the foreseeable future and that borders still matter in our global society (Diener and Hagen 2010, 4; Herzog and Sohn 2016, 53). If anything, globalization renders territoriality even more important, and while the location of modern borders and frontiers might not be changing, their function and significance are rapidly evolving (Atzili 2012, 14). Indeed, in the United States and many other countries, borders are in the process of becoming more open to the flow of goods, information, investment, and collaboration but simultaneously less open to the flow of people. This paradox is created when borders become transition zones that are open to communication in some places but remain a closed frontier characterized by mistrust in other places (Diener and Hagen 2010, 10).

The complexity and versatility of frontiers and borders can be seen in action in debordering and rebordering processes that happen all the time (Amilhat Szary and Giraut 2015, 4,13). The building and toppling of the Berlin Wall, the increasing militarization of the Mexico-US border, and the reordering of parts of Eastern Europe after civil and secular wars are all examples of these processes in recent times. Frontiers and borders have always been and will always be active forces that shape societies.

There is much work in this area for bioarchaeologists. The questions raised in this volume demonstrate how rich and nuanced the interpretations are when information from human remains are added to archaeological and/or historical reconstructions. This area of study for bioarchaeologists can be considered a new frontier, a place to push into with our questions, theories, and data in order to see what new ideas emerge about how people at the edges are affected and what kind of agency or resistance they use to avoid being killed or forced into particular kinds of social arrangements. It will be exciting to see the new areas of study that emerge in this field.

References

Alvarez, R. R., Jr. 1995. "The Mexican-US Border: The Making of an Anthropology of Borderlands." *Annual Review of Anthropology* 24: 447–470.

Amilhat Szary, A.-L., and F. Giraut. 2015. "Borderities: The Politics of Contemporary Mobile Borders." In *Borderities and the Politics of Contemporary Mobile Borders*, edited by A.-L. Amilhat Szary and F. Giraut, 1–19. London: Palgrave Macmillan.

Anderson, M. 1996. *Frontiers: Territory and State Formation in the Modern World*. Cambridge, UK: Polity Press.

Anderson, J., and L. O'Dowd. 1999. "Borders, Border Regions and Territoriality: Contradictory Meanings, Changing Significance." *Regional Studies* 33(7): 593–604.

Atzili, B. 2012. *Good Fences, Bad Neighbors: Border Fixity and International Conflict*. Chicago: University of Chicago Press.

Diener, A. C., and J. Hagen. 2010. "Introduction: Borders, Identity, and Geopolitics." In *Borderlines and Borderlands: Political Oddities at the Edge of the Nation-State*, edited by A. C. Diener and J. Hagen, 1–14. Plymouth, UK: Rowman & Littlefield.

Donnan, H., and T. Wilson. 1999. *Borders: Frontiers of Identity, Nation and State*. Oxford: Berg.

Herzog, L. A., and C. Sohn. 2016. "The Cross-Border Metropolis in a Global Age: A Conceptual Model and Empirical Evidence from the US-Mexico and European Border Regions." In *International Boundaries in a Global Era: Cross-Border Space, Place and Society in the Twenty-First Century*, edited by L. A. Herzog and K. J. Hayward, 50–70. London: Routledge.

Lambert, N. and Clochard, O. 2015. "Mobile and Fatal: The EU Borders." In *Borderities and the Politics of Contemporary Mobile Borders*, edited by A.-L. Amilhat Szary and F. Giraut, 119–137. London: Palgrave Macmillan.

Lightfoot, K. G., and A. Martinez. 1995. "Frontiers and Boundaries in Archaeological Perspective." *Annual Review of Anthropology* 24: 471–492.

Williams, J. 2006. *The Ethics of Territorial Borders: Drawing Lines in the Shifting Sand*. London: Palgrave Macmillan.

Contributors

Angelica Bălos is a specialist in historical monuments. She works as an inspector for the Romanian Ministry of Culture's Department of Cultural and National Heritage, Hunedoara County, which is dedicated to the conservation and protection of archaeological sites. She is an Iron Age field archaeologist and has directed or co-directed several long-term excavations, notably at Piatra Detunata (Brasov County) and Măgura Uroiului (Hunedoara County).

Jonathan D. Bethard is assistant professor in the Department of Anthropology at the University of South Florida. He is interested in broad research questions related to bioarchaeology and forensic anthropology. He received his academic training at the University of Tennessee and has conducted archaeological fieldwork in the United States, Peru, and Romania.

Michele R. Buzon is professor in the Department of Anthropology at Purdue University. She currently co-directs an excavation at Tombos in Sudanese Nubia with Stuart Tyson Smith of the University of California, Santa Barbara. Her research examines health, identity, and migration during sociopolitical transitions in ancient Nubia.

Alfredo Coppa is full professor in the Department of Environmental Biology at the Sapienza Università di Roma. He was president of the Italian Anthropology Association in 1997–1999 and won the national prize awarded by the Accademia dei Lincei for physical anthropology in 2007.

Tosha L. Dupras is professor and chair of anthropology at the University of Central Florida. Her research is focused on stable isotope analysis for the reconstruction of diet and mobility, paleopathology, juvenile osteology, and growth and development. She has been associated with the Dakhleh Oasis Project in Egypt since 1995 and joined the Dayr al-Barsha expedition in Egypt in 2004.

Andre Gonciar is an experienced field archaeologist and geophysicist. He is currently the field director of ArchaeoTek's Geophysics Program and Roman Villa and Settlement Excavation and Survey Project and co-director of Archaeo-Tek's Medieval Cemetery Funerary Excavations and experimental workshop. His main focus is prehistoric social and political evolution patterns during the Bronze and Iron Age.

Amanda T. Groff is associate lecturer of anthropology at the University of Central Florida. Her primary area of research uses stable isotopes to determine the migration and mobility of ancient individuals. She has been associated with the Caracol Archaeological Project in Belize (2002–2010) and the Pietramarina Project in Italy (2012–2014) and is currently associated with the Dakhleh Oasis Project in Egypt (2007–).

Ryan P. Harrod is assistant professor of anthropology at the University of Alaska Anchorage. His research interests include bioarchaeology and paleopathology. He is interested in questions about identity, inequality, social control, and violence.

Virginia Lucas is a PhD student at the University of Nevada, Las Vegas. She specializes in the identification and interpretation of animal skeletal remains. She has worked on zooarchaeological assemblages in the southeastern United States. Presently, her research focuses on faunal exploitation practices of the Virgin Branch Ancestral Puebloans in Nevada, as well as trade economies and networks of these people.

Debra L. Martin is professor of anthropology at the University of Nevada, Las Vegas. She is an expert in human osteology and bioarchaeology and conducts research in the areas of nonlethal violence and inequality, gender differences and paleopathology, and the bioarchaeology of human experience with a focus on groups living in risky and challenging desert environments.

Kimmarie Murphy is associate professor of anthropology at Kenyon College in Ohio. She holds a PhD in biological anthropology from Indiana University. Trained as a biocultural anthropologist, she is interested in understanding contemporary patterns of health and nutrition as a way of interpreting diet and disease in the past. Her research focuses on human osteology with an emphasis on paleopathology and stable isotope analysis.

Evan Muzzall earned his PhD in anthropology from Southern Illinois University Carbondale in 2015. He is currently instructional services lead at the UC Berkeley Social Sciences D-Lab, where he teaches many of the R and machine learning workshops. He previously taught bioarchaeology at San Francisco State University and forensic anthropology and data science for Upward Bound at UC Berkeley and was a visiting scholar in the UC Berkeley Human Evolution Research Center.

Selin E. Nugent is a postdoctoral researcher for the Centre for Anthropology and Mind at the University of Oxford and a research affiliate with the Institute for the Study of the Ancient World at New York University. Her research centers on social collaboration, organizational structures, and complex systems among mobile pastoralists and other highly mobile populations in Bronze Age through the Medieval period in Eurasia. She conducts fieldwork in Anatolia and the South Caucasus.

Zsolt Nyárádi is a medieval archaeologist from the Haáz Rezső Múzeum in Székelyudvarhely (in Romanian: Odorheiu Secuiesc). His research focuses on the realities of long-distance influences at the local level; dynamic interactions on a practical and material level, and the expansion and expression of medieval religious currents in small Székely communities.

Anna J. Osterholtz is assistant professor in the Department of Anthropology and Middle Eastern Cultures at Mississippi State University. She specializes in the analysis and interpretation of commingled and fragmentary human skeletal assemblages and has worked with such assemblages in North America, Europe, the Near East, and the Mediterranean. Her research focuses on the relationship between the living and the dead and on the social roles that manipulation and body processing can play within societies and how those relationships and social roles can be interpreted based on assemblages where remains can no longer be identified as discrete individuals.

Claudia Radu is a PhD candidate in archaeology at the Babeș-Bolyai University in Cluj-Napoca, Romania. Her doctoral research explores the features of the Migration period population that inhabited Transylvania, Romania, from both a biological and a cultural perspective. Her research interests focus on social bioarchaeology, Migration period burial practices, theoretical archaeology, and paleopathology.

Contributors   281

Claira Ralston is a PhD student at the University of Nevada, Las Vegas. She specializes in the identification and analysis of human and animal skeletal remains. Her research interests are situated within the sociopolitical narrative of captive-taking and slavery practices in the southwestern United States. Currently, her research focuses on a biocultural approach to reconstructing the lived experiences of marginalized communities living in and around New Mexico in the eighteenth and nineteenth centuries.

Stuart Tyson Smith is professor in the Department of Anthropology at the University of California, Santa Barbara. He currently co-directs an excavation at Tombos in Sudanese Nubia with Michele R. Buzon of Purdue University, focusing on the dynamics of colonialism, cultural interactions, and identity between ancient Egypt and Nubia.

Andrei Soficaru is a researcher at the "Francisc I. Rainer" Institute of Anthropology in Bucharest, Romania, where he has worked since 1999. His research interests include bioarchaeology, paleodemography, and paleopathology from late antiquity to the modern period, mainly in southeast Romania. He has published many studies covering the Upper Paleolithic to the middle of the twentieth century.

Cristina I. Tica is a PhD candidate in the Department of Anthropology at the University of Nevada, Las Vegas. Her field of study is bioarchaeology. Her research interests are the study of late antiquity in Eastern Europe, frontier and borderlands studies, migration studies, Eurasian Steppe nomads of the Iron Age and late antiquity, Sarmatian groups from the Great Hungarian Plain, trauma and violence studies, paleopathology, and biogeochemical analyses.

Mark P. Toussaint is a PhD candidate in the Department of Anthropology at the University of Nevada, Las Vegas. His research interests include the Bronze Age of Central Europe, cross-cultural constructions of gender, ethnogenesis, the development of social stratification, the bioarchaeology of embodiment, and ancient DNA studies.

Katie Marie Whitmore is a PhD candidate in the Department of Anthropology at Purdue University. Her interests include a life course approach to health, social constructions of age, and impairment/disability in the ancient Nile Valley.

Aaron R. Woods is a PhD candidate at the University of Nevada, Las Vegas. He earned bachelor's and master's degrees from Brigham Young University. His current academic research focuses on the role of small sites in community systems, the importance of experimental archaeology and replicative studies, and chipped-stone tool use.

Guðný Zoëga is the head of the Archaeological Department of the Skagafjordur Heritage Museum, North Iceland. She holds a PhD in archaeology from Oslo University. Recently her focus has been on settlement history, mortuary archaeology, and the bioarchaeology of early Christian households and household cemeteries.

Index

Page numbers in *italics* refer to illustrations.

Abandonment, 90, 217

Actinomycosis, 169

Activity markers, stress and, 221–22

Activity pattern evidence, in bones, 150

Adderley, P., 162, 178

Adrianople, 190, 204

Age: of children and terminology used, 256; of death in Roman Egypt, 90; death with sex and, 219–20; distribution at Kelduda-lur and Seyla, *170*; distribution at Telek-falva Reformed Church, 260; Iceland and patterns associated with, 169–73; LEH by sex and, *146*; M141 cranial fragments by sex and, 194, *195*

Agriculture: Iceland and, 164–65; in Iron Age, 110; Mierzanowice Culture and, 56; Roman Empire and, 35; Sântana de Mureş Culture and, 20

Alans, 190

Alfedena, 275; dental data, *118*; discussion, 121–23; grave goods, 112; in historical context, 109–11, *111*; materials and methods, 113–17; neighbor-joining clustering from, *120*; results, 117–21; social differentiation, origins of, 110–11; trauma and, 112–13; weapons at, 112

Alyha, 62

Amani (deity), 144

Amarna and Post-Amarna periods (ca. 1390 to ca. 1295 BCE), 139

Amenhotep II (Egyptian Pharaoh), 139

Amenhotep III (Egyptian Pharaoh), 139

American Southwest, 213

Amheida, 98

Ammianus Marcellinus, 35, 190, 203–4

AMTL. *See* Antemortem tooth loss

Amun-Re (deity), 144

Analyses of variance (ANOVA), 108, 116–17, *119*, 121, 123

Ancestral Puebloans (Anasazi), 212; activity and stress markers, 221–22; border areas, *213*; ceramics and, 216–17; Chaco Branch, 216, 217; discussion, 223–24; Fremont and, 7, 214–25; Kayenta Branch, 216, 217, 219–25; materials and methods, 218–19; Mesa Verde Branch, 216, 224; results, 219–20; rock art, 214; with traumatic injuries and intergroup conflict, 222–23; Virgin Branch, 216–17, 219–25

Anderson, M., 273

Andritoiu, I., 234

Anemia, 24, 28, 146, 221, 240

Animal husbandry, 18, 56, 165, 262

Animals: activity with bones, 196, 205; bivalves, 247–48; bones of, 191, *245*; burials, 137; gray wolf at Măgura Uroiului, 244, *245*; pack, 85; ritual use of, 244–46; sacrifices, 143, 242–44

ANOVA. *See* Analyses of variance

Antemortem tooth loss (AMTL), 67, 147–48, *148*, 153, 173

Antemortem trauma, 29, 69, 71, 74, 198

Anukis (deity), 144

Apennine Mountains, 109

Apprenticeships, 85, 88, 98, 99, 100

Aras River Basin, 45, 51

Arboreto, 113

Archaeological Isotopes Laboratory, 49

Archaeology, of children, 255–56

ArchaeoTek, 236

Ariès, Philip, 265

Arizona State University Dental Anthropology System (ASUDAS), 108, 113–14, 116, 118, *120*, 121–22

Armenia, 45, 46, 52
Art, on rock panels, 214, 224, *246*
Artaxiad dynasty, 46
Askut, 151
ASUDAS. *See* Arizona State University
  Dental Anthropology System
Asyut, 96
Aufderheide, A. C., 22, 145, 192, 219
Augustus (Roman emperor), 44, 45
Aurelia Marsis, 87
Aurelian (Roman Emperor), 19, 20
Aurelius Psais, 87
Avars, 15, 190

Babia Góra II, 56–57, 59
Baczyńska, Barbara, 63
Bălos, Angelica, 236
Baptism, 263, 266
Barbarians, 5; Danube frontier and, 188;
  defined, 13–14, 36; identity, 16; role of,
  14–15; Târgşor and, *14*, 19, 28. *See also*
  Roman Empire
Barth, Fredrik, 56, 107
Bartlett's tests for homoscedasticity, 114–15
Basketmaker II, 212, 214
Basketmaker III, 214, 216, 217
Bass, William M., 219
Bastarnae, 20
Batn-el-Hajar, 137
Baxter, J. E., 256
Beads, 19, 46, 58, 63, 112, 144
Beaumont, J., 267
Bell Beaker Culture, 59
Bereavement, 265, 267
Berlin Wall, 277
Bethard, J. D., 266
Bioarchaeology: of frontiers and border-
  lands, 3–5; Telekfalva Reformed Church,
  analysis, 258–62, *259*, *260*
Biodistance approach. *See* Biological dis-
  tance approach
Biogeochemical findings, 47–51
Biological distance (biodistance) approach,
  6, 108–9, 116, 121–23
Biological kinship, 115–16; expression of,
  108; relevance of, 107
Bivalves, 247–48
Black, S., 63
Black Sea, 20, 41, 188, 189
Bögöz community, 267
Bones: activity pattern evidence in, 150;

animal activity with, 196, 205; of animals,
  191, *245*; antemortem trauma in, *29*, 69,
  71, 74, 198; apatite results with tooth
  enamel, 90–96, *99*, *101*; CDFs, 30–32, *31*,
  198, 222–23, *238–39*; cranial landmarks,
  113, *115*, 116; cribra orbitalia, 22, 24–25,
  146–47; decapitation, 71, *71*, *72*, 105;
  diseases and, 28; entheses, 64, 72–73,
  150, 218–19, 221; femurs of mice, 91;
  fibula, 242; Fracture Freshness Index
  and, 196; long, 22, 25, 147, 149, 152, 202,
  242, 246–47, 258, 261; at M141, *195–97*,
  197–98, *199–202*; mandible fracture, *72*;
  osteoarthritis, *67*, 150; with osteological and biogeochemical findings, 47–51;
  osteoperiostitis, 148–49, 152; oxygen and,
  84; periosteal reaction, 22, 25–27, *27*, 242;
  porotic hyperostosis, 146–47; skeletal
  populations, 108, 167; surface modifications, *197*; tibiae, 25, *27*, 31, 65, 242;
  trauma, 29–33, *32*, 149–50. *See also* Teeth
Book of the Dead, 142
Borderlands: bioarchaeology of, 3–5; in context, 5–8; frontiers and, 2, 277; portrayal
  of, 2; with social theory, 206; as viewed
  by Naum, 162–163
Borders: bioarchaeology of, 3–5; in context,
  5–9; as counter-power sites, 273; defined,
  2–3; disputes, 273; Fremont and Pueblo,
  213, 214–16; frontiers and, 55, 162–68, 273,
  276–77; Mexico-US, 277; paradox of, 277;
  role of, 1–3
Bottles, small glass, 46
Boundary-bending bioarchaeological
  scholarship, 8, 252, 267, 275
Bowing, of long bones, 261
Bowlby, John, 265
Brigham Young University, 224
Bronze Age, 5, 73, 110, 234, 276. *See also*
  Mierzanowice Culture
Brooks, S., 63
Brucellosis, 169, 176
Bruzek, Jaroslav, 63
Buikstra, J. E., 63, 150, 168, 169, 192, 219
Bulgars, 190
Burebista (King of Dacia), 18
Burials: animal, 137; ceramics and, 43, 46,
  51, 110, 143, 144, 152; of children and
  women, 8, 237; *cillíni* and, 263; data and
  social analyses, 169; elite class and, 46–
  47; Ibida, 21; Kerma-style, *143*, 143–44;

Sântana de Mureș Culture, 21; sex and orientation of, *67, 68,* 69; Târgşor, 21; Telekfalva and social context of, 262–65; westward-facing, 43–45. *See also* Funerary practice; *specific burials*
Burneshas ("sworn virgins"), 62
Butler, Judith, 61
Buzon, Michele R., 139

Callatis, 194
Campovalano, in ancient Italy: dental data, *118*; discussion, 121–23; grave goods at, *112*; in historical context, 109–11, *111*, 275; materials and methods, 113–17; neighbor-joining clustering from, *120*; results, 117–21; social differentiation, origins of, 110–11; trauma and, 112–13
Cannibalism, 214
Cannon, A., 265
Canyon del Muerto, 214
Carpathian Arch, 253, *257*
CDFs. *See* Cranial depression fractures
Ceauşescu, I., 255
Celts, 162–63
Ceramics: Ancestral Puebloans and, 216–17; burials and, 43, 46, 51, 110, 143, 144, 152; elite class and, 20; feasting pits and, 44, 236; in Ibida, 18; Kerma-style, 143; pottery and, 7, 20, 58, 112, 139, 191–92, 205, 216; in South Caucasus, 46
Chaco Branch Puebloans, 216, 217. *See also* Ancestral Puebloans
Chaco Canyon, 214
Children: archaeology of, 255–56; baptism of, 263, 266; bioarchaeological analysis, 258–62; burials of women and, 8, 237; *cillíni* and, 263; frontal bone fragment of newborn from, *202*; in Iceland, 166, 171; infant mortality, 171, 176, 262, 265, 267; in Roman Egypt, 85, 87–88, 98, 100; terminology used with ages of, 256; trauma in, 238–40. *See also* Telekfalva Reformed Church
Christianity, advent of, 160, 166, 176–77
Churches: farmstead, 166–67; Hungarian Reformed, 263; Roman Catholic, 263; as sacred space, 163; Skagafjörður Church Project, 167; slaves and, 174. *See also* Telekfalva Reformed Church
Cillíni (separate burial grounds for infants and older children), 263

Circum-Carpathian Epi-Corded Culture Circle, 58, 59
Clochard, O., 274
Clothing, 62, 85, 199, 203, 205
Cocoş, R. S., 253
Coffin graves, 174–75, *175*
Coins, 18, 20–21, 43–44, *44*, 51, 256, 258, *258*
Colonization: frontier and, 2; in historical context, 135–38; Iceland and, 163–64. *See also* New Kingdom period
Comorbidity, Ibida and Târgşor samples, 28, 33
Connolly, W. E., 206
Constantine, 15
Constantinople, 15, 18
Cook, K., 265
Copper Age, 110
Corded Ware Culture, 59, 60
Counter-power, borders and frontiers as sites of, 273
Cranial depression fractures (CDFs), 30–32, *31*, 198, 222–23, *238–39*
Cranial fragments, from M141, *200*; by age and sex, 194, *195*
Cranial landmarks, 113, *115*, 116
Cribra orbitalia, 22, 25; anemia and, 24; in Ibida sample, 24; at Măgura Uroiului, 240, *241*; in Târgşor sample, 24; Tombos, 146–47
Croft, Paul, 244
Csáky, Kata, 264–65
Cultures, 107; American Southwest, 213; Bell Beaker, 59; Circum-Carpathian Epi-Corded, 58, 59; Corded Ware, 59, 60; Fremont in context, 215–16; frontiers and, 187–88; Great Basin area, 213; languages and, 188–89; Mierzanowice, 56–74; Otomani-Füzesabony, 58–59, 73; Romanization and, 16–17; Sântana de Mureş, 19–21; "stabilized pluralism" and, 20; Únětice, 58, 73; women and Nubian, 151–52. *See also specific cultures*
Cut marks, on long bones, 246–47

DacFest, 236
Dacians, 20, 188, 236; with Dragon carving, 246, *246*; Hallstatt period and, 246
Dakhleh Oasis, *86*, 87, 89; materials and methods, 90–91; results, 92–96
Danube frontier, Roman Empire and, 187–90

Index   287

Danube River, Roman Empire and, 15–16
DDE. *See* Defects of dental enamel
Decapitation, 71, *71*, 72, 105
Decebal (King of Dacia), 18
Defects of dental enamel (DDE), 168, 171, *173*, 174
Degenerative joint disease, 168, 169, 173, 174, 176
Dehumanization, 203–4, 207
Demographics: human remains on Romanian frontier, 237, *237*; Ibida, 22, *23*; Roman Empire, 22–24, *23*, 35–36; Târgşor, *23*, 24
Denarii, 43–46, *44*
Dennell, R. W., 2
Dental data, *118*
Dental enamel, 48–49, 90–91, 168, *173*, 266
Dental metrics, 113–17, *114*
Dettman, David, 49
Deviant behavior, 206, 263
Dioskouroi (deity), 111
Diseases: bones and, 28; brucellosis, 169, 176; degenerative joint, 168, 169, 173, 174, 176; health and, 145–50, *148*, 152–53; infectious, 25, 146, 165, 168–69, 171, 176, 221, 240; LEH, 67, 71, 145–46, *146*, 152–53; leprosy, 98, 101–2; mobility and, 101; plague, 205; risk, 65; scurvy, 169, 174, 176, 222, 240–42, 260–61, 264; syphilis, 169; tuberculosis, 169, 176, 219
Disputes, borders, 273
Dobrudja, 188, 194, 253, 267n3
Donnan, H., 3
Dragon carving, 246, *246*
Drinking water, 83–84, 191

Ecosystem, 48
Egypt: chronologies of, *137*; grave goods, 142, *142*; in historical context, 135–38; immigrants from, 138; jewelry, 144; migration from, 139; Nubia and, 6, 135–52, *136*, 273–74; temples and, 138. *See also* Roman Egypt, mobility and
Elite class: Barbarian, 16; in Bronze Age, 110; burials and, 46–47; ceramics and, 20; heart scarabs and, 142, 151; Nubia and, 144, 152; pyramids and, 141; Romans, 176
Ellis, L., 20
Enamel. *See* Teeth
Enarees, 61
Entheses, 64, 72–73, 150, 218–19, 221

Environment, Iceland with challenges, 163, 164–65, 166, 171
Environmental Isotope Laboratory, 49
Escalante Drainage Survey, 224
Ethnic identity, 6, 16, 20, 154
Etruscan pottery, 112

Famine, 35, 164, 177
Farafara Oasis, 98
Farmstead churches, 166–67
Faunal remains, Romanian frontier and, 242–48
Feasting: activities, 51; at Măgura Uroiului, 246–48; pits, 44, 236; rituals and, 247; sacrifice and, 8; wares, 111
Fehér, Andrea, 264–65
Females: Keldudalur and heights of, 171, *172*; with LEH, 146
Females, in Roman Egypt: mean age of death and, 90; mobility for adult, 98–99; oxygen isotope data for, 92–93; socioeconomic activities and, 85–88; tooth enamel and bone apatite results, 92–93, 99
Femoral shaft, head and, *196*
Femur fragments, from M141, *201*
Fibula, 242
Finland, 163
Finlay, N., 263
Fiore, 112
Fisher, A., 22, 33
Floca, O., 234
Fracture Freshness Index, 196
"Francisc I. Rainer" Institute of Anthropology, 21
Fremont, 7, 217–18, 225; activity and stress markers, 221–22; border areas, *213*; in cultural context, 215–16; with head collection, trophy, 214, 224; Kayenta Branch Puebloans and, 224; rock art, 214; sex and age at death, 219–20; traumatic injuries, 222–24; violence with Pueblo and, 214–16
Frontal bone of newborn, from M141, *202*
"Frontier consciousness," 187
Frontiers: bioarchaeology of, 3–5; borders and, 55, 162–68, 273, 276–77; characteristics of, 55–56; colonization and, 2; concept of, 252–53; in context, 5–9; as counter-power sites, 273; cultures and, 187–88; defined, 2, 55–56, 162; identity

and, 274; "Norse," 162–63; role of, 1–3;
Roman Empire, 15–18
Funerary cones, 141
Funerary figurines (*ushabtis*), 142, 151
Funerary practice, Şərur Valley, 5, 41–42;
burials, 21, 43–45; foreign identity and
local interactions at Oğlanqala, 51–53;
mortuary assemblage, 46–47; osteological and biogeochemical findings,
47–51; South Caucasus during Roman
campaign, 45–46

Gaius Caesar, 44, 45–46, 51, 52
Gebel Barkal, 144
Gebelein, 96
Geib, Phil, 224
Geller, Pamela, 60–61, 62
Gender: mobility and, 98–102; with mobil-
ity and sex, 85–90; Neolithic rock art,
110; tooth enamel and bone apatite
results, 90–96, 99, 101
Gender, in Mierzanowice Culture: as
construct, 55–56; Enarees and, 61; grave
goods and, 57–58; power and, 56, 73, 275;
sex and, 57, 59–62, 66, 73–74
Genetic sex typing, 266
Germany, 205
Getae population, Romanization of, 188
Glen Canyon, 224
Gloucester, 205
GNU Image Manipulation Program, 116
Gold, 47, 58, 138, 142, 150
Goths, 15, 20; Huns and, 35; Romans and,
190, 203–5; soldiers, 204
Grasshopper Pueblo, 217
Grave goods: Alfedena, 112; Campovalano,
112; Egypt, 142, 142; gender and, 57–58;
Ibida, 18–19; Iceland, 169; jewelry as, 112;
Sântana de Mureş Culture, 21; Tombos,
142, 142; *unguentaria*, 46
Gray wolf, at Măgura Uroiului, 244, 245
Great Basin, 213
Great Salt Lake area, 214
Greek language, 188
Greenland, 160, 166, 171, 174
Grémaux, René, 62
Grief, 265, 267

Haáz Rezső Múzeum, 256
Haddow, S. D., 98
Hallstatt period, 246

Handbook of the North American Indians
(Smithsonian Institute), 212–13
Hat brim line (HBL), 30, 32, 238
Hawkey, Diane E., 150
HBL. *See* Hat brim line
Heads: CDFs, 30–32, 31, 198, 222–23,
238–39; cranial landmarks, 113, 115, 116,
194, 195, 200; femoral shaft and, 196; HBL
and, 30, 32, 238; trauma, 219, 223–24;
trophy collection of, 214, 224
Health: New Kingdom period and indica-
tors of, 145–50, 153; oral, 147–48, 148,
153; osteoperiostitis, 148–49, 152. *See also*
Diseases
Heart scarabs, 142, 151
Hercules (deity), 111
Hermopolis, 88
Herodotus, 61
Heterogeneity, 17, 110
Hijras, 62
Histria, 194
Homosexuality, 60–61
Howard, Julie, 214
Hradisko, 205
Hreppr (municipality system), 163, 178
Hrísbrú, 171, 176
Human remains, on Romanian frontier:
demography, 237, 237; pathology, 240–42;
trauma, 238–40
Hunedoara County Ministry of Culture, 236
Hungarian Reformed Church, 263
Hungary, 58, 253, 262, 267n4
Huns, 15, 35, 190, 204
Hwame, 62
Hydatidosis, 169
Hyksos people, 137

Ibida (M141), political violence in: bone
surface modifications in, 197; cranial
fragments by age and sex from, 194, 195;
cranial fragment with perimortem bone
modification from, 200; Danube frontier
and, 187–90; dehumanization and, 203–
4, 207; discussion, 198–205; evidence of,
7, 207–8; femoral shaft and head from,
196; femur fragment with postmortem
bone modification from, 201; formation
process of, 199; frontal bone fragment of
newborn from, 202; materials and methods, 192–94; results, 194–98; site of, 189,
190–92, 193; with social theory, 206–7

Index   289

Ibida (Slava Rusă), 13, *14*, *29*; as archaeological site, 18–19; burials, 21; ceramics
in, 18; comorbidity and, 28, 33; cribra
orbitalia and, 24; demographics, 22, *23*;
grave goods, 18–19; necropolis at, 194,
195, 200; periosteal reaction and, 27,
27; porotic hyperostosis and, 24; stress
conditions and, 25; trauma, 31, 33; vault
at, 194, 195
Iceland: age, patterns associated with,
169–73; agriculture and, 164–65; children
in, 166, 171; colonization and, 163–64;
discussion, 175–78; environmental challenges, 163, 164–65, 166, 171; frontiers and
borderlands, 162–68; grave goods, 169; in
historical context, 7, 160–63; land ownership in, 166; materials and methods,
168–75; sex differences, patterns associated with, 174; social analyses of burial
data, 169; social reactions, 165–68; status
differences, patterns associated with,
174–75; with transport back to Norway,
177; women in, 166
Identity: ethnic, 6, 16, 20, 154; formation, 1,
41, 46; frontiers and, 274; local interactions at Oğlanqala and foreign, 51–53; in
Mierzanowice Culture, 59; Tombos and,
273–74
Immigrants, Nubia with Egyptian, 139
Infanticide, 266
Infants: baptism for, 263, 266; mortality,
171, 176, 262, 265, 267. *See also* Children
Innse Gall, 162–63
Institute of Anthropology at the Romanian
Academy, 192
Ireland, 263
Iron Age, 44; agriculture in, 110; indigenous
populations in, 188; necropolis, 113. *See
also* Italy, Iron Age in; Romanian fron-
tier, in Iron Age
Isis (deity), 47, *47*
Ismant el-Kharab. *See* Kellis
Isotopes: laboratories, 49; oxygen, 6,
48–51, *50*, 83–84, 90–91, 92–97, 96–97;
results, 92–96; strontium, 48–51, *50*,
139, *141*
Italy, Iron Age in: Campovalano and
Alfedena in, 109–13; in historical context,
6, 107–8; materials and methods, 113–17;
results, 117–21; social differentiation,
origins of, 110–11

Jaeger, M., 59
Janetski, Joel, 214
Jewelry, 58, 109; Egyptian and Nubian, 144;
as grave goods, 112; rings, signet, 46–47,
47; Żerniki Górne case study and, 63
Justinian (Roman Emperor), 34, 191

Kápolnásfalva village, 262
Karr, L. P., 192
Kayenta Branch Puebloans, 216; activity
and stress markers, 221–22; in cultural
context, 217; Fremont and, 224–25; sex
and age at death, 219–20; traumatic
injuries, 222–23. *See also* Ancestral
Puebloans
Keldudalur, 160, *161*, 164, 167; age distribution at, *170*; coffin graves in, *175*; DDE
at, 168, 171, *173*, 174; discussion, 175–78;
grave goods, 169; heights of females and
males at, 171, *172*; materials and methods,
168–75; pathologies summary at, *173*; sex
distribution at, *170*
Kellis (Ismant el-Kharab), 86; history of,
89–90; oxygen isotope ranges from,
96–97; patrilocality in, 87–88; slavery
in, 87
Kempisty, Andrzej, 63
Kerma: burials in style of, *143*, 143–44;
ceramics, 143; traumatic injury at, 150; as
urban center, 137
Kerma Classic period (ca. 1750–ca. 1550
BCE), 150
Kharga Oasis, 98
Khnum (deity), 144
Killgrove, K., 36
Kissonerga-Mylouthkia, 244
Komar, D., 202, 203
Krueger, H. W., 91
Kulubnarti, 96
Kush, 138, 141–42

Labor: apprenticeships, 85, 88, 98, 99, 100;
imported, 190; slavery and, 85, 87, 89, 99,
102, 174, 176
Laboratory for Bioarchaeological Sciences,
91
Lahr, Marta Mirazón, 240
Lambert, N., 274
Land (*terra*), 206
Land ownership: in Iceland, 166; women
and, 87

Languages, 188–89
Laqueur, Thomas, 61
Latin, 188
Lava flows, 165
Leasing contracts, 87
LEH. *See* Linear enamel hypoplasia
Leprosy, 98, 101–2
Lesions, on long bones, 149
Lewis, M. E., 256
Lillehammer, G., 255
Limbo, 263
Limes, 15–17, 19, 188
Linear enamel hypoplasia (LEH), 67, 71, 145–46, *146*, 152–53
Long bones, 202; bowing of, 261; cut marks on, 246–47; growth, 152, 258; growth disruption, 147; lesions on, 149; periosteal reaction, 22, 25, 242
Lovejoy, C. O., 63
Lowell, Julia, 217
Lucas, Virginia, 242
Lucius Caesar, 44

M141. *See* Ibida, political violence in
Măgura Uroiului: animal sacrifice at, 242–44; with animal use, ritual, 244–46; cribra orbitalia at, 240, *241*; Dacian dragon carving at, 246, *246*; demography of human remains at, 237, *237*; feasting at, 246–48; geography of, *235–36*; gray wolf at, 244, *245*; with mortuary monument, excavation of, *236*; nonhuman species at, *243*; Romanian frontier and, 235–36; trauma, *238*, 238–40, *239*
Magyars, 254, 267n4
Mahieu, E., 192, 194
Maiden Castle, 205
Males: Keldudalur and heights of, 171, *172*; with LEH, 146; weapons and, 111
Males, in Roman Egypt: mean age of death and, 90; mobility for adult, 100–102, *101*; oxygen isotope data for, *94–95*; socioeconomic activities and, 88–89; tooth enamel and bone apatite results, 94–96, *101*
Mandible, fracture of, *72*
Marcomannic Wars, 205
Mariotti, Valentina, 64, 218
Marriage, 6, 87, 98, 99, 275–76
Mars (deity), 111
Martian, I., 234

Martin, Debra L., 240
Massacres, 203, 204–5, 207, 224
Mass graves, 205. *See also* Ibida (M141), political violence in
Maya people, 135
Meindl, R. S., 63
Mendes, 96
Merbs, Charles F., 150
Merymose, 139
Mesa Verde Branch, 216, 224. *See also* Ancestral Puebloans
Mexico-US border, 277
Mice femurs, 91
Middle Kingdom period (ca. 2050–ca. 1650 BCE), 137–38
Mierzanowice Culture: agriculture and, 56; Bronze Age and, 56–59; discussion, 70–73; with frontiers, definition and characteristics, 55–56; sex and gender, theorizing of, 60–62; sex and gender in, 59–60, 66, 73–74; Żerniki Górne case study, 62–70
Migration: Kayenta Branch Puebloans and, 217; to Nubia, 139; rates, 262; tribal, 139–40; Virgin Branch Puebloans and, 217
Military: Nubia and Egyptian, 137–38, 139, 151; Roman campaigns, 45–46, 188, 190, 203–5; soldiers, 14, 47, 88–89, 139, 204; Viking raids, 166
Miscarriages, 264–65
Mobility: diseases and, 101; female adult, 98–99; of goods and people, 85–90; immigration and, 138; male adult, 100–102, *101*; oxygen isotopes and, 6. *See also* Roman Egypt, mobility and
Mogollon pueblos, 217
Moldavia, 253, 267n3
Molnár, M., 255
Molto, J. E., 98
Montagne de Campania, 112
Moravia, 56
Mortuary assemblage, Şərur Valley, 46–47
Mughal, M. Z., 261
Mundelsheim, 205
Municipality system (*hreppr*), 163, 178
Murdock, G., 262, 263
Mureş River, 234
Murphy, E. M., 263
Murphy, K., 168, 173
Mut, 98

Nádleeh, 62
Nail, Thomas, 2, 4
Nanda, Serena, 62
Napatan period (ca. 1400–ca. 650 BCE), 138, 144, 152
Naum, M., 162–63
Naxçıvan Archaeological Project, 43, 53
Necropolis: at Ibida, 194, 195, 200; Iron Age, 113; from Târgşor, 19
Neolithic rock art, 110
New Kingdom period: discussion, 150–54; health indicators, 145–50, 153; in historical context, 135–38, 154–55; Tombos in, 6, 138–44, *140*, *142*, 146–47. *See also* Egypt; Nubia
Nile Cataracts, *136*, 136–37, 138–39, 151
Nile Valley: adult male mobility in, 101–2; oxygen isotope ranges from, *96–97*; strontium isotopes in, *141*; trade routes and, 85, 137
"Norse frontiers," 162–63
Norway, 160, 177
Nubia: chronologies of, *137*; Egypt and, 6, 135–52, *136*, 273–74; elite class and, 144, 152; jewelry, 144; Kerma, 137; migration to, 139; rebellion in, 151; temples in, 138, 144; Tombos, 6, 138–44, *140*; trade routes and, 85; with women and culture, 151–52
Nyárádi, Zsolt, 256

Oğlanqala, *42*; foreign Identity and local interactions at, 51–53; Period II and, 44–45
Ohio State University, 49
Old Stone Age, 89
Olexa, L., 59
Olive oil, 85, 88
Oral health, 147–48, *148*, 153
Oram, R., 162, 178
Orăştie Mountains, 234
Ortner, D. J., 22, 168, 192, 219
Osteoarthritis: defined, 150; by sex and burial orientation, *67*
Osteological findings, 47–51
Osteoperiostitis, 148–49, 152
Osterholtz, Anna J., 202–3, 264
Otomani-Füzesabony Culture, 58–59, 73
Ottoman Empire, 254–55
Outram, A. K., 192, 196
Oxygen isotopes, 6, 48–49; analysis, 83–84, 90–91, 96–97, *96–97*; data for females in Roman Egypt, *92–93*; data for males in Roman Egypt, *94–95*; with strontium values, *50*, 50–51
Oxyrhynchus papyri collection, 85

Paiute, 217
Pakot, L., 262
Parker, B. J., 2, 55, 162
Parowan Valley, 213, 223
Parr, R., 102
Parthian Empire: ceramics in, 46; Romans and, 42, 45, 52
Patakfalva village, 264
Pathology: burial orientation and dental, 68; human remains on Romanian frontier, 240–42; at Keldudalur and Seyla, *173*
Patrilocality, 87–88, 98, 99
Pecos Classification System, 212
Pérez, Ventura R., 206
Period II, 44–45, 51
Periosteal reaction, 26; Ibida and, 27, *27*; long bones, 22, 25, 242; Târgşor and, 27
Perry, M. A., 256
Phenice, T. W., 63
Phraataces (King of Parthia), 45
Pinhasi, R., 261
Plague, 205
Point of Pines, 217
Poland, 19, 56, 58
Political violence. *See* Ibida, political violence in
Porčić, M., 73
Porotic hyperostosis, 25; in Ibida sample, 24; in Târgşor sample, 24; in Tombos, 146–47
Pottery, 7, 20, 58, 112, 139, 191–92, 205, 216. *See also* Ceramics
Power: counter-, 273; gender and, 56, 73, 275
Pregnancy diets, 264
Pretuzi, 108, 113
Prokopios of Caesarea, 188
Prostitutes, 87
Puebloans. *See* Ancestral Puebloans
Pueblo III period (1150–1285 CE), 216, 217
Pueblo II period (900–1150 CE), 216, 217
Purgatory, 263
Pyramids, 141

Ralston, Claira, 242
Ramesses II (Egyptian Pharaoh), 139
Raymond, Nicole, 223
Rebellion, in Nubia, 151

Redfern, R. C., 34
Regensburg-Harting, 205
ResearchGate (website), 234
Res Gestae divi Augusti, 45
Riggs, Charles, 212, 217
Rights, transmitting of, 107–8
Rings, signet, 46–47, *47*
Rituals: animals used in, 244–46; feasting and, 247
Rivera, Frances, 240
Rock art, 214, 224, *246*
Rocky Mountains, 213
Rodríguez-Martín, C., 22, 145, 192, 219
Rodseth, L., 2, 55
Roman Catholic Church, 263
Roman Egypt, mobility and, 6, 103; in archaeological context, 85–90; discussion, 96–102; isotope analysis, 83–84, 90–91, 96–97; materials and methods, 90–91; results, 92–96
Roman Empire, 13; agriculture and, 35; coins, 18, 20–21, 43–44, *44*, 51; comorbidity and, 28, 33; cribra orbitalia and, 22, 24–25; Danube frontier and, 187–90; Danube River and, 15–16; demographics, 22–24, *23*, 35–36; discussion, 33–35; elite class in, 176; frontier, 15–18; funerary practice and South Caucasus during, 45–46; materials, 21; methods, 22; military campaigns, 45–46, 188, 190, 203–5; Parthians and, 42, 45, 52; periosteal reaction, 25–27, *27*; political violence, 7, 206–8; porotic hyperostosis and, 24–25; results, 23–33; Sântana de Mureş Culture and, 19–21; Târgşor and, *14*, 19, 21, *23, 24,* 27–28, *29,* 31–33; trauma, 29–33, *32*; violence in, 5, 16, 45. *See also* Ibida; Ibida, political violence in
Romanian frontier, in Iron Age, 8; in context, 233–35; faunal remains and, 242–48; human remains and, 237–42; Măgura Uroiului and, 235–36, *235–36*
Romanization, 16–17, 188
R Statistical Computing Package, 65, 117
Rubin, Gayle, 61
Russell, Nerissa, 242, 244

Sacred space, 163, 263
Sacred springs (*veris sacri*), 113
Sacrifices: animals, 143, 242–44; feasting and, 8

Sādhins, 62
Samnite samples, 108, 113
Sangro River Valley, 112
Sântana de Mureş Culture: agriculture and, 20; grave goods, 21; Roman Empire and, 19–21
Sarmatians, 20, 188
Satet (Egyptian consort), 144
Saxe-Goldstein interpretive framework, 107
Scarabs, 139, 142, 151
Scavi Mariani, 113
Schaafsma, Polly, 214, 224
Schattmann, A., 264
Scheuer, L., 63
Schrader, Sarah A., 150
Schut, Henk, 265
Schwarcz, H. P., 91
Scurvy, 169, 174, 176, 222, 240–42, 260–61, 264
Scythia Minor: Târgşor, *14*, 19, 28; trade and, 20–21. *See also* Ibida; Roman Empire
Scythians, 61
Sea ice, 165
Separate burial grounds for infants and older children (*cillíni*), 263
Serapis (deity), *47, 47*
Sergi Museum, 113
Sex: AMTL by, 148, *148*; death with age and, 219–20; dental pathologies by burial orientation and, *68*; differences and associated patterns, 174; distribution at Keldudalur and Seyla, *170*; gender, mobility and, 85–90; genetic typing, 266; LEH by age and, *146*; M141 cranial fragments by age and, 194, *195*; Mierzanowice Culture with gender and, 57, 59–62, 66, 73–74; osteoarthritis by burial orientation and, *67*; teeth with location or, 120–21, *121*; trauma by burial orientation and, *68, 69*
Seyla, 160, *161,* 164, 167; age distribution at, *170*; coffin graves in, 174–75, *175*; DDE, 168, 171, *173,* 174; discussion, 175–78; grave goods, 169; materials and methods, 168–75; pathologies summary at, *173*; sex distribution at, *170*
Şərur Valley: Aras River Basin and, 45; mortuary assemblage, 46–47; oxygen isotopes and, 48–49. *See also* Funerary practice, Şərur Valley

Index   293

Shapiro-Wilk tests, 114
Siamun (Egyptian Pharaoh), 141–42
Sierra Nevada Mountains, 213
Signet rings, 46–47, *47*
Siikala, A.-L., 163
Siikala, J., 163
Skagafjörður Church Project, 167
Skagafjörður region: in historical context, 160, *161*, 177–78; with religious reality, emergence of, 7
Skeletal populations, 108, 167
Slava Rusă. *See* Ibida
Slavery, 85, 87, 89, 99, 102, 174, 176
Slavs, 15, 190
Slovakia, 56, 58–59
Smith, Stuart T., 139, 144, 151
Smithsonian Institute, 212–13
Social context, of burial at Telekfalva, 262–65
Social differentiation, in ancient Italy, 110–11
Social reactions, Iceland, 165–68
Society for American Archaeology, 1
Socioeconomic activities, in Roman Egypt, 85–89
Sofaer, Joanna, 63
Soldiers, 14, 47, 88–89, 139, 204
South Caucasus, *42*; ceramics in, 46; in historical context, 41–43; during Roman campaign, 45–46
Spierling, Karen, 263
"Stabilized pluralism," culture and, 20
Stafanović, S., 73
Status, differences and associated patterns, 174–75
Steckel, Richard H., 149
St. Peter's Cathedral, 113
Strei River, 234
Stress: activity markers and, 221–22; conditions in Ibida samples, *25*; entheses, 64, 72–73, 150, 218–19, 221
Stroebe, Margaret, 265
Strontium isotopes, 48–49; in Nile Valley, *141*; with oxygen values, *50*, 50–51; Tombos, 139
Suchey, J., 63
Sullivan, C. H., 91
"Sworn virgins" (*burneshas*), 62
Syphilis, 169
Szarbia Zwierzyniecka, 57, 60
Székelyföld, 8, 252–56, 267n2. *See also* Telekfalva Reformed Church

Székely people, 267n1, 267n4
Szentegyházasfalva village, 262

Târgșor, *14*, *29*; as archaeological site, 19; burials, 21; comorbidity samples and, 28, 33; cribra orbitalia and, 24; demographics, *23*, 24; periosteal reaction and, 27; porotic hyperostosis and, 24; trauma, 31–32
Taroy fortress, 139
Teeth, 98; AMTL, 67, 147–48, *148*, 153, 173; dental data, *118*; dental enamel, 48–49, 90–91, 168, *173*, 266; dental metrics, 113–17, *114*; dental pathologies by sex and burial orientation, *68*; enamel and bone apatite results, 90–96, 99, *101*; LEH, 67, 71, 145–46, *146*, 152–53; with location or sex, 120–21, *121*; mandible fracture, *72*; oral health and, 147–48, *148*, 153; oxygen and, 84
Tehat, 87
Telekfalva Reformed Church, 241; age distribution of recovered individuals, *260*; bioarchaeological analysis, 258–62, *259*, *260*; case study, 256–65, *258*, *258*; with research continued, 265–67; social context of burial, 262–65
Temples, 138, 144
La Tène, 244
Terra (land), 206
Terra Dacica Aeterna, 236
Terrere (terrorize), 206
"Territory," violence and, 206
Terrorize (*terrere*), 206
Thebes, 141, 144
Thracians, 188–89
Thutmose I (Egyptian Pharaoh), 138, 153
Thutmose IV (Egyptian Pharaoh), 139
Tibiae, *25*, *27*, 31, 65, 242
Todd, M., 263
Todd, T. W., 63
Tombos: cribra orbitalia and porotic hyperostosis, 146–47; grave goods, 142, *142*; health indicators, 145–50, 153; identity and, 273–74; in New Kingdom period, 6, 138–44, *140*; Taroy fortress and, 139
Trade: Nile Valley and, 85, 137; in Roman Egypt, 85–90; Scythia Minor and, 20–21
Trajan (Roman Emperor), 18, 19
Transporters, professional, 88
Transylvania: "golden age" of, 254; Székely-

föld and, 8, 252–56; Telekfalva Reformed Church, 241, 256–65, 258, *258–60*

Transylvania: An Ancient Romanian Land (Ceauşescu), 255

Trauma: antemortem, *29*, 69, 71, 74, 198; bones, 29–33, *32*, 149–50; by burial orientation and sex, *68*, 69; Campovalano and Alfedena with, 112–13; head, 219, 223–24; in human remains on Romanian frontier, *238*, 238–40, *239*; with injuries and intergroup conflict, 222–24; in M141 bones, 197–98; violence and, 65

Tribal migration, 139–40

Tryphon (weaver), 85

Tuberculosis, 169, 176, 219

Tukey's Honest Significant Difference test, 108, 116, 117, *119*, 121

Turner, Frederick Jackson, 188

Ubelaker, D. H., 63, 150, 168, 169, 192, 219

Únětice Culture, 58, 73

Unguentaria (small glass bottles), 46

University of Arizona, 49

University of Central Florida, 91

Uroi Hill, 234

Ushabtis (funerary figurines), 142, 151

Valens (Roman Emperor), 204–5

Vault at Ibida, 194, *195*

Velleius Paterculus, 45

Verdery, K., 206

Veris sacri (sacred springs), 113

Vikings, 160, 166, 176, 178. *See also* Iceland

Villa, P., 192, 194

Violence: dehumanization and, 203–4, 207; with Fremont Pueblo interactions, 214–16; massacres, 203, 204–5, 207, 224; in rock art, 224; in Roman Empire, 5, 16, 45; "territory" and, 206; trauma and, 65, 149–50. *See also* Ibida, political violence in

Virgin Branch Puebloans: abandonment and, 217; activity and stress markers, 221–22; in cultural context, 216–17; Fre-

mont and, 224–25; sex and age at death, 219–20; traumatic injuries, 222–23. *See also* Ancestral Puebloans

Volcanic eruptions, 165

VPDB, 91

VSMOW, 91–97

Wadi Halfa, 96

Walker, Phillip L., 219

Wallachia, 253, 267n3

Wari people, 135

Water: drinking, 83–84, 191; samples, 48–49; sea ice, 165; supply, failure of, 90

Weapons, 21, 109, 149; at Alfedena, 112; bronze, 58; males and, 111

Weaving, 85, 88, 111

Weren, 141

Weston, Darlene A., 149

Wetherill, Richard, 214

Wet nursing, 87

Whitehead, N. L., 206

Whitehouse Pueblo exhibit, 217

Williams, H., 273

Wilson, T. M., 3

Wine, 20, 85, 87, 88, 145, 264

Women: burials of children and, 8, 237; with grief, 265, 267; in Iceland, 166; infant mortality and, 171, 176, 262, 265, 267; land ownership and, 87; with miscarriages, 264–65; Nubian culture and, 151–52; pregnancy diets for, 264

Wood, J. W., 34

Workers, compulsory, 88–89

World War I, 267n3

World War II, 234, 249n1, 254

Wright, L. E., 91

Ylimaunu, T., 163

Żerniki Górne case study, 62; with clusters, distance between, *69*; jewelry, 63; methods, 63–65; results, 65–70, *68*

Zoëga, G., 168, 173

Bioarchaeological Interpretations of the Human Past: Local, Regional, and Global Perspectives

EDITED BY CLARK SPENCER LARSEN

Ancient Health: Skeletal Indicators of Agricultural and Economic Intensification, edited by Mark Nathan Cohen and Gillian M. M. Crane-Kramer (2007; first paperback edition, 2012)

Bioarchaeology and Identity in the Americas, edited by Kelly J. Knudson and Christopher M. Stojanowski (2009; first paperback edition, 2010)

Island Shores, Distant Pasts: Archaeological and Biological Approaches to the Pre-Columbian Settlement of the Caribbean, edited by Scott M. Fitzpatrick and Ann H. Ross (2010; first paperback edition, 2017)

The Bioarchaeology of the Human Head: Decapitation, Decoration, and Deformation, edited by Michelle Bonogofsky (2011; first paperback edition, 2015)

Bioarchaeology and Climate Change: A View from South Asian Prehistory, by Gwen Robbins Schug (2011; first paperback edition, 2017)

Violence, Ritual, and the Wari Empire: A Social Bioarchaeology of Imperialism in the Ancient Andes, by Tiffiny A. Tung (2012; first paperback edition, 2013)

The Bioarchaeology of Individuals, edited by Ann L. W. Stodder and Ann M. Palkovich (2012; first paperback edition, 2014)

The Bioarchaeology of Violence, edited by Debra L. Martin, Ryan P. Harrod, and Ventura R. Pérez (2012; first paperback edition, 2013)

Bioarchaeology and Behavior: The People of the Ancient Near East, edited by Megan A. Perry (2012; first paperback edition, 2018)

Paleopathology at the Origins of Agriculture, edited by Mark Nathan Cohen and George J. Armelagos (2013)

Bioarchaeology of East Asia: Movement, Contact, Health, edited by Kate Pechenkina and Marc Oxenham (2013)

Mission Cemeteries, Mission Peoples: Historical and Evolutionary Dimensions of Intracemetery Bioarchaeology in Spanish Florida, by Christopher M. Stojanowski (2013)

Tracing Childhood: Bioarchaeological Investigations of Early Lives in Antiquity, edited by Jennifer L. Thompson, Marta P. Alfonso-Durruty, and John J. Crandall (2014)

The Bioarchaeology of Classical Kamarina: Life and Death in Greek Sicily, by Carrie L. Sulosky Weaver (2015)

Victims of Ireland's Great Famine: The Bioarchaeology of Mass Burials at Kilkenny Union Workhouse, by Jonny Geber (2015; first paperback edition, 2018)

Colonized Bodies, Worlds Transformed: Toward a Global Bioarchaeology of Contact and Colonialism, edited by Melissa S. Murphy and Haagen D. Klaus (2017)

Bones of Complexity: Bioarchaeological Case Studies of Social Organization and Skeletal Biology, edited by Haagen D. Klaus, Amanda R. Harvey, and Mark N. Cohen (2017)

A World View of Bioculturally Modified Teeth, edited by Scott E. Burnett and Joel D. Irish (2017)

Children and Childhood in Bioarchaeology, edited by Patrick Beauchesne and Sabrina C. Agarwal (2018)

Bioarchaeology of Pre-Columbian Mesoamerica: An Interdisciplinary Approach, edited by Cathy Willermet and Andrea Cucina (2018)

Massacres: Bioarchaeology and Forensic Anthropology Approaches, edited by Cheryl P. Anderson and Debra L. Martin (2019)

Mortuary and Bioarchaeological Perspectives in Bronze Age Arabia, edited by Kimberly D. Williams and Lesley A. Gregoricka (2019)

Bioarchaeology of Frontiers and Borderlands, edited by Cristina I. Tica and Debra L. Martin (2019)

Printed in the United States
By Bookmasters